PERSONS IN COMMUNION

PERSONS IN COMMUNION

An Essay on Trinitarian Description
and Human Participation

with special reference to Volume One of
Karl Barth's *Church Dogmatics*

Alan J. Torrance

T&T CLARK
EDINBURGH

T&T CLARK LTD
59 GEORGE STREET
EDINBURGH EH2 2LQ
SCOTLAND

Copyright © T&T Clark Ltd, 1996

First published 1996

ISBN 0 567 09740 4

British Library Cataloguing-in-Publication Data
A catalogue record for this book is available
from the British Library

Typeset by Trinity Typesetting, Edinburgh
Printed and bound in Great Britain by Biddles Ltd, Guildford

Contents

v

Preface

This study has resulted from doctoral research which I submitted to the University of Erlangen in Germany but which I undertook while in different locations around the world over a period of a decade. Initially begun in the University of Cambridge, it was interrupted by moves to teaching positions first in the University of Erlangen and then in the University of Aberdeen before I was appointed to the chair of theology in Knox Theological Hall, Dunedin, New Zealand. A year's sabbatical leave in 1992, generously provided by the University of Otago and the Presbyterian Church of Aotearoa-New Zealand, meant that I was finally enabled to complete my research.

This has meant that a large number of people have helped and influenced me as I wrestled with the issues under discussion. To them I owe a debt of gratitude. Professor Nicholas Lash, my initial supervisor in Cambridge, was encouraging and supportive during the initial stages of the research. Professor Alasdair Heron, who appointed me to be his 'academic assistant' in the University of Erlangen has offered invaluable personal support over many years and much excellent advice – not least with respect to the revision of the thesis into its present form. Insightful comments on the original thesis offered by Professor Reinhard Slenczka, also of Erlangen, have proved to be of inestimable value in the process of editing it for publication.

Given that the research was completed following many years of teaching and graduate supervision, it will be of no surprise that my most influential teachers during much of this time have been my students from whom I have learned a great deal. There are too many to list here but the following former postgraduates require special mention: Dr Marty Folsom, Dr Chris Gousmett, Dr Bruce Hamill, Dr Susan Patterson (on whose research I draw in my final chapter), Dr Murray Rae (an invaluable friend and dialogue partner) and Rev. Graham Redding (a 'church theologian' and good friend). Others who have deepened my insights into the Christian Gospel by their friendship and support include Dr Jeremy S. Begbie, Dr Douglas Campbell, Dr and Mrs Sandy Ross, Rev. and Mrs John Sinclair, Rev. Robert Walker, Rev. Selwyn Yeoman, Mrs Natalie Yule Yeoman, Professor Peter Skegg and his wife Elizabeth and finally my sisters, Heather and Marion.

Since coming to King's College, London in 1993, Professor Colin Gunton, whose writings I have long admired, has become a source of theological inspiration and warm personal support and encouragement. Our weekly research seminars which bring into dialogue an impressive list of colleagues – Professors Michael Banner and Paul Helm and Drs Douglas Farrow, Brian Horne and Francis Watson – have come to provide a further rich source of inspiration.

There is no-one, however, to whom I owe a greater theological debt than my father, Professor James B. Torrance. Without his enthusiasm, unceasing help and encouragement and theological insight, not to mention the Christian witness and nurture provided over the years by my mother, there would be no book at all.

Clearly, the extent of theological input implied by those named above warrants a considerably finer volume than this. It is important to emphasise, therefore, that none of them should be held even partly responsible for the shortcomings of this book. For these my only indebtedness is to myself!

To my children, Andrew, Peter, Robert and David, I owe many interruptions to my research – interruptions, however, of the most welcome kind. Whether their violin practice in the background can be counted as offering insights into the harmonies of the Christian life may be open to question but the extent of their incalculable contribution to the harmony of family life is beyond doubt.

My fondest gratitude, however, is to my dear wife, Jane, to whom this volume is dedicated and who knows so much more about sustaining persons in communion than I do.

Since the completion of this book, a number of potential resources have emerged too late to be taken into consideration in this volume. Chief among these is Bruce L. McCormack's masterly volume, *Karl Barth's Critically Realistic Dialectical Theology: its Genesis and Development 1909–1936*, Clarendon Press, Oxford, 1995. The excellent historical analysis and discussion of Barth which he has undertaken here serve as an invaluable resource in furthering the contemporary trinitarian debate which this volume is so eager to encourage.

Abbreviations

J. B. L.   *Journal of Biblical Literature*

J. S. N. T. Supplement   Journal for the Study of the New
                          Testament Supplement Series

J. T. S.   *Journal of Theological Studies*

R. G. G.   *Die Religion in Geschichte und Gegenwart,*
                          ed. K. Galling, Tübingen, 1957–65

S. J. T.   *Scottish Journal of Theology*

Introduction

The principal aim of this book is to examine three closely associated and interrelated theological issues. These are, first, the question of the propriety or otherwise of describing the 'members' of the Trinity as 'persons'; second, the manner in which language functions in the context of trinitarian description, and, third, the question of the underlying models of the theological enterprise as these characterise the nature of human participation within it. It will be suggested that these three interrelated questions are of fundamental significance for the shape and orientation of theology and dogmatics as a whole — and of particular importance for establishing the foundations of theological anthropology.

The *form* which this analysis takes is that of a critical evaluation of Barth's exposition (in Volume One of his *Church Dogmatics*) of theological method, the relationship between issues of semantics and ontological issues (as reflected particularly, for example, in his discussion of the concept of *vestigia Dei*) and his arguments in favour of the term *Seinsweise*, which he prefers to that of *Person* ('mode' or 'way' of being), when referring to the Father, the Son and the Holy Spirit. It is here that we find what Colin Gunton has described as the 'Achilles' heel' of Barth's theology.[1] As we shall seek to show, it testifies to a weakness in his thought which is linked to the revelation-orientation of his theology. That is, Barth opts for a revelation model of the theological task which led (paradoxically) to an inadequate interpretation of God's Self-communication – to the extent that this requires a more

---

[1] This was a comment made to me in private conversation.

1

satisfactory exposition of the triune communion than Barth's categories enabled him to offer.

In the light of our analysis we shall offer a critique of Barth's 'revelation model' as it shapes and conditions the whole orientation of his discussion and exposition of the doctrine of the Triunity, of the nature of revelation and of theological language.

From a critical examination of Barth's interpretation of these issues we shall turn to consider several other recent approaches to the question of triune personhood representative of the modern ecumenical debate, namely those of Karl Rahner (whose approach in this area will be seen to echo some of the primary weaknesses of Karl Barth's discussion), John Zizioulas and Catherine Mowry LaCugna (whose approach will, in turn, be seen to echo the weaknesses of John Zizioulas' approach). Reference will also be made to the approaches of Eberhard Jüngel, Jürgen Moltmann, Wolfhart Pannenberg and others. However, it is important to note that our principal concern here is not to offer a survey of this debate. Rather, our primary intention is to focus on the manner in which certain particularly influential theologians serve to exemplify a combination of important strengths while, at the same time, exhibiting some serious methodological weaknesses in addressing the subject. These discussions will serve in turn to undergird our conclusions as to the nature of trinitarian description, the model of the theological enterprise that may best serve and underlie it and, finally, the fundamental significance for the theological programme as a whole of a proper appreciation of the nature of the relationship between 'semantic' and 'doxological' participation. It will be suggested that a worship-oriented model of the grounds of theological articulation is more satisfactory than that which informs Barth's exposition in the opening volume of his *Church Dogmatics.*

On initially setting out on this project, it was my intention to focus specifically on the question how far it is appropriate and useful to speak of trinitarian 'persons'. It soon became clear, however, from reading a wealth of material which broached this issue from different theological perspectives that, although the matter of terminology is important and deserves serious consideration in itself, the central issues which largely determine our answers to this question go much deeper. They concern, first, how we interpret theological semantics, that is, the meaning and function of the terminology involved in theological description, and, second, the theological models which undergird our 'God-talk'. Too often, it seems, discussions of triune personhood are pursued either, on the one hand, with a naïvely 'essentialist' conception of meaning and 'objectivistically referentialist' view of semantic function (or both) or, on the other hand, a prior (theologically *a priori*) agenda conceived with recourse to some particular theme – such as, for example, a certain model of the logic of revelation or an abstract 'personalist' agenda. Such options too easily misrepresent the enterprise of theological description as this stems from an *a posteriori* and 'participative' consideration of the actual, 'ontic' nature of the Gospel as it would interpret itself to us on its own grounds.

Consideration of these issues meant that some sustained discussion of the traditional analogy debate and the often confused rendering of the *analogia entis* issue could not be avoided. As a result, I found myself obliged to devote a whole chapter (chapter three) to a consideration of the nature of analogy in preparation not only for discussing the *vestigium Dei* question later in the same chapter (which is particularly relevant to the 'material', ontological issues raised by our analysis), but also for the re-examination of the nature of theological semantics (in dialogue with contemporary developments in the philosophy of language) in chapter five.

In sum, the main thrust of this book can be summarised in the following terms.

First, we seek to show that to approach theology and the doctrine of God exclusively from the perspective of a model of the structure of revelation, as represented by the opening volume of the *Church Dogmatics* – and also by Karl Rahner's discussion of the Trinity – is, in the final analysis, inadequate. Although a doctrine of revelation is essential for Christian theology not only materially but also formally, divine communication cannot be separated from a proper theology of divine communion. Theologically interpreted, communication presupposes the category of communion and not the other way round. Dogmatically speaking, therefore, the *mirifica communicatio* requires to be interpreted in integration with, and from the perspective of, a proper doctrine of the *mirifica commutatio* and the further *mirifica communio*. At the level of christology the prophetic office of Christ may not be separated from the priestly, revelation may not be separated from reconciliation and the atonement and, hence, theology and theological description may not be separated from worship. The triune grounds of divine communication repose on a communion intrinsic to the Triunity as this creates and sustains the communion with God and with one another which is intrinsic to the very being of the New Humanity. The theology of revelation requires to be articulated, therefore, within this context and not the other way round.

Second, just as Christian dogmatics must take place within the context of church dogmatics, theological statement stems from a context of doxological participation which includes within it what we shall term 'semantic participation'. An ecclesial theology of revelation, therefore, necessitates a doctrine of semantic participation which in turn requires a much fuller and more careful interpretation of the philosophy of language within the theological context than has generally been offered – not least by Karl Barth. What is more, ecclesial, doxological and semantic participation require a theologically profounder doctrine of the sacraments than has generally characterised, not least, Reformed theology — despite the penetrating (and too little known) insights into the nature of these in Calvin's *Institutio*.

Third, a proper doctrine of semantic participation within the context of ecclesial communion serves to suggest constructive ways forward beyond the impasse of the *analogia entis/analogia fidei* dispute that has proved to be the cause of so much intra-ecclesial confusion within the ecumenical debate. We require to think in terms of an *analogia communionis*.

Fourth, whereas Barth showed powerfully that there is an *intrinsic* relationship between the event of revelation and the subjective perception of it, we seek to explore further the extent to which intrinsic relationships are to be found on the divine side: a) between God's Being and God's Being-in-communion; and b) between God's Being-in-communion and God's Being-in-communication as this involves a further intrinsic relationship between the person and work of the Logos. These intrinsic relations on the divine side will be seen to have their counterpart on the human side in a parallel intrinsic relation between a) human being and being-in-communion; and between b) human being-in-communion and epistemic participation in the reconciling event of revelation.

Finally, in the light of our respective analyses it should become clear: a) that it is not only possible to describe the members of the Trinity as 'persons', but that this is both meaningful and appropriate; and b) that the 'commandeering' of this terminology integrates effectively with that form of semantic participation which stems from, and takes the form of, 'doxological participation'.

Despite the apparently 'abstract' nature of the utilisation of the term 'persons' in the trinitarian context, it may nevertheless be seen to present a richer, more constructive and, indeed, ultimately more concrete means of theological expression than is enabled or facilitated by the term *Seinsweisen*. Properly interpreted, the term 'person', when used within the context of the doxological model outlined in the course of the discussion, should be seen, on the one hand, to obviate many of the problems feared by both Karl Barth and Karl Rahner, while serving, on the other hand, a theology of communion which obviates some of the potential weaknesses which, we shall suggest, are to be found in the expositions of LaCugna and, to a lesser extent, John Zizioulas.

Throughout our discussion Karl Barth's exposition of method, revelation and the Trinity will function as something of a 'foil' for our own exploration of the issues outlined above. This is not due to any disrespect for this theological giant, but for precisely the opposite reason. It is my firm conviction that Barth's insights into the nature of theological method and his courageous exposition of these in the face of the influence of Neo-Kantianism on European theology, on the one hand, and of *Kulturprotestantismus* on the self-understanding of large areas of church life, on the other, are as profoundly relevant for the theological task today as they were then. The intention of this book is not to undermine this but rather to build upon it. It is appropriate, therefore, that it is to an analysis and exposition of Barth's discussion of theological method that we devote our opening chapter.

1

Theological Description and the Content of Theology in Volume One of *Church Dogmatics*[1]

It is not possible to assess Karl Barth's conclusions as to the nature and structure of the identity of God and the propriety, or otherwise, of describing God as a Triunity of 'persons' without exploring his understanding of the nature of theological description, the dynamics of theological language and the underlying question of theological warrant.

Problematic as it is, however, for the purposes of theological exposition, it is also not possible (and Barth is supremely aware of this) to deal with methodological issues in abstraction from the consideration of the 'subject-matter' of theology. It is impossible, therefore, to engage in the discussion of *formal* issues without consideration of the *material* issues which penetrate every level of epistemological, semantic and ontological analysis.

---

[1] I have chosen to confine myself in this chapter to an exposition of the primary text of *Church Dogmatics*, Volume One, Part 1. When referring to the German text (*Die Kirchliche Dogmatik: Erster Band, Die Lehre vom Wort Gottes: Prolegomena zur Kirchlichen Dogmatik, Erster Halbband*, Munich, 1932) I shall use the abbreviation 'K. D. 1. 1' and when referring to the English translation I shall adopt the abbreviation 'C. D. 1. 1'. The *Church Dogmatics* will be quoted in translation with reference being made to the German only when it is deemed important for the issue under discussion. The translation used, unless stated otherwise, will be the 2nd edition, translated by G. W. Bromiley (Edinburgh, 1975). There are some misprints in certain small-print sections of the English translation, e.g. pp. 338 and 356, where the sense is either undermined or, in the latter case (where 'begreiflicher' is translated 'inconceivable'), seriously distorted. On the rare occasion where the translation requires to be modified the necessary alterations have been introduced.

Consequently, our discussion of Barth's conception of the nature and function of theological language is inseparable from some parallel consideration not only of his understanding of the Being and Act of God but also of his interpretation of the doctrine of the Church, his theology of reconciliation, his pneumatology and, indeed, his theological anthropology.

The need for this could be demonstrated and justified, of course, by appeal to the hermeneutical circularity which is integral to all such enterprises whatever the subject-matter may be. Common to every consideration as to how we go about exploring an area are the necessary and irreducible circularity of inter-questioning between the subject-matter and the methods adopted, and the further necessity of interpreting any one domain in terms of its interrelations with other domains.

However, it is *not* primarily for reasons of a general academic nature (i.e. reasons which are deemed to apply universally in critical research) that this issue is of such mandatory importance for exploring the thought of Karl Barth. Rather, what we must be aware of here is that at the very heart of Barth's interpretation of theology there is an insistence on the integration of content and its 'dis-covery' which is quite unique to theology and which involves a very specific kind of 'circularity'. This circularity is not – indeed, it cannot be – recognised hypothetically and in advance of (*a priori* to) a consideration of the subject-matter, but is discovered *a posteriori* to be of the very essence of the case owing to the uniquely dynamic and subject-involving nature of that of which the theologian speaks – and *speaks* through being *compelled* to speak. This is bound up with the fact that theological talk, as Barth understands it, is not a voluntary human activity or form of human self-expression[2] (where one gives voice to one's views about the divine) but derives from a compulsion to speak grounded in the Word without whose agency there is no form of speech that can be deemed to be adequate – without

---

[2] 'Man has as such no possibility of uttering the Word of God' (*C. D.* 1. 1, 52; *K. D.* 1. 1, 53). Again, 'Dogmatics is not by nature a general *gnosis* of God and the world' (*C. D.* 1. 1, 81); 'Dogmatik ist nun einmal keine allgemeine Gott-Welt-Gnosis' (*K. D.* 1. 1, 83).

which, indeed, there is no form of warrant or justification for any such speech at all.[3] It should become clear from our discussion, therefore, that much of the disagreement between Barth's position and various other trends in theology with their suppositions as to the nature of divine attribution stems from a failure to appreciate fully the import and ramifications of this insistence.

An 'in depth' exploration and appreciation of these methodological issues is therefore vital for an assessment of Barth's approach and his conclusions as to the manner in which we may or may not refer to the three members of the Trinity as 'persons'.

Barth's Perspective on the Task of Dogmatic Theology

It must also be made clear from the outset that Barth is not concerned with building a theological system – a 'Barthian' theology.[4] Consequently, there is no series of independent or

---

[3] Here again, we must insist that this denial is not grounded in any *a priori* determinations resulting, for example, from the arguments of Hume's *Dialogues Concerning Natural Religion* . This is a negative assertion made *a posteriori* in the light of God's being toward us as Word, the God who *is* his Word to us. Barth comments, 'Hence it is only subsequently, *a posteriori*, exegetically and not in the sense of demonstrating the Church's commission, that we may rightly consider whether even the thought of God's Word being revealed outside the known existing Church is possible for one who has not previously come to be acquainted with real proclamation within the Church ...' (*C. D.* 1. 1, 57–8; *K. D.* 1. 1, 58).

[4] Barth repudiated the notion that there is some series of 'Barthian' theological 'principles' as is made clear not least from his reply to a letter from Pastor Max Schoch. Pastor Schoch had written in a letter to Barth on 7 June 1967, 'I am not a Barthian. I understand by this one who draws certain principles from your works and fights with these principles.' Barth replied, 'Many thanks for your letter. I myself am not a Barthian according to your definition or in any other sense.' (9 June 1967; *Karl Barth's Letters 1961-68* (trans. by Geoffrey Bromiley), Edinburgh, 1981, 255.)

Barth's repudiation of any theology which baptises principles either formal or material is reflected not least in his criticisms of Moltmann's *Theologie der Hoffnung* (Munich, 1965) and Pannenberg's *Grundzüge der Christologie* (Gütersloh, 1964). Indeed, it was their perceived tendency to introduce foreign 'principles' and to build either an eschatological or christological system in the light of these which determined that neither was the 'child of peace and promise' for which he had longed! Cf. ibid., 174–6 and 177–9.

self-contained building blocks which can be distinguished and interrelated in a systematic way. Rather, and as we shall continually emphasise, he is committed (at least in intention) to a process of *a posteriori* theological articulation and description not merely at the material level but at the methodological level also, in such a way that the integratedness of his conclusions is not bound up with any subjective or rationalistic form of *systematic* rigour but, rather, with the integrity of the subject-matter which is the all-transforming Reality of God in his Self-givenness in an act of reconciliation – an event which involves methodological and epistemological reconstruction of the academic, theological enterprise. This poses a problem for those wishing to expound Barth's thought, in that the very nature of his approach means that issues are described from different perspectives (and in the light of different concerns) in a manner that attempts to follow through the implications of the Self-giving Reality with which we are engaged in the revelation of God in his Word. The consequence of this is that Barth continually reiterates certain central themes, albeit from different perspectives and within different contexts. This is integral to the nature of his method. For this very reason, this process of reiteration becomes frustratingly difficult to 'distil away' in the process of critical exposition and analysis.

Theology and the Being of the Church

The only possibility of a conception of dogmatic knowledge remaining to us on the basis of Evangelical faith is to be marked off on the one hand by the rejection of an existential ontological possibility of the being of the Church and on the other hand by the rejection of the presupposition of a constantly available absorption of the being of the Church into a creaturely form, into a 'There is.' On the one side we have to say that the being of the Church is *actus purus*, i.e., a divine action which is self-originating and which is to be understood only in terms of itself and not therefore in terms of a prior anthropology. And on the other side we have also to say that the being of the Church is *actus purus*, but with the accent now on *actus*, i.e., a free action and not a constantly available connexion, grace being the event of personal address and not a transmitted material condition. On both sides we can only ask how it may be otherwise if the being of the Church is identical with Jesus Christ. If this is true, then the place from which the way of dogmatic knowledge is to be seen and understood can be neither a prior anthropological possibility nor a subsequent ecclesiastical reality, but only the present moment of the speaking and hearing of Jesus Christ Himself, the divine creation of light in our hearts.[5]

The immediate significance of Barth's emphasis on the primacy of the existence of the Church for the theological task, as reflected in this statement, is his categorical refusal to address the question, 'How is human knowledge of revelation possible?' For the theologian to ask such a question would imply either a) that there is, or can be, doubt as to whether revelation is known or b) that 'insight into the possibility of knowledge of divine revelation' can be expected from the 'investigation of human knowledge'. The former is a *de facto* repudiation of the fact that revelation has taken place. (And, as will become clear below, the revelation event for Barth is necessarily a 'success' event, to use a phrase taken from Gilbert Ryle.)[6] The latter is, at best, a form of disobedience in the face of revelation in that it seeks to validate the particularity of the revelation event with recourse to universal structures which are deemed to be more foundational. To the extent that Barth identifies the revelation event with the Being of God, such a move to establish the possibility of human knowledge of revelation in terms of an appeal to universal structures in human knowing, outlined by the human subject in abstraction from God's Self-disclosure, is tantamount to the affirmation that such structures are more foundational than the Being of God! Offering a foretaste of Bonhoeffer's exposition of the Logos as the Counter-Logos or Anti-Logos with respect to the human logos, Barth outlines the fallacy here in ecclesiological terms, 'if the contradiction of human reason is made the subject of enquiry and its overcoming the goal, the sphere of the Church is abandoned

---

[5] *C. D.* 1. 1, 41 (*K. D.* 1. 1, 41).
[6] See footnote 9 below.

and "another task" is indeed substituted for the task of dogmatics'.[7]

The implication of this is both simple and also radical, namely that, contrary to traditional methodological assumptions especially within the domain of theological apologetics, we do not and must not begin dogmatic, theological investigation outside of the givenness of God to and for humankind, that is, outside the context of what has traditionally been termed 'special revelation' – an expression which quite appropriately leads Barth to ask if there is any form of revelation that is not 'special'! In so far as this Self-disclosure includes our knowing processes and takes place within the Body of Christ, to affirm that there is 'special' revelation but not to allow it to determine theological method and the whole process of the definition of terms would be a form of disobedience or rebellious self-assertion before God. This would involve a *de facto* repudiation of God's Self-gift within the context of the Church and ultimately a determination to engage with something other than the Being of God (a *tertium quid*) which is not, and cannot be, *God* in so far as it is affirmed to be or to exist independently of the context of God's Self-gift.

The Non-neutrality of the Theologian

To be 'absolutely neutral in relation to God' is to be 'absolutely hostile' to God ('schlechterdings gegen ihn').[8] Non-commitment before the revelation event, i.e. before the reality of the Self-giving disclosure of God (what amounts to repudiation of the '*success*'[9] of the event of revelation which is intrinsic to it), is a form of the withdrawal of self from the One with whom one is created to be in communion and from

---

[7] *C. D.* 1. 1, 29 (*K. D.* 1. 1, 28). Cf. also Dietrich Bonhoeffer, *Christology*, (Eng. trans. by John Bowden), London and New York, 1966, section entitled 'The Christological Question', 27–37.

[8] *C. D.* 1. 1, 47–8 (*K. D.* 1. 1, 48).

[9] Christoph Schwöbel writes in a manner which echoes Barth's approach, '"Revelation" is in this sense a "success word" (G. Ryle) which presupposes the reception of the communication ...' (*God: Action and Revelation*, Kampen, 1992, 92.)

whom, in the event of revelation, one receives 'the divine creation of light' in one's heart – a form of epistemic communion, that is, which includes the intellect as much as the will. Any claimed reserve or sustained 'critical distance', therefore, on the part of the theologian in relation to the revelation event, far from being a testimony to the reliability and objectivity of the theologian, constitutes precisely the opposite.[10]

The form of approach which cultivates this myth of critical detachment or 'disengagement'[11] is typified in what Barth regards as the misleading supposition that revealed truth can be identified with doctrinal truths, where these are conceived as having a propositional life of their own as detached embodiments of divinely revealed Truths ('veritates a Deo formaliter revelatae').

As Barth expresses his perception of the matter,

> The very reserve with which one can confront the truth of a doctrinal proposition, the possibility of a purely theoretical attitude to it, and, in objective correspondence to this possibility, the idea of a purely material and impersonal presence of truth in the proposition – this is what makes the equation of *veritas revelata* and the doctrinal proposition suspect, and more than suspect in our view.[12]

---

[10] At the level of secular philosophy, there are parallels here with John Macmurray's analysis of abstract thought as a temporary detachment from action, for the sake of action, and thus as to be conceived as a negative act – a withdrawal from the field of epistemic engagement – rather than as a positive one. It must not, therefore, be identified with a rational response to the object of philosophical investigation, since any such supposition is to participate in the Cartesian confusion which failed to recognise the primacy of the practical over the theoretical, of the participatory over the speculative or cognitive. In a not unrelated manner, Michael Polanyi sets out to demythologise the myth of detachment for the sake of scientific objectivity in *Personal Knowledge* (Chicago, 1958). He sees the passionate, personal commitment of the scientist as being of the essence of the objective, heuristic engagement with the nature of reality rather than a barrier to it.

[11] Cf. Colin Gunton's exposition and discussion of Taylor's use of this term in the opening chapter of *The One, The Three and the Many: God, Creation and the Culture of Modernity* (The 1992 Bampton Lectures), Cambridge, 1993.

[12] *C. D.* 1. 1, 270–1 (*K. D.* 1. 1, 286).

This requires a reassessment of the question of truthfulness such that it is conceived neither in terms of successful, objective reference projecting across the gulf between the human and the divine (i.e. in terms of a 'correspondence theory of truth'), nor in terms of internal consistency within a system of propositions or ideas (i.e. in terms of a 'coherence theory of truth'), but in terms of what is customarily assumed to be a quite foreign category, one that is subjective and ethical, namely *obedience* – the obedience of thought and of mind. Theological truthfulness is a form of intellectual obedience before the Reality of God. Here, Barth comes close to interpreting truth in 'performative' terms. However, the truth–performance connection here is not bound up with any autonomous human performance, but with the divine speech-act performed in and through the ambiguous event of God's Self-veiling/unveiling in the human context. Truthfulness is ultimately to be found, therefore, in and through the divine event of Self-communication in the Church, where the obedience of the human hearer is included within the divine speech-act and where God is 'heard', and therefore conceived, in a creative divine *act* of the reconciliation of the human mind to himself.[13]

Consequently, theological or 'dogmatic' truthfulness and objectivity are not sustained by an attitude of 'detachment' and cannot be reduced merely to a property of propositional truths. The truth of God is not embodied in, or communicated by, dogmatic exposition, but rather communicates and embodies itself in and through the Word who utters himself in and through the Church's proclamation – that is, to the extent to which the Church is true to its task (the performance of

[13] This echoes Calvin's insistence that *scientia Dei ex oboedientia nascitur*. Rowan Williams' slightly dismissive comment that this is simply 'Calvin's irresistible grace rendered into epistemological terms' ('Barth on the Triune God' in S. W. Sykes (ed.), *Karl Barth – Studies of his Theological Methods*, Oxford, 1979, 158) fails to engage sufficiently either with the force of Barth's argument or, indeed, with the problems confronting an alternative approach. It also ignores the fact that Barth's very contemplation of the notion of rebellion suggests a rather different scenario from that of a hyper-Calvinist determinism. A fuller discussion of Williams' critique will be offered in chapter 2.

which it is the task of dogmatics to serve). This means that

what is under debate in dogmatics is the Church's fundamental relation of obedience to its Lord in respect of its proclamation ... A dogmatics which it (the Church) might not pursue, in whose enquiry it did not wholly participate as in the enquiry about its whole existence, a dogmatics which might let itself be crowded into the corner of religious intellectuals or the intellectually religious, could only be a poor, useless and tedious dogmatics which it would be better not to pursue at all. We pursue dogmatics because, constrained by the fact of the Bible, we cannot shake off the question of the obedience of Church proclamation. The question of its obedience includes that of its truth. But the question of its truth can be put only as the question of its obedience. As the question of its obedience it is the question of its dogma.[14]

The Inseparability of Formal and Material Considerations

Barth stresses the impropriety of the separation of formal and material considerations and of the introduction of any form of prior or 'foundational' philosophical prescription at the methodological, epistemological or ontological level.[15]

For Barth, 'prolegomena to dogmatics are possible only as part "als ein Teilstück" of dogmatics itself'.[16] The reason for this is bound up with the fact that valid God-talk cannot be said, in the face of the Word of God, to be a free human option grounded in human possibilities and conditions defined and deemed appropriate in advance. For this reason, as we discuss below, Barth is very suspicious of words beginning with 'pre' or 'pro' (in German, *vor*). Eberhard Jüngel echoes Barth's concern by taking up prepositions which imply logical or ontological priority and then predicating them *of God* in such a way as to make this point quite explicit: '... das Sein Gottes

---

[14] *C. D.* 1. 1, 274-5 (*K. D.* 1. 1, 290-1).

[15] It is this feature to which Jüngel refers when he argues that 'Barth's doctrine of the Trinity as dogmatic interpretation of God's self-interpretation possesses an anti-metaphysical and anti-mythological significance.' (Jüngel, *The Doctrine of the Trinity: God's Being is in Becoming*, (Eng. trans. by Horton Harris), Edinburgh, 1976, 29.)

[16] *C. D.* 1. 1, 42 (*K. D.* 1. 1, 41).

geht und eben so allem menschlichen Fragen zuvorkommt'[17] ('the Being of God proceeds, and thus precedes all human questioning'[18]); 'Die theologische Frage nach dem Sein Gottes denkt *nach*, eben: dem Sein Gottes. D. h. aber, daß das Sein Gottes, nach dem theologisch gefragt wird, *vorausgeht*. Das Prädikat ist streng zu nehmen. Gottes Sein geht der theologischen Frage *nach* diesem Sein *voraus*; es ist nicht etwa dieser Frage voraus*gesetzt*.'[19] ('The theological question concerning the Being of God *reflects* on the Being of God. This means, however, that the Being of God which is the subject of theological inquiry *precedes* the question. The predicate is to be taken strictly. God's Being *precedes* the theological inquiry after this being; it is not in any way *presupposed* by this inquiry.'[20]) By this technique Jüngel echoes Barth's concern to emphasise that it is the Being of God alone which conditions and preconditions the event of revelation – not some *tertium datum*. The significance of this for evangelical dogmatics is that it 'realises that all its knowledge, even its knowledge of the correctness of its knowledge, can only be an event, and cannot therefore be guaranteed as correct knowledge from any place apart from or above this event. In no circumstances, therefore, can it understand the account which is to be rendered in prolegomena as an attempt to secure such a guarantee.'[21]

An event of theological knowing is not, therefore, a human product defined from prior, humanly contrived, formal constraints. Rather, it is an event of knowing God which is an act of God's freely becoming the 'object' of our knowing and this is an event in and for God whose Being *becomes* 'God's Being-as-Object'.[22]

This is possibly one of the most difficult claims for the theologian to take seriously, since it involves the sacrifice of

---

[17] Eberhard Jüngel, *Gottes Sein ist im Werden. Verantwortliche Rede vom Sein Gottes bei Karl Barth: Ein Paraphrase*, Tübingen, 1976, 10.

[18] Jüngel, *The Doctrine of the Trinity*, xx.

[19] Jüngel, *Gottes Sein ist im Werden.*, 9 (his italics).

[20] Jüngel, *The Doctrine of the Trinity*, xix.

[21] *C. D.* 1. 1, 42 (*K. D.* 1. 1, 42).

[22] For a full discussion of this see Jüngel, op. cit., Chapter 2.

the widely endorsed academic ideal of philosophers of religion to the extent that they interpret it to be of the essence of their endeavour and academic accomplishment to establish grounds and truth criteria on the basis of which the truth of their conclusions can receive ratification, or the opposite. However, we must, in Barth's words, 'accept the fact that only the Logos of God Himself can provide the proof that we are really talking about Him when we are allegedly doing so'.[23]

Barth's approach here insists on a radical integration of form and content which he sees to be obligatory in the light of a proper appreciation of the agency of God. This is highlighted in his discussion by his suggestion that in John 10:30 and 17:11 the terms 'Father' and 'Son' could be substituted for 'form' and 'content'.

> The statement that 'I and the Father are one' (10:30), or '… that they may be one even as we are' (the Father and the Son, 17:11), obviously does no more than underline the fact that in John believing is equally both coming from the known Father to the unknown Son and also coming from the known Son to the unknown Father. There can hardly be anything contrary to the sense of John if in this context we substitute for Father and Son the concepts of form and content in their distinction and unity.[24]

This is a suggestion, however, which carries with it risks of its own! There could be an opposing danger, which we shall examine below, of reducing the material to the formal in a manner which depersonalises God. (We shall argue that Barth's use of the metaphor of address to describe the Trinity by way of an exposition of the structure of the revelation event itself comes too close to making precisely this kind of mistake.)

---

[23] *C. D.* 1. 1, 163 (*K. D.* 1. 1, 169). One might add here that, as T. F. Torrance has shown in his writings, the impossibility of establishing the truth of one's conclusions about reality on grounds internal to the reasoning of the subject is of the essence of scientific objectivity.

[24] *C. D.* 1. 1, 176 (*K. D.* 1. 1, 183). Later on, Barth emphasises further the radical impropriety of operating with a dichotomy between form and content, adding, 'The distinction between form and content cannot be applied to the biblical concept of revelation. When revelation is an event according to the Bible, there is no second question as to what its content might be. Nor could its content be equally well manifested in another event than this' (*C. D.* 1. 1, 306.)

Critical reflection on the formal process and methodological issues of dogmatic thinking occurs only subsequently to, and in the light of, the Word of God spoken.

Only when and to the extent that such a Word of God is spoken by God Himself to the Church is there any right or sense in speaking about God in the Church. Only when there is such a Word of God is there a criterion, namely, this Word itself, of the correctness of such speech and therefore of the correct criticism and correction of such speech, i.e., of dogmatics. In the prolegomena to dogmatics, therefore, we ask concerning the Word of God as the criterion of dogmatics. In so doing, and therefore already on the way, we give an account of the way which we tread.[25]

Consequently, we must reflect the approach of the 'older dogmaticians' and their tendency to anticipate such 'material dogmas' as the doctrine of reconciliation, the Holy Spirit, faith and the Church. The greater the anticipation here, the greater the likelihood of achieving true clarity. As to Barth's own programme, he concludes his 'Introduction' to the *Church Dogmatics* by making the following point:

The most striking anticipation of this kind will consist in the fact that we shall treat of the whole doctrine of the Trinity and the essentials of Christology in this connexion, namely, as constituent parts of our answer to the question of the Word of God. We cannot pose the question of formal dogma without immediately entering at these central points upon material dogma. Indeed, what is thought to be formal dogma is itself highly material in fact.[26]

The question that will recur throughout this discussion is how far this 'anticipation' in Barth actually takes the form, despite all that he has said, of a formal 'predetermination'.

It may be noticed that his talk of the event which cannot be anticipated, which is new and which is inseparable from the condition of its recognition which is given with it in the event, is reminiscent of the argument in Kierkegaard's *Philosophical*

---

[25] *C. D.* 1. 1, 43 (*K. D.* 1. 1, 43).
[26] *C. D.* 1. 1, 44 (*K. D.* 1. 1, 43).

Fragments. Here the pseudonymous Climacus offers vigorous opposition to any approach which suggests that the Moment, which, he will argue, must include the condition for the recognition of the Truth, is to be construed in terms of the instantiations of forms, concepts or ideals already immanent in the mind of the pupil and which are simply brought to birth (*maieuesthai*) by a process of facilitation or 'midwifery' on the part of the Teacher (that is, by *paideia*).

There is, however, a significant difference between Barth's argumentation and that in which Climacus engages. And it is worth examining this briefly in order to bring out the precise nature of Barth's discussion. Climacus introduces his discussion by asking the question 'How far does the Truth admit of being learned?' In this way he poses the problem as to how we can learn that which is entirely new. This he does by considering the 'pugnacious proposition' of the *Meno*, namely that 'one cannot seek for what he knows, and it seems equally impossible for him to seek for what he does not know. For what a man knows he cannot seek, since he knows it; and what he does not know he cannot seek, since he does not even know for what to seek.'[27] This question becomes the ground of his consideration of what amounts to a form of the hermeneutical circle showing that either we do not and cannot ever learn anything new or the condition of the recognition of that which is entirely new is given with it. The whole study becomes a) an exploration of the radical difference, indeed, incompatibility between Socratic idealism, as this exemplifies a radically distortive form of foundationalism when utilised in the interpretation of Christian thought (as in Hegel), and the faith interpreted in terms of itself, and also b) an exploration of the internal coherence and cogency of the Christian faith understood on the basis of its own premises. Climacus argues, for example, that the Moment through which we come into relationship with the Truth would have to take the form of an act of redemption which would constitute a necessary condition for

---

[27] Søren Kierkegaard, *Philosophical Fragments* (Eng. trans. by David Swenson and Howard Hong), Princeton, 1967, 11.

the acquisition of knowledge of the divine of which one is otherwise in ignorance – this unique and decisive Moment, filled with the eternal (and which he further suggests would involve an event of incarnation), might properly be described as 'the fulness of time'.[28]

The *Philosophical Fragments* functions as a brilliant exposé of the incompatibility of Christian theology not only with idealism but with all other forms of foundationalism that suggest that the conditions for the interpretation, recognition and acknowledgement of God and revelation are immanent within us and sufficient for the task. It seeks, moreover, to establish what we might call a methodological apologetic where the incarnation is interpreted in terms of the possibility of the realisation of certain hypotheses and possibilities. This suggests the assumption that this methodological principle can be discerned at the *formal* level independently of one's being taken into the Moment, that is, into the hermeneutical circle. And this suggests that the necessity of the Moment itself, although it is interpreted as an event, may be seen as a necessary postulate within a formal argument. To the extent

---

[28] Ibid., 18. It should be added that Climacus' attempt to demonstrate *a priori* the essential conditions of the (Christian) alternative to the Socratic includes arguments for a great deal more than the above. It includes, for example, the attempt to establish that non-Socratically conceived 'ignorance' would require to be conceived as *culpable* ignorance on the part of the human subject – establishing, in other words, the Pauline emphasis on the culpability of our cognitive alienation. 'And still we have not said all that is necessary; for by his self-imposed bondage the learner has brought upon himself a burden of guilt, and when the Teacher gives him the condition and the Truth he constitutes himself an Atonement, taking away the wrath impending upon that of which the learner has made himself guilty' (ibid., 21).

Murray Rae argues that Kierkegaard himself did not, however, hold to the Western *ordo salutis* – that soteriological system which supposes that we must first know law in order to know sin and thereby come to repentance and the consequent reception of grace, thus implying that law is epistemically prior to grace and grace conditional upon repentance. Kierkegaard appreciated that repentance, the perception of our error, is a theologically *a posteriori* perception to the extent that it reposes on the knowledge of grace given in and given by that same grace. Cf. 'By Faith Transformed: Kierkegaard's Vision of the Incarnation.', Doctoral thesis, University of London, 1995, which constitutes an outstanding exposition of Kierkegaard's theology.

that this is successful, *material* exposition is taking place, and this by consideration of the necessary implications of universally interpretable hypotheses. In short, if Climacus is seeking to establish the coherence and cogency of the incarnation, he would appear to be hoist on his own petard.

This, however, it should be added, should be seen as reflecting a weakness not in Kierkegaard's own position, but in that of Climacus, one of which Kierkegaard is fully aware.[29] Consequently, we are not suggesting that there are grounds here for supposing any methodological incompatibility between Barth's theological emphases and those of Kierkegaard himself. Indeed, Murray Rae's impressive analysis of Kierkegaard's theological position means that one cannot but be impressed by the remarkable theological parallelisms between the two thinkers.[30] The purpose of our discussion here, however, is simply to emphasise the difference between the kind of *theological* argument Barth adopts against foundationalism in the first volume of his *Church Dogmatics* and Climacus' famous critique in the *Fragments*. The similarities apparent at a superficial level do not suggest parallel methodologies.[31]

---

[29] This is almost certainly one of the reasons why he presented these arguments under the name of the non-Christian Climacus and not under either his own name or that of the Christian Anti-Climacus. Moreover, Climacus himself appears at various different places in the *Philosophical Fragments* (esp. chapters one and two) to be struggling with this problem. He was aware, it seems, that there could be argued to be a subliminally 'Socratic' bent to his rejection of Socratic interpretations of Christian thought.

As for Kierkegaard, his primary aim here, it would seem, was essentially to articulate and expose, through Climacus, the suppositions inherent in interpretations of the Christian faith from immanentist or idealist principles, and to show that the incompatibility between these and the kinds of claims that Christianity might make when interpreted on its own grounds should be plain to any thinking agnostic! Kierkegaard did not regard this as the exposition of Christian thought from the inside – hence the pseudonym. Again, for a lucid discussion of this issue, cf. Murray Rae, 'By Faith Transformed'.

[30] Indeed, it would appear that a great deal is to be gained by examining these parallels, not least for the sake of a proper appreciation of the impressive insight and theological cogency of both thinkers!

[31] Kierkegaard was fully aware that progress made on the basis of common ground (even negative common ground) in philosophical dialogue runs the risk

Barth's approach is quite simply incompatible with explanations of theological method or theological epistemology which begin by seeking to address a problem. He simply would not begin an examination of any theological claim, formal or material, with a consideration of a 'how' question (as Climacus does), nor would he frame any exposition of these within the context of a 'how' question![32] To do so would be to seek to interpret and affirm the Logos on the basis of a prior ratification of our *logoi*. For Barth this would amount to a subtle form of disobedience.

In sum, Barth found himself totally opposed to theology moulded by *a priori* premises (be they formal or material) which were endorsed as being establishable independently of the exposition and articulation of the becoming of the Word,

of failing to distinguish between two different hermeneutical circles – one hypothetical, anticipatable and ultimately subjective, the other actual and given in such a way that its rationale is radically and objectively dependent on the 'event' or free act of this givenness.

Barth himself thought that theologians should attend the school of Kierkegaard although he also thought that they should move beyond him to greater objectivity. (Cf. T. F. Torrance, *Karl Barth: An Introduction to his Early Theology 1910–1931*, London, 1962, 30f., where he discusses Barth's desire to move beyond the 'cancerous subjectivism' from which Kierkegaard was not able to free himself. Barth desired a real theological objectivity – 'What he needed above all was to break through to concrete relations with the living God.')

[32] Barth's views are echoed with clarity and conciseness in Dietrich Bonhoeffer's impressive discussion of the primacy of the 'Who?' question over the 'How?' question in christology. The 'How?' question, he argues, affirms the 'human, classifying logos' and risks assimilating the counter-logos into itself. Christology must operate from methodological and presuppositional 'silence'. 'When the Counter-Logos appears in history, no longer as an idea, but as "Word" become flesh, there is no longer any possibility of assimilating him into the existing order of the human logos. The only real question which now remains is: "Who are you? Speak for yourself!" The question, "Who are you?", is the question of dethroned and distraught reason; but it is also the question of faith ...' ('Introduction' to *Christology* (transcribed from the lecture notes of his students), Eng. trans. by Edwin Robertson, London, 1978, 29–30.) It is interesting to note the extent to which Bonhoeffer's discussion echoes Kierkegaard's discussion and critique of the Socratic method.

the *Event* (lit. *e-venire*) of which functions as its own *Apo-logia* at both the material and formal levels.[33]

But what is also crystal clear, not least in his repentance of the mistakes in his early theology, his debate with Przywara and also his dialogue with Emil Brunner, is that Barth was not only totally opposed to such *a priori* claims, he was also totally opposed to any *a priori* **repudiation** of such claims.[34] Any such *a priori* repudiation is itself a form of 'natural theology' – and *a fortiori* not a form of *theology*, as Barth defined it, at all! What is important to appreciate is that Barth should not be interpreted as engaged in an *a priori* repudiation of claims made independently of the Gospel, as Brunner would appear to interpret him as doing.[35] That there is, indeed, rather more openness on Barth's part than either Brunner and many of Barth's critics are willing to acknowledge is reflected in his comment: 'There is talk of revelation outside the Bible too, and we have no reason to say that this is absolutely impossible.'[36]

Barth's theological method means that *negative* repudiations should also be grounded in the positive acknowledgement of God's free giving of himself to be proclaimed and thus spoken. The sole force of God's 'No!' is his 'Yes!' and this applies to the whole process of theological affirmation and negation.

This speech-act of the Word of God, by the free grace of God, bankrupts any perceived need to make offerings before 'foreign' theories or starting-points conceived as affirmable in advance. The force of his negations was, in his mind, the *authority* attaching to the event of the Word. Actual knowledge of God suggests that it alone is the ground of our consideration of what is possible before God and what is not possible, what

---

[33] He also refused to proceed from any ratifying of claims of the 'synthetic *a priori*' variety as if they possessed the authority to condition the manner in which we think, positively or negatively, about the nature of the event of revelation.

[34] For Barth, the '(r)eal rejection of natural theology can come about only in the fear of God.' ('No! Answer to Emil Brunner', Eng. trans. in *Natural Theology*, edited by John Baillie, London, 1946, 76.)

[35] Cf. section entitled 'Barth's False Conclusions' in *Nature and Grace*, Eng. trans. in *Natural Theology*, edited by John Baillie, 19–22.

[36] *C. D.* 1. 1, 331 (*K. D.* 1. 1, 350).

is appropriate and inappropriate, both formally and materially. 'Even knowledge of the impossibility of knowledge of the Word of God outside its reality is possible only on the presupposition of this real knowledge.' ('Auch die Erkenntnis der Unmöglichkeit der Erkenntnis des Wortes Gottes außerhalb ihrer Wirklichkeit ist nur möglich unter Voraussetzung dieser wirklichen Erkenntnis.')[37] In other words, Barth's insistence that the 'No!' is grounded solely in a prior 'Yes!' is as relevant with respect to the repudiation of forms of 'natural theology', Idealism or liberal theology as it is in the ethical domain or, indeed, any other. This is not to deny that there is a philosophical task for philosophers to engage in, but their results are not to be conceived either negatively or positively as falling within the domain of theology or preparing the ground in which the claims of the Word may take root.

Parallel to this, Barth also believed that our decisions as to what is possible beyond the Church must also be grounded alone in what is given within the context of God's Word as witnessed within the Church: 'it is only subsequently, *a posteriori*, exegetically and not in the sense of demonstrating the Church's commission, that we may rightly consider whether even the thought of God's Word being revealed outside the known existing Church is possible for one who has not previously come to be acquainted with real proclamation within the Church.'[38]

Any eagerness to continue in any other vein Barth interprets as a *de facto* repudiation of the validity of God's Self-utterance

---

[37] *C. D.* 1. 1, 197 (*K. D.* 1. 1, 206). It is not at all Barth's concern to find support for his critique of natural theology and of *a priori*, 'philosophical' reasoning by appealing, for example, to Hume or any other expositions of the inadequacy of natural religion. The suspicion of natural theology has nothing to do with philosophical debates as to whether or not it works. What is unambiguously clear is that, if the Word of God warranted this kind of engagement, Barth would support it whether or not the philosophers were happy about it! One can also see here why he was so keen to repudiate the term Barthianism as it implies that there is a Barthian 'system' or formal approach being advocated and submitted for the task of theological analysis.

[38] *C. D.* 1. 1, 57–8 (*K. D.* 1. 1, 58). Clearly, this is particularly relevant for an assessment of the status of the argument in chapter two of Kierkegaard's *Philosophical Fragments*.

whether or not what is hit upon by the natural theologian or 'philosopher of religion' happens to be true and relevant.[39] This is the main thrust of his repudiation of the wisdom of natural theology and, indeed, of the notion of an *analogia entis.*[40] The force of Barth's approach should be interpreted affirmatively, rather than negatively, as a sustained and consistent affirmation and endorsement at the methodological level of an objective, *a posteriori* approach – in so far as this is dictated by faith. His concern to be true to this is reflected not least in the very manner in which he uses the terms 'must' and 'cannot'. As Colin Gunton rightly (if too tentatively) observes, these 'might almost be called analytic *a posteriori* statements'.[41] In contrast, therefore, to all forms of what might loosely be termed 'foundationalism', i.e. approaches which start with a prior ontology, deontology, methodology, metaphysic or anthropology, Barth interprets all relevant, describable features of theological method as

---

[39] One wonders whether the bitterness and confusion which has been associated with the debate concerning natural theology is not bound up in part with confusion over the terms used. One suspects that what is sometimes seen as being repudiated by Barth is a theology of nature or what is given to men and women as their *humanum* where both of these are assumed to be the concern of a programme of theology entitled 'natural theology'. Neither of these fears are grounded. Barth's concern is for reverence before the Word who exists as freedom and not as 'object' and who is the Word of creation as much as of God's reconciling act of revelation. Barth's concern relates to any conclusions or suppositions that do not show that they take the facticity of this with sufficient seriousness at either the formal or material levels. It is arguably confused to see this as reflecting opposition to a form of 'theology'!

[40] Barth's consistency here is reflected in his openness to the 'content of truth in even the so-called analogia entis: *quum igitur christiana fides hominem de Deo... instruit... fit in homine quaedam divinae sapientiae similitudo* (Thomas Aquinas, *Summa contra Gentiles, II, 2).' (C. D. 1. 1, 239; K. D. 1. 1, 252.*) He is happy to affirm such a *similitudo* just as he is also concerned to affirm the ascription to human beings of an 'aptness to receive the Word of God'. He writes, 'There can be no receiving of God's Word unless there is something common to the speaking God and hearing man in this event, a similarity for all the dissimilarity implied by the distinction between God and man, a point of contact between God and man, if we may now adopt this term too.' (*C. D.* 1.1, 238; *K. D.* 1. 1, 251.)

[41] *Being and Becoming: The Doctrine of God in the Theology of Charles Hartshorne and Karl Barth,* London, 1978, 130.

requiring to be articulated from the knowledge of faith as this is described *a posteriori* from within the context of the givenness of revelation for faith in the Body of Christ. Justification for this, moreover, reposes nowhere else than on the content or substance of that faith given in and with the event of revelation that constitutes it.

It is perhaps to labour the point still further to add that when Barth uses the word 'presupposition' ('Voraussetzung'), as he does when he refers to 'the presupposition of this real knowledge of the Word', Barth really means 'post-supposition' ('Nachaussetzung'). It is *nach* with regard to the revealing act of God and it is only *vor* in so far as it is *therefore and for this reason* epistemologically prior to any statements that we might make, methodological or otherwise, about God or indeed method. Any 'pre-ness' ('Vorheit') attaching to a methodological or epistemological statement results from its 'post-ness' ('Nachheit') at this deeper level. And Barth is not advocating an *a posteriori* method because he is (negatively) an 'anti-foundationalist' or 'anti-idealist', but because theological articulation is neither prompted by, nor motivated by, but actually *derives* at the most fundamental level from the *interruption* of our apperception by the Gospel in the form of the speech-act of God. The very nature of this event he sees as denying him the right to ratify any approach which implies that we can operate with prior, extraneous conditions on our thinking about the Word of God.

In other words, there is no *a priori*, 'philosophical' or formal argument against foundationalist argumentation operating here. What we have is no more than an expression of the *a posteriori* conviction that in the face of the givenness of God for speech in the context of the reconciled community of the Church, and as this is to be identified with God's presence, any attempt to step outside this and establish conditions upon God's speech *must* (analytic *a posteriori!*) involve a form of disobedience, a failure to think out of God's freedom and therefore a failure to let God be God.

In the light of the critical givenness of God for speech within the domain created and sustained by God's being Revealer, Revelation and the Condition/Context of revelation (the Revealedness), any recourse to God as given within or conditioned by such theories or absolutised dogmas is analogous to believing not only that God-talk but that God himself (since the Word of God *is* God) is conditioned within the human domain by what may be described as established 'software applications' (foundational formal instructions) on the one hand, or 'saved data files' (the truths of the 'tradition') on the other – to use contemporary computer-jargon!

One of the most seductive forms of this error Barth finds, like Helmut Thielicke,[42] in the 'Cartesianism' which has so moulded the development of European theology. Barth cites the following claim by Wobbermin as an example: 'The I-experience establishes for man the surest certainty for reality that he can conceive of or that is possible for him at all. It is the presupposition ... of all validation of reality with reference to the external world.'[43] What he is offering is an existentialist form of what Alvin Plantinga has described in his Gifford Lectures (1986-7) as 'Classical Foundationalism'.

In radical contrast to this, Barth argues that the 'fact of God's Word does not receive its dignity and validity in any respect or even to the slightest degree from a presupposition that we bring to it. Its truth for us, like its truth in itself, is grounded absolutely in itself.'[44]

This *a posteriori* repudiation of the claim of 'foundationalist' approaches to provide access to human certainty or theological surety stems from a *positive* affirmation, namely that 'The procedure in theology ... is to establish self-certainty on the certainty of God, to measure it by the certainty of God, and thus to begin with the certainty of God without waiting for the validating of this beginning by self-certainty.'[45]

[42] Cf. Helmut Thielicke's *Der Evangelische Glaube*, Tübingen, 1968, the opening two parts of which offer an extensive discussion of European theological approaches moulded by a Cartesian methodology and agenda.

[43] *C. D.* 1. 1, 195 (citing G. Wobbermin, *Systematische Theologie, Vol. 2*, 1921, 455) (*K. D.* 1. 1, 203).

[44] *C. D.* 1. 1, 196 (*K. D.* 1. 1, 204).

[45] Ibid.

Our judgement as to how far the apparent circularity here is only a circularity if interpreted from within a Cartesian perspective, how far it is valid and/or scientific, should become clear as we progress. Suffice to say that for Barth there could be no possibility of standing outside the standpoint of faith and affirming the validity either of this statement or what it presupposes. The most that may be discerned outside of faith is the self-referential incoherence involved in any attempt to seek to establish outside the faith a claim that includes the methodological implication that that claim can only be perceived within the context of faith! Perhaps here dialogue with the secular philosopher can indeed find agreement!

The Necessity of the Semantic Revision of Theological Terminology

There is a further point, here, which we have touched on but to which we must draw particular attention as it is critical for our present discussion of Barth's approach to the theological use of the term 'person'. The impropriety of an *a priori* approach relates no more specifically to our interpretation of method and our ways of knowing than to our understanding of the function of the terminology which belongs to the discipline of theology.

In every question that is asked suppositions are made which relate to the meaning of the terms used. These suppositions which are inevitable and potentially innocent become less than innocent if we fail to appreciate their provisionality or 'sketch-like' quality.[46] If this happens, the answer to a question, no matter how careful, can function as a *de facto* ratification of a prior conceptuality in a manner which undermines the very possibility of critical dialogue with these suppositions. We must appreciate here the emphases of Wittgenstein and, more recently, of the Hintikkas concerning the extent to which language actually creates and conditions thought rather

---

[46] Suppositions here can too easily become, in Collingwood's language, 'relative presuppositions' or more sinisterly 'absolute presuppositions' which are so fundamental to one's frame of reference that one is not even aware one is presupposing them. (*Essay on Metaphysics*, Oxford, 1940.)

than the other way round.[47] Semantic naïveté here too easily
endorses a 'social construction of reality' (to borrow the
expression used by Peter Berger and Thomas Luckmann[48])
rather than the theological reconstruction of our sociality!
Barth is profoundly aware of the fact that the meaning of
language is to be interpreted in terms of the conventions
governing its use rather than some isolated, accompanying
'thought' or 'idea' in the mind of the speaker. Referring to the
words that constitute the material of proclamation and the
'raw material' of dogmatics, he writes, in a manner which
anticipates the insights of the later Wittgenstein, 'these words
*acquire their meaning through the associations and connexions in
which they are used*'.[49] This implies that meaning is a product of
the public domain. Consequently, the meaning of a term is
neither to be understood simplistically as its reference nor
merely as the mode of designation of its reference, as Frege
argued,[50] but rather, as Wittgenstein was to show in his
Philosophical Investigations, in terms of the complex rules of use
and language-games constituted and governed by public
conventions.[51] This means that dogmatics must continually
ask the question as to how far the 'specific usages' are adapted
or not to their purpose of serving God's Word.[52] Essential,
therefore, to the critical task of dogmatics in its service of

[47] Cf. Wittgenstein, *Philosophical Investigations*, Oxford, 1967, and also Merrill B.
and Jaakko Hintikka, *Investigating Wittgenstein*, Oxford, 1986.
  [48] Peter L. Berger and Thomas Luckmann, *The Social Construction of Reality: A
Treatise in the Sociology of Knowledge*, New York, 1966.
  [49] *C. D.* 1. 1, 78 (italics mine) (*K. D.* 1. 1, 79).
  [50] See his essay 'Über Sinn und Bedeutung', the English translation of which
may be found in P. Geach and M. Black (eds.), *Translations from the Philosophical
Writings of Gottlob Frege*, Oxford, 1952.
  [51] Fergus Kerr points to the fundamental agreement here between Wittgenstein
and Barth drawing attention to the fact that Wittgenstein read the first volume
of Barth's *Church Dogmatics*. (*Theology after Wittgenstein*, Oxford, 1986.)
  [52] 'Here as elsewhere these words acquire their meanings through the
associations and connexions in which they are used. By virtue of these meanings,
talk about God becomes in every age specific and distinctive talk. It is in a
plenitude of such specific usages that it exists at any given time for dogmatics, and
in general the dogmatic question will be whether and how far this talk, i.e., the
sense in which the words are employed in it, is adapted or not to its purpose of
serving God's Word.' (*C. D.* 1. 1, 78; *K. D.* 1. 1, 79.)

proclamation is the critical assessment of 'yesterday's proclamation' and the extent to which its content is determined by the meanings attached to its words and how far these meanings have been altered by changes in the rules of use of these terms.[53] In this way, therefore, 'Scientific dogmatics must devote itself to the criticism and correction of Church proclamation and not just to a repetitive exposition of it'.[54] If this is not a continual task – and if any particular concept or word is absolutised – then we may find ourselves absolutising semantic regulations (i.e. suppositions) extrinsic to the revelation event. Secular subliminal legislation at the semantic level would thereby condition the dynamic of grace!

This issue is linked directly by Barth to the challenge of avoiding 'tacit' and illegitimate forms of what I have referred to as 'foundationalism' in the manner in which we take over terms which carry with them fixed conventions of usage. This is reflected not only in his discussion of the word 'science' in connection with his description of dogmatics as 'science', but also in his discussion of the concept of 'knowledge'. Barth's self-consistency here is expressed clearly in his careful explanation of how he allowed the word 'knowledge' to function in his broaching the topic of theological knowledge.

> When knowledge was defined earlier as acquaintance with the reality of an object which is self-confirmed in the subject, this was meant to be only a sketch of the problem of knowledge and not an anticipatory interpretation. Any interpretation at this stage would mean philosophical and epistemological definition. But the problem of knowledge cannot be presupposed with such distinctness here even as a problem if we are not to incur the most serious risk of anticipating the answer in the presupposition in a very definite and perhaps most inappropriate way. *What knowledge means as knowledge of God must in no case be introduced in a definitive form into investigation of this question.*[55]

It is due to a seductive failure to appreciate this that so many theological questions are reduced to anthropological ones, not least the question of knowledge of God. A prior concept

---

[53] *C. D.* 1. 1, 78 (*K. D.* 1. 1, 80).
[54] *C. D.* 1. 1, 281 (*K. D.* 1. 1, 298).
[55] *C. D.* 1. 1, 190 (italics mine) (*K. D.* 1. 1, 197).

of knowledge is used which means that the question 'How is God known?' is reduced (explicitly or implicitly) to questions concerning the possibility of the extension of our concept of knowledge to include a reality such as God. As this assumes that God can only be 'known' if and in so far as this previously defined conception of knowledge can include within its domain such an 'object' as God is assumed to be, another (anthropological) question is addressed, namely, 'How *can* God be known?', that is, 'How can we encompass God within the prior domain of this knowing activity?' Or, to put the matter more concretely, 'How can God belong to the class of "objects knowable by human beings"?' Immediately the matter has been approached in this way a form of 'foundationalism', which regulates the usage of terms, serves to define the theological task in such a way that the crudest of theological mistakes is made, that is, God is reduced to membership of a class defined with recourse to predeterminable, human capacities.[56]

The fact that we have spent so much time on the issues raised in this section is due not least to our concern to emphasise the illegitimacy which Barth would find in approaching God-talk and theological anthropology with a prior ontology of personhood or predefined category of personhood (particularly one defined from an essentially anthropological base) – that is, in baptising a concept whose use was not critically redefined by the theological context in which it is used. We shall see that Barth's critique of the way the concept has been used in the past is a form of criticism of yesterday's proclamation on grounds which have received expression in this section. The extent to which his conclusions were correct and the alternative he provided appropriate will be discussed in chapter four.

The Identity in God of Word and Act

In parallel to his refusal to support the operation of a form–content dichotomy in his theological programme, and his consistent refusal to engage in approaches which we have

---

[56] Cf. *C. D.* 1. 1, 191 (*K. D.* 1. 1, 199).

described as 'foundationalist', Barth also stresses at the ontological level the identity – rather than mere correspondence – in God of Word and Act. 'God's Word is itself God's act.'[57] God's Word is 'enacted Divine event'.[58] Consequently, whenever God speaks to man the content of the speech is a *concretissimum*.[59] To put it another way, when God speaks, there is no point in looking about for a related act.[60] God's speech is act just as God's Being as Being is pure event.[61] Just as there can be no dichotomy between God's Word and Act, neither can, nor rather must, God's Work and Essence be conceived as being of two different kinds.[62]

One obvious implication of this is that there are no grounds for operating in theology with a dichotomy between God's speaking and its being heard of a kind to which we may be accustomed at the level of human discourse. If God always speaks concretely a Word of personal address then its being heard is integral to the same act of God. This point is made by Barth, not with recourse to a theory of the *logical* necessity of

---

[57] *C. D.* 1. 1, 147 (*K. D.* 1. 1, 153). It is this that gives rise to Horst Pöhlmann's comment that Barth is committed to an 'actualistic ontology'. Cf. Horst Georg Pöhlmann, *Analogia entis oder Analogia fidei?, Die Frage der Analogie bei Karl Barth,* Göttingen, 1965, 119. He suggests also, 'Man kann deshalb ohne Übertreibung von einem Panaktualismus Barths sprechen.' (ibid., 117.) As I shall argue further in chapter four, it is not Barth's concern or intention to seek to universalise an actualistic concept of being. His emphasis on the *a posteriori* nature of theological articulation precludes this kind of ontological agenda. For his criticism to work Pöhlmann requires to show that Barth's grounds for his refusing to operate theologically with a dualism between God's being and act are foreign to an *a posteriori* theological description of the New Testament notions of the divine Presence, Glory, Word and the identification of the Redeemer as 'Immanuel'.

[58] *C. D.* 1. 1, 59 (*K. D.* 1. 1, 60).

[59] *C. D.* 1. 1, 140 (*K. D.* 1. 1, 145).

[60] *C. D.* 1. 1, 143 (*K. D.* 1. 1, 148).

[61] Eberhard Jüngel, *The Doctrine of the Trinity,* 27.

[62] Ibid., 33: 'But because for Barth God's work and essence are not of two different kinds, it is for him impossible that the reality of God and the reality which owed its existence to God's work should be related to each other as two different ontological strata and even less that they should fall apart as two worlds separated through a chorismos (division).'

It would be of value to consider Eberhard Jüngel's exposition of Barth's thought here but this will be reserved for the next chapter when we shall consider more fully Barth's understanding of the Being of God.

the divine utterance being heard, but with recourse to the coinherence of the person of the Word in Jesus Christ and the Holy Spirit. When we speak of the Holy Spirit,

> we are always speaking of the event in which God's Word is not only revealed to man but also believed by him. We are always speaking of the way in which the Word of God is so said to this or that man that he must hear it, or of the way in which this or that man is so open and ready for the Word of God that he can hear it.

In this coinherence of the Word and the Spirit (so stressed by Athanasius in his affirmation of the *homoousion* both of the Son and of the Holy Spirit as the *sine qua non* of God's Self-communication to humanity and of the very possibility of *theologein*) resides the grounds of the inseparability of God's Word (conceived as personal address) and its reception by the human subject. As God's Word is never an address into thin air the divine address includes its hearing. An implication of this is that we

> must believe in our faith no less than in the Word believed, i.e., even if we think we can and should regard our attitude to God's Word as positive, even if we confess our faith, we can regard it as positive only as it is made possible and actual by God, only as the miracle of the Holy Ghost and not as our own work.[63]

This brings us to a further implication of this identity between Word and Act, between Essence and Work, namely to the essentially *personal* nature of God's Self-communication as it is affirmed in and through this integration. Its personal nature is highlighted by the refusal to countenance any conceptual reduction of God's Word. It can be interpreted neither as a describable entity nor as an objective reality. Further, there is no possibility of defining it with recourse to a general model of truth – not even as its most supreme *exemplar*. Rather, it is *the* truth *precisely* by virtue of its being God's speaking person – '*Dei loquentis persona.*'[64] This means,

---

[63] *C. D.* 1. 1, 182 (*K. D.* 1. 1, 190).
[64] *C. D.* 1. 1, 136 (*K. D.* 1. 1, 141). Barth uses the same Latin phrase later on (p. 304), where he again stresses the irreducibly concrete particularity of the divine

again, that it is not to be conceived as *an* objective reality but
rather as *the* objective reality where this objectivity reposes
precisely in the fact that it is also subjective, 'the subjective that
is God'.[65]

This irreducibly 'personal quality' of God's speaking and
the consequent impossibility of detaching God's Word from
God's speaking (and therefore from God's personal Being-
toward-us) points further to the fact that God's Word is as
unanticipatable and unrepeatable by human beings as God's
Being is unanticipatable or unrepeatable. Just as human
beings cannot be the authors of the personal Being of God,
neither can they anticipate nor repeat the Word of God by
virtue of the fact that it *is God* in God's free, personal Being.
This means, naturally, that what God speaks can never be
known or true anywhere in abstraction from God himself. 'It
is known and true in and through the fact that He Himself says
it, that He is present in person in and with what is said by
Him.'[66] It also carries with it the further implication that God's
act of speech creates the conditions of its being understood.
The Truth of God's Word and the event of its communication
within the Church cannot be interpreted in terms of
possibilities or potentialities immanent within the human
subject in particular or the created order in general. Any
inner truth created within the human subject, any coming to
articulation of the Word of Christ, is created and brought
about by the Truth which is 'purely external' and therefore by
a free act of God's *eudokia*.[67]

---

address in revelation as this is to be identified with the Being of God. Here he
writes, 'According to Scripture God's revelation is God's own direct speech which
is not to be distinguished from the act of speaking and therefore is not to be
distinguished from God Himself, for the divine I which confronts man in this act
in which it says Thou to him. Revelation is *Dei loquentis persona*.'

[65] *C. D.* 1. 1, 136 (*K. D.* 1. 1, 141): 'It is the objective reality, in that it is also
subjective, the subjective that is God.'

[66] 'The personalising of the concept of the Word of God, which we cannot avoid
when we remember that Jesus Christ is the Word of God, does not mean its
deverbalising.' (*C. D.* 1. 1, 138.) It is its personal nature which underscores its
verbal quality. To emphasise the former serves to strengthen, rather than to
detract from, the latter.

[67] *C. D.* 1. 1, 148 (*K. D.* 1. 1, 153). Barth here refers to Mt. 11:26; Gal. 1:15 and
Eph. 1:9.

It is in his exposition of this personalising (though not de-verbalising) of the concept of the Word of God, necessitated by the identification of the Word of God with Jesus Christ, that we have Barth's initial (and rather individualistic) discussion of the attribution of personhood to God in the *Church Dogmatics.*

> To be person means to be subject, not merely in the logical sense, but also in the ethical sense: to be free subject, a subject which is free even in respect of the specific limitations connected with its individuality, able to control its own existence and nature both as particular form and also as living development, and also able to select new possibilities of existence and nature. If we consider what this implies, it will not occur to us to see in this personalising of the concept of God's Word a case of anthropomorphism. The doubtful thing is not whether God is person, but whether we are. Can we find among us even one man whom we can call this in the full and proper sense of the term? But God is real person, really free subject.[68]

(The criticism that Barth's concept of God as 'really free subject' echoes idealist or Hegelian concepts of God as pure subjectivity will be addressed below in chapter four.) What seems to suggest itself here is an individualistic tinge to Barth's conception of divine personhood, an individualism that is challenged, as we shall see, by the notions of divine personhood to be found, for example, in the theologies of Yannaras, Zizioulas, Moltmann, Gunton and LaCugna, to mention just a few contemporary names noted for their views on this matter.[69]

---

[68] *C. D.* 1. 1, 138-9.

[69] It may, of course, be pointed out that these names share some of the same roots. LaCugna is profoundly influenced by Zizioulas as is clear from her book (Catherine Mowry LaCugna, *God for Us: The Trinity and Christian Life,* New York, 1991). Moltmann sees his doctrine of the Triunity with its, arguably, *pluralistic* conception of the divine community as resulting from ecumenical discussions with the Orthodox at the Commission for Faith and Order in 1978 and 1979 (*The Trinity and the Kingdom of God* (Eng. trans. by Margaret Kohl), London, 1981, xv), and interprets his exposition as an attempt to integrate Western and Eastern insights rather as Zizioulas has sought to do. We might also add that his latest writing on the subject owes a great deal to Christos Yannaras (cf. *History and the Triune God* (Eng. trans. John Bowden), London, 1991, xii) and, indeed, is endorsed by him (see ibid., 183, note 6). Finally, John Zizioulas also seems to have

To speak of divine personhood is, for Barth, to speak of the free subjectivity of God in his love for humankind and therefore it is to speak of the possibility of objective God-talk where its reference penetrates to the very Being of God in and through the Self-referring of the Word by grace. It is to make divine subjectivity the ground of the objectivity of the Church's proclamation and its subsequent liberation from an otherwise 'Babylonian captivity' of its language and conceptuality in prior forms of semantic regulation.

This is certainly not to suggest, however, that the *human* concept of personhood is basic to a proper theology. Rather, it is to say that the personal nature of God, as this is defined for us *a posteriori* in and through the Act of God, is essential to the possibility of theology. And it also leads to the affirmation that the liberation or, rather, recreation of human beings for personhood is the subsequent condition at the human level of the epistemic communion which stems from this free act of God's grace.

One of the prime concerns of this whole discussion, however, will be to assess how far Barth succeeded in being true to his intentions in this regard, that is, how far Barth *did* ultimately succeed in allowing a radically *a posteriori* redefinition of divine personhood actually and effectively to take place in and through his own modelling of revelation.

The Eschatological Tension in Human Existence

If the anthropology of the Reformed tradition has been associated with the doctrine of 'total depravity' – despite, paradoxically, the remarkable confidence in the rational capabilities of human beings of certain hyper-Calvinists – sight is too often lost of the fact that in Calvin this was not a foundational dogma. It was grounded in the affirmation of the grace of God in relation to which humanity could affirm its absolute value in Christ and subsequently and *by contrast* its own worthlessness as this describes humanity in its alienation

been influenced by Christos Yannaras, whom he clearly regards as an ally ('On Human Capacity and Incapacity, A Theological Exploration of Personhood', *S. J. T.* 28 (1975), 408, n. 2).

from God. Anticipating Calvin, Luther expresses the epistemic implications of the basicality of grace in the following way: 'No creature can come to this knowledge [of the Word]. For Christ alone revealeth it to it in the heart itself. Thus falleth to the ground all merit, all powers and faculties of reason, and availeth naught for God.'[70] As suggested by this quotation from Luther (which Barth cites and endorses), the failure to take seriously the fact that we live in the sphere of grace, that we are participants in the *regnum gratiae*, can only lead to massive epistemological and methodological confusion and a fatal failure to distinguish between the Truth of the Reality of God and the products of our own forms of intellectual alienation and confusion. It is, moreover, the *a posteriori* nature of this perception that means that it cannot be ignored – it is a consequence of the Gospel and arrived at deductively. That this facet of our humanity has been so overlooked derives from the fact that the tendency of so much theology (not only Catholic Thomism but also Neo-scholastic Calvinism with its emphasis on the knowability of God in the created order by the light of natural reason) has been to dismiss this acknowledgement of the intellectual alienation or fallenness of humankind as a denigratory, *a priori* supposition which doubts the goodness of God's creation, rather than as an unavoidable conclusion derived *a posteriori* before the factuality of God's grace, God's righteousness and God's creative goodness as these are defined in and through Christ.[71]

---

[70] Sermon on Mt. 11:25-30, 1527, W.A., 23, p. 689, 1.4, quoted by Barth, *C. D.* 1. 1, 185 (*K. D.* 1. 1, 192).

[71] Two further factors have been influential here: first, there is the subliminal appeal, deeply ingrained within European thought, of 'tripartite' anthropology (defining the person in terms of the three faculties of reason, will and emotion). This introduces a dichotomy between the reason or the intellect and the will, relating sin exclusively to the domain of the latter. Second, the continuing method characteristic of the Western *ordo salutis* (law/nature – sin – grace) and its need to postulate a universally and naturally recognisable (by the light of natural reason) *Anknüpfungspunkt* in the human person which requires the formal integrity and reliable function of our rational capacities and their innate natural ability to perceive what is and what is not God's will. Our *sensus moralis* becomes the *sine qua non* of the whole operation as it is otherwise impossible to hold the human subject responsible for sin. The extent and nature of human

For Barth, it is absolutely critical that Christian theology take into account, at the formal as much as at the material level, the fact that we live not in the *regnum gloriae* but in the *regnum gratiae.* If we belonged to the former, there would be no need either for any 'special talk about God', or for our being addressed by God. Similarly, there would be no need for the Church. This is one area in which Barth sees much modernist theology (he cites the examples of Paul Tillich and Otto Dibelius)[72] as falling seriously short. Immanentist theologies which co-posit God and humanity operate on the basis of the supposition that there is no real tension between the two spheres or two 'times'. As such, *a priori* assumptions come into operation which refuse to take seriously the eschatological tension of the New Testament as it bears testimony to the inadequacy, imperfection and incompleteness attaching to our present ability to know God. This incompleteness and alienation includes not only certain areas of our knowledge (or absence of it) that we can nevertheless determine and circumscribe, but our very awareness of and ability to gauge the extent, range and ramifications of our epistemic *lack of communion.* In other words, not only is our lack of appreciation of the inadequacy of our knowledge of God endemic to the problem here but the fact that we cannot, in advance of the address of the Word of God and reconciliation to it, determine appropriately where our knowledge of God is reliable and where it is not. This has inescapable implications at the formal level every bit as much as at the material level. Furthermore, if one were to

alienation is thereby restricted to the domain of the will, to the realm of the individual's autonomous choice. Why this is endorsed so strongly is due to an underlying contractual interpretation of the relationship between God and the human self and the attendant need to think in terms of the category of 'just reward'. In other words, a Western juridical interpretation of God's will (with categories quite foreign to the essence of the Pauline interpretation of our being made righteous through the faithfulness of Christ) has served to condition *a priori* certain essential features of Western theological anthropology. Cf. Douglas Campbell, *The Rhetoric of Righteousness in Romans 3:21–26,* J. S. N. T. Supplement, Sheffield, 1992.

[72] *C. D.* 1. 1, 63 (*K. D.* 1. 1, 64).

attempt to deny this, one would have to establish that what is literally the *Sub-stantia* of Christian theology has either no real significance at the formal level at all, or that that which it *does* have can be interpreted as accommodated within limits which are determinable *a priori*, that is, in advance of the gracious address to humanity which *is* the Person of the Word of God (*Dei loquentis persona*). This latter alternative would imply that we can know infallibly that the very fact of this possibility can itself be determined reliably as a possibility in advance. It is difficult to see how any such argument could interpret itself as taking seriously the fact that we do not belong to the *regnum gloriae*.

The point we are making represents essentially an 'ontic' issue rather than a temporal one. The essence of the eschatological tension must be perceived within the perspective of the present lack of fully realised communion with God. This in turn is perceived in the light of the promise of the realisation of such communion by the act of God's establishment of the *regnum gloriae* as the context in which the fullness of *his* glory includes the fullest realisation of *ours* – what might be called the 'beatific participation'.[73] In advance of, or outside of, this state of intellectual and empirical communion with God, God is not given for the natural purview of human beings. The issue here, as we have just mentioned, clearly does not therefore relate to any arbitrary 'temporal placing' of human history in relation to the eternal, but to the breach of humanity's communion with God. At the same time, it directs us on the one hand to the divine freedom which means that God is not an object for our examination in the context of this alienation, and on the other hand to the divine promise, as this reposes in and includes the *realised*

---

[73] There is a need for a 'reconstruction' of the concept of beatific vision not only in the light of the critique of ocularism in contemporary philosophy (cf. Richard Rorty's *Philosophy and the Mirror of Nature,* Princeton, 1979), but more specifically in the light of a properly theological concept of communion which precludes the element of detachment inherent within visualist metaphors and encourages a more dynamic, holistic and subject-involving concept of knowledge of God.

eschatological dimension – namely, God's interruption into this brokenness in Christ. The latter holds forth the prospective vision of the final completion of the new creation and realisation of the new humanity and thus of humanity's epistemic powers at every level.

The implications of eschatology for the theological enterprise are summarised by Barth in the following way:

> We are asking about the concrete present of God's Word between the times, a present that is as certain as it is inconceivable, as unique as it is ever new. Naturally the reality of revelation stands beyond the concept, even and precisely the concept derived from the Bible and proclamation. We cannot try to deal with the reality. Neither in proclamation nor in dogmatics can we produce the attested past and promised future as a present. Nor can we think that in any present that we can produce we are producing this past or this future. We are dealing with the concept of revelation, i.e., with the present of God's Word between the times. But we are still dealing with a concrete concept of revelation, with a concrete present of God's Word.[74]

One implication of this is that there is no place, therefore, for an ontology of personhood which assumes that the concept of the person possesses the status of a 'natural' bridge between the times, between the *regnum gloriae* and the *regnum gratiae*. If a concept is provided which possesses a realised eschatological function, then this will be conceived and defined *subsequent* to the theology of grace and will not be presupposed by it.

The Provisional Nature of Dogmatic's Forms of Expression

Barth perceives a continual need for the 'direction of Christian thought and speech to its own contemporary responsibility'.[75] The fact that Christian truth is about the Self-communication of the Truth, in such a way that our formulations of the truth

---

[74] *C. D.* 1. 1, 291 (*K. D.* 1. 1, 309). It may be noted that Barth has little time for concepts of revelation 'in general' or notions of 'general revelation'. This is reflected, for example, when he insists that the root of the doctrine of the Trinity is in revelation – 'not in any revelation, not in a general concept of revelation, but in the concept of revelation taken from the Bible' (*C. D.* 1. 1, 332; *K. D.* 1. 1, 351).

[75] *C. D.* 1. 1, 16 (*K. D.* 1. 1, 15). It might be added that Barth's views here were to have a profound influence on Pope John XXIII.

cannot, therefore, be identified with that Truth, means that dogmatics asks not what tradition has said, but rather what the Truth, as it is witnessed in and through the tradition, dictates that we must say to the *present* of our alienated condition – not in order that it may be contained in, or translated into, propositional form, but in order that the Truth's Self-communication *as* the Word might be served by means of our proclamation. Consequently, 'dogmatics does not ask what the apostles and prophets say but what we must say on the basis of apostles and prophets'.[76] Thus,

> Dogmatics is preparation for Church proclamation. It formulates statements that have to be pondered before Church proclamation formulates its statements. But it is by this relation that the statements of dogmatics must be tested. They should never stand in the air (perhaps as statements constructed for the sake of logical or philosophical or moral completeness) in such a way as to be unintelligible as preparation for Church proclamation and intelligible only as pure gnosis.[77]

This is the ground of his disagreement with the Roman Catholic conception of the nature of dogmatic theology where 'a dogma is a truth of revelation defined by the Church and dogmatics is the collection of these dogmas and commentary on them'.[78] For Barth, dogma is 'simply the kerygma tested, provisionally purified, and reduced to a correct formula by the church'.[79] Consequently, there is no ground for taking the further step of interpreting dogmas as '*veritates a Deo formaliter revelatae*'[80] which may exist *in vacuo*. There must be a clear distinction between *the Church's expressions of the truth* (in and through which the Church seeks to articulate the reality of God's promise to us, 'Lo! I am with you always', as this constitutes the context of God's judgement of

[76] *C. D.* 1. 1, 16 (*K. D.* 1. 1, 15).
[77] *C. D.* 1. 1, 280 (*K. D.* 1. 1, 297).
[78] *C. D.* 1. 1, 265 (*K. D.* 1. 1, 280).
[79] *C. D.* 1. 1, 82 (*K. D.* 1. 1, 84).
[80] *C. D.* 1. 1, 266 (*K. D.* 1. 1, 281).

grace) and *the Truth itself* which can never be identified with a set of human propositional statements.

> The dogma which dogmatics investigates cannot then, be the *veritas ab Ecclesia definita*. The *veritas ab Ecclesia definita* is itself the question of dogma. It can and should guide dogmatics. But it cannot seek to be the dogma which is the goal of dogmatics.[81]

Clearly, this applies not only to dogmatic statements as a whole but to the individual words and concepts used. The term 'person', therefore, does not, on this account, have of itself any necessary or definitive status by virtue of its place in traditional trinitarian formulations. A *concept* is not in itself to be regarded as an object of faith or as an element of it.

The Relationship between Proclamation and Dogmatic Theology

It would be quite inappropriate to draw the conclusion from what has been said either that the only form of meaningful or relevant talk about God is proclamation or that theology itself is a form of proclamation. Proclamation is the 'presupposition' of theology, its 'material' and its 'practical goal', but it is not its content or task.[82] 'One cannot and should not expect to hear the content of proclamation from dogmatics.'[83] Dogmatics serves church proclamation but is not itself proclamation.[84] There is a need here, however, to be clear about how Barth understands this differentiation and the task

---

[81] *C. D.* 1. 1, 267 (*K. D.* 1. 1, 282–3).

[82] *C. D.* 1. 1, 51 (*K. D.* 1. 1, 51).

[83] *C. D.* 1. 1, 79 (*K. D.* 1. 1, 81). 'As compared with Church proclamation dogmatics does not have access to a higher or better source of knowledge which is to be sought in the fact that only here does Christian thought begin, or that thought is here more exact comprehensive and profound than in simple preaching.' (*C. D.* 1. 1, 83; *K. D.* 1. 1, 85.)

[84] 'Dogmatics serves Church proclamation. Its relation to this should be seen as parallel to what was called *pistis* and *gnosis* in the early Church and what has been called *credere* and *intelligere* since Augustine, *pistis* or *credere* being understood as the simple reproduction and propagation of the content of the message in a way which unreflectingly corresponds to what has been heard, *gnosis* or *intelligere* as the scientific investigation of this correspondence.' (*C. D.* 1. 1, 8; *K. D.* 1. 1, 85.)

of theology *vis-à-vis* proclamation as this relates to the language we use and the way it is conceived as functioning.

> Proclamation is human speech in and by which God Himself speaks like a king through the mouth of his herald, and which is meant to be heard and accepted as speech in and by which God Himself speaks, and therefore, heard and accepted in faith as divine decision concerning life and death, as divine judgement and pardon, eternal Law and eternal Gospel together.[85]

When human talk about God aims to be proclamation this means that it aims to serve the Word of God in such a way that it points to its prior utterance by God himself. There is no respect in which such human talk may assume that it is *itself* the Word of God or that the human pointer may be sanctified – there is no possibility of men and women *uttering* the Word of God. Conversely, when we understand the unity of Act and Being in God, between God's Word and Being, it is clear that God is always the free and unconditioned ground of God's own Self-communication and thereby not to be confused in his Word with any human word.[86] It is by grace alone, and certainly not by any accuracy of reference accomplishable by human endeavour, that the Word of God is communicated. The Word of God communicates himself. Alienated and sanctified humanity is involved in this by grace alone as that which is foreign to the nature, being and content of this Word. Consequently, any attempt on the part of man to utter God's Word, and thereby usurp God's place, is a subtle form of 'blasphemous rebellion' ('gotteslästerlicher Aufruhr').[87] This option is open neither to the preacher nor to the theologian!

If proclamation is not to be interpreted in these terms (as the Self-communication of God by God and through God, and where God *is* Word in his becoming for us), then what claims to be proclamation can ultimately only take the form of self-

---

[85] *C. D.* 1. 1, 52 (*K. D.* 1. 1, 52).

[86] Barth is being totally consistent, therefore, when he affirms that God may speak to us through Russian Communism, a flute concerto, a blossoming shrub, or a dead dog ... through a pagan or an atheist...' (*C. D.* 1. 1, 55; *K. D.* 1. 1, 55).

[87] *C. D.* 1. 1, 52–3 (*K. D.* 1. 1, 53).

exposition, where what is being expounded or communicated is not God or God's Being-Word, or God's presence with us by grace, but the preacher's views on 'god', morality, culture or whatever. In the long run proclamation as self-exposition will turn out to be a 'superfluous and impossible undertaking'.[88]

In the light of this and with respect to the task of the theologian, although the task of theology is inseparable from proclamation (just as it is also inseparable from the being of the Church as the field of God's Being-Word), the God-talk of the theologian is not in itself proclamation. The aim of the theologian is not the same as that of the minister of the Word, which, as Barth interprets it, is to serve the Word of God by seeking to become a means by which God speaks. This occurs in such a way that what is uttered is meant to be heard and accepted in faith as a form of human speech in and by which God himself speaks. Neither, secondly, is the task of the theologian free self-exposition! The task of the theologian is to talk about *God* to men and women in the service of proclamation as this is grounded in *the Event of God's being toward us as God's Word*. As we have already stressed, 'Dogmatics is not by nature a general *gnosis* of God and the world.'[89] It is not an end in itself. It has place and justification as a critical theory, *gnosis* or speculation only to the extent that it serves its aim responsibly – that is, its responsibility to the Word as the theme of proclamation – and where this aim is the correct performance of proclamation.[90]

This form of secondary service may take different forms – in theological education the theologian has a didactic role in which his or her talk about God educates people and thereby functions as a kind of 'technical sub-structure' for the understanding of proclamation in so far as it involves teaching and instruction about the Church. But the most central task of theology proper is its duty to reflect upon proclamation in

---

[88] *C. D.* 1. 1, 64 (*K. D.* 1. 1, 65).

[89] *C. D.* 1. 1, 81 (*K. D.* 1. 1, 83).

[90] 'In sum, since dogmatics does not imply a higher possibility of Christian life, since it may not advance an independent source of knowledge and since it cannot claim as theory an autonomous role and significance, therefore the subject-matter of Christianity does not exist for it any other way than as it is found in Christian proclamation.' (*C. D.* 1. 1, 8; *K. D.* 1. 1, 87.)

such a way that it 'confronts it as a court of criticism', testing the coherence of modern proclamation over and against the original and dominant being of the Church and giving directions for its correct and relevant continuation.[91]

This means that it will at times have a proclamatory function, but that essentially it is not proclamation but rather science, instruction and investigation. This of course does *not* mean that it stands back from faith. Rather, it operates from faith, from within the Body of Christ and in the field of God's Being as Revealer, Revelation and Revealedness, even though the primary aim or function of its God-talk is not itself to be a means of the direct Self-communication of God's Word.

What emerges distinctively from this interpretation of proclamation and theology is that the critical controls upon proclamation, and therefore the critical controls upon the specific claims and *vocabulary* of theology in relation to God and God's purposes, are internal to God's Word. Recognising the freedom of God in God's Word leaves no room for forms of *Kulturprotestantismus*, for example, which attach critical authority to prior forms of human self-understanding, whether they be conceived collectively, socially or individually. The function or critical control upon our God-talk belongs to the Word and the Word alone.[92]

> Church proclamation, as regards its content, cannot let itself be questioned as to whether it is in harmony with the distinctive features and interests of a race, people, nation, or state. It cannot let itself be questioned as to its agreement with the demands of this or that scientific or aesthetic culture ... A proclamation which accepts responsibilities along these or similar lines spells treachery to the Church and to Christ Himself ... Far better no proclamation at all than this kind.[93]

This adds further force to our earlier point that, for Barth, matters of theological terminology and expression may not be

[91] *C. D.* 1. 1, 51 (*K. D.* 1. 1, 51). Further on, Barth adds, 'In dogmatics criticism and correction of talk about God can be practised only on a specific section of the whole world of past and future Church proclamation.' (*C. D.* 1. 1, 79; *K. D.* 1. 1, 81.)

[92] Cf. *C. D.* 1. 1, 140 (*K. D.* 1. 1, 145).

[93] *C. D.* 1. 1, 72 (*K. D.* 1. 1, 73).

dictated by critical criteria or controls attaching to any social or political or 'politically correct' philosophy – or, as this will concern us later on, personalist ontology!

It is the free act of God in the event of God's Word and that alone which it is the task of the Church to proclaim – a task which is accomplished by the grace of God alone (where 'grace' here refers not to some static divine disposition but to the dynamic, Self-giving activity of God within the context of alienated humanity). And it is this Word in its human form which the Church proclaims that is the content of dogmatic theology. As such the critical controls upon dogmatics do not belong to it itself, but stand over and against it and are known and perceived through faith alone and, therefore, by the free grace of God alone. The task of theology is to serve the Word, not claiming to be the agent of the Word, but in full recognition of the fact that precisely *there* is theology's point of reference and it neither *may* nor *can* look elsewhere for it.

The significance of this for decisions about theological terminology is twofold.

a) First, there is a radical freeing of terms. There is a freedom in the human task of articulation and there is no *a priori* reason why a wide range of terms and metaphors may not be drawn upon to express the most fundamental theological truths. The articulation of proclamation is not locked into any series of 'given' terms or established human concepts. There is no ecclesial 'imprimatur' which is exercised in relation to any particular finite set of concepts.

b) Second, there is simultaneously a rigorous critical control on the terms we use which is the givenness of the revelation event and the apodeictic or categorical demand and obligation that we be as true as humanly possible to this in and through our speech – speech which is by grace, in the service of grace and, indeed, *translucent* in this respect.

The Methodological and Epistemological Significance of Divine Freedom

Two quite distinct points must be made here.

a) First, as we have already suggested, Barth may be seen to be *the* theologian of divine freedom, emphasising the free life of God over and against all that we would consider necessary, possible, real and unreal. To recognise divine freedom is to give theological primacy to the actual over and against human conceptions (i.e. preconceptions) of the necessary – it is to allow one's thinking to be controlled by the former and not the latter. The God who gives himself to be known in Christ is the God who makes this known to be a revealing in freedom and not from any external constraint or compulsion.[94] This is due not least to the fact that God has

> actually, though not necessarily, created a world and us ... His love actually, though not necessarily, applies to us ... His Word has actually, though not necessarily, been spoken to us. The purposiveness we find in proclamation, the Bible and revelation is thus a free and actual purposiveness by no means essential to God Himself.[95]

A great deal may be, and perhaps ought to be, said here, but it is the methodological implications of this that are of particular relevance to our discussion of the nature and task of dogmatic theology and the function of its language. In Barth's own words, 'In both its investigations and its conclusions it must keep in view that God is in heaven and not on earth, and that God, His revelation and faith always live their own free life over against all human talk, including that of the best dogmatics.'[96] This means that in all correlating of the divine and the human we 'must not think away the free basis that this correlation has in God...'[97] The counterpart of this is that this freedom also belongs to the Church's proclamation, it reflects

[94] '(W)e must always bear in mind that the "God for us" does not arise as a matter of course out of the "God in Himself", that it is not true as a state of God which we can fix and assert on the basis of the concept of man participating in His revelation ...' (*C. D.* 1. 1, 172; *K. D.* 1. 1, 179.)

[95] *C. D.* 1. 1, 140 (*K. D.* 1. 1, 144). Barth continually makes similar comments as, for example, in his discussion of 'The Speech of God as the Mystery of God': 'We know ourselves only as those addressed by God's Word, but precisely as those addressed by God's Word we must know God as the One who addresses us in freedom , as the Lord, who does not exist only as He addresses us, but exists as the One who establishes and ratifies this relation and correlation, who is also God before it, in Himself, in His eternal history.' (*C. D.* 1. 1, 172; *K. D.* 1. 1, 179.)

[96] *C. D.* 1. 1, 85-6 (*K. D.* 1. 1, 88).

[97] *C. D.* 1. 1, 172 (*K. D.* 1. 1, 179).

the ever new dynamic of God's engagement in grace with the specific and concrete contexts in which we find ourselves, or, rather, in which God finds us. 'Like the subject-matter of Christianity, Church proclamation must also remain free in the last resort, free to receive the command which it must always receive afresh from that free life of the subject-matter of Christianity.'[98]

God is free and thus the subject-matter of proclamation is free. In so far as proclamation is the ground of dogmatics and not the other way round, the vocabulary of the Church cannot be fixed. However, it must also be emphasised that the Church cannot usurp this freedom in such a way that it becomes Lord over its own message and vocabulary. There is no room for any subjective libertarianism (which is a form of bondage) where humanity becomes subject to the dictates of the alienated conceptuality and language of its culture, be it past or present. Rather, the freedom of the Church exists precisely in its responsibility before the liberating freedom of God. Dogmatic theology serves to remind the Church of this and, therefore, of the need for a propriety and objectivity of terminology and conceptuality.

b) Second, to say that Barth's genius is reflected in his ability to work through the formal, epistemological and methodological implications of divine freedom immediately raises the question as to whether there may not be an *internal* inconsistency in his own approach here – whether, that is, this very argument itself does not repose on a prior *concept of divine freedom*. May his exposition not be said to have presupposed (that is, to have been *determined* by) certain prior suppositions about what it must mean for God to be free with respect to our knowledge of the divine? Such an approach would, by virtue of being an *a priori* form of argument, be nothing less than a *de facto* denial of divine freedom. It would itself betray the very criteria on the basis of which it operates. In sum, for Barth to be consistent the *very recognition* of the divine freedom must be embraced by (and, therefore, fall *within the compass of*) that

---

[98] *C. D.* 1. 1, 87 (*K. D.* 1. 1, 89).

same divine freedom, that is, recognised and submitted to in a manner whereby our very conceptions of divine freedom are *themselves* freely conditioned by God.

In other words, Barth's argument that recognising the divine freedom involves engaging in reverent and objective *a posteriori* theology, that is, theological enquiry 'out of' the Word of God, must *itself*, in order to be consistent, be grounded in the recognition of the free agency of God in and through our articulation of God in his Word to us.[99] Any validity of the

[99] It is precisely this *a posteriori* reverence to which Bonhoeffer refers in the opening sentence of his lectures on christology when, quoting Kierkegaard's dictum 'Be silent, for that is the absolute', he writes, 'Teaching about Christ begins in silence.' This silence is the silence that is necessitated by our standing before the Logos, a silence which is not the soul chattering away to itself but the silence of the human logos before the One who from the human side may best be defined as the 'Counter-Logos' or 'Anti-Logos'. (Cf. the opening paragraph of his *Christology*, Eng. trans. by John Bowden, London and New York, 1966, 'Introduction: The Christological Question'). To acknowledge the freedom of God is to be committed to such silence, not least at the methodological level. What we must notice here is that Bonhoeffer would be being inconsistent if he was recommending this silence as something to be created and sustained by the subject. What he is talking of cannot be a human accomplishment, it must rather be a gift of the Logos in the act of his speech. At most, it can be a criticism of foundationalist forms of approach where Bonhoeffer is telling such theologians that the filters are not articulating but rather creating the message they are hearing.

Bonhoeffer's famous stress on the theological priority of the 'Who question' over the 'How question' is a clear expression of Barth's influence on him. It is as we answer the Who question that both our theoretical and pragmatic concerns (*vis-à-vis* epistemological, methodological, ethical and other problem-solving issues) are defined, or redefined, in an appropriate manner and addressed. Barth is making a related point when he writes, 'In practice the nature of the biblical answer to the question: Who is God in His revelation? is such as to answer at once the two other questions: What is He doing? and: What does He effect? ... The first question that must be answered is: Who is it that reveals Himself here? Who is God here? and then we must ask what He does and thirdly what He effects, accomplishes, creates and gives in His revelation.' (*C. D.* 1. 1, 297; *K. D.* 1. 1, 313.)

To repeat, the methodological point that we are concerned to make is *not* that a personalist ontology demands that one refuse to ask 'How' questions before 'Who' questions but rather the *a posteriori* one that the relevant How questions are in fact addressed in and through the Who question and, moreover, that propriety before the reality of God, therefore, requires us to ask the Who question before the How questions. The Bible's primary witness relates to 'who the God is whom it attests as self-revealing'. As this God is presented to us in and through this self-revealing we discover that 'this God will and can make Himself manifest in no

process of argumentation here, and its conclusions *vis-à-vis* the freedom of God, must *itself* be owed to the free God who is known consequent upon his freedom and in such a way that this consequentiality applies in the very recognition and understanding of this divine freedom and of its specific, concrete character. If we appear to labour this point, it is because it is an important one. If Barth were inconsistent here, it would seriously weaken his central arguments. His entire conviction that we recognise the methodological and epistemological significance of divine freedom must, to be consistent, repose on an *a posteriori* expression not only of the *facticity* but also of the *nature* of divine 'freedom' – of the meaning which the concept acquires when used of God. It must not repose on some predetermined anthropomorphic or anthropocentric 'mapping' of the concept.

  Barth's perception of the *primordial* significance of the divine freedom and the extensive implications of this is best reflected in his repudiation of approaches which operate from a prior ontology or anthropology by appealing to the notion of the divine freedom. He writes, 'In this light one can also see how dubious it is to set the doctrine of the Word of God in the framework of an anthropology. In that case the

---

other way that in the That and the How of this revelation. He is completely Himself in this That and How.' (*C. D.* 1. 1, 297; *K. D.* 1. 1, 313.)

  There is no separation therefore in God between the Who, the What and the How. The latter two questions will not answer the first and, asked on their own, threaten to undermine the very possibility of an appropriate asking of the first. When we ask, or, rather, are brought to ask the first, however, the latter two are addressed in an integrated manner.

  It should also be added here that the answer to the Who question is not revealed by flesh and blood but rather given 'from above' in an act that recreates the subject – Simon becomes Peter. Cf. here Hans Urs von Balthasar's discussion of this issue in his book, *On Prayer* (Eng. trans. by A. V. Littledale), London, 1973, 48ff. He writes, 'Simon, the fisherman, before his meeting with Christ, however thoroughly he might have searched within himself, could not possibly have found a trace of Peter. Yet the form "Peter", the particular mission reserved for him alone, which till then lay hid in the secret of Christ's soul and, at the moment of this encounter, was delivered over to him sternly and imperatively - was to be the fulfilment of all that, in Simon, would have sought vainly for a form ultimately valid in the eyes of God and for eternity' (49).

freedom of the divine purpose for man can be asserted only at a later stage, while it is really denied by the starting-point.'[100]

But are there any pointers which suggest that Barth really is consistent by acknowledging himself, in his own approach, the conceptual transcendence of the divine freedom? It would seem that his use of the concept of the 'inconceivable *novum*' is pertinent here. The fact that the Word of God represents an 'inconceivable *novum*' over against the conceptualities and capabilities of the human mind is an essential coefficient here safeguarding the internal consistency of Barth's appeal to the notion of divine freedom. This *novum* testifies not simply to the goodness of God *vis-à-vis* alienated humanity but also to the ultimate unanticipatability ('freedom' being the positive ground of this) of God in this context – and where this unanticipatability does not simply refer to the failings of our subjective, creaturely capacities, but to the nature or agency of God revealed as Lord.[101] Barth's use of the term *novum* directs us to an acknowledgement on his own part that his arguments repose on a primordial ground that is neither formally nor materially predeterminable in any sense whatsoever and with respect to which we do not operate on the basis of conceptual deductions – as that includes any utilisation of the concept of freedom.

A great deal of testimony can be found to the correlation in Barth between material affirmations made *a posteriori* in the face of God's Word and the consequent questioning of assumptions made at the formal level. However, there will always be – not least in the context of the concept of freedom – an irreducible, dialogical circularity whereby one operates from 'sketchy' provisional suppositions and concepts in the light of which material conclusions are reached but in such a

---

[100] *C. D.* 1. 1, 140 (*K. D.* 1. 1, 145).

[101] *C. D.* 1. 1, 194. Later on, Barth discusses further this issue, emphasising the connection between the freedom of God, the lordship of God ('Lordship means freedom') and revelation's consequent requirement that it be understood out of itself as 'that self-contained *novum*' (*C. D.* 1. 1, 306; *K. D.* 1. 1, 323). As we discuss in chapter two, we cannot support Moltmann's criticism of Barth as operating with a nominalist conception of the divine freedom. Barth is doing something much more profound than simply attributing *potentia absoluta* to God!

way that these in turn are allowed to question, to redefine and to correct the nature of any original 'sketchy' suppositions and conceptualities and thus to reassess formal suppositions made on that basis. The fact that 'one has to start somewhere' is therefore acknowledged but *without* its being used to warrant any illegitimate, 'foundationalist' approach.[102]

We must avoid, therefore, describing the circularity involved here as a necessary heuristic pattern or technique of human discovery. Rather, it is what emerges as the form of God's Self-presentation in a context of *metanoia* and thus of an ever-continuing process of sanctification at the theological and epistemological levels – a process initiated and governed by God in and through the free dynamic of God's Word and the event of its being heard.[103] In and through this process what comes to be known is not simply what is actual in the light of sets of possible worlds considered in advance but the radically new knowledge of what *is* possible, most notably, the possibility of knowing the Word of God. The very awareness of this is consequent upon, and therefore subsequent to, knowledge of that Word.[104] All this must be affirmed (in the light of God's

---

[102] In theology the observation that 'one has to start somewhere' is simply a *descriptive* truism, which means that one has to have started somewhere. It may not serve as a *prescriptive* ratification which endorses whatever starting-point suits the ends of the enquirer! Properly interpreted by the theologian it means that 'one finds oneself having started somewhere but that this somewhere is now acknowledged as having possessed provisional, incidental or contingent status'.

[103] The content of the divine Word will be, amongst other things, 'the limitation of his (the recipient's) existence by the absolute "out there" of his Creator, a limitation on the basis of which he can understand himself only as created out of nothing and upheld over nothing. It will also be a radical renewal and therewith an obviously radical criticism of the whole of his present existence, a renewal and a criticism on the basis of which he can understand himself only as created out of nothing and upheld over nothing. It will also be a radical renewal and therewith an obviously radical criticism of the whole of his present existence, a renewal and a criticism on the basis of which he can understand himself only as a sinner living by grace and therefore as a lost sinner closed up against God on his side.' (*C. D.* 1. 1, 194; *K. D.* 1. 1, 202.)

[104] Knowledge of the possibility of the knowability of the Word of God, Barth suggests, 'stands in the freedom of God. Grace would not be grace if God could not give and also refuse us this reality and with it this possibility too. The knowability of the Word of God stands or falls, then, with the act of its real knowledge, which is not under our control.' (*C. D.* 1. 1, 224; *K. D.* 1. 1, 235–6.)

freedom), not as a necessary predicate of the divine nature, but as 'dis-covered' through God (i.e. dis-closed) to be of the very essence of God's personal subjectivity in his Self-communication through his Word and by the Spirit. Here 'God's Word, is no mere thing; it is the living, personal and free God.'[105]

A negative consequence of this, as Barth emphasises, is that there is no possibility of our operating in theology on the basis of immanentist suppositions. Here he cites Schleiermacher and Tillich as exemplifying this kind of approach. Immanentist affirmations are most obvious as ontological statements. However, they may receive equal, though less obvious, endorsement at the epistemological, hermeneutical and semantic levels in such a way that

> the ideas of speech, word, proclamation and preaching ... must obviously disappear in the general concept of operation or movement or even meaning which embraces God and man, which is in some way the vehicle of the existence of each and all of us, and which somehow ... is to be articulated by us. But then Logos in its isolation as word spoken back and forth necessarily becomes one symbol among many others.[106]

In the contemporary theological debate forms of (Wittgensteinian) semantic foundationalism or immanentism may also be criticised on this score – together with the forms of 'neo-fideism' that attend them. If language is to be conceived along the lines suggested by Merrill and Jaakko Hintikka, as a universal medium and as included in 'world' as a 'given' of thought, and if this insight is to be appropriated within the theological domain, one is required to safeguard the assertion that our language, and linguistically sustained forms of thought, are 'commandeered' in and through the revelation event and that God is not necessarily immanent due to some inherent all-pervasiveness of the semantic conditions of human thought.

[105] *C. D.* 1. 1, 198 (*K. D.* 1. 1, 206).
[106] *C. D.* 1. 1, 62–3 (*K. D.* 1. 1, 63–4).

The 'Scientific' Nature of Theology

In concluding this chapter it is pertinent to consider briefly Barth's claim that dogmatics is a science. There are two reasons for this. First, the term is central to Barth's exposition of his theological method, appearing in the opening statement of the *Church Dogmatics*. This requires us to ask again whether he thereby imports predetermining, methodological suppositions from elsewhere under the auspices of this term – thereby generating an inconsistency.

Second, his use of the term provides, we shall argue, a useful 'case study' in his approach to language as it is used in the theological context. This relates to the manner in which he will refuse to define 'theological science' with recourse to methods pursued in other disciplines and *yet retains the word* – despite the potential for dubious transfers of connotation, mediated, for example, by Marburg Neo-Kantian thought and its utilisation by Barth's teachers, for example.

The underlying question, therefore, is: how far and in what way does Barth's approach allow the application of words in the theological domain on the basis of some continuity of meaning with their usage in non-theological contexts, given the apparent stress in his theology on the discontinuity between these various domains? As should become clear, the discussion of this issue serves as a useful way of summarising some of the key principles already mentioned.

Barth uses the term 'science' to express several closely related features proper to theology: a) the vulnerability and responsibility of church statements – and the critical function of theology in relation to these; b) the provisionality and non-*a priori* nature of its forms of investigation in the light of the *a posteriori* givenness of its object. The criticism and correction of the Church's talk about God is to be carried out 'in the light of the being of the Church, of Jesus Christ as its basis, goal and content';[107] c) that theology is a human concern with a

---

[107] *C. D.* 1. 1, 6 (*K. D.* 1. 1, 4).

definite object of knowledge;[108] d) that its path of knowledge is appropriate to and specifically defined by its own subject-matter;[109] and e) that it is required to give account of this both to itself and to others.

Barth comments,

> Its scientific character consists in its orientation, in its conscious orientation, in what must always be its conscious orientation, to the question of dogma which is raised by the existence of the Church. When the enquiry is pressed with this orientation, or, as we might also say, with this objectivity, then dogmatics takes place as a science.[110]

At the same time, however, Barth is also quite emphatic that for theology 'it would not make the slightest difference to its real business if it had to rank as something other than science'.[111]

> It does not recognise the need to understand and legitimate itself as a science at all. Nor does it recognise as normative for itself the general concept of science at all. Nor does it recognise as normative for itself the general concept of science that is authoritative today. Nor does it recognise any obligation to oppose to this another concept which will include and therefore justify itself.[112]

In other words, the word is provisionally and conditionally appropriated by theology to serve its own purposes. In no respect is it to be conditioned by scientific methods or ontological apperceptions endorsed within other domains.[113]

---

[108] Barth was using the concept of theology as a science to emphasise precisely this when he wrote much earlier, in *The Epistle to the Romans*, that 'to be scientific means to be thrown up against reality. The reality of theology is its unconditional respect for the peculiarity of its chosen theme.' (*The Epistle to the Romans*, trans. Edwyn C. Hoskyns, London: 1933, 531.) See also Barth's emphasis on the 'specificity' of that which calls itself a science, *C. D.* 1. 1, 283 and 287 (*K. D.* 1. 1, 299–300, 305).

[109] The understanding of dogmatics as a science 'means that it consciously and explicitly treads its own very specific path of knowledge as specifically defined by its object' (*C. D.* 1. 1, 287; *K. D.* 1. 1, 305).

[110] *C. D.* 1. 1, 275 (*K. D.* 1. 1, 292).

[111] *C. D.* 1. 1, 8 (*K. D.* 1. 1, 6).

[112] *C. D.* 1. 1, 275 (*K. D.* 1. 1, 291).

[113] *C. D.* 1. 1, 8 (*K. D.* 1. 1, 6).

The only witness that other sciences might provide is their capacity to remind the theologian of the need for fidelity within his or her own field and with respect to his or her own axioms and methods.

Far from the term 'science' being advocated, as may be supposed, to boost the theologian's sense of self-respect in the academic context, for Barth it serves rather to remind the theologian that it is *only* a science and that it is thus 'secular'.[114] Indeed, one of Barth's concerns in appropriating the word is the purpose of keeping scientists humble! It serves, he suggests, to remind scientists that theology does not take 'the heathenism of their understanding seriously enough to separate itself under another name, but that it reckons them as part of the Church in spite of their refusal of the theological task and their adoption of a concept of science which is so intolerable to theology'.[115] In other words, far from any attempt to subsume dogmatics under a foreign category of science, he suggests that, properly understood, scientists should interpret their own enterprise as belonging within the domain of the Church.

The answer to our first question is quite clear, therefore. The term 'science' is defined by Barth for utilisation within the theological domain, and he ignores any other attributes which might be peculiar to the enterprise as it is understood outside the Church. His decision is a tactical one, therefore. He simply assesses the respective benefits of taking the term on board (and allowing it to be redefined accordingly) or rejecting it. This exemplifies that specific form of semantic freedom to be enjoyed within theology.

This anticipates our second question, to which we return later. Why is it that Barth is willing to claim the term 'science'

---

[114] Barth's refusal to regard dogmatics as in any way elevated by its self-understanding with regard to the academic character of its scientific methods is rather delightfully reflected when he writes, 'It is certainly as well to reflect that at any moment it is possible that the question of dogma may be put and answered much more seriously and fruitfully in the unassuming Bible class of an unknown country parson than in the most academic discussion imaginable.' (*C. D.* 1. 1, 279; *K. D.* 1. 1, 296.)

[115] *C. D.* 1. 1, 11 (*K. D.* 1. 1, 10).

for use within the context of dogmatics while being so much less enthusiastic about doing the same with the notion 'person' used of the members of the Trinity – citing its misuse within the realm of secular philosophies which he so strongly believed require radical conceptual revision by theological input?

Conclusion

In this chapter our task has been quite simply that of expounding Karl Barth's central methodological concerns as they are stated in Volume One (Part 1) of his *Church Dogmatics*. We have sought to map out selected features which, we have suggested, embody certain central facets integral to the orientation of his approach and subsequent exposition of his doctrine of God. We have also set out to describe how these elements coinhere and interconnect. In our next chapter we shall examine how Barth applied these to his doctrine of God (within the same volume of his *Church Dogmatics*) and assess how consistent he was in his task. Later in our discussion we shall move on to assess other models of the 'grammar' of theological exposition, with the aim of setting out an alternative approach which, we shall argue, may be more consistent with the force of these methodological principles than his own exposition of the divine Triunity turned out to be.

2

Revelation, Reiteration and the Divine Identity

Writing on the relationship between action and revelation in God, Christoph Schwöbel comments, 'The point of the concept of self-revelation is that the self-disclosure of God is the unified mode of the actualisation of God's creative, reconciling and perfecting action.'[1] It is precisely such an integration of the doctrine of revelation with those of creation and reconciliation which Karl Barth saw to be so seriously lacking in the mainstream of European theology – not least in the dichotomies resulting from Marburg Neo-Kantianism.[2] In this chapter we shall be attempting to do three things. First, we shall outline two reasons for the compartmentalisation within Western theology (referring mainly to the Reformed tradition in which Barth stood) which involved a bifurcation between the revelation event and the divine identity and consequent dichotomies between the revelation of God's creative purposes and that of God's redemptive purposes. It will be suggested that these dichotomies, together with the attendant depersonalisation of revelation, may be seen to have borne tragic social and political costs throughout the Christian world. Second, we shall discuss the manner in which Barth sought to address these problems through a radical reintegration of the divine identity with the event of revelation.

---

[1] *God: Action and Revelation*, Kampen, 1992, 92.

[2] See my discussion of this in 'Christian Experience and Divine Revelation in the Theologies of Friedrich Schleiermacher and Karl Barth' in *Christian Experience in Theology and Life*, ed. I. Howard Marshall, Edinburgh, 1988, 83–113, and also 'The Self-relation, Narcissism and the Gospel of Grace', *S. J. T.* 40 (1987), 481–510.

Finally, we shall assess the implications of Barth's own programme for his interpretation of divine Triunity and God's triune personhood. The question which will attend and underlie our approach concerns whether Barth's own exposition encourages a more fully 'personal' conception of the revelation event. It is our contention that his exclusive use of a 'revelation model' rather than a 'worship model' obscures the concept of communion in God.

The Reformed tradition has too often failed to integrate adequately the doctrine of revelation with the doctrines of creation and reconciliation. This may be seen in particular in the development of 'Federal Theology'.[3] Two closely associated reasons for this stand out.

The first lies with the Western *ordo salutis* and the role of the nature-grace model in conditioning its understanding of revelation.[4] The second takes the form of a confused conception of the grammar of revelation. Both of these involve a deeply inadequate conception of the divine identity.

The Western *Ordo Salutis* and its underlying Model of Revelation

In his important book *The Clue to History*, John Macmurray offers a 'broad-brush' outline of what he sees to be a threefold apperception underlying Western culture. First, there is the influence of the aesthetic-contemplative apperception which characterised the Hellenic mind and which is the legacy of Greek culture. Second, he refers to the pragmatic orientation which owes its origin more specifically to the influence of

---

[3] Cf. David Weir, *The Origins of the Federal Theology in 16th-Century Reformation Thought*, Oxford, 1990.

[4] For 'in depth' analyses of the *ordo salutis* underlying the developments of federal theology cf. Richard A. Muller, 'Perkins' *A Golden Chaine*: Predestinarian System or Schematised *Ordo Salutis*', *Sixteenth Century Journal* 9. 1 (1978), 69–81; *Christ and the Decree, Christology and Predestination in Reformed Theology from Calvin to Perkins*, Grand Rapids, 1986; Weir, op. cit., chap. 2, 'The Background to the Prelapsarian Covenant', and, finally, James B. Torrance, 'The Concept of Federal Theology – Was Calvin a Federal Theologian?' in *Calvinus Sacrae Scripturae Professor*, ed. Wilhelm H. Neuser, Grand Rapids, 1994, 15–40.

Latin or Roman thought with its sophisticated legal categories.
Third, he discusses the 'Hebrew consciousness' and its shaping
of the Christian tradition in terms of relational and personal
categories.[5] It is not our task to investigate the 'genetic'
influences of which he speaks – although his second category
is relevant to our concerns. What we would wish to take from
this, however, is Macmurray's insistence on the need for an
awareness of the dangers of imposing in our very questions an
apperception which is quite foreign, and indeed inappropriate,
to Judaeo-Christian thought and culture. When this is done
our questions threaten to be hermeneutically distortive as we
seek to articulate the dynamics of New Testament thought
and theology.

This kind of mistake is reflected in the Western tendency to
interpret theology and revelation from a deontological
standpoint in natural ethics and moral law, and where the
concept of universally accessible universal law is thus
interpreted as defining universal conditions of the divine
acceptance of humanity. Relationships are thus mapped in
contractual terms with recourse to notions of legal requirement
and condition. The influence of this is mirrored in the
soteriological architectonic of Western theology, its *ordo salutis.*

The Western order of salvation, as it has moulded European
Christianity (Catholic and Protestant) for generations, takes
the following general form: *Law* (inscribed in the human
heart) is the necessary presupposition for an *awareness of Sin,*
which is the impetus for *Repentance,* through which we may
experience *God's Grace and Forgiveness* and know the joy of
Reconciliation.

This model is internally driven to interpret the most basic
form of revelation as God's 'general' revelation conceived in
legal terms. God's will is inscribed in the created order to be
perceived by natural reason through the universal *sensus
moralis,* that is, the moral conscience. Our consciences are
conceived as transcending cultural conditioning in so far as
they provide a natural and universal *cum-scientia* (*suneidesis*),

---

[5] Cf. *The Clue to History,* London, 1938, especially, chapter 2 ('The Hebrew
Consciousness'), 16–41.

a 'with knowing' with God of God's purposes for humanity as these are written into the human heart, that is, within the created order. Consequently, the Western *ordo salutis* was characterised at the *epistemological* level by the primacy of law and nature over grace. That is, it is God's legal purposes for humankind which we apprehend in the first instance, and it is only in the light of this primary revelation that we can recognise and interpret God's redemptive purposes as these are revealed in Christ. The latter perfect the former. It is in the light of the prior perception of God's will and legal purposes for humankind that we interpret God's redemptive purposes.[6]

The objects of this mode of perception, therefore, are essentially prescriptive, normative or ethical data which are foundational, i.e. 'given', and which are identified with God's will as expressed in divine 'laws'. Scholastic Calvinism identified these with 'federal' conditions of divine acceptance, and its theological programme was defined in these terms with various further categories and distinctions (as between 'general' and 'special' grace or 'efficient' and 'sufficient' grace) added to fill out this deontological frame of reference.

---

[6] This becomes particularly clear in the concept of a *foedus naturale*, conceived as a prelapsarian covenant, in strong contrast to Calvin, Zwingli and Bullinger's concept of the covenant of grace (*foedus gratiae*), conceived as a postlapsarian covenant made for sinners after the Fall and conceived therefore as the promise of salvation fulfilled in Christ.

David Weir suggests that it was Ursinus' *Major Catechism* of 1562 which first put forward the concept of a *foedus naturale*.

Question 10: What does the divine Law teach?

Answer: What sort of covenant in creation God had entered into with man; but which pact man would have conducted himself in that service, and what God would require of him after beginning with him a new covenant of grace ...

Question 36: What is the difference between the Law and the Gospel?

Answer: The Law contains the covenant of nature initiated in creation by God with man, that is, it is known to man by nature; ('lex continet foedus naturale in creatione a deo cum hominibus initium, hoc est, natura hominibus nota est') and it requires from us perfect obedience to God, and it promises eternal life for those who keep it, and threatens eternal punishments for those who do not fulfil it. But the Gospel contains the covenant of grace, that is, existing but not known naturally: it shows to us the fulfilment in Christ of his justice, which the law requires, and its restoration in us through the Spirit of Christ: and it promises eternal life by grace because of Christ to those who believe in him. (Weir, op. cit., 104 ff.)

This feature of Western Christianity was further reinforced by contractual models of God's acceptance of humankind[7] (stemming originally from the influence on Western thought of Tertullian), which further confirmed the interpretation of revelation as the divine *dissemination of information* concerning God's character and requirements. The rise of Federal Theology in Britain and the United States and the development of the Westminster tradition in particular exemplified this in the manner in which it operated with the Calvinist conception of a *duplex cognitio* or a twofold knowledge of God – the first being mediated through nature and relating to the revelation of God's will and legal purposes, the second mediated through Christ and relating to the revelation of God's redemptive purposes.[8]

[7] Ursinus' definition of a 'covenant' is found in his *Catechesis religionis Christianae*, Question 18: What the covenant of God is ('quod sit foedus Dei').
Answer: A covenant in general is a mutual pact between two parties, where one obligates the other to certain conditions for doing, giving, or receiving something, employing signs and external symbols for solemn testimony, as a confirmation that the promise may be inviolable. From here certainly the definition of the covenant of God is deduced. For it is a mutual pact between God and man ... ('Foedus in genere est mutua pactio duarum partium, qua altera alteri certis conditionibus obligat ... Hinc facile colligitur definitio foederis Dei. Est enim mutua pactio inter Deum et hominibus.') (Cf. Weir, op. cit., 109, 114.)

[8] I would agree with T. H. L. Parker (*The Doctrine of the Knowledge of God: A Study in the Theology of John Calvin*, Edinburgh, 1952) over against Edward A. Dowey (*The Knowledge of God in Calvin's Theology*, New York, 1952) that this was not taught by Calvin. It is interesting that Calvin himself saw and stated explicitly that, as a result of sin, no human being will now see God as Creator who has not first seen Christ as Redeemer. This means that theologically we should start with God the Redeemer in order to know God the Creator. Nevertheless, Calvin still believed that as a point of order in exposition we should follow the historical order and begin with creation.
E. David Willis suggests that the difference in interpretation of Calvin reflects 'the divisions established by the Barth–Brunner debates'. He comments, 'These two Calvin scholars may not be called Brunnerian and Barthian, but certainly in their interpretations of Calvin one is more receptive to the insights of Brunner and the other to those of Barth.' (*Calvin's Catholic Christology*, Leiden, 1966, 103.)
The problems in determining which was more accurately representing Reformed thought are reflected in the following comment by Alasdair Heron, 'While Brunner's interpretation of Calvin was weak at many points – as Barth took a somewhat mischievous delight in pointing out – his claim to stand more clearly than Barth in the line of Calvin was not without foundation ... Barth, unlike

These approaches tended to endorse an interpretation of revelation in essentially impersonal terms as the communication of divine law, that is, of legal purposes and of contractual conditions of acceptance and salvation. More generally, this suggested that the form of divine revelation concerned essentially the revelation of *data*[9] and *truths* (ethical and legal) about the nature and character of God.

In sum, there was a tendency, not only within the Western Roman tradition but in the Reformed tradition in which Barth himself stood and which he so sought to revise, to interpret God's general purposes for humanity – and thus the function of revelation – as primarily legal rather than filial, as essentially contractual rather than covenantal (unconditional),[10] and thus conceived in terms of *Lex* (a contractual framework of conditions) rather than *Torah* (the declaration of God's prior and unconditioned covenant purposes for Israel). Interpreting the function of revelation along these lines led to its being seen as essentially an event of *communication* rather than of *communion*.

All this meant that revelation (together with redemption) was construed as an essentially extrinsic act of God rather than as a *creative* and *reconciling* event of divine communion with human persons on the part of the God who has his Being in communion. The consequence was the failure to perceive that, as Barth would emphasise, it is *within the act of grace* that we find the conditions for the interpretation of God's general, covenant purposes for humankind within the created order –

Brunner and unlike Calvin too, insisted in his mature work on unfolding every aspect of Christian faith in the light of Jesus Christ and *only* in that light.' (*A Century of Protestant Theology*, Guildford, 1980, 88.)

[9] For example, Ursinus' 'signs and external symbols' constituting the *certae conditiones* of the *mutua pactio* between God and man – see footnote 7 above.

[10] Cf. J. B. Torrance's analysis of the confusion in the use of the term *Foedus* in 'Federal Theology' (which so shaped Reformed thought in the English-speaking world), and the inability to distinguish between the concept of covenant conceived as unconditional (*diatheke*) and contract (*suntheke*, in Aristotelian thought) which is conditional by definition: 'Covenant and Contract, a study of the theological background of worship in seventeenth-century Scotland', *S. J. T.* 23 (1970), 51–76; cf. also his article 'The Contribution of McLeod Campbell to Scottish Theology', *S. J. T.* 26 (1973), 295–311.

and not vice versa.[11] It is in God's Word to humanity (perceived as the one through whom and for whom all things were made) that we have the hermeneutical key to God's creative purposes, to the ultimate *telos* and purpose of the created order.

Paradoxically, what we witness here, and what Barth failed to interpret adequately, is a flawed doctrine not simply of revelation but more fundamentally of *creation* – of the divine creativity. Revelation and reconciliation are *intrinsic*, and not *extrinsic*, to God's act of creation and their theological exposition should, therefore, be included within it. The creation of communion (as this includes epistemic at-one-ment and the *metanoia* intrinsic to the reconciling event of revelation) is not a peripheral or subordinate event but, rather, one that is central and integral to the divine creativity conceived in its totality – God's purpose here is integral to the event of *creatio ex nihilo* and not incidental to it.[12]

---

[11] Cf., for example, *C. D.* 3. 1. chap. 9, sect. 41 ('Creation and Covenant'). Here he argues that 'the purpose and therefore the meaning of creation is to make possible the history of God's covenant with man which has its beginning, its centre and its culmination in Jesus Christ. The history of the covenant is as much the goal of creation as creation itself is the beginning of this history' (42).

[12] It would seem that the confusions leading to this situation result from a confused conception of divine temporality where God's purposes are ordered in terms of the perceived *temporal* priority of creation over redemption where creation is interpreted narrowly in terms of what we might call 'original' creation and where this 'originality' is defined with recourse to created time rather than in the light of an ontological ordering of events – and where 'originality' is not to be defined in terms of the historical ordering of events in created time but in terms of the ontological grounds of an event with spatio-temporal co-ordinates. The essential form of the fallacy witnessed here constitutes what D. C. Williams refers to as the 'myth of passage' ('The Myth of Passage', *Journal of Philosophy*, 48, no. 15 (July 1951)). Barth's discussion of created time in the context of his discussion of 'divine constancy' and of human time in the context of divine time serves to obviate this. However, Barth's programme is not without its critics here and Richard Roberts is particularly vehement in his criticism in his essay, 'Barth's Doctrine of Time: Its Nature and Implications', in *Karl Barth – Studies of his Theological Methods*, ed. S. W. Sykes, Oxford, 1979, 88ff. This is reprinted in his *A Theology on Its Way? Essays on Karl Barth*, Edinburgh, 1991, in which he interprets Barth's 'isolationism' as bound up with his concept of time. We need only refer to Bruce D. Marshall's outstanding critique of this book to draw attention to the serious failure on Roberts' part to understand Barth. Far from endorsing Roberts' critique of Barth, Marshall exposes the extent to which Barth's theology (with its grasp of the ontological significance of God's freedom) offers a

A second reason which was responsible for the fragmentation of theology in the West and which is exposed by Barth's reinterpretation of the form and grammar of revelation results from the projection of a simplistic conception of the grammar of revelation on to Christian 'revelation'. As we discussed earlier, every concept carried over into theology brings with it suppositions relating to its ordinary context of use. However, when sight is lost of the fact that the *Vorverständnis* relating to the secular use of a term is provisional, an *impropria loquutio* can emerge where semantic suppositions assume the status of relative *pre*-suppositions and determine the form of theological exposition.[13] This has happened to some extent with the term 'reveal'. The customary rules of use attaching to this term as used in the transitive imply the following kind of structure where one subject (in this case the divine subject) reveals something to another.

significant critique of Roberts and his fashionable (and historically all too dangerous) desire for an 'immanent starting-point' (46), one which is in 'the cultural *Sitz im Leben* of the theologian' (197):

> Roberts supposes that for Barth God's eternity and the time we actually inhabit are opposites; this assumption underwrites his alternating criticisms that in the *Church Dogmatics* God's eternity either keeps him from making contact with time, or allows God to be temporal only by including a peculiar sort of time which is not our own. For Barth, though, God's relation to the world is founded ontologically in his freedom. This means that God may in no respect be conceived either as necessarily identified with the world (and so unfreely bound to it) or as necessarily opposed to the world (and so unfreely limited by that to which he stands opposed). As an attribute of his freedom, God's eternity is not his opposition to mundane time, but his transcendence of the opposition between time and timelessness. In the freedom unique to him, therefore, the eternal God has the capacity to (and in incarnation does) enter time genuinely and completely; the contact of this God with our time signals neither its destruction nor his, but the conquest of our time's corrosive divisions. The coherence of this way of conceiving God's relation to the world (which is not at all unique to Barth) is again another matter. It is surely, however, a matter with which attempts to assess Barth's account of 'eternity and time', not least one which sees this as the key to an isolationist reading and criticism of Barth, should come to grips (*J. T. S.*, 44, 1993, 458.)

[13] Or, worse, *absolute pre*-suppositions – that is the term Collingwood uses to describe those categories of interpretation which are so deeply ingrained within our epistemic processes that we cease even to be conscious of them.

S^1 (the divine subject – God/the Holy Spirit) reveals x (propositional truth or 'idea' or information or a facet of something) to S^2 (the human subject) where the 'revelation' is interpreted by the human subject in terms of y (conditions of interpretation internal to the subject – semantic/epistemic conditions; cultural apperception; moral *cum-scientia*; 'faculties'...)

Adopting this kind of model can lead one to postulate a distinction (which too easily becomes a disjunction) between the being of S^1 and the being and nature of x. Moreover, a further distinction is assumed between the being of S^1 and the act of 'revealing' where the latter is regarded as an extrinsic event – an action quite distinct from the *being* of the agent.[14]

If there is any correlation between x and S^1 then this is conceived in 'referential' terms rather than 'ontological' terms. The object x is a different kind of thing altogether from the subject S^1 in that it takes the form of information (*inscribed* in 'Scripture' or within nature) or ideas (or ideals) or indeed dogmas (the '*veritates a Deo formaliter revelatae*' mentioned above – truths which have been formally revealed by God).[15] At the same time there is presupposed by this model a kind of parallelism about the revelation axis such that

---

[14] On this model, communication is clearly indirect and mediated by external 'media'. The activity implies that there are ideas in the mind of S^1 which he wants to communicate to S^2. He therefore *codifies* these ideas in words (or actions) and utters them. This requires that S^2 hears and *decodifies* them. Eric Mascall has used this argument to critique certain forms of English radical empiricism (logical positivist analysis), since it limits the communication of knowledge to a) the five senses and b) discursive thought, thereby limiting verifiable statement to being one of two kinds – either empirical statements or analytical statements. This fails to take account of immediate – though mediated – personal, intuitive knowledge where 'the intellect uses the sensible phenomenon as an *objectum quo*, through which it passes to the apprehension of the *objectum quod* which is the intelligible trans-sensible being.' (Eric L. Mascall, *Words and Images*, London, 1957, chap. 4, sect. 2, 'Things, Persons and God', 70.) Mascall's argument reflects John Baillie's earlier advocacy of the notion of a 'mediated immediacy' by way of which he sought to integrate his own idealism with a personalist concept of knowing. (*Our Knowledge of God*, London, 1939, chap. 4, sect. 16, 'A Mediated Immediacy', 178–98.)

[15] *C. D.* 1. 1, 266 (*K. D.* 1. 1, 281).

there is a further disjunction between the being of x and that of S^2. This means S^2 is regarded as receiving revelation x in such a way that the revelation received remains essentially extrinsic to the being and constitution of S^2. This must be the case, it is assumed, for the simple reason that the rational subject is essentially determined *in advance* of the revelation occurrence, is presupposed by it and therefore, in some sense, ontologically foundational to it. Receiving revelation x may of course influence S^2 such that S^2 acts differently in the future on the basis of the additional information acquired as a result of the act of revelation. However, this model fails to communicate the extent to which revelation relates irreducibly to the form or being of S^2.

The event of revelation in Christ concerns his gift of his life in our humanity in his communion with the Father, and it is into participation in this that we are brought by a 'radically' *creative* act of the Spirit. The participation which results is, therefore, formative and re-formative of our thought patterns and only in-formative in so far as it *also* involves the simultaneous reconstitution of our apperception. Revelation, therefore, is not simply the feeding of data into predetermined software as if we were all born with incorrigibly pre-programmed 'ROM' chips! Human alienation involves the confusion (the computer jargon is 'corruption') of our epistemic software, and the creative and reconciling event of revelation in Christ by the Spirit addresses a programming problem, therefore, and not merely data deficiency.

Taking the two models together we should now be able to see the extent to which the Western *ordo salutis* and the revelation model intermesh with one another in mutual reinforcement. The result is:

1) a dichotomous interpretation of the relationship between revelation and redemption, and the introduction of a bifurcation between the Being of God and God's specific redemptive acts, where the former can be described in general terms in advance of a consideration of the latter;

2) the consequent restriction of the theology of creation within the human domain to a static interpretation of an (historically) 'original' creation of innate and formally ade-

quate conditions of rational and moral perception and interpretation;[16]

3) an attendant dichotomy between general and special revelation where interpretations of the former serve to condition the latter;

4) a contractual/legalistic concept of divine purposes for humanity which fails to take account of the extent of God's primary affirmation of humanity – encouraging, at best, a synergistic and, at worst, a Pelagian interpretation of human obligation and human value;

5) an anthropological exposition grounded in an *incurvatus in se* analysis and description of human nature – where these initial conditions determine and interpret themselves in such a way that divine endorsement of the analysis is included within it.

In sum, these models make a foundational assumption of an absolute *extrinsicity* between the Being and Act of God and therefore between the Being of God and the epistemic processes in terms of which we interpret revelation.

The dangers to society of the forms of 'religion' to which this model of 'revelation' gives rise can be seen throughout the course of this century, not least in the Germany of the 1930s, in the apartheid regime in South Africa and also more recently in the Balkans. It is witnessed, indeed, throughout the Christian and also the Islamic world. When an identification is made between either the dictates of a written text (conceived as embodying infallible divine instructions to 'the religious' – a verbal fundamentalism) or the dictates of an exclusive culture (whose forms or way of life are conceived as

---

[16] There are three forms of this. First, there is the Platonic-Augustinian appeal in his exemplarism and illuminationism to an intrinsic likeness between ideas in the divine mind and ideas in the human mind. Second, in the Western 'Stoic' tradition (as it influenced later Puritan Calvinism), with its appeal to God as the author of natural law who has endowed the human mind with the faculty of reason as it is able to 'read off' the laws of nature and moral law. Third, there is the Thomist concept of an intrinsic likeness between cause and effect and therefore between the Creator and the created order. (This latter we shall discuss fully in chapter three.)

exemplifying God's universal purposes for 'those living this religious way of life' – a fundamentalism of culture) and divine revelation (the Word of God), we have the conditions for violence and intolerance defined not by 'theology', but by the identification between the divine on the one hand and human forms of life and expression on the other that may be termed 'religion' or, more accurately, 'civil religion'.

Christian 'religion' of this kind takes place when, instead of radically reinterpreting nature in the light of grace, our prior interpretation of nature becomes the basis of our interpretation of grace and its compass – what amounts to a 'reification' (and deification) of human law.[17] There is not space to explore this further, but it is relevant to note that whereas the Puritan theology behind the American constitution prescribes the universally discernible conclusion that all human beings can perceive by the light of natural reason that it is the will of God revealed in the natural order that all people are created equal, in South Africa an identical theology of revelation led, in Afrikaner theology and politics, to a diametrically opposite conclusion – one that derived from the same epistemological premises and a parallel doctrine of the perspicuity of nature. There the generally revealed organisation of God's creative purposes was perceived, by the light of natural reason, to justify separate ethnic development and a very specific social ordering along ethnic lines. For several decades the Gospel was assumed to perfect the orders of creation – *gratia naturam perficit*.[18] Similar issues relate much more widely in the Church,

---

[17] For a particularly profound exposition of the relationship between grace and law between the Kingdom of God and the State and for the grounding of the divine 'No' in the 'Yes', cf. Eberhard Jüngel's book, *Mit Frieden Staat zu Machen* (Eng. trans. *Christ, Justice and Peace*, Bruce Hamill and A. J. Torrance, Edinburgh, 1992).

[18] See my discussion of the theological grounds of the interpretation of the divine will with special reference to the manner in which Reformed theology has operated in the South African context, 'On the Theological Derivation of 'Ought' from 'Is'" in *Religious Studies in Dialogue; Essays in Honour of Albert C. Moore*, Dunedin, 1991, 195–204.

See also Cf. H. J. B. Combrink, 'Perspektiewe uit die Skrif', in J. Kinghorn (ed.), *Die NG Kerk en apartheid*, Capetown, 1986, 219–23. An example of the kind of position that I would criticise here is to be found in the 1975 report of the

of course, to the interpretation of God's purposes for men
and women. Here again, very different views can be found
operating from identical theological assumptions *vis-à-vis* our
capacity to 'read off' God's 'generally revealed' purposes for
humankind by *incurvatus in se* means.

For Barth, these kinds of approach lead too easily to our
attaching papal infallibility to our own particular
Weltanschauungen.[19] This he saw all too clearly in the case of
the Church's struggle with *Kulturprotestantismus* and attendant
interpretations of God and revelation which appeal to prior,
foundational categories of self-understanding – anthropological,
racial, cultural and nationalistic. Barth's reaction was to insist
that to let God be God is, and must be, to allow our
interpretation not only of the content of revelation but of its
grammar and form to be defined precisely from within the
context of that revelation itself.

(white) Nederduitse Gereformeerde Kerk on race relations, entitled *Ras, Volk en
Nasie en Volkeverhoudige in die Lig van die Skrif* (also published in English under the
title *Human Relations and the South African Scene in the Light of Scripture*). Cf. Douglas
Bax's useful summary and evaluation of the recent N. G. K. report, *A Different
Gospel: A Critique of the Theology Behind Apartheid,* Johannesburg n.d. In the report
of the Dutch Reformed Church, 'Human Relations and the South African
Scene', it is argued (13) that 'ethnic diversity is in its very origin in accordance
with the will of God for this dispensation'. (Quoted by John de Gruchy in *The
Church Struggle in South Africa,* London, 1979, 71. Cf. also pp. 201–2 for further
relevant discussion.) This led to the theological conviction that the 'ideal
condition' was one of separate development on the basis of the scriptural
endorsement of autogenous development where the diversity of peoples reflected
a divine dispensation. D. S. Bax, *A Different Gospel,* 7.

J. Botha argues in 'A Critical View of the Use of the Scriptures in the Kairos
Document' (*Orientation: International Circular of the Potchefstrom University for
Christian Higher Education,* Mar 1988, 92–3) that in 'apartheid theology the ideal
of the diversity of nations as a given of Creation (and thus God's will) functions
… to shape the entire reading of the Bible'. See also my article, 'Forgiveness; the
Essential Socio-political Structure of Personal Being', *Journal of Theology for
Southern Africa* 56 (1986) 47–59.

[19] 'On the basis of instinct and reason one man may proclaim one thing to be
an "ordinance of creation", another man another thing – according to the liberal,
conservative or revolutionary inclinations of each. Can such a claim be anything
other than the rebellious establishment of some very private *Weltanschauung* as
a kind of papacy?' (*Nein,* Eng. trans. by John Baillie, *Natural Theology,* London,
1946, 87.)

The Primacy of the 'Who' Question over the 'How' Question

Barth interpreted the weaknesses we have outlined in terms of the Western tendency to approach theological investigation with pragmatic 'How' questions as these assumed a predominant, and distorted, soteriological and epistemological bent – and where theological considerations are couched in terms of a prior, unconditioned anthropology. This meant that there was a failure to appreciate the extent to which the Judaeo-Christian tradition (where it reflected the Hebrew 'apperception') interpreted normative obligations in terms of a prior and primary concern with the question as to *who* Yahweh is and *who* Jesus Christ is – a question which immediately invites a response which interprets ethical requirements not as the *conditions* of grace and of God's acceptance of humankind, but as the *obligations* of God's prior and unconditional faithfulness toward, and acceptance of, humankind.

If, as we have suggested, there is a hermeneutical imperative to be clear about the distinction between these two, there is also a theological imperative. As Bonhoeffer would argue in his lectures on christology (under Barth's influence), it is of critical importance to affirm the priority of the 'Who' question over the 'How' question if the Logos is to be recognised as God's own, free Logos and not to become the divine ratification of our own *logoi*.[20] Our understanding of the Logos who is God cannot be framed by the solutions we produce to our 'How' questions, with their preconceived formalistic and programmatic assumptions, i.e. where the solutions are defined with recourse to our own prior frames of reference, as these functioned to define the problems! As Bonhoeffer suggested, it is necessary to interpret the Logos as the one who stands as the Counter-Logos or Anti-Logos[21] with respect to our prior

---

[20] *Christology*, Eng. trans. by John Bowden, London and New York, 1966, cf. especially his 'Introduction'.

[21] The expression 'Anti-Logos' can easily involve confusion. What is meant here is not the identification of the Logos with the human repudiation of the human logos! Bonhoeffer is not advocating anti-rationality or irrationality, as is too often

logoi and conceptual systems. It is only the 'Who' question which allows that methodological or epistemological reverence or 'silence' with which all theology must begin. It is only as we are brought to ask that question that the Logos is given the space to define *who* he is, the *manner* in which he is known and the *condition* of our recognising him – the condition being none other than the Logos himself.

This serves to characterise the intention and direction of Barth's discussion of 'The Triune God'. From the beginning he points to the failure of Western thought and its commitment to addressing 'the That and the What of God, as though these could be defined otherwise than on the presupposition of the Who'.[22] As he points out, the traditional approach has often been to follow the 'far too obvious and illuminating scheme: How do we know God? Does God exist? What is God? and only last of all: Who is our God?'[23] When this happens the doctrine of the Trinity is only stated at a later stage in dogmatics and is not given 'the first word as that which gives us information on the concrete and decisive question: Who is God?'[24]

Barth's decision to discuss the doctrine of the Trinity right at the start of his *Church Dogmatics* is a move of decisive significance for the entire programme. The theological reason for this is his determination to begin by addressing the 'Who' question, that is, by seeking to allow the 'object' of theology to redefine the word traditionally used of that object, namely 'God'. In his own words, 'this is the point where the basic decision is made whether what is in every respect the very important term "God" is used in Church proclamation in a manner appropriate to the object which is also its norm'. In other words, Barth is refusing to assume even that we know

thought (e.g. in I. Howard Marshall's critical review of *Christology* in *Evangelical Quarterly* 38: 242–4). Rather, Bonhoeffer is advocating a profoundly objective and rational form of engagement by insisting on the objective revision by the Logos of our subjective categories of thought.

[22] *C. D.* 1. 1, 301 (*K. D.* 1. 1, 317).

[23] Ibid. This echoes John Calvin's emphasis in his *Institutio* that the primary question in theology does *not* concern *an sit deus* or *quid sit deus* but rather *qualis sit deus*.

[24] Ibid.

what we mean when we use the term 'God'. The theological enterprise begins, therefore, with the intention not to offer any *a priori* ratification of assumptions at the methodological, epistemological or even semantic level. This means that the 'Who' question involves a making provisional not only of our methods and epistemic assumptions, but of the very language we use to denote the subject of the first question we ask in theology. To ask 'Who is our God?' in a manner true to the thrust of a genuine 'Who' question means the giving up of the term for redefinition in the very act of posing the question.[25] It is this approach and this approach alone which can allow the object of theological investigation to liberate the Western mind from the *a priori* assumptions associated with a 'concept' of God.

Related to this is the fact that the doctrine of the Trinity is to be given the *first* word rather than the last as in so many volumes of systematic theology where it features at the end as a speculative addendum of questionable relevance.[26] This is because it articulates the manner in which we are given, by means of Scripture, an answer to the 'concrete' and 'decisive' question: 'Who is God?' And, further, because it is the doctrine of the Trinity which 'basically distinguishes the Christian doctrine of God as Christian, and therefore what already distinguishes the Christian concept of revelation as Christian, in contrast to all other possible doctrines of god or concepts of revelation'.[27]

[25] Saul's 'Who' question on the Damascus Road, 'Who are you, Lord?' (Acts 9:5), shows the extent to which his prior understanding of God and God's purposes *vis-à-vis* Israel (as understood in the context of his late Judaism) were being shattered and requiring to be remoulded in the light of his encounter with the risen Lord (with the Logos).

[26] Two examples written during the period in which Barth was developing his own doctrine of the Trinity illustrate the point: Theodore Haering's *The Christian Faith: A System of Dogmatics* (Eng. trans. John Dickie and George Ferries, London, 1913), where the section entitled 'The Trinity' constitutes the brief and final subsection at the very end of his dogmatic exposition (pp. 913-4); John Dickie's *The Organism of Christian Truth: A Modern Positive Dogmatic* (London, 1930), where the doctrine of the Trinity is not discussed properly until the brief, final section of the entire exposition (pp. 401-5) which has the title 'The Final Synthesis – the Doctrine of the Trinity'.

[27] *C. D.* 1. 1, 301 (*K. D.* 1. 1, 318).

To recapitulate here on our primary emphasis in the first chapter, and as Barth expresses it in his *Göttingen Dogmatics*, the radical redefinition of the theological enterprise in the light of the *Who* question suggests that 'All reflection on how God *can* reveal himself is in truth only a "thinking after" ("Nachdenken") of the fact that God *has* revealed himself.'[28] This applies not only to the form and grammar of revelation, but to the consideration of both its content and its scope as also of the relationship of revelation to other doctrines. All these issues and questions are to be determined *a posteriori* to the revelation event itself since, for Barth, the entire theological enterprise is to be an exercise in *Nachdenken* – as David Ford has argued in an essay on Barth's method[29] – and as Rowan Williams also confirms in his essay in the same volume.[30]

As has been argued above, this does not mean that Barth advocates an empiricist approach, at least not in any subjectivist sense. To the extent that the theology of revelation is *a posteriori* and bound by its subject-matter it will be uniquely objective in that it is concretely and specifically determined by its object. Such objectivity in theology reposes on what Eberhard Jüngel describes as the event of God's 'becoming-object-for-us' in revelation, an event which includes the reconciliation of our minds.[31]

The Primacy of Proclamation

The *Nachdenken* which is of the essence of the theological task suggests that the task of dogmatics is a derivative one. Its 'presupposition' (as also its 'practical goal') is proclamation, where proclamation is that specific form of 'human speech in and by which God Himself speaks ... and which is meant to be heard and accepted as speech in and by which God Himself

[28] Karl Barth, *The Göttingen Dogmatics, Instruction in the Christian Religion, Volume 1*, (Eng. trans. by Geoffrey Bromiley) Grand Rapids, 1990, 151.

[29] 'Barth's Interpretation of Scripture' in *Karl Barth — Studies of his Theological Methods*, ed. S. W. Sykes, Oxford, 1979, 55–87.

[30] 'Barth on the Triune God' in ibid., 149.

[31] *The Doctrine of the Trinity: God's Being is in Becoming* (Eng. trans. by Horton Harris), Edinburgh, 1976.

speaks ...'[32] If proclamation is not defined in this way, it can only become an extravagant form of self-exposition thereby reducing theology to an anthropocentric 'general gnosis of God and the world'.[33] If this is not to be so its task is faithfully to recognise that it is precisely *there* in the Word that its point of reference is to be found.

Three features of the Word in the event of revelation referred to in the previous chapter require further emphasis at this point, all of which relate to the derivative and secondary nature of the theological task conceived as the reverent, faithful and *a posteriori* 'thinking after' God's address in the revelation event.

a) God's Revelation is its own Ground   God's revelation is both its own ground and the ground of our acknowledgement that it is its own ground. It is not subject to any other prior or foundational categories. And, reiterating one of the emphases of chapter 1 above, Barth's concern here is to stress not that revelation *can necessarily* have no higher or deeper ground in terms of which it can receive verification or validation, but rather that it *has* no such higher ground and this fact belongs to the nature of the revelation itself. This is despite the fact that the former might well be argued to be the case, although that would inevitably raise two questions, namely: 'From what grounds is that affirmed?' and 'Are these grounds in themselves prescribed by the Self-revealing God or are they also brought to the task from foreign fields?' The question of any such regress does not arise for Barth, as his approach here sets forth an *a posteriori* description both of what the givenness of God's revelation suggests in terms of the logic of its givenness (which is integral to the content given[34]) as also in terms of the 'subject-matter' given!

---

[32] *C. D.* 1. 1, 52 (*K. D.* 1. 1, 52).

[33] *C. D.* 1. 1, 81 (*K. D.* 1. 1, 83).

[34] For Barth there is no form–content dichotomy in revelation. 'When revelation is an event according to the Bible, there is no second question as to what its content might be. Nor could its content be equally well manifested in another event than this.' (*C. D.* 1. 1, 306; *K. D.* 1. 1, 323.)

According to Holy Scripture God's revelation is a ground which has no higher or deeper ground above or below it but is an absolute ground in itself, and therefore for man a court from which there can be no possible appeal to a higher court. Its reality and its truth do not rest on a superior reality and truth. They do not have to be actualised or validated as reality from this or any other point ... On the contrary, God's revelation has its reality and truth wholly and in every respect – both ontically and noetically – within itself. Only if one denies it can one ascribe to it another higher or deeper ground or try to understand and accept or reject it from the standpoint of this higher or deeper ground.[35]

Even its acceptance from some higher ground involves its denial! 'Revelation is not made real and true by anything else, whether in itself or for us. Both in itself and for us it is real and true through itself.'[36]

Reference may be made here to Barth's extensive discussion of the *vestigium trinitatis* and the use by the Christian tradition of imported models of threeness as a means for interpreting the Triunity. After discussing a whole series of such triadic principles, conceived within the Christian tradition as '*vestigia*', Barth comments by way of summary,

The moment it [the theologoumenon of the *vestigium trinitatis*] is taken seriously it leads plainly and ineluctably into an ambivalent sphere in which in a trice, even with the best will in the world, we are no longer speaking of the God of whom we want to speak and whose traces we meant to find but of some principle of the world or humanity, of some alien God. The original intention was to speak of God's revelation. But what happened was talk about the world and

----

[35] *C. D.* 1. 1, 305 (*K. D.* 1. 1, 321–2). Dan Hardy once made the comment in a seminar discussion that in the final analysis Barth's theology is not really 'grounded'. This is a common criticism which immediately raises the question as to what kind of 'grounding' we require. Too often this kind of criticism is couched (grounded?) in a failure to appreciate the strengths of Barth's argumentation at this point in the *Church Dogmatics* and one is left wondering what kind of alternative grounding could withstand the rigour of Barth's analysis of the theological challenges here. The issue is the same as that raised by the 'isolationist' charge and the desire among many of Barth's critics to operate from 'common ground', a general 'point of connection' ... a *tertium quid*!

[36] Ibid.

man, and this talk, understood as talk about God's revelation, necessarily wound up by being talk against God's revelation. The conqueror was conquered. This game cannot yield serious results. Taken seriously it can be only a profanation of holy things.[37]

This issue becomes particularly relevant to our discussion when we consider the importation into some recent trinitarian exposition of political principles (as we see in Moltmann,[38] Boff[39] and Geervarghese Mar Osthathios[40]),[41] or, indeed, personalist or anthropocentric principles (as appear to a certain degree in the argumentation of Catherine Mowry

[37] *C. D.* 1. 1, 344 (*K. D.* 1. 1, 363).

[38] *Trinität und Reich Gottes*, Munich, 1980, (especially chap. 6).

[39] *Trinity and Society* (Eng. trans.), Maryknoll, 1988 (especially chap. 1, sect. 1, 'Trinity, Society and Liberation'). There is a tendency in this book to allow a programme of liberation, egalitarianism and the structures of society to condition the interpretation of the Trinity. This is given warrant by way of his notion of society as the 'sacrament of the Trinity' (13).

[40] *Theology of a Classless Society*, London, 1979. Here, again, a vision of human sociality threatens to become the condition of trinitarian exposition.

[41] Cf. Ted Peters' interesting critique of the fashionable trend in appealing to the doctrine of the Trinity to confirm an ideal of sociality. His critique is relevant even if his use of the term 'personality' is unfortunate. 'Social doctrines of the Trinity, though increasingly popular, are, in my judgement, wrongheaded. What attracts social trinitarians is the category of community rather than personality for understanding God.' He continues, 'Sometimes contemporary theologians pit the Cappadocian fathers over against Athanasius or Augustine so as to root the contemporary view in an ancient precedent of plurality in harmony. The point usually advanced is this: if loving relationships of a nonsubordinationist or egalitarian type can be found within the being of God, then this could become a model or paradigm for loving relationships in human society. As a model, the Trinity would serve as an ethical ideal. Our moral task would be one of copying God – that is, of reorganizing society so that nonhierarchical and mutually supportive relationships would provide peace and harmony. The function of the doctrine of the Trinity then, according to social theorists, would not be to construct a conceptual understanding of the gospel; rather, it would be to serve as a heuristic device for motivating and directing social change.' He continues, 'The problem with this is that the social doctrinalists have chosen the wrong symbol. The doctrine of the Trinity is a second order symbol, a conceptual apparatus constructed for the purpose of clarifying the more primary symbols of Father, Son, and Holy Spirit.' (*God as Trinity: Relationality and Temporality in Divine Life*, Louisville, 1993, 184–5.)

LaCugna[42] and, to a lesser extent, in the earlier writing of John Zizioulas[43]).[44]

It must also be noted, however, that, yet again, Barth continues by insisting, 'This does not mean, however, that the game can be forbidden in principle ...'[45] Any rejection must be *a posteriori* and on the basis of material, theological argumentation *vis-à-vis* general statements of foundational truths or specific improprieties in particular examples.

b) The Epistemological Impossibility of Revelation   Barth conceives of revelation as an 'impossible possibility' and consequently 'unanticipatable and therefore contingent'. It is the 'self-unveiling, imparted to men, of the God who by nature cannot be unveiled to men'.[46] It is significant that Rowan Williams chooses this theme to open his important article on Barth's doctrine of the Trinity. He writes,

> That man should hear the Word of God is an impossibility revealed to man by that very Word. It is this essential strangeness in the event of man's hearing the Word to which Barth's discussions of revelation again and again return; and this sense of strangeness is of major importance in the whole of Barth's analysis of the nature of man's encounter with his Lord, since it at once raises the question of how the impossibility of revelation is compatible with the fact that the Word is heard. It raises the question, that is to say, of where the possibility of revelation is grounded. How is it that God can abrogate the principle *homo peccator non capax verbi divini* (*C. D.* 1. 1, 407)?[47]

The significance of this again concerns the impropriety of prior ontologies which may accommodate God's Self-bestowal and the essentially trinitarian structure of this 'possibility'.

---

[42] Cf. *God for Us: The Trinity and Christian Life*, New York, 1991.

[43] This is more obvious in his article 'On Human Capacity and Incapacity : A Theological Exploration of Personhood', *S. J. T.*, 28, (1975) – not least in his use of existentialist philosophy to expound personhood – than in his book, *Being as Communion: Studies in Personhood and the Church*, New York, 1985.

[44] Cf. Wolfhart Pannenberg's useful, if brief, discussion of personalism in his article, 'Person' in *R. G. G.* Dritte Auflage, V Band, 230–5, especially 233–4.

[45] *C. D.* 1. 1, 344 (*K. D.* 1. 1, 364).

[46] *C. D.* 1. 1, 320 (*K. D.* 1. 1, 338).

[47] 'Barth on the Triune God' in *Karl Barth – Studies of his Theological Methods*, 147.

As Williams emphasises, the issue here is at least in part a soteriological one relating to the epistemological significance of sin and the fact that we live between the times. Quoting Luther's insistence that grace exposes the fact that 'all powers and faculties of reason ... availeth naught for God',[48] Barth stresses that theology takes place within the sphere of grace, that is, we are members of the *regnum gratiae* and not yet of the *regnum gloriae*. Consequently, we must never confuse the Truth of the Reality of God and our own provisional formulations of the truth – as these are inevitably fraught with intellectual alienation and confusion.[49]

c) God's Lordship and Freedom and the Consequent Novelty of Revelation Again, we must return to the theme of freedom as this is included within the notion of God's Lordship. In the event of revelation God is free and, as we have noted already, 'we must not think away the free basis that this correlation has in God ...'[50] This is because 'God reveals Himself as the Lord'.[51] There is in Barth the tightest conceivable interrelating of the Lordship of God, God's freedom in the event of revelation and the promulgation of the Kingdom of God.

To understand this we are required to ask the question: 'What is meant by "Lord"?' Barth's somewhat tautological-sounding answer yet again exemplifies his refusal to operate on the basis of predetermined definitions of the terms he uses:

To be Lord means being what God is in His revelation to man. To act as Lord means to act as God in His revelation acts on man. To acquire

[48] Sermon on Mt. 11:25–30, 1527, W. A., 23, p. 689, 1.4, quoted by Barth, *C. D.* 1. 1, 185 (*K. D.* 1. 1, 192).

[49] We see through a mirror darkly, what we know we know – by grace alone, and, therefore, *a posteriori*. Furthermore, our knowing belongs to a present which must be distinguished from the attested past on the one hand and the promised future on the other.

[50] *C. D.* 1. 1, 172 (*K. D.* 1. 1, 179). 'God's presence is always God's decision to be present. The divine Word is the divine speaking. The divine gift is the divine giving. God's Self-unveiling remains an act of sovereign divine freedom.' (*C. D.* 1. 1, 321; *K. D.* 1. 1, 339.)

[51] *C. D.* 1. 1, 295 (*K. D.* 1. 1, 311) *et passim.*

a Lord is to acquire what man does in God when he receives His revelation – revelation always understood here in the unconditional sense in which it encounters us in the witness of Scripture.[52]

Lordship is present in revelation because its reality and truth are so fully self-grounded, because it does not need any other actualisation or validation than that of its actual occurrence, because it is revelation through itself and not in relation to something else, because it is that self-contained *novum*.[53]

The argument here is not that the concept of revelation entails that revelation must *necessarily* be new. This may, indeed, be suggested, as Stewart Sutherland argues (and powerfully so) in an essay on the concept of revelation.[54] Rather, Barth's argument is that this revelation *is* new, that the annunciation of its newness is intrinsic to the event and that the recognition of its newness belongs to the recognition of the event.

Barth's concept of Lordship requires careful interpretation and, as is suggested by the way in which he explains the term, precisely what he means by it requires to be interpreted in the light of the event to which it is used to refer – and not only the *content* of the revelation event but its very form.[55] That is, the term is used to describe, or perhaps to denote, the manner of God's relation to humankind, but at the same time the term is claimed and defined by that event itself. So what can we say, therefore, about the meaning of the term as this begins to be defined by its use? First, and as we have already stressed,

---

[52] *C. D.* 1. 1, 306 (*K. D.* 1. 1, 323).

[53] Ibid.

[54] 'The Concept of Revelation' in *Religion, Reason and the Self: Essays in Honour of H. D. Lewis*, eds. S. R. Sutherland and T. A. Roberts, Cardiff, 1989, 35–45. The following quotation exemplifies an approach which would support much of what is said above, but from a much more *a priori* standpoint: 'There is always "news" in what is revealed.' He continues, 'Since I have already by implication ruled out … the possibility that the "news" which is to be revealed is simply a matter of information or facts which have so far eluded us, there must be some alternative account of what is new about the truths of revelation' (43).

[55] 'God reveals Himself as the Lord; in this statement we have summed up our understanding of the form and content of the biblical revelation.' (*C. D.* 1. 1, 314; *K. D.* 1. 1, 331.)

revelation is its own ground – it is not subject to other prior or foundational categories. Second, God is free in God's revelation. God is both the condition and the author of God's Self-revelation. It designates Godhead where, for Barth, 'Godhead means in the Bible freedom, ontic and noetic autonomy.'[56] And, third, it means that the event of revelation falls within the context of the purposes of the furtherance of God's Kingdom: revelation is 'always in all circumstances the promulgation of the *Basileia tou theou...*'[57]

The essential methodological thrust of Barth's notion of the divine Lordship involves the insistence that, far from having a merely informative function, revelation has a relational and conceptually reorganisatory function involving, to borrow a phrase from Dan Hardy, a 'creative reordering' of our conceptualities and world-views. This is initiated on the part of the divine I *for the sake of* the recipient thou. The Lordship of God in revelation is a Lordship which is *for* humanity and not over and against it, and God's freedom constitutes precisely God's freedom to liberate humanity from the bondage of ultimate, foundational principles, laws and constraints foreign to our free participation in the Kingdom.

The *Material* Implications of Barth's Notion of Freedom

By way of an integrative summary of the elements outlined above, Barth writes,

> By the fact that He speaks as an I and addresses by a Thou God announces His kingdom and differentiates this intimation from all speculations about freedom, lordship, or Godhead such as man might perhaps engage in even without revelation. As freedom, lordship and Godhead are real and true in God Himself and only in God Himself, being inaccessible and unknown if God Himself, this I, does not speak and address by a Thou, so, in God Himself, they are the meaning of the event that the Bible calls revelation.[58]

---

[56] *C. D.* 1. 1, 307 (*K. D.* 1. 1, 323).
[57] *C. D.* 1. 1, 306 (*K. D.* 1. 1, 323).
[58] *C. D.* 1. 1, 307 (*K. D.* 1. 1, 324).

This quotation summarises the critical point which we made in chapter 1, namely that the way in which terms such as 'Lordship' and 'freedom' function when applied to God is such that they require redefinition in this context. This semantic transformation is, moreover, inseparable from the context of their inclusion within this event of revelation. In other words, we do not know in advance precisely what is meant by 'freedom' or 'Lord'. The very thrust of Barth's argument is that a revision of the very meaning of these terms is given in the event of revelation.[59]

This brings us to consider the serious criticisms which Jürgen Moltmann has levelled at Karl Barth's use of the notion of freedom – criticisms that integrate with Moltmann's belief that Barth does not offer an adequately 'communal' or 'social' conception of the Triunity of the divine persons and lapses accordingly into monarchianism.

What Moltmann objects to is a perceived 'nominalist fringe' of the doctrine of *potentia absoluta* which, he suggests, underlies Barth's concept of freedom. Here he points to Barth's arguments that God could have remained satisfied with himself and with the impassible glory and blessedness of his own inner life, that God has no need of us, that God is Self-sufficient and that his election of humanity as covenant partner is the result of a prior Self-election, a prior decision which is the free overflowing of the divine goodness in and for the other – 'He ordains that He should not be entirely self-sufficient as He might be.'[60]

Moltmann asks:

> What concept of liberty is Barth applying to God here? Is this concept of absolute freedom of choice not a threat to God's truth and goodness? Could God really be content with his 'impassible glory'? Does God really not need those whom in the suffering of his love he loves unendingly?[61]

[59] As has already been emphasised, to fail to acknowledge this is to fail to accept the function of revelation at the formal level (i.e. in relation to the status of our concepts and semantic frameworks) and that in the event of revelation the terms we use are redefined in and through this event.

[60] *C. D.* 2. 2, 10.

[61] Jürgen Moltmann, *The Trinity and the Kingdom of God: The Doctrine of God*, Eng. trans. by Margaret Kohl, London, 1981, 53. (The original German text reads:

Moltmann's argument continues as follows:

If God is the truth in that he corresponds entirely to himself, then his revelation can only be true if he entirely corresponds to himself in that revelation. That is to say, not to reveal himself and to be contented with his untouched glory would be a contradiction of himself. And if he himself determines not to be sufficient for himself (although he could be so), then there is after all a contradiction between his nature before and after this decision; and this would mean a contradiction between his nature and his revelation. The reasoning 'God could', or 'God could have', is inappropriate. It does not lead to an understanding of God's freedom. God's freedom can never contradict the truth which he himself is.[62]

There are at least three different arguments concealed within this protest and I shall seek to distinguish these and deal with them in turn.

First, Moltmann argues from the fact that what God *is* toward humanity, God *is* in himself – there is an absolute correspondence between God as he *is* in himself and what he *is* toward us. The very fact, therefore, that God reveals himself would suggest that God is not content with existing in 'untouched glory'. Consequently, to say that God is revealed, or may be revealed, is to imply that God is not actually in himself what he is toward us.

This argument suggests that God reveals himself in terms of states and propensities. Barth, however, is suggesting that in and through all this God reveals himself as Lord, as free in and through this commitment to humanity. God is this in his revelation and, in so far as God is this in and through the act of revealing, God is this eternally and antecedently in himself.

If God were not free in this sense then there could be no ontological distinction between God's *hypostasis* and God's personal *ekstasis*. Indeed, on this approach it would be difficult to avoid conceiving of God as ontologically determined by extrinsic conditions. This would mean that the hypostasis of

'Braucht Gott wirklich diejenigen nicht, die er im Leiden seiner Liebe unendlich liebt?', *Trinität und Reich Gottes,* 68.)

[62] *The Trinity and the Kingdom of God,* 53. (*Trinität und Reich Gottes,* 69.)

this world is defined in terms of *its* ek-static conditioning of the hypostasis of God rather than the other way round. Loving participation would be defined in terms of a necessary ontological identification leading to a position more closely resembling a form of pantheism than the panentheism in terms of which Moltmann wishes to describe his position.

Second, the general form of Moltmann's argument can be translated into the old argument that the notion of decision internal to God is incoherent. To make a decision is to bring about a change in time, and if this can in any sense be said to involve a change in the being of the one who makes this decision then, applied to God, this means that God *is not* following (subsequent to) his decision what he *was* before (prior to) this decision. This implies a contradiction between the two natures at the two different temporal points.

The first thing to point out is that this is a puzzling argument coming from one committed to a patripassian position, as it closely resembles the argument used in the patristic period to establish divine *impassibility.* The argument that ontological change involves contradiction in the divine Being is the chief argument against theopassianism in all forms. It is argued by those opposing theopassian views that if God is not identical at time t^1 to what God is at time t^2 then God is not fully real at one or other of these points. That is, if God is in any way conditioned by factors external to the Godhead then God is less than fully real – be it either at t^1 or at t^2. Moltmann is appealing to a form of this argument in relation to the decision *internal* to the Godhead, and he does so by tacitly assuming that such a divine decision even in this context involves intra-divine temporal change.

This argument presupposes that we can think of decision in God as possessing an absolute 'before' and 'after' in God's time. That is, it involves carrying over into the divine realm implications relating to human decision-making, namely that there is invariably a 'before and after'.[63] If 'decision' is used of

---

[63] 'If the eternal origin of the creative and suffering love of God is seen as lying in God's decision of will, then time's "beforehand–afterwards" structure has to be carried over into the divine eternity as well; and we have to talk about a divine

God, however, it is used analogically and metaphorically, although 'reality depicting' it must be used in a manner appropriate to the divine being. One must not think of a 'before' and 'after' in God in a manner which subsumes God within categories of (absolute) linear time, and Barth's notion of divine freedom does not do this. This is not to say that the concept of divine decision is vacated of its content to the point of meaninglessness. Rather, it communicates a great deal about the *ekstasis* of God in relation to that which is not eternal and thus contingent. The point is that such notions do not, however, require an absolutisation of time or the supposition of an absolute all-inclusive history within which both the Being of God and that of the created order are subsumed together – as is supposed in this reference to a 'before and after' in God. They do not involve a notion of decision in which there is absolute change in the divine intention. The notion of election communicates a free personal *ekstasis* of God *vis-à-vis* the contingent, non-necessary realm and requires to be conceived as taking place in eternity (or 'divine time'), making human notions of temporal co-ordinates, and the conclusions we draw in the light of these, inappropriate. It is not least for this reason that Barth speaks of 'God's time' and the 'divine constancy', thus obviating a false form of reasoning from the human context and preserving the notion (essential to the Godness of God) that ontological statements are made descriptively and in an *a posteriori* manner, and not by way of deductive reasoning from the conditionedness of the created order.

Third, Moltmann points to the impropriety of the 'God could' or 'God could have' style of argument. This would seem to be a much more forceful argument. However, two sentences further on he uses a logically identical argument to

---

nature *before* this decision and a divine nature *after* it. There would be no other way of defining the decision more closely. But that would mean that God has two natures: describing his nature before his self-determination, we would have to say that God is in himself blessed and self-sufficient; whereas describing his nature afterwards, we would have to say that God is love – he chooses man – he is not self-sufficient.' (*The Trinity and the Kingdom of God*, 53–4.)

establish this very impropriety. He writes, 'God's freedom can never contradict the truth he himself is.' In other words, God could not have acted in a manner which contradicts his nature – where this divine nature is defined by Moltmann in the light of a series of *deductive* conclusions which a) relate to the nature of God's participation in the suffering of the human context as defined in terms of Moltmann's panentheism, and b) presuppose the absolute two-way identification between the events described as divine acts on the one hand with the divine nature on the other – where this is determined by way of a principle of necessary correspondence. That Moltmann does not argue his case in a more careful manner is a pity, as his argument would have been much stronger had it been framed in different terms. Forms of argument which run 'God could ...' or 'God could have ...' are theologically dubious. Why? Precisely because they tend to be less than reverently *a posteriori* – tending, that is, to be derived (though not always) from deductions from principles which emerge from human reasoning from God's acts followed by the projection of 'necessary consequences' back into the Godhead. This *can* lead to ways of thinking which take the form of a *de facto* rejection of revelation. Moreover, in so far as they tend to make recourse to conceptual implications derived from within the realm of human experience, they can also be anthropomorphic – a feature of which Moltmann's own argument savours. These are issues which Moltmann might have learned from Barth!

What emerges in Moltmann is a style of argumentation reminiscent of the Arminian–Calvinist debate. However, in this context what is being wrestled with is not the paradox involved in speaking of human freedom but the apparently paradoxical nature of freedom in God when parallelisms are presupposed between divine and human decision-making processes and a common temporal framework is assumed! If Moltmann's arguments were to succeed, he would be required to explain how the divine *ekstasis* does not collapse into a pantheistic divine *hypostasis*, leading to a mysticisation and sacramentalising of suffering (where divine and human suffering became mutually identified and indistinguishable) where even to conceive of a divine proffering of ultimate liberation for humanity would be profoundly difficult. As Karl Rahner has argued, with Moltmann in mind,[64] it is precisely God's free participation which offers hope to humanity, and it is precisely this free participation that speaks of God's love which must not, therefore, be conceived in terms of a form of ontological compulsion expounded in a mechanistic fashion. God is not 'suffering-driven' in any mechanical sense. God is God-driven as the freely loving God who participates ek-statically within the human context. Clearly, this involves a Self-determination on the part of God, but free Self-determination is not necessarily arbitrary, as Moltmann would seem to fear. To speak of God's Self-determination in these terms is to predicate precisely the opposite of any arbitrariness in God here. There is no suggestion in Barth that this is a spontaneous or wilful event occurring to God at some point within the temporal process! Barth's argument is that it is the Being of God which is revealed in Christ and on the cross, and that there is a real correspondence – indeed, identity – between the event of the free participation of God by grace and the loving and 'constancy'[65] of God in eternity.[66] As Barth himself writes: 'what we have here is not an abstract revelation of Lordship but a concrete revelation of the Lord, not Godhead but God Himself, who in this freedom speaks as an I and addresses by a Thou'.[67] It is this, moreover, that underlies Barth's willingness to acknowledge the element of truth in patripassianism.

Moltmann's perception that Barth operates with a monarchianism that betrays a nominalist approach to divine freedom fails, therefore, because he himself operates with a

---

[64] *Karl Rahner im Gespräch* 1, eds. P. Imhoff and H. Biallowons, Munich, 1982, 245f.

[65] Cf. *C. D.* 2. 1, 491ff.

[66] Colin Gunton rightly emphasises that God's eternity is not to be conceived as non-temporality. 'There is a kind of temporality in God, which preserves both the ontological distinction of God from the world and the real relation God has with it. God's eternity is not non-temporality, but the eternity of the triune life.' ('Barth, the Trinity, and Human Freedom', *Theology Today* 18, no. 1 (April 1986), 318.)

[67] *C. D.* 1. 1, 307 (*K. D.* 1. 1, 324).

nominalist conception of the divine nature on the one hand and generic conceptions of freedom and lordship on the other. A proper appreciation of God's lordship and freedom, and an attendant sense of the consequent 'novelty' of God's Self-bestowal in the event of revelation, together with an awareness of the semantic and epistemic implications of all this, mean that the form, character and nature of every aspect of God's grace and communion with human beings in love require to be thought *out of* the event of God's Self-bestowal and not adjudicated, affirmed or, indeed, 'named' from a point elsewhere. This requires that all our terminology be used in the light of its being 'commandeered' in this self-same event.

There is a semantic and pre-conceptual *sacrificium* required here if nominalism is to be avoided, and that is something that Moltmann appears unwilling to make. It is not a sacrifice that scholastic Calvinists have been willing to make either. And it is this which explains the nominalism of Calvinist notions of divine freedom in the 'eternal decrees', notions which Barth would turn on their head later in the *Church Dogmatics*.[68]

To appreciate what is involved here is of critical importance if Barth's own arguments *vis-à-vis* the application of the term 'person' in the trinitarian context are to be understood and if (departing from Barth) the term is to be used *appropriately* with respect to the members of the Trinity – that is, without the importation of a whole series of deductive (and latently nominalist) arguments.

In sum, taken together, the arguments outlined in both this and the previous section are integral to Barth's unambiguous insistence that theology in the light of the Word must take the form of a faithful *Nachdenken* – the essential reason being that 'God's Word is no mere thing; it is the living, personal and free God.'[69] It must be acknowledged that throughout his argumentation Barth does indeed use the terms 'must' and

---

[68] *C. D.* 2. 2, *passim* (see, in particular, his discussion of double predestination and reinterpretation of the terms of the debate, 169ff.).

[69] *C. D.* 1. 1, 198 (*K. D.* 1. 1, 206).

'cannot'. However, these require to be understood in terms of the 'analytic *a posteriori*' status of the claims made and not as reflecting any latent nominalism.

Barth's Reinterpretation of the Structure of Revelation

We now come to the more immediate question: what does the obedient *Nachdenken* tell us about the structure of revelation itself? Further: what does this lead us to affirm about the nature of the divine identity? And, finally: do Barth's conclusions reflect a faithful *Nachdenken*, i.e. are they appropriate to the nature of that with which we are dealing in the revelation event?

'If we really want to understand revelation in terms of its subject, i.e. God,' Barth writes, 'then the first thing we have to realise is that this subject, God, the Revealer, is identical with His act in revelation and also identical with its effect.' ('... dann müssen wir vor allem verstehen, daß dieses ihr Subjekt, Gott, der Offenbarer, identisch ist mit seinem Tun in der Offenbarung, identisch auch mit dessen Wirkung.')[70] 'God Himself is not just Himself. He is also His self-revealing.'[71] He continues, 'It is from this fact, which in the first instance we are merely indicating, that we learn we must begin the doctrine of revelation with the doctrine of the triune God.'[72] Furthermore, the Trinity itself is witnessed in the structure of revelation, as is reflected, Barth argues, in the statement, '*God* reveals Himself. He reveals Himself *through Himself.* He reveals *Himself.*' This is to say that God is the Revealer, the Revelation and the Revealedness. Revelation suggests that, in terms of the traditional model outlined above, God is not simply S^l, but also x and y.

Two features immediately stand out here in contrast to our previous model. First, the disclosure event is radically 'irreflexive and asymmetrical', to borrow terms used by Christoph Schwöbel. Second, whereas both the structure of the Western *ordo salutis* and the traditional model of the form

---

[70] *C. D.* 1. 1, 296 (*K. D.* 1. 1, 312).
[71] *C. D.* 1. 1, 298 (*K. D.* 1. 1, 315).
[72] *C. D.* 1. 1, 296 (*K. D.* 1. 1, 312).

of revelation suggested an *extrinsicity* between the Being of God, the act of revelation and the apprehension of that in the subject, Barth's interpretation involves a *radical* and *irreducible intrinsicity* in this respect – an intrinsicity, indeed, which may appear to suggest the influence on Barth of Hegelian idealism.[73]

The intrinsicity that we find to be involved here is the result of Barth's insistence that the event of revelation, to the extent that it actually takes place, 'is not another over against God. It is the same' – a reiteration of God. In the biblical understanding of revelation God is the 'revealing God and the event of revelation and its effect on man'.[74] All three parts of the equation (S^l, x and y) are to be identified as the God whose Being *is* in this becoming and for whom this becoming *is* his Being. God *is*, that is, God 'takes place', in revelation in such a way that God *is* the becoming which is the event of hearing. God *is* the condition of the reception of God's Word in the human subject.

In no way for Barth does the hearing of revelation belong to humanity independently of the actual, ontic presence of God.

Here we witness, as T. F. Torrance has shown, the extent to which Barth is indebted to the thought of Athanasius.[75]

---

[73] We suspect this is what David Ford has in mind when he implies a closeness of Barth to Hegel with respect to his concept of rationality in his essay 'Conclusion: Assessing Barth' in *Karl Barth – Studies of his Theological Methods*, ed. S. W. Sykes, 196.

Rowan Williams in his essay in the same volume, 'Barth on the Triune God', is more explicit in drawing parallels between Barth's desire to minimise human freedom of response before the Word and the idealist 'obsession with what has been called the "concrete universal"' which 'arose from the desire to ground knowledge securely in an ontology of participation'. He continues spelling out the parallelism by commenting '*das absolute Wissen*, Hegel's final synthesis of consciousness and self-consciousness, is the level at which the divisions and contradictions of prior levels are overcome by the finite subject's identification with, recognition of itself in, Absolute Spirit, the one and universal self-thinking thought ... the finite self's participation in the One'. However, Williams also acknowledges Barth's insistence on 'the total strangeness of God and man to each other' which 'turns the Hegelian system on its head' but does so in a manner that suggests 'a recognizable similarity of pattern, something of a mirror-image'. (Ibid., 188.) We shall return to the question of the connections between Hegelian Idealism and Barth later on in the discussion.

[74] *C. D.* 1. 1, 299 (*K. D.* 1. 1, 315).

[75] *Karl Barth: Biblical and Evangelical Theologian*, Edinburgh, 1990. Cf. the sections in chapter 6 entitled: 'Karl Barth and Athanasius' (160–2), 'The

Athanasius had affirmed the *homoousion* not only of the Son but also, in his *Letters to Serapion*, of the Spirit, and argued a) that these two affirmations were the *sine qua non* of knowledge of God and the possibility of *theologein* (theologising) as opposed to *muthologein* (mythologising), and b) that this was the grounds of knowledge of God (*dianoia*) as opposed to the blind projection of opinions (*epinoiai*) into the infinite on the part of human beings who are, in Paul's words, '*echthroi te dianoia*' (Col. 1:21). In direct parallel, Barth identifies the Being of God not only with the Revealer but with the Revelation and also with the condition of its perception, that is, in terms of the dynamic presence of the Spirit as the Spirit freely indwells the one who hears to the extent that he or she has ears to hear. The very means of the perception of God – the One by whom God is recognised, as well as the One in whom God is perceived, is 'very God from very God'. This is not grounded in any logical necessity, any more than Athanasius' insistence is grounded in a Hellenising of the Gospel; their common perception is that there is here an *objective*, theological and epistemological necessity which is discovered *a posteriori* through an unfolding of the divine Self-givenness in revelation – through the perception of *who* Jesus Christ is and *who* the Spirit is, that is, as the One who brings us into epistemic communion with the Father in and through the Word.[76]

Before turning to our next task, which is to address the ramifications of this approach for Barth's interpretation of the triune identity, we must first consider certain anthropological and semantic problems which emerge here.

a) The Question of a Potential Circularity   If Barth's account offers a radical critique of the *extrinsicity* involved in

---

Doctrine of the Homoousion' (166-7) and 'The Doctrine of the Homoousion and Revelation' (170–4) and chapter 7 (*passim*).

[76] Yet again, the relevant questions here are 'Who' questions and not 'How' questions. For an example of Barth's refusal to engage in consideration of 'How' questions in exploring the ontological issues raised here cf. *C. D.* 1. 1, 367 (*K. D.* 1. 1, 387).

the more traditional approach discussed above, a different problem emerges with his alternative approach. The intrinsicity inherent in Barth's alternative programme seems to involve a potentially damaging circularity.

This relates to Barth's refusal to affirm the validity of the 'How' question of the knowledge of revelation owing to the fact that on his account the 'How' question cannot be answered outside the sphere of revelation. His account suggests that within the sphere of revelation one is compelled to affirm that the *sine qua non* of the reception of revelation is 'participating within its sphere'. If asked how one knows this to be the case, the answer is that one knows this to be the case and can only know it to be so by virtue of one's being within the sphere of this event. What is more, there are no subjective means of entry or points of access into this sphere, since the event reposes in a free, divine act – an event of personal address and neither a 'constantly available connection' ('kontinuierlich-vorfindliche Beziehung') nor a 'transmitted material condition' ('übertragener dinghafter Zustand').[77] In other words, the apparent circularity here is the consequence of affirming that God is not only the revelation but the absolute condition and means of its apprehension. It is when one is inside this context of revelation, within this circle, that one appreciates a) the bankruptcy of claims (methodological and epistemological) made from outside this context of revealedness, and b) that human endeavour of itself offers no means of access.

Here we have the grounds of perhaps the most strongly felt objection to the kind of approach with which Barth is identified. There is perceived to be an endorsement here of privileged access to God and God-talk.[78] That there should be privilege in such a context clearly raises ethical questions – a criticism which relates to the assumed (but invalid) belief that such an

----

[77] *C. D.* 1. 1, 41 (*K. D.* 1. 1, 41).

[78] In other words, it is assumed to involve a form of élitism – a betrayal of 'equality of opportunity' at the theological level!

approach necessarily involves the denigration of 'natural' human capacities.[79]

Several forms of response may be provided in defence of the apparent advocacy of an 'inner circularity' as this is implied by the intrinsicity we have described.

a) It can be said that this is quite simply an unavoidable feature of the uniquely dynamic and subject-involving nature of this particular subject-matter.

b) It may also be said that this is the consequence of human alienation which necessitates that theology be undertaken from within the communion of the Body of Christ, that is, from within the specific context of participation in the (*quodammodo*) reconciled perception of the New Humanity as this involves the free and creative action of God.

c) It may be argued that this is the case in any scientific community – that one cannot appreciate, interpret or evaluate the relevant claims that are made without participating in the particular community, within its language-games, the sphere of the operation of its metaphors, the understanding of its formulations ... and so on. Such a response, however, does not grasp the nettle, since within the academic context there is at least the theoretical possibility of one's becoming part of this perceiving community by virtue of some endeavour on one's own part, whereas this is clearly not the case in the context of divine revelation interpreted in these terms.

d) Further, the response may be given that what we have described as 'extrinsic' models of revelation themselves involve

---

[79] This connects with Rowan Williams' comment (part of which we have referred to above) that 'The revelatory event and experience is not only unitary but infallible, God guaranteeing the divinity of his Word, miraculously grasping man through the uncertain medium of worldly happening and bringing him into the single true event of the divine being. It is Calvin's irresistible grace rendered into epistemological terms.' (op. cit., 158). One suspects Barth might respond by saying that if the revelatory event and experience was not unitary and lacked a sense of certainty, if the divinity of God's Word was not guaranteed in and through the event, if it did not grasp the human self and bring it into the single true event of divine being, then it would surely be less than straightforward to justify describing such an event as a real *disclosure* of God to a confused and alienated humanity at all!

a circularity (with similarly exclusive ramifications), in that the endorsement of prior, epistemic conditions in knowledge of God on *a priori* grounds is circular and, therefore, may also be argued to involve an ultimate 'fideism' that can be equally exclusive. (Most manifestations of *odium theologicum* exemplify precisely this!)

e) Finally, it may be suggested that, if Barth's circularity appears to be exclusive at the anthropological level, that is, of human beings, the alternative appears to be methodologically exclusive at the theological level, that is, of God!

The most coherent response in support of Barth is surely a theological one which questions or, indeed, denies the implied assumption that the possession of this kind of knowledge is either a) morally commendable, or b) may be believed to be from the inside, or c) may be perceived to be by those outside the sphere of this event. If there is no potential for self-congratulation, on the one hand, or ethical condemnation, on the other, then there is no possibility of theological élitism, on the one hand, or criticism for the failure on anybody's part to endorse or appreciate the warrant of the position, on the other. In other words, the self-authenticating event of Self-disclosure is simply an *event* and never an *accomplishment* at the human level.

This response leads, of course, to the conclusion that the Christian faith and the theological affirmation integral to it can neither be advocated nor commended by appeal to any universally (or independently) endorsable features. Further still, the participation of believers in the event of proclamation is not anything they should or may actively attempt. Rather, participation in the event of proclamation will be inherent in what they are as persons, to the extent that their personhood is constituted by the event of becoming a 'member' of Christ's Body, that is, to the extent that the Spirit is, by grace, dynamically present in their lives and words and as their personhood is constituted by this creative presence. Any creative increase in the population of the Body of Christ will be explicable purely and simply in terms of the dynamic *ekstasis* of the Spirit of God. In other words, any

Anknüpfungspunkt will, in the final analysis, always be describable solely in terms of the concrete life and activity of the Holy Spirit within the Body of Christ as the latter exemplifies and lives out the Gospel of grace and God's unconditional and inclusive valuing of persons. That to which we are brought to witness is a Self-authenticating event of the divine Self-disclosure – it is not a form of disclosure for which we may bear positively any responsibility whatsoever.

Consequently, any apparent exclusiveness on the part of God suggested by the inclusiveness stemming from the intrinsicity we have described will be addressed not by defining knowledge of God with recourse to necessarily inclusive, programmatic principles, but in terms of something which is even more dynamic than is implied by Moltmann's metaphor of the 'openness' of the life of God. What we would wish to denote is closer to what Daniel Hardy describes as 'an unsurpassably active abundance'[80] or 'overflow of life',[81] yet where this abundance 'has its own intrinsic character or energetic homogeneity …'[82]. This points to an inclusiveness that is active and not merely passive – with the resulting perception that the door will invariably be opened and opened *from within* as and when anyone knocks on it, is brought to it or, indeed, falls against it. The Christian God is dynamically active as a seeking, vivifying, transforming and reconciling Agent – One whose love does not merely suffer but *actively* opposes, in and through the Body of Christ, all that which would negate the *telos* of the created order.

From within the event of revelation the inclusiveness which we witness may be seen to contrast with the exclusiveness of approaches which repose on 'religious' human endeavour or human capacity. Religion defined in this manner is rarely inclusive! To suggest, moreover, that the existence of 'independent' or extrinsic grounds of affirming God's existence or purposes would be fairer is to succumb to a myth

---

[80] Daniel W. Hardy, 'Theology, Cosmology and Change' (unpublished paper presented to the Society for the Study of Theology, Cardiff, 1993), 16.

[81] D. W. Hardy and D. F. Ford, *Jubilate: Theology in Praise*, London, 1984, 73.

[82] 'Theology, Cosmology and Change', 16.

that forms the subtext of so much criticism of Barth's views here – not least from within the Anglo-Saxon world. This myth suggests, quite simply, that human beings are naturally and properly 'free' to accept God (in a human act of faith) or, indeed, to reject God (by way of a similarly free and 'responsible' act), and that any proposal, therefore, that for human beings to be really free in this regard requires an event of liberation is an affront to human dignity, rationality, responsibility and agency.

b) Does Barth's Revelation Model involve the Notion of a Private Language?   But there is a further issue which we must address and which concerns the *semantic* implications of the intrinsicity which I have described. Does revelation, interpreted in this manner, not lead to a kind of private language, a semantic isolationism which would be avoided by a model which endorsed more general, public conditions of knowledge of revelation? Does the suggestion that the defining of theological terms takes place within the revelation event not lead to an esoteric notion of meaning in this context? Anthony Thiselton criticises Rudolf Bultmann on precisely this score. Bultmann's advocacy of 'deeper levels of meaning' where the language of the New Testament is interpreted in terms of existential categories internal to the subject falls foul, he argues, of Wittgenstein's critique of 'private language'.[83] For terms to be meaningful they must adhere to rules of meaning which are public. Even if these are to change, they cannot change privately. As Wittgenstein has argued with reference to his 'beetle in the box' analogy, we cannot define the meaning of a term by looking into some supposed private or internal realm of meaning. The incoherence of any such suggestion he illustrates in the following way: 'Suppose everyone had a box with something in it: we call it a "beetle". No one can look into anyone else's box, and everyone says he

---

[83] Cf. his section entitled 'The Hermeneutical Significance of the Argument about Private Language and Public Criteria of Meaning' in *The Two Horizons, New Testament Hermeneutics and Philosophical Description with special reference to Heidegger, Bultmann, Gadamer and Wittgenstein*, Exeter, 1980, 379–85.

knows what a beetle is only by looking at his beetle.' Wittgenstein concludes that the thing in the box 'has no place in the language-game at all; not even as something: for the box might even be empty'. One cannot even 'divide through' by the thing in the box as 'it cancels out, whatever it is'.[84] The very notion of a private language is thus incoherent. Any change of meaning must necessarily be conceived as a public process involving a change of public rules grounded in facets or features that are not only publicly discernible but perceived publicly to be publicly discernible. The objection becomes still more serious, to the extent that, as Jaakko and Merrill Hintikka suggest,[85] language may be argued to be the universal medium of reality to the extent that our thought processes and the very possibility, therefore, of interpreting the world are linguistically constituted. Our very cognition, to the extent that it is language-bound, cannot therefore be private. If the revelation event is such that we cannot make use of public language, the question emerges as to if and how we can think about it at all, let alone articulate what we find.

Eberhard Jüngel argues that the doctrine of the Trinity serves the same purpose for Barth that demythologising does for Bultmann, in that it rescues God-talk from the charge of anthropomorphic projection.[86] God is not simply fitted into predetermined contexts of meaning. The revelation event is, moreover, an event in which 'language is "commandeered"'.[87] What is vital to note, however, is that this is not conceived as happening privately but within the context of the shared life of the Body of Christ, the community of the Church. It is

---

[84] *On Certainty* (1950–51), Germ. and Eng., Oxford, 1969, sect. 293.

[85] *Investigating Wittgenstein*, Oxford, 1986.

[86] *The Doctrine of the Trinity*, 22. He writes, 'Paradoxical as it may sound, the doctrine of the Trinity in Barth's theology (1932) has the same function as the programme of demythologising in the theology of Rudolf Bultmann … If we understand Bultmann's programme as the concern for appropriate speech about God (and therewith about man) and if we view the fulfilment of this concern as a concern not to objectify God or let him be objectified as an It or He, but to bring him to speech as Thou and thus to speak of him appropriately, then we shall not fail to recognize a conspicuous parallelism to the significance which Barth attributes (and gives) to the doctrine of the Trinity.'

[87] Ibid., 12.

grounded, therefore, in a *public* tradition.[88] Theological thought and articulation take place, therefore, where the theologian participates in the community-forming event of the triune God in which language is commandeered from the human side in *Christ's* own reception and appropriation, as a social human being, of knowledge of God.

Early in the *Church Dogmatics*, Barth seems to have been aware of the force of this modern concern and affirms, prior to Wittgenstein's influence, that the meaning of terms is their use in the public domain. (As we have already mentioned, Wittgenstein himself read the first volume.) What Barth's position requires him to say, therefore, is that, although family resemblances between the meanings of terms span the divide between the Church and secular society, the meanings of the terms we use are transformed, the rules of use extended metaphorically, by the language-commandeering event which takes place in the irreducibly social Body of Christ. Christian dogmatics is always, therefore, a *church* dogmatics.[89]

So, for example, Barth argues that the very term 'God' receives redefinition (acquires new rules of use, that is) within the context of the revelation event, within the context of the Body of Christ – it is given a new meaning that is defined by its 'norm' ('Kriterium').[90] What must also be clear is that the same will apply to the term 'person' if it is to be used of God in any way at all.

Reiteration and the Divine Identity

This brings us finally to consider Barth's definition of the term 'God' as this is conditioned by his interpretation of

---

[88] Here we see one of the major differences between Barth and Bultmann. Bultmann conflated the Marburg Neo-Kantian conception of the *Individuum* as the home of *Religion* with the existentialist emphasis on the *Existenz* of the self. The 'deeper meaning' of the kerygma was to be interpreted with recourse to this inner realm of the individual self.

[89] Wittgenstein would not repudiate this, in that family resemblances are open and do not involve a term's having a predetermined essential meaning. The rule-governedness in the use of terms does not imply that the totality of these rules are determined and fixed *a priori*.

[90] *C. D.* 1. 1, 301 (*K. D.* 1. 1, 317).

revelation – a feature which has led Barth himself to be perceived by Moltmann as 'Western' in his theology and by Colin Gunton as being driven too much by the post-Enlightenment concern with epistemology as this has characterised Western thought.

Barth's reinterpretation of the structure of revelation led him, as we have seen, to a concern with the divine identity. God is identified not only as the Revealer but also as the Revelation and the Revealedness. If God ceases to be any one of these, God ceases to be God (in so far as God *is* the fullness of the divine speech-act in the event of revelation[91]) and revelation ceases to take place.

But defining God in this way resulted in Barth's giving massive prominence to the metaphor of the divine address to humankind, that is, God's 'speech' – 'God's own direct speech, which is not to be distinguished from God Himself, from the divine I which confronts man in this act in which it says Thou to him'.[92] He sought, moreover, (in his own words) to 'treat of the whole doctrine of the Trinity and the essentials of Christology ... as constituent parts of our answer *to the question of the Word of God*'.[93] This led him to expound the Trinity in a manner which raises questions, first, as to how far his own approach was *itself* characterised by the reverent *Nachdenken* that he advocated and, second, whether the emphasis on *Nachdenken* is not itself subliminally misleading – whether *nach* should not be interpreted as qualifying a participative form of *being* conceived in more integrated and holistic terms than those denoted by his emphasis on 'Nach-denken'.[94]

[91] 'God's Word is itself God's act.' God's Being is in Becoming. God's speech is act just as God's Being as being is pure event. (*C. D.* 1. 1, 147; Jüngel, op. cit., 27.)

[92] *C. D.* 1. 1, 304 (*K. D.* 1. 1, 320).

[93] *C. D.* 1. 1, 44, italics mine (*K. D.* 1. 1, 43).

[94] This is certainly not to seek to polarise the two or to imply that we can exist in any meaningful sense without thinking! Rather, it is to stress that our thinking not only shapes, but is shaped by, our whole socially participative and semantically moulded apperception. Our proper functioning at the cognitive level is thus inseparable from our social participation and communal being. Cf. the final footnote in this book referring to Alvin Plantinga's discussion in *Warrant and Proper Function*, Oxford, 1993.

The Triune Nature of God's Being-with-us in the Event of Revelation

a) **The Task of Theological Expression** The Bible declares that God's Being with humanity is the event of revelation. This statement, understood in terms of God revealing himself as the Lord, Barth describes as 'the root of the doctrine of the Trinity'.[95]

As such it involves two things: first, over and against a nominalist approach, Barth affirms that 'the statement of statements about God's Trinity cannot claim to be directly identical with the statement about revelation or with revelation itself. The doctrine of the Trinity is an analysis of this statement, i.e., of what it denotes.'[96] This means that we must distinguish carefully between our formulations – the language we use – and the realities we seek to denote by way of these:

> we should take ... with Calvin the insight that in doctrine as such we are always dealing with *impropria loquutia* as regards the object, that the explanation as such, in so far as it is different from the text, in so far as it must work with concepts alien to the text, might be gladly 'buried' if a right understanding of the text could be assured in some other way.[97]

The articulation of God within the context of language-games (and the human thinking irreducibly connected with, and indeed shaped by, these) should be conceived as methodologically posterior, therefore, and demanding the dynamic and continual reformation, restructuring and reordering of our language. If a slightly naïve referentialism is suggested by Barth's comment here, it is not necessitated. We can say that the (language-mediated) communion of our being with God, which demands and involves the propriety of our (language-engendered) thought, requires the continual reconciliation of our language-world (thought-world). This involves the *metanoia* of our *noiein* in such a way that the pressure of interpretation, reinterpretation and reordering

---

[95] *C. D.* 1. 1, 307 (*K. D.* 1. 1, 324).
[96] *C. D.* 1. 1, 308 (*K. D.* 1. 1, 325).
[97] *C. D.* 1. 1, 309 (*K. D.* 1. 1, 326).

involves a directionality which is *from* God's Word (what Hardy describes in terms of the 'information density' of God) *to* humanity and not the other way round.[98]

Second, it is to suggest, he argues, 'that the statement or statements about the Trinity of God purport to be indirectly, though not directly, identical with the statement about revelation'.[99] Consequently, the dogma of the Trinity is to be regarded 'as a necessary and relevant analysis of revelation, and we thus think that revelation is correctly interpreted by the dogma'.[100]

If this prompts one to ask whether the Trinity is derived, for Barth, by way of an analysis of the form of revelation rather than its content, his answer would be to deny that a valid distinction may be drawn here. What is given in revelation, as in proclamation, is not 'information' detached from its reference and independent of its *modus cognoscendi.* What is given (or, more accurately, Self-giving) is *God* in a reconciling act where the triune Being-in-act of God reveals by virtue of this Being-in-act precisely this Being-in-act! The doctrine of the Trinity is thus not 'read off' the information content of revelation independently of its givenness. Rather, there is an absolute integration of form and content in revelation, every facet of which requires to be expressed in terms of the divine Triunity.

b) Barth's Rejection of Modalism   It is precisely here that we see that, if Barth is not guilty of monarchianism, he is equally eager not to advocate any form of modalism that undermines the reality of what is given in revelation. In his own words,

> We are not saying that the doctrine of the Trinity is merely the interpretation of revelation and not also an interpretation of the God who reveals Himself in revelation. ... If we are dealing with His

[98] Cf. D. W. Hardy's discussion of the second person in terms of the concept of 'information density', in 'Christ and Creation' in *The Incarnation*, ed. T. F.Torrance, Edinburgh, 1981.

[99] *C. D.* 1. 1, 309 (*K. D.* 1. 1, 326).

[100] *C. D.* 1. 1, 310 (*K. D.* 1. 1, 326–7).

revelation, we are dealing with God Himself and not, as Modalists in all ages have thought, with an entity distinct from Him.[101]

We are dealing, moreover, with the divine Thou who addresses us in and through proclamation and, indeed, in every *Seinsweise* that is the reiteration of God in freedom. God *is* what is revealed and God *is* the means of that revelation.[102] As Eberhard Jüngel confirms, here 'the significance – not the final, but certainly a primary significance – of the doctrine of the Trinity for Barth consists in ensuring over against subordinationism on the one hand and modalism on the other, that God becomes "neither an It nor a He": "he remains Thou".'[103] It is this integrity of the divine address that underlies the perception that without the human Jesus, God is not God.

God does not exist *behind* that which reveals God. God is not mediated by that which is not God, God is nothing less than identical with God's revelation –

---

[101] *C. D.* 1. 1, 311 (*K. D.* 1. 1, 328–9).

[102] Barth says of the modalism of Noetus of Smyrna, Praxeas, Sabellius and Priscillian, as well as of Schleiermacher 'they did indeed assert the substantial equality of the trinitarian 'persons' but only as manifestations behind which God's one true being is concealed as something other and higher, so that one may well ask whether revelation can be believed if in the background there is always the thought that we are not dealing with God as He is but only with a God as he appears to us. If the *tropos apokalypseos* is really a different one from the *tropos huparxeos* and if the *huparxis* is the real being of God, then this means that God in His revelation is not really God. To take this unreal God seriously as God is to be diametrically opposed to monotheism even though it was and is the point of the distinction to protect this. The result is ... that belief in revelation necessarily becomes idolatry.' (*C. D.* 1. 1, 353; *K. D.* 1. 1, 372.)

In his important book *Von Den Kirchenvätern zu Karl Barth* (Amsterdam, 1993) E. P. Meijering argues not only that Barth himself pushes too far in the direction of modalism (in the first volume of the *Church Dogmatics*), but that he seems to have misinterpreted the patristic critique of Sabellianism. He writes, 'Barth ist sich des Unterschiedes zwischen der patristischen Kritik am Sabellianismus und seiner eigenen wohl nicht bewusst, jedenfalls schweigt er hierzu gänzlich' (57). Earlier he stresses that 'sein Hauptargument gegen den Sabellianismus ist nicht klassisch'. And, again, '... gegen den Sabellianismus... führt Barth ein Argument an, das gerade nicht traditionell ist. ... Mit seiner Kritik will er offenbar nicht den historischen Sabellianismus sondern Schleiermacher treffen. Das klassische Argument gegen den Sabellianismus ist anderer Art, nämlich dass nach seiner Lehre der Sohn keine Entität neben dem Vater ist' (53).

[103] *The Doctrine of the Trinity*, 22.

the fact that God takes form does not give rise to a medium, a third thing between God and man, a reality distinct from God that is as such the subject of revelation. This would imply that God would be unveilable for men, that God Himself would no longer need His revelation, or rather that God would be given up into the hands of men, who, God's form being given Him, could more or less control God as he does other realities.[104]

God *is* in God's Being toward us, God is and remains the Thou which he is in his address and which his address brings us to speak in response.

Despite all this, there are modalist tinges in certain features of his discussion. Posing the question as to whether Barth does incline toward a modalist interpretation of the Trinity, Alasdair Heron comments, 'In line with the general Augustinian trend in the West, while Barth emphasises both the unity and the threefoldness within God, he tends to give effective priority to the former.' Heron then goes on to make a profoundly important observation which points to what is, in our opinion, the essential weakness in Barth, one which haunts the *Church Dogmatics* throughout – namely that 'God's triple *reiteration of himself* is much more prominent than his *relation to himself;* the note of "otherness" is more muted than that of "self-expression"; tritheism is sensed to be a greater threat than Sabellianism.'[105] It is this that lies behind William Hill's description of Barth as a 'trinitarian modalist' – trinitarian because the three are not united by some fourth essence, but a modalist because, he argues, there is only one seat of divine subjectivity.[106] Whether it is possible to be a 'trinitarian modalist' in this way is open to doubt. However, Hill's comment does direct us to some consideration of the divine singularity which underlies Barth's exposition.

c) The Metaphor of Address and Divine Singularity   The question emerges as to whether Barth's exposition of revelation as divine address does not give rise to an inordinate stress on

---

[104] *C. D.* 1. 1, 321 (*K. D.* 1. 1, 339).
[105] A. I. C. Heron, *The Holy Spirit*, London, 1983, 167.
[106] *The Three-Personed God*, Washington, 1982, 113–24.

a divine singularity conceived in logical terms. Even if Barth may be defended against the charge of modalism (an issue to which we shall return in chapter four), it is difficult to deny that there is at least a detrimental 'anhypostaticism' in his doctrine of revelation. This undermines the significance for revelation of the communion internal to God into which humanity is taken by the Spirit in and through the vicarious humanity of the Word made flesh. Our adoption in Christ and participation through the Spirit must be essential elements of an interpretation of revelation which is concerned to take seriously not least at the *formal* level both Christ's humanity and ours.

One key reason for this is the influence on the shape of his theology of the singularity implicit in his exposition of revelation. First, a singularity seems to be implied in the various forms in which Barth poses the 'Who' question, for example: 'Who is God?' (301), 'Who is our God?' (301), 'Who is the self-revealing God?' (303), 'Who is He?' This apparent singularity would not be a problem if it were clear that the very posing of the 'Who' question were itself to be interpreted as an act of God in such a way that asking the 'Who' question included as its object the very dynamic of this asking. The genuine posing of the 'Who' question on the part of a human subject is a participatory act and requires to be interpreted in trinitarian terms. Second, Barth places a heavy if not controlling emphasis on a) God's direct speech ('Gottes eigenes unmittelbares Reden'[107]) – his notion of the *Dei loquentis persona*[108] – and b) the confrontation ('gegenübertreten') of the divine I ('Ich') with the human subject. This means that the singularity of the divine subject – that is, the addressing, confronting *Individuum*, integral to his revelation model – leads him to underplay the foundational importance for interpreting the divine identity of the notion of the triune *perichoresis*, where unity is defined not in terms of the singular identity of the free divine subject,[109] but in terms of the divine

[107] *K. D.* 1. 1, 320.
[108] 'Offenbarung ist *Dei loquentis persona*' (ibid.).
[109] *C. D.* 1. 1, 138–9 (*K. D.* 1. 1, 142–3).

communion.[110] In contrast to this, Barth's approach at this formative and, indeed, determinative point in his theological exposition suggests an exclusive reference to divine personhood in the singular – as expressed by his summarising statement: 'Offenbarung ist *Dei loquentis persona.*'[111]

If the personal 'Who' question is to be posed with respect to God, is it not the case that this question is posed within a context of participatory communion, of *theopoiesis,* where God is conceived in much more dynamic terms than merely as a confronting, addressing *Individuum* – the *Dei loquentis persona?* May it not be that God should be conceived as reconciling, communicating Triunity, where 'communication' is integral to a wider event of triune communion? This would suggest that there is no address of the human subject which is not integral to the human subject's being brought to participate within that same triune communion where what speaks and addresses *is* this 'receiving into communion' by grace. The 'Who' question, asked in this context, invites an answer that speaks not simply of the 'anhypostatic' movement from God to humanity but of an embracing speech-act of the Father inseparable from the enhypostatic and 'participation-accomplishing' movement of the Son to the Father on our behalf in and through the liberating, recreating, transforming and enlightening presence of the Spirit. This inclusive, perichoretic dynamic of the grace of God does not repose in

---

[110] Colin Gunton's exposition of the concept of *perichoresis* is particularly useful here. He writes, 'The central point about the concept is that it enables theology to preserve both the one and the many in dynamic interrelations. It implies that the three persons of the Trinity exist only in reciprocal eternal relatedness. God is not God apart from the way in which Father, Son and Spirit in eternity give to and receive from each other what they essentially are.' (*The One, the Three and the Many,* Cambridge, 1993, 163–4.)

[111] *K. D.* 1. 1, 320. Unfortunately, the apparently personalist stress in Barth's insistence on the centrality of the 'Who' question over the 'How' question seems to have the effect of compounding the problem further. If the 'Who' question, posed not of the Father or the Son or the Spirit but of the divine *Ich* is conceived as the primary question in theology, unless it is set and defined very firmly within the context of participatory communion, then the singularity implicit in the question leads too easily to the illicit projection on to God of the notion of an absolutely singular subject.

one who is singular and *also* triune but in the One whose very singularity *is* this Triunity.[112] In other words, the 'Who' question directs us to a much richer dynamic than that of the confronting, addressing divine *Ich*. And it should not be asked, therefore, in a manner which allows, at the subliminal level, the localisation or individualisation of its object. In sum, the 'Who' question, asked of the Triunity of God, must include a corresponding 'Where is God' question, which reformulates and deepens our asking of the 'Who' question. God is not only before but also behind, not merely above but also below – a dynamic, we might add, that is not served well, however, by incoherent polarisations between so-called 'Christology from above' and 'Christology from below'![113]

The issue here is highlighted in the statement Barth makes earlier in the volume where he discusses the human experience of God, perhaps rather surprisingly *prior* to his discussion of God's Triunity. There he argues that, 'the experience of God's Word involves a relation of man as person to another person, naturally the person of God'.[114] ('... es sich in der Erfahrung vom Worte Gottes um ein Verhältnis des Menschen als Person zu einer anderen Person, natürlich zu der Person Gottes, handelt.'[115]) It would seem that there is a subliminal orientation which interprets God's engagement with humanity too definitively on a model of inter-personal address or, bearing in mind the indefinite article (*einer*), even subsuming this engagement within a class of individuals-in-relation. If this influences Barth's thought in any way at all, then it would be difficult for him to conceive of three persons in the

---

[112] At various points in his *Church Dogmatics*, not least in Volume Four, Barth's exposition seems to be in accord with this. It is only a pity that he did not work through the epistemological implications of this more consistently in his exposition of methodology and its relationship to the doctrine of God.

[113] Cf. Nicholas Lash's discussion, 'Up and Down in Christology', *New Studies in Theology 1*, eds. S. W. Sykes and D. Holmes, Duckworth, 1980, 31–46. The fullest and most perceptive analysis of this debate and the confusions therein is to be found in Colin Gunton's *Yesterday and Today: A Study in Continuities in Christology*, London, 1983.

[114] *C. D.* 1. 1, 205.

[115] *K. D.* 1. 1, 214.

Godhead in this sense of the term. To do so would commit him either to three different forms of address (or conversations) or to the 'three manikins' notion of which he is so critical.

We shall now go on to examine the extent to which his additional 'verbal' metaphors of repetition and reiteration and his analogical reference to 'saying the same thing in a threefold way' may be construed as undermining further the notion of an intra-trinitarian communion which would appear to be necessary if we are to identify what God is in himself with what God is toward us.

d) The One God in Threefold Repetition[116] The differentiation within God which he seeks to denote by the term *Seinsweise* is expressed by Barth by way of a series of verbal metaphors. He speaks, for example, of a 'threefold sense' ('dreifacher Sinn') in the statement 'God reveals Himself as Lord',[117] of 'saying the same thing three times'[118] and also of 'repetition' or 'reiteration' ('Wiederholung') where the unity of the divine identity is described in terms of a *repetitio aeternitas in aeternitate*[119] – where God is 'sein eigener Doppelgänger', his own *alter ego*.

Barth's argument would appear to be summed up in the statement that, when we are speaking of the Trinity as it expresses God's revealing himself as Lord, we are saying 'the

---

[116] 'Der Name des Vaters, des Sohnes und des Geistes besagt, daß Gott in dreimaliger Wiederholung der eine Gott ist ...' (*K. D.* 1. 1, 369).

[117] 'God reveals Himself as the Lord; in this statement we have summed up our understanding of the form and content of the biblical revelation.' (*C. D.* 1. 1, 314; *K. D.* 1. 1, 331.) Cf. also *C. D.* 1. 1, 307 (*K. D.* 1. 1, 324): 'The statement ... that God reveals Himself as the Lord ... we call the root of the doctrine of the Trinity.'

[118] *C. D.* 1. 1, 332 (*K. D.* 1. 1, 351). This is, of course, an extremely difficult metaphor to interpret within any kind of philosophy of language. Is he saying that the sense ('Sinn') is different but the reference ('Bedeutung') is the same? This would suggest an incipient modalism. (We might note that, in the same passage, he also speaks of 'the three elements of veiling, unveiling and impartation', and 'form, freedom and historicity', as being relevant for defining revelation as the root and ground of the doctrine of the Trinity, suggesting that this conclusion may be regarded as a 'genuine finding' ('ein wirkliches Ergebnis') in this respect.

[119] *C. D.* 1. 1, 353 (*K. D.* 1. 1, 373).

same thing three times in three indissolubly different ways'
('dreimal unauflöslich anders dreimal dasselbe').[120]
In this section, entitled 'Unity in Trinity', he writes,

> The name of the Father, Son and Spirit means that God is the one
> God in threefold repetition, and this in such a way that the repetition
> itself is grounded in His Godhead, so that it implies no alteration in
> His Godhead, and yet in such a way also that He is the one God only
> in this repetition, so that His one Godhead stands or falls with the fact
> that He is God in this repetition, but for that very reason He is the one
> God in each repetition.[121]

All this points to Barth's keenness to expound the threeness
in God in terms of linguistic metaphors. These portray what
Rowan Williams describes as an 'expressive view of language'
and a 'linear model of God's Trinitarian utterance'. To
criticise a one-sidedness in Barth here is *not* to deny that, as
Catherine Mowry LaCugna emphasises, 'God by nature is self-
expressive, God seeks to reveal and give Godself ...' and that
'This is consistent with the biblical images of a God who is
alive, who is ineluctably oriented "other-ward", who is plenitude
of love, grace and mercy overflowing.'[122] Nor is it to deny, as
Karl Rahner argues, that the Logos is the Father's Word 'in
which the Father can express himself ...'[123] However, it *is* to
emphasise that the grammar of this *other-ward* orientation is
realised in a dynamic of communion that, by the Spirit,
completes the other-ward or anhypostatic dynamic in a
consequent 'in-ward' dynamic. This is realised in an act of
'vicarious' gathering of humanity in a salvific parallel to –
indeed, participation in – the home-coming of the Son. As
such it corresponds to the enhypostatic dynamic in the
incarnation whereby the '*ex-pressive*' nature and giving of God
is completed in a bringing of humanity to participate in the
life of God – where this is a sharing not just *with* but *in* the
'given' communion of God.

---

[120] Ibid.
[121] *C. D.* 1. 1, 350 (*K. D.* 1. 1, 369).
[122] *God for Us: The Trinity and Christian Life,* 230.
[123] *The Trinity* (Eng. trans. by Joseph Donceel, London, 1970), 32.

Barth's use of the notion of *Wiederholung* and exposition of it may be seen, therefore, to clarify what he intends to convey in and through the term *Seinsweise*. It also presents us with some insight as to how he perceives the divine Triunity.

Prior to a discussion of the priority in revelation of the second person of the Trinity,[124] Barth repeats that the form and content of biblical revelation are summarised by the statement, 'God reveals himself as Lord.'[125] 'The question now', he continues, 'is whether we must take this statement in a threefold sense ("in einem dreifachen Sinn") without infringing the unity ("Einheit") of its content or whether we must take it in its unified[126] content ("als einheitlich in seinem Gehalt") without infringing its threefold sense.'[127] In order to assess the validity or otherwise of Moltmann's critique of Barth's thought here as being 'monotheistic' and 'Western', we shall have to interpret carefully a) how Barth balances the oneness and the threeness in his understanding of God's Self-revelation, and b) the extent to which his interpretation of

---

[124] 'Historically considered and stated the three questions answered in the Bible, that of revealer, revelation and being revealed, do not have the same importance. The true theme of the biblical witness is the second of the concepts, God's action in His revelation, revelation in answer to the question what God does, and therefore the predicate in our statement. Within this theme the two other questions, materially no less important, are answered. Similarly the doctrine of the Trinity, when considered historically in its origin and development, is not equally interested in the Father, the Son and the Holy Ghost. Here too the theme is primarily the second person of the Trinity, God the Son, the deity of Christ.' (*C. D.* 1. 1, 314–15; *K. D.* 1. 1, 332.)

Here Barth makes a distinction between historical importance and logical or material importance. Only the former applies to the Son as against the other members of the Trinity. Historically, the Son is of prime importance in that the question of the Son gave rise to the other two questions as a necessary counterpart to the Son: 'the question of the Father on the one side and that of the Spirit of the Father and the Son on the other' (*C. D.* 1. 1, 315; *K. D.* 1. 1, 332). Hence the order in 2 Cor. 13:13 (Christ, God, Spirit) is the most authentic form of the biblical witness in this matter.

[125] 'God reveals Himself as the Lord; in this statement we have summed up our understanding of the form and content of the biblical revelation.' (*C. D.* 1. 1, 314; *K. D.* 1. 1, 331.)

[126] One suspects that 'unified' is the best translation of *einheitlich* in this context. 'Unitary' would perhaps be more appropriate to Barth's line of thought.

[127] *C. D.* 1. 1, 314 (*K. D.* 1. 1, 331).

God's 'Self-revelation, as Lord' may function as a formal principle or dictum which conditions his interpretation of God's triune Being. To do this we must examine his exposition of these issues.

Barth argues that God exists for men and women 'in His own special form which cannot be mistaken for any other'. He continues, 'But he does so truly and concretely, so that those concerned can say without any speculation or metaphor: Immanuel, God with us! so that without any fiction or self-deception they can say Thou to Him and pray to Him. That is what self-revelation is.'[128] In other words, his Self-unveiling is a 'taking form' whereby God is his 'own alter ego in His revelation' ('in seiner Offenbarung sein eigener Doppelgänger'). This is not to be conceived as necessarily the case. Rather, it is an event – 'an event that cannot be explained by or derived from either the will or act of man or the course of the world at large'.

This step of unveiling on the part of God means quite simply that there is 'something new in God, a self-distinction of God from Himself, a being of God in a mode of being that is different from though not subordinate to ("nicht untergeordneten") His first and hidden mode of being ("verborgenen Seinsweise") as God, in a mode of being ("Seinsweise"), of course, in which he can also exist for us'. Consequently, he continues,

> the very fact of revelation tells us that it is proper to Him to distinguish Himself from Himself, i.e., to be God in Himself and in concealment, and yet at the same time to be God a second time in a very different way, namely, in Self-manifestation ('in sich selbst und verborgen Gott zu sein und nun zugleich ganz anders, nämlich offenbar') i.e., in the form ('Gestalt') of something He Himself is not.'[129]

It is significant that Barth uses the term *Seinsweise* here. In this context it is used both of a) the first and hidden mode of being of God, and b) of God in his act of unveiling. This testifies to the fact (as emphasised above) that there are no

---

[128] *C. D.* 1. 1, 316 (*K. D.* 1. 1, 333).
[129] *C. D.* 1. 1, 316 (*K. D.* 1. 1, 334).

modalistic connotations to be found specifically in the way in which he uses *Seinsweise*, since it would be absurd to interpret God's eternal being in and for himself as a 'mode of God's being' where the word was being interpreted in a modalist sense. However, it may be to state the obvious to point out that it is also clear here that 'inter-relationality' is not built into this conceptuality. There is no essential 'communion' apparent between the two *Seinsweisen* referred to here.

When Barth refers to a *Seinsweise* of God he is referring to God himself in a manner which takes cognisance of the fact that God does not always have being in precisely the same way and yet the unitary identity of God is not to be placed in question. The language for which he opts here involves speaking of a reiteration or a repetition ('Wiederholung') of God.

What is clear in his discussions of this concept is that he is concerned to leave no room whatsoever for any form of subordinationism. The *Seinsweisen* are, as Barth continually reminds his reader, *nicht untergeordnet* – a feature that clearly requires to be distinguished from the 'subordination' for which he does argue later in the *Church Dogmatics*.[130] If God is toward us in a way of being, then God *is* in this way of being. This *is* God, nothing less than God and, therefore, nothing less than God in God's full divinity. The point here is quite simple: in all God's ways of being, God remains the divine subject, and the divine I cannot have predicated of it different levels of reality or different proportions of divinity. All such forms of quantification of the divine are inappropriate and, indeed, less than reverent![131]

This point is further clarified when Barth comments that

all the attributes which characterise the Yahweh of Israel, His righteousness ... goodness and faithfulness ... His glory and also His

---

[130] In Volume Four, he argues that we are required to endorse the 'offensive fact' that 'there is in God Himself an above and a below, a *prius* and a *posterius*, a superiority and a subordination' (*C. D.* 4. 1, 201).

[131] 'The divine essence would not be the divine essence if in it there were superiority and inferiority and also, then, various quanta of deity.' (*C. D.* 1. 1, 393; *K. D.* 1. 1, 414.)

Word and Spirit, the wisdom of the later Old Testament, and the countenance which is anthropomorphically – or should we say not at all anthropomorphically – ascribed to Him, His arm, His hand, His right hand, all these are sometimes referred to as though they were not just in or of Yahweh but were Yahweh Himself a second time in another way ('sondern eben anders noch einmal Jahve selbst'). Revelation means that all these human, all too human concepts are not just that, are not just descriptions and representations of the reality of Yahweh; they are themselves the reality of Yahweh.[132]

This brings out clearly the appeal for Barth of the metaphor of 'repetition' or 'reiteration' ('Wiederholung') and the other synonyms associated with it. It serves to suggest self-differentiation without threatening the absolute Self-identity of God in these self-differentiations. This move is essential to the very structure of his offering an alternative theological form of approach to those characterised either by a) the *analogia entis*, or b) the reduction of theology to merely symbolic self-expression – where there is no intrinsic connection between the symbol and that which is arguably (i.e. on what grounds?) symbolised.

But this immediately encourages us to ask which of the other semantic rules associated with this metaphorical language apply to the use of the term *Seinsweise?* Does it imply 'free identification' (in the sense that reiteration or repetition is an optional act) on the part of the divine subject with the relevant *Seinsweisen?* Are the second and third *Seinsweisen* of the Trinity to be seen as free events of God's Self-reiteration? That Barth would not draw any such conclusion is suggested not least by his opposition to the notion that the Father is the causal source of divinity – although even here his argumentation requires careful interpretation. He writes, 'God's trinitarian name of Father, God's eternal fatherhood, denotes the mode of being of God in which He is the Author of His other modes of being', and yet he eagerly follows Calvin in affirming that the Son is *autotheos* in the fullest sense (and

---

[132] *C. D.* 1. 1, 316 (*K. D.* 1. 1, 334).

not *deuterotheos*).[133] In sum, Barth's metaphor of repetition, the 'noch einmal' clearly does not, however, imply a free act of causal responsibility in an act of self-replication.[134] It is not the case that, for Barth, the Father is the essential and original Being of God in the manner which suggests that the Son and the Spirit are two causally derivative modes of being of the Father. As quoted above, 'The divine essence would not be the divine essence if in it there were superiority and inferiority ... The Son and the Spirit are of one essence ("eines Wesens") with the Father.'[135] This stands despite the case, Barth adds, that the Father is 'from Himself alone' in a way that the others are not from themselves alone.[136]

Clearly, therefore, he does not intend the metaphor of repetition or reiteration to imply a) notions of causal priority or contingency in God, or b) any super-ordination or sub-ordination in God, that is, any way of Being of God which is less a *Seinsweise* than others and more truly a *Sein*. If this is the case, however, is it not possible to express rather more precisely and less ambiguously the key features which Barth is indeed seeking to articulate by way of this metaphor?

To conclude, not a great deal should be inferred from this metaphor of a divine *Wiederholung* taken on its own! It clearly seeks to express that there is a plurality in God's being in the revelation event – 'diese dreifache Weise von Sein'.[137] It

---

[133] 'Because God is the eternal Father as the Father of the Son, and with Him the origin of the Spirit, therefore the God who acts in reconciliation and redemption, and who reveals Himself as the Reconciler and Redeemer, cannot be a second and third God or a second and third part of God; He is and remains God *unus et individuus* in His work as in His essence.' (*C. D.* 1. 1, 395; *K. D.* 1. 1, 416.)

[134] This is made particularly clear in his radical distinction between the terms Father and Creator used of God. Whereas the former is used of the first 'mode of being', the latter is used of all the 'modes of being'. (*C. D.* 1. 1, 394; *K. D.* 1. 1, 414–15.) There is, moreover, no connection to be made between God as Father and the originating relationship as known in the creaturely context, or indeed the creative relationship between God and the created order. Cf. *C. D.* 1. 1, 393 (*K. D.* 1. 1, 414) .

[135] *C. D.* 1. 1, 393 (*K. D.* 1. 1, 414).

[136] Ibid.

[137] *K. D.* 1. 1, 315. The English reads: ' this threefold mode of being' (*C. D.* 1. 1, 299).

expresses the need carefully to predicate number – there is a subject *and* a predicate in revelation. There is a 'Wieder'. Second, it intends to affirm the identity of subject and predicate – it is not a second, it is an 'again'. Finally, there is an underlying concern to make clear that what is under discussion here is not to be seen as either quantifiable or divisible despite the need to appeal to the concept of number. The metaphor of repetition combines multiplicity and full identity at one and the same time without implying the notion of constituent, quantifiable 'parts'.

These concerns are reflected in the following paragraph.

> The name of Father, Son and Spirit means that God is the one God in threefold repetition ('in dreimaliger Wiederholung'), and this in such a way that the repetition ('Wiederholung') itself is grounded in His Godhead, so that it implies no alteration in His Godhead, and yet in such a way also that He is the one God only in this repetition, so that His one Godhead stands or falls with the fact that He is God in this repetition, but for that very reason He is the one God in each repetition.[138]

Eberhard Jüngel summarises Barth's argument in the following way,

> In revelation, therefore, we have to do with *one* internally-distinguished being of God. The *oneness* of this internally-distinguished being of God is grounded in the fact that revelation is 'not an other over against God' but 'a reiteration of God'. In that God *can* reiterate himself, in that he *executes* this reiteration and in that he *has* thus reiterated himself, the internally-distinguished being of God becomes recognisable in its *differentiation*.[139]

However, the metaphor has serious weaknesses. Granting that it may be construed in such a way as to avoid modalistic tendencies,[140] it cannot, however, avoid the fact that it seems

---

[138] *C. D.* 1. 1, 350 (*K. D.* 1. 1, 369).

[139] *The Doctrine of the Trinity*, 16–17.

[140] Although, as I shall discuss further in chapter 4, a number of commentators (Moltmann, Meijering and LaCugna, for example) suspect precisely such a weakness in Barth here.

to detract from any sense of a mutuality between the *Seinsweisen*. The metaphor does not imply that the category of communion is appropriate to conceiving of the relationship between these eternal 'repetitions', indeed, rather the opposite. This is further raised when he writes:

> What we hear when with our human ears and concepts we listen to God's revelation, what we perceive (and can perceive as men) in Scripture, what proclamation of the Word of God actually is in our lives – is the thrice single voice of the Father, the Son, and the Spirit. This is how God is present for us in His revelation. This is how he obviously creates a *vestigium* of Himself and His triunity.[141]

However, as Moltmann points out rather bluntly,

> to understand God's threefold nature as eternal repetition or as holy tautology does not yet mean thinking in trinitarian terms. The doctrine of the Trinity cannot be a matter of establishing the same thing three times. To view the three Persons merely as a triple repetition of one and the same God would be somewhat empty and futile.[142]

If the metaphor of repetition is to be used to establish the singularity of the divine identity in the threeness, this requires to be qualified by a much more profound doctrine of *perichoresis* than Barth seems willing to offer in this context. However, in fairness to Barth, it should be added that he *does* affirm that in relation to the trinitarian names 'we have to distinguish *alius–alius–alius* but not *aliud–aliud–aliud*'. However, it should also be pointed out that Barth makes this point *not* to seek to undermine any impersonal feature latent in the metaphor, but simply to make it clear that we are not dealing here with 'parts of a whole or individuals of a species'.[143]

Critical Evaluation

Barth's concept of the trinitarian *Seinsweisen* obscures the concept of communion in God. Whereas the heart of the New

---

[141] *C. D.* 1. 1, 347 (*K. D.* 1. 1, 367).
[142] *The Trinity and the Kingdom of God*, 141–2.
[143] *C. D.* 1. 1, 350 (*K. D.* 1. 1, 369).

Testament suggests that there is communion between the Father, the Son and the Holy Spirit, we find ourselves asking whether there is or can be communion between *Seinsweisen* – as Cornelius Plantinga expresses it, 'modes do not love at all. Hence they cannot love each other.'[144] Barth's concept of a confronting or addressing *Individuum* threatens to dominate where a reverent *Nachdenken* might encourage the interpretation of the divine identity more fully in terms of a creative conception of the triune communion – where what we term (metaphorically) 'revelation' or 'unveiling' is the transformative and informative reordering of our thought and perception as this is intrinsic to our participation, by grace, within that same communion.

As we shall explore further in chapter 4, the fact that Barth opts, albeit with some hesitation, for the term *Seinsweise* (in place of the term 'person') when speaking of the members of the Trinity does not help to redress this imbalance. If Barth is to adopt the term *Seinsweise* because of its apparent neutrality he risks the charge of naïveté here through his failing to appreciate the extent to which *Seinsweise* is less than neutral – to the extent that it undermines the notion of mutuality and of relatedness within the divine identity as these are conveyed by the term *person* when it is given proper theological currency.[145]

This gives rise to two brief questions.

1) Is it not the case that an *a priori* element is beginning to feature here stemming from his analysis of the logical structure of revelation – one which threatens to mould his doctrine of God?

To be fair to Barth, it is certainly not the case that he intended to offer a 'grammatical' or 'rationalistic' proof of the Trinity.[146] He is quite adamant that it was not his view that the dogma of the Trinity could be derived from the general

---

[144] 'The Threeness/Oneness Problem of the Trinity', *Calvin Theological Journal* 23, no. 1 (April 1988), 49.

[145] This is not to say, however, that Barth was a modalist – or indeed subordinationist, despite perceived inadequacies in his doctrine of the Spirit.

[146] *C. D.* 1. 1, 296 (*K. D.* 1. 1, 312).

truth of any formula. But the question still remains as to whether his articulation of the divine identity in terms of the logical structure of the event of revelation is not more a reactive interpretation of revelation than an exposition of the Triunity in a manner which can be described as a 'thinking after' the New Testament witness.

2) Whereas Barth's metaphors of speech expose powerfully the inadequacy, indeed poverty, of the divine identity portrayed in the models outlined earlier in this chapter and whereas they certainly obviate many of the forms of confused modalism and subordinationism that have haunted the West, is it not the case that they leave open the question as to whether the human element in the event of revelation is being taken seriously, and whether the enhypostatic element in the Gospel is not being deprived of its proper place within the doctrine of *revelation* (as opposed to merely the doctrine of reconciliation) by an exclusively anhypostatic emphasis?

When Barth expounds the Word in terms of the divine Lordship, and adopts the metaphor of the King speaking through his herald, it is the prophetic and kingly offices of Christ which predominate. But it would seem that Christ's vicarious humanity – the *humanity*, that is, of *his* vicarious Amen to the divine address as this is taken into the life of God – and thus his continuing priesthood risks being subordinated.[147] If, as Barth himself suggests, the event of

[147] Despite the fact that Barth makes use of the notion of the *triplex munus* (prophet, priest and king) to interpret the person and work of Christ, in Volume Four, when he expounds the continuing ministry of Christ, he stresses the continuing kingly and prophetic offices of Christ (the 'Royal Man') but neglects the continuing priesthood – the continuing vicarious humanity of Christ. This is probably out of a fear of Roman or Anglo-Catholic notions of priesthood and eucharistic sacrifice which might call in question the 'once and for all' (*eph' hapax*) nature of Christ's finished work. It would appear that Protestant bias may have led him astray!

In private conversation with James B. Torrance, Markus Barth (Karl Barth's son) recounted that, prior to his father's death, when he was lecturing on the *Epistle to the Hebrews* in Basle and reflecting on the priesthood of Christ, he commented to his father that he had not dealt with this in Volume Four of his *Church Dogmatics*. Karl Barth acknowledged this deficiency and commented that, if he were writing on these subjects again, he would pay more attention to the continuing priesthood of Christ.

revelation includes its acknowledgement, these two dynamics cannot be separated. A faithful *Nachdenken* should not allow any separation either between the prophetic and the priestly or between the anhypostatic and the enhypostatic. Similarly, no dichotomy should be made here between the God–humanward and the human–Godward, or between proclamation and worship, between the divine address and the gift of *koinonia*, between the preaching of the Word (on which Barth was so strong) and the celebration of the sacraments (on which he was less so). All of these should find fully integrated expression within a proper exposition of that event of communion which is grounded in the triune identity and which includes that 'informing', epistemic and semantic atonement that is 'revelation'.

In this light it may justifiably be argued that for Barth the revelation model received prominence, as Wingren suggests, at the cost of other models. It is, indeed, our view that a 'worship' or 'communion' model[148] is preferable to the extent

---

Alasdair Heron rightly points to a Zwinglian strain in Barth's doctrine of the sacraments. He comments, 'Behind Barth ... lies a somewhat zwinglian rejection of "sacramentalism", sharpened up by Barth's own insistence that the so-called "sacraments" of Baptism and the Eucharist are not to be looked upon as vehicles of God's action, but of ours: they are witness and sign and response to the one response to the one sacrament which is Jesus Christ himself.' (*Table and Tradition: Towards an Ecumenical Understanding of the Eucharist*, Edinburgh, 1983, 157.) This emphasis on our activity rather than our being brought by the Spirit to participate in Christ's continuing and vicarious activity would seem to lie behind Barth's slightly one-sided emphasis on the preaching of the Word and our responding to the Word in worship. Jesus is not only prophet and thus bearer of the Word, but the truly worshipping human being (bone of our bone, flesh of our flesh) in communion with the Father in the Spirit. He is the priest of our worship, our *leitourgos*. Such an emphasis integrates with a proper concept of the work of Christ in substitution (*Stellvertretung*) as not only the 'Judge judged in our place' in a once and for all atonement for sin, but also as substitute in the sense of the one who stands in for us today in worship – the one true worshipper, who worships *for* us, *with* us and *in* us. The liturgical implications of an integrated conception of substitution, representation and participation point to the centrality of Christ's presenting us in himself to the Father as God's beloved children and drawing us into his communion with the Father by the Spirit.

[148] This will be expounded in our concluding chapter as suggesting an integrated model of 'doxological and semantic participation'.

that this would offer, on the one hand, a more integrative conception of the theological programme as a whole and, on the other, a profounder exposition of the one *Anknüpfungspunkt*, the point of contact (at-one-ment) between the divine and human, which is not simply an event of divine address but the whole humanity of Christ in his life of communion with the Father, as we are brought not merely to 'connect with' it but to participate in it by the Spirit.

The adoption of this kind of model would not only have addressed the dichotomies of so much traditional Western thought (not least by undermining the contractualism of the Western *ordo salutis* and impersonalist notions of revelation), but would encourage a fuller appreciation of revelation as a creative, perichoretic and participative event, one whose *telos* is the integrated reordering of our humanity for the fullness of participation in the triune life of God.

3

Theological Language, Vestigiality and the Question of Continuity between the Human and Divine Realms[1]

Prior to discussing the propriety, or otherwise, of using the term 'person' of the members of the Trinity, Barth engages in a discussion of the nature of theological language or, more specifically, the ontological issues that relate to the function of theological language. What becomes clear is that his understanding of the way language functions and of the

[1] We must stress that it is not the purpose of this chapter to rehearse, yet again, the debates concerning Barth's interpretation of the *Vaticanum* on the *analogia entis* and the question of the extent of his reliance on Przywara's account (cf. Jüngel, 'Die Möglichkeit Theologischer Anthropologie auf dem Grunde der Analogie', *Barth-Studien*, Gütersloh, 1982: 'Barth wendet sich gegen denjenigen Gebrauch des Analogiephänomens, der von E. Przywara unter dem Titel der analogia entis ausgewiesen wurde...' (210, fn. 1)). Neither can we discuss the accuracy of Przywara's representation of Catholic orthodoxy nor the validity of Hans Urs von Balthasar's discussion of these matters, let alone Henri Bouillard's further analysis of the thought of all three nor, finally, Colm O'Grady's analysis of all the above! Although these issues are important we have decided not to focus specifically on these debates not only because this would require a book in itself if they were to be considered adequately but because it is not, for our purposes the most economical way of dealing with the central substantive issues. Our primary concern here is with the theological debate concerning analogy as it still continues. Consequently, we have elected to focus on the specific matters raised by Mondin's influential reinterpretation and reclassification of St Thomas' theory of analogy (which in many respects supersedes the interpretations of Przywara and von Balthasar) and his subsequent critique of Barth's account. It is in the light of this more contemporary Thomist critique that we shall attempt to assess the validity or otherwise of Barth's central theological emphases.

nature of reference profoundly influences his decision to opt for *Seinsweise* rather than *Person*.

This is not my only reason, however, for devoting a chapter to a discussion of theological language. The issues raised by the analogy debate are of central importance here not least when it comes to assessing approaches which argue for the use of the term 'person' from what might be called a 'personalist' base. John Zizioulas suggests that the concept of the person is possibly the only concept that can be predicated properly and without the risk of anthropomorphism of both the divine and human realms.[2] In other words, it is suggested that this concept has unique referential potential in that it can span both domains – it constitutes a primordial ontological and thus *semantic* bridge between the theological and anthropological spheres. If this can be argued to be the case then the concept stands to serve as a building block of the most fundamental importance underpinning theological ontology and method. The critical question for us to consider here concerns the *grounds* on which such claims may be assessed.

Later in his *Church Dogmatics* Barth expressed willingness to endorse the interpretation of the *analogia entis* formulated (under his influence) by Söhngen in a manner which would suggest an openness to certain features of Zizioulas' approach. Henri Bouillard argues that Barth's arguments here reflect an 'evolutionary curve' in his thought.[3] And Hans Urs von Balthasar (Barth's friend 'from another shore' who so influenced him in this area) has argued similarly that there is to be found in Barth a progressive passage from dialectic to analogy.[4] Our principal task here, however, is not to assess

---

[2] He writes of the notion of personhood, that, if properly understood, it is 'perhaps the only notion that can be applied to God without the danger of anthropomorphism.' 'On Human Capacity and Incapacity: A Theological Exploration of Personhood', *S. J. T.* 28 (1975), 419–20.

[3] *The Knowledge of God*, London, 1969, 124.

[4] Von Balthasar interprets Barth's understanding of analogy in the following way: 'The creature has his origin in God in such a way that it owes to God not only the power of receiving but also the power of responding. Or better yet: it also receives the power of responding, and responding in such a way that this autonomous answer itself is a supreme acceptance. This is called theological

developments in Barth's thinking, but to engage much more specifically with the theological issues at stake.[5] For this reason we shall be considering Barth's particularly significant discussion of Söhngen's work.

Our primary concern will be to analyse the ontological and methodological issues underlying the *analogia entis* debate as these relate to impinge on the grounds of the affirmation of

analogy.' (*Karl Barth*, Cologne, 1952, 123.) This interpretation, which allows the recognition of a 'secondary subject' within the event of grace, is argued by von Balthasar to result from a move beyond the pure dialectic of the *Römerbrief* which threatened to dissolve into the event of revelation the subjects of the event, that is, God and the creature. In the *Church Dogmatics*, it is argued, Barth presupposes a creature who has its own particularity and consistency and who participates as a subject in this revelation. (Cf. Bouillard's discussion of von Balthasar in *The Knowledge of God*, 124.)

Colm O'Grady similarly focuses on this dimension as being of key significance for the discovery of common ground across the ecumenical divide here. He refers to the fact that, 'Barth speaks of man's adaptability to enter into the covenant partnership with God', and continues, 'Adaptability or susceptibility obviously presupposes a good being and activity proper to an already existing man. God can use man and his thoughts and words to express his Word. In this Barth does not seem to differ from the concept of "analogy of being" expounded by certain Catholic authors, with whom he was in dialogue.' (Here O'Grady mentions Söhngen and Przywara): *The Church in Catholic Theology: Dialogue with Karl Barth*, London, 1969, 7–8. See also O'Grady's companion volume, *The Church in the Theology of Karl Barth*, London, 1968, 93.)

It is difficult to avoid the suspicion that the search for commonality on the part of these writers tends to say more about their own concerns and programmes than about what Barth was wishing to stress as central to the theological debate. The question as to whether Barth can allow the human subject to be seen as a 'good being' with a 'consistency' and activity proper to itself is to lose sight of the central issue. At the anthropological level the central question for Barth concerned the nature of cognitive acknowledgement which, as Barth sees, does not allow itself ultimately to be explained in terms of the free and independent rational subjectivity of the (*echthros*) human mind. To take due cognisance of this is not to make *a priori* rejections of human capacity and it is certainly not to downplay the essence of what it is to be truly human. Barth's own concern is the reverse, that it is too easy in this debate to overvalue that which is not 'truly' human and which in the end denigrates a theological interpretation of the fullness of God's creative purposes for human beings and *a fortiori* what *is* truly human.

[5] It is noteworthy that there was an eagerness right to the end of Barth's life to find a constructive *rapprochement* between his and von Balthasar's rendering of analogy.

divine personhood.[6] As it is not possible to go into this issue in a single chapter in anything like as extensive a manner as is required by the topic, we have opted to focus our exposition on one of the most significant recent studies of analogy – namely that of Battista Mondin. This work exemplifies the recent reformulation of the theory of analogy in Catholic theology that has taken place under the influence of Gilson and others. Our theological analysis of the issues raised be Barth will be couched, therefore, in a critical dialogue with Mondin's assessment of Barth's views from within the perspective of the Neo-Thomist reclassification of analogical predication and reinterpretation of the views of St Thomas Aquinas.

---

[6] The expression *analogia entis* is being used here as shorthand for the *a priori* assumption of an ontological continuity between the divine and human realms which is argued to underlie and is justifiably presupposed, therefore, by theological statement independently of the consideration of God's Self-revelation in the person of Christ. Giving a more precise definition is difficult given its interpretation by different theologians in such widely varying ways. This is reflected in Bouillard's comments with regard to Barth's interpretation of the *analogia entis*, 'Pour être juste, il faut ajouter qu'il a été orienté sur cette voie par l'un de ses critiques catholiques, le P. Przywara.' (Henri Bouillard, *Karl Barth: Parole de Dieu et Existence Humaine*, Vol. 3 (or Vol. 2, Part 2), Aubier, 1957, 212.) Further on, he refers to the differences among the Catholic theologians engaging with Barth on the topic. 'L'interprétation et le jugement de Balthasar concordent très largement avec les nôtres. Mais il importe de signaler la différence de terminologie. Adaptant à sa propre perspective les concepts définis par Przywara, par Barth et par Söhngen, Balthasar donne au vocabulaire de l'analogie un sens assez particulier.' (Ibid., 216.)

It is an open question, moreover, as to whether analogy, as interpreted by Przywara, is really representative of Catholic orthodoxy. And it also requires to be asked whether the analogy issue is as central to Catholicism and Catholic theology as he suggests (for example, in his book, *Polarity: A German Catholic's Interpretation of Religion* (Eng. trans. by A. C. Bouquet), London, 1935, where it serves as the dominant theme or principle) and as Barth was led to assume. Karl Rahner seems nervous about the degree of prominence that it came to acquire – something for which he blames Przywara. 'As far as the doctrine of analogy is concerned, we shall have to admit if we are honest that it was E. Przywara who first elevated it from being a modest study somewhere in logic or general ontology to being a really important nodal point of theological discourse.' (*Theological Investigations V* (Eng. trans. by Karl-H. Kruger), London, 1966, 59.) Similarly, Andrew Louth comments, 'It may be doubted now whether *analogia entis* may be regarded as the point of Roman Catholic theology as E. Przywara presented it.' ('The Doctrine of the Knowability of God in the Theology of Karl Barth', M.Th., Univ. of Edinburgh, 1968, 77.)

The structure of this necessarily complex chapter will therefore be as follows:

a) an introductory raising of the question as to whether personhood may be conceived as a *vestigium Dei*;

b) a brief consideration of the 'traditional', Thomist exposition of analogy and the nature of theological reference as expounded by Phelan – a representative of the traditional Thomistic interpretation of analogy who was writing during the same period in which Barth was expounding his own critique of the *Vaticanum* and the *analogia entis*;

c) an exposition of Mondin's critique of the traditional Thomist rendering of Aquinas (as this is attributed to Cajetan's misinterpretation of the thought of St Thomas) and his reclassification of Thomas' interpretation of analogy;

d) a critical dialogue with Mondin's subsequent critique of Barth's position from within this revisionary restating of St Thomas' position. This will serve the context of some further discussion of what precisely Barth *was*, and *was not*, rejecting in his repudiation of the *analogia entis*; and, finally,

e) some re-examination of Barth's own discussion in the context of his qualified endorsement of Söhngen's views.

Our intention in and through this is to seek to analyse the ingredients of a more constructive and coherent way forward than either traditional Thomism, or more recent reclassifications of Thomas' views, or, indeed, Karl Barth himself could offer.

It should become plain that there is a profoundly interesting, *intrinsic* connection and interrelationship between how we conceive of triune personhood and the manner in which we conceive of the functionality of theological language. Precisely how this may be envisaged will only finally be explored in chapter 5, where we engage with still more recent philosophical studies of the dynamics and function of language and correlate this with some consideration of the nature of Christian worship.

Is Human Personhood a *Vestigium Dei*?

A central and obvious question raised by the personhood debate concerns whether there may be argued to be 'traces' of the divine Being in human personhood which might automatically and straightforwardly warrant the application of the term 'person' to both the divine and human contexts.[7] Can we affirm that there is some kind of *vestigium dei* (or *trinitatis*) immanent either within the created order or, indeed, the new order – the New Creation? Clearly, to affirm the former, at least, would be to commit oneself to some form of *analogia entis*.

The concept of a *vestigium trinitatis*, so influential in Western thinking, is traced by Barth to the Platonist exemplarism of Augustine where, he writes, it assumes

> an analogue of the Trinity, of the trinitarian God of Christian revelation, in some creaturely reality distinct from Him, a creaturely reality which is not a form assumed by God in His revelation, but which quite apart from God's revelation manifests in its own structure by creation a certain similarity to the structure of the trinitarian concept of God, so that it may be regarded as an image of the trinitarian God Himself.

As such this would commit us to 'an essential trinitarian disposition supposedly immanent in some created realities quite apart from their possible conscription by God's revelation'.[8] The implication, in this approach, of a genuine *analogia entis* where there are deemed to be traces of the triune Creator in created beings, by virtue of their createdness, may give rise, Barth fears, to a 'second root' of the doctrine of the Trinity alongside that of revelation – that is, where the doctrine of God is expounded not merely out of revelation in its concrete and specific forms but out of the created order interpreted in its own light by the created mind, i.e. by the additional 'light' of natural reason. If this is the case a further question follows for Barth, namely: 'Which of the two roots of the doctrine of the Trinity that together call for consideration

---

[7] Although Rahner has misgivings about the intra-trinitarian use of the term 'person', his transcendental anthropology constitutes a confident exposition of continuity between the divine and human realms – and suggests little nervousness, for example, about the semantics of the word 'spirit' as used in this context.

[8] *C. D.* 1. 1, 334 (*K. D.* 1. 1, 353).

is the true and primary root, and which is the derivative and subsidiary [lit. "descending"] one?'[9] Is the biblical doctrine simply the confirmation of a knowledge of God which can be gleaned quite independently from God's revelation in creation? 'Do we not have in this idea of the *vestigium trinitatis* an ancient Trojan horse which one day ... was unsuspectingly allowed entry into the theological Ilium, and in whose belly ... we can hear a threatening clank ...?'[10] Despite Barth's later much discussed speculations concerning 'lights of creation'[11] – a conception of which Moltmann makes a great deal in his Gifford Lectures[12] – these same convictions on the matter of *vestigia trinitatis* are echoed in Volume Four. Referring back to the first volume, he writes, 'There can be no proper or direct *vestigium trinitatis*, no direct and complete correspondences to the triunity of God, apart from God's own being and life and therefore within the creaturely world.'[13] In other words, the central issue here is not one from which Barth seems to have moved in the later volumes of his *Church Dogmatics*.

However, on the other side of the debate the question remains as to whether there is any real possibility of language – and the human thought forms which are intrinsically bound up with language – and therefore of God-talk *of any kind* if we do not hold to some kind of continuity of meaning (as this involves ontological continuity) across this supposed gulf. If there is a radical, semantic discontinuity here how is it possible to speak of God? And furthermore, how is it possible to think

---

[9] *C. D.* 1. 1, 335 (*K. D.* 1. 1, 354). The Bromiley translation runs: 'Which of the two roots of the doctrine of the Trinity that both call for consideration is the true and primary root, and which is a secondary "runner"?' The word in the German text which is translated by 'runner' is *Senkling*. This suggests that the translator assumed that what was actually intended was *Sendling*, meaning 'messenger' or 'emissary'. This is clearly a mistake. Barth was using the word *Senkling* from the noun *Senken* in a graphic way to mean 'the subsidiary one' or 'the descending one'.

[10] *C. D.* 1. 1, 335–6 (*K. D.* 1. 1, 355).

[11] *C. D.* 4. 3. chap. 16, sect. 2 ('The Light of Life'), *passim*.

[12] *God in Creation: An Ecological Doctrine of Creation* (Eng. trans. by Margaret Kohl), London, 1985, see esp. chapter 3 §3, 'The World as Promise and Anticipation' (60–5).

[13] *C. D.* 4. 2. 338.

of God given that, as Wittgenstein has shown, our cerebral processes necessarily function in and through the rule-governed, social context of linguistic activity as it has its grounding in the created, social order? Still further, how are we to avoid the problem (discussed in chapter two) of resorting to some form of spiritualised 'private language', i.e. of endorsing a subjective, indeed esoteric, reinterpretation of the meaning of our terms which recognises no coincidence or semantic overlap with the meaning they have in the public realm?

Some limited discussion of the philosophical background of this debate is unavoidable if we are to propose an alternative framework which can succeed finally in drawing the sting from such questions.

The Question of Analogy in its Basic Form

The analogy debate derives from what Frederick Ferré describes as a 'perplexity' created by apparently contradictory axioms inherited from both the Bible and philosophy. Put simply, this 'perplexity' is generated by 'the *prima facie* conflict between repeated Biblical warnings that God is wholly incommensurable with his creation and vivid Biblical imagery depicting things divine combined with fairly explicit statements on the Deity's purposes, emotions, and characteristic modes of behaviour'.[14] Christian theologians find themselves committed to axioms which appear to contradict each other:

> On the one hand, God, to be the God of the Bible or of the philosophers, must be so utterly different from all finite created beings that no statement with God as referent can mean what it would mean if it had any other referent ... and any claim to knowledge of God would seem profoundly threatened. On the other hand, however, genuine knowledge of God – of some kind – must be insisted upon if God has somehow been revealed to men. Statements about God must not be totally unintelligible; the terms attributed to him must

---

[14] 'Analogy in Theology', by Frederick Ferré, in *The Encyclopaedia of Philosophy*, Vol. 1, ed. Paul Edwards, New York, 1967, 94.

continue to mean something; the loss of univocality in regard to God must not be allowed to drive theological talk into sheer equivocation.[15]

So how are we to conceive of the status of those statements which, Christian theologians claim, incorporate their knowledge of God? Clearly, we have to affirm that these statements are neither entirely equivocal nor wholly univocal. It is not possible for them to have no ultimate bearing on the Being of God nor may they mean exactly the same thing when applied to God as when applied to humankind. The former would mean that all theological statements were purely mythological, the arbitrary projection of human images and concepts on to that which transcends the created order, and the latter would commit us to anthropomorphism which fails to recognise the divine Infinitude and Transcendence – that God may not be subsumed under the category of created reality. It is for these reasons that theological statements are claimed to function *analogically* where 'analogy' constitutes a third category which may not be reduced to either of the previous two.

Thomist thought has traditionally defined this third category or theological option in fairly specific ways. Our concern will be to consider how far Barth broke with the Thomist solution to this quandary and, further, to assess the extent to which he was actually required to do so – since this has substantial ramifications for the whole matter of attributing 'personhood' to God.

Despite the fact that the approach ascribed to Thomas Aquinas has informed and moulded the Christian Church's understanding of this central issue for well over half a millennium, what would seem to be the comparatively straightforward task of expounding, comparing and contrasting the very different approaches advocated by Aquinas, on the one hand, and by Barth, on the other, has been complicated by the fact that the exposition and systematisation of Aquinas by the fifteenth-century Thomist

[15] Ibid.

Cardinal Thomas Cajetan (which has been widely adopted over several centuries – and which was essentially the approach assumed by Barth to be that of Aquinas) has been argued in recent years by certain Catholic philosophical theologians to be not only flawed but thoroughly inadequate as an interpretation of Aquinas' thought.

Our first task, therefore, must be to establish the essential differences between two divergent approaches to the thought of St Thomas. This discussion will also serve to focus attention on the key issue raised by the problem of analogy, which concerns not the manner in which terms are used but the nature of the cosmology controlling their use. As Bouillard concludes in his discussion of analogy, 'Tout vocabulaire est légitime, pourvu qu'on s'entende.'[16] That to which we require to pay attention in these debates concerns not the terms we use but the nature of the cosmology or ontology underlying the theory of analogy operative in any particular theology. It is this which governs whether the terms being used are being used in legitimately *theological* ways, that is, where their use is characterised by proper function and theological warrant.[17]

St Thomas' Theory of Analogy as Traditionally Interpreted

Despite being widely regarded as the father of the theory of analogy, St Thomas offered neither an extensive nor a systematic analysis of the nature of analogical predication.[18] It was left, therefore, to his later disciples particularly Cajetan, but also Sylvester of Ferrara and John of St Thomas – to offer a systematic exposition of his theory.

It is the interpretation of St Thomas' theory of analogy, worked out in the tradition of Cajetan, which we shall investigate first, and it is to Gerald Phelan's rendering (*Saint*

---

[16] Henri Bouillard, *Karl Barth: Parole de Dieu et Existence Humaine*, Vol. 3 (or Vol. 2, part 2), 217.

[17] The notions of 'proper function' and 'warrant' are borrowed from Alvin Plantinga, who utilises them in a different, although not unrelated, context.

[18] 'His texts on the notion of analogy are relatively few, and in each case they are so restrained that we cannot but wonder why the notion has taken on such an importance in the eyes of his commentators.' (Etienne Gilson, *The Christian Philosophy of St Thomas Aquinas*, (trans. L.K. Shook), New York, 1956, 105.)

Thomas and Analogy, which appeared as recently as 1941)[19] that we shall turn as a widely respected modern rendering of the traditional approach.

Forms of Predication   Phelan begins by establishing the traditional tripartite classification of types of predication as follows:

a) *Univocal predication:* terms which are predicated univocally mean exactly the same thing when predicated of different objects. For example, in the two statements, 'an oak is a *tree*', 'an elm is a *tree*', 'the word *tree* designates an intrinsic formal constituent of both the oak and the elm which each equally possesses and by reason of which they are the same, although for other reasons they may differ'.[20]

b) *Equivocal predication:* equivocal terms are those which, although identical in sound or in their written form, 'do not signify any such formal constituent but mean something totally different when predicated of diverse things'.[21] For example, the term 'pen' is being used equivocally when used of a writing instrument on the one hand and of an enclosure for sheep on the other.

c) *Analogical predication:* analogical terms, however, have 'a meaning which is neither entirely the same nor entirely different when predicated of diverse objects. For example, when I say that my dinner was *good* and my shoes are *good*, the word *good* does not signify any common constituent of both my dinner and my shoes, but it does indicate that the relation between my dinner and what a dinner ought to be, on the one hand, and my shoes and what shoes ought to be, on the other hand, is similar. *Proportion-ately speaking* both dinner and shoes may be called good.'[22]

In many cases of what are popularly termed 'analogies' what is designated is simply, Phelan suggests, a resemblance

---

[19] Gerald B. Phelan, *Saint Thomas and Analogy*, The Aquinas Lecture, Milwaukee, 1941.
[20] Ibid., 14.
[21] Ibid.
[22] Ibid., 14–15.

or likeness (real or imaginary) between various objects. In the majority of cases what is signified is purely the univocal participation in a common formal constituent or possibly even a fictitious or imaginary likeness as, for example, in the statement 'That cloud is like a ship.'[23]

After distinguishing authentic forms of analogy from such pseudo-analogies Phelan asserts that there are three ways remaining in which two or more things may be said proportionately to participate in a common characteristic.[24]

1) The common character or *ratio* belongs really and truly to each and all of the participants, in the same way but in unequal degrees of intensity or under conditions of existence which are not identical. Men and dogs are equally animals but they are not equal animals; the common character which makes them both animals really and truly belongs to each, but it does not exist in dogs and human beings under the same conditions of existence. This, he suggests, is what is usually referred to as the *Analogy of Inequality* or the *Analogy of Generic Predication.*

2) The common character or *ratio* belongs properly to only one of the participants but is attributed by the mind to the others. Health, for instance, belongs properly speaking only to an organism but, because of the relation in some order of causality which other things like food, medicine, exercise, bear to the health of the organism, these too are called healthy. This is traditionally called the *Analogy of Attribution.*

3) The common characteristic or *ratio* belongs really and truly to each and all in proportion to their respective being (*esse*). This is the *Analogy of Proportionality.*

It is in the light of this threefold classification that the heart of Aquinas' theory of analogy, as traditionally understood, is

---

[23] Phelan adds that the term 'analogy' is also used in the sciences and in philosophy where reasoning by analogy is simply what Aristotle calls the rhetorical method of persuasion by *example*. It is also adopted in mathematics where it is used to designate the proportion of one quality to another. However, none of these meanings of the term analogy, he argues, 'signify more than a superficial resemblance between things, or at most a univocal participation in a generic, specific or accidental characteristic. None of them satisfy the strict requirements of analogy proper.' (Ibid., 18.)

[24] Ibid., 18–19.

expounded. In the Thomistic doctrine of analogy, Phelan claims, 'the basic proposition ... in its strict and proper meaning, is that **whatever perfection is analogically common to two or more beings is intrinsically (formally) possessed by each,** not, however, by any two in the same way or mode, but by each **in proportion to its being**'.[25]

Knowledge is possessed by human beings, by angels and by God, but not in the same way. The way in which human beings know is proportionate to the being which humans have, the way in which angels know is proportionate to the being which angels have and, likewise, the way in which God knows is proportionate to the being which God has. This is not to say that there is a direct equivalence between these proportions, but rather that there is a proportion of proportions. 'There is thus a strict proportion of proportions in which the terms of one proportion are not proportionate to the terms of the other proportion, but the whole proportion between the terms on one side of the relation is proportionate to the whole proportion between the terms on the other side of the relation.'[26]

Therefore, if we say that 'God knows', we are saying that God knows in a way appropriate to God and that this corresponds proportionately to the relation between human beings and their knowing, where human beings know in a way appropriate to human beings. Therefore we can assert analogically that 'God knows', but in doing so we are not ascribing to God human knowledge and we are not, therefore, speaking anthropomorphically of God. In this way we respect the divine transcendence and the categorial difference between God and humankind, that is, we acknowledge the divine incommensurability with the created order.

Phelan explains that 'what is stated is that the proportion between knowledge and angel holds, i.e. angels know as angels are; and that the proportion between knowledge and man holds, i.e. men know as men are; and further (and finally) that there is a proportion between the way the first

[25] Ibid., 22.
[26] Ibid., 23.

proportion holds and the way the second proportion holds'.[27] However, this betrays the fact that in the analogy of proper proportionality, so understood, two claims are being made – firstly, that the predication holds analogously for all the creatures (and the Creator!) named, and, secondly, that there is an analogy between the proportionality which exists between the analogates and the properties predicated of them. But is this second statement not just another statement of the same form as the first? And is this second statement moreover necessary? We shall return to this question later.

On this traditional interpretation all other forms of analogy fail for one of the following two reasons: [28]

either a) the perfection or character which is predicated of two or more beings is possessed intrinsically by only one of the beings in question and is merely transferred by the mind to the others as, for example, when one says that an organism is healthy and exercise is healthy (an 'analogy of extrinsic attribution');

or b) the perfection or character which is predicated of two or more beings, although possessed intrinsically by each of the beings in question, is possessed by all in the same manner or mode (i.e. the term is used univocally), albeit in unequal degrees, as, for example, when one says that men and women are animals and dogs are animals (an 'analogy of inequality').

Cajetan's 'analogy of proportionality', however, 'demands that the analogated perfection be not univocal either in its being or in the concept of it, but, on the contrary, that it both exist intrinsically in all of the analogies and in each according to a different mode'.[29]

This means that there is neither *ontological univocity* between the analogues nor *logical univocity* with respect to the terms used. Put simply, this means that neither can the analogues (God, men, angels etc.) be regarded as beings of the same kind (i.e. possessing ontological univocity), nor can that which is predicated of them be construed as being the same

[27] Ibid., 24.
[28] Ibid., 25.
[29] Ibid., 28.

property in the various cases (i.e. possessing conceptual or 'logical' univocity). This, as Phelan sees it, is true analogy, 'for it is *in being* (essendo) that all beings are one yet the very being (esse) by which they are one is diverse in each, though proportionate to the essence of each'.[30] This conception of analogy provides, therefore, a kind of unifying cosmological principle grounded in the universal participation of everything in 'being'. It is for this reason that the Thomist approach to the doctrine of analogy is referred to as the *analogia entis*.

Analogy construed in this manner is interpreted as the principle in terms of which one can account for the *diversity* of beings in addition to their *unity*. It becomes the metaphysical principle in terms of which one can be true simultaneously to the emphases of Heraclitus on the one hand (all is becoming, everything is in a state of flux) and to those of Parmenides on the other (all is being, everything *is* only in so far as it is not in a state of becoming or flux).

> The Heraclitean-Parmenidean dilemma can be overcome only by the recognition of the intrinsic, formal, necessary, entitative unity of that which is actually diverse. The basis of diversity in beings is the division of being by potency and act – existence (esse) is diversified by essence (or form) and in beings in which there is diversity within the essence that diversity is caused by the composition of matter and form ... Yet within that very diversity, unity is present by reason of the intrinsic order of all that is in any way whatsoever, to the act of existence, really and formally, though proportionately, possessed by each. The unity of beings in being is necessarily an analogical unity. Were it univocal, diversity would be unintelligible; were it equivocal, nothing would be intelligible. And it is for this reason that St Thomas says: 'In analogicals it is not *diverse realities* which fall under consideration but *diverse modes* of existence of the self-same reality.'[31]

This 'diversity' Przywara interprets as the 'tension' of the created order. Defining the *analogia entis*, he argues that 'the creaturely is the *analogy* of Deity' in the following manner:

[30] Ibid., 29.
[31] Ibid., 38–9.

It is like Him, through the possession of a unity of essence and existence, but even in this similarity it is unlike Him, because in Deity the unity of essence and existence is that of identity, whereas in that of creation the unity is one of tension. Since now the relationship of essence and existence is of the *esse* of 'being', Deity and the creation are in 'being' like and unlike, i.e. analogous to one another: *analogia entis* = analogy of being.[32]

What is of importance for our conclusion is to notice here that God is ultimately, particularly on Phelan's model, not only integral to but *integrated within* this 'analogical whole'.

Two questions which we shall be asking concern whether a) this is true to the nature of God to the extent that he is, precisely as Creator, transcendent and fundamentally different from all existents which are essentially contingent (as Ferré's comments suggested); and b) whether the very different ontological identification with the created order which stems from the affirmation of the *homoousion*, as this safeguards divine freedom, does not render inappropriate and unnecessary any such universal ontological framework as a means of undergirding theological description.

First, however, we shall consider how far this traditional rendering of the Thomistic view of analogy is true to St Thomas' own thinking on the matter.

The Reinterpretation of Aquinas' Theory of Analogy

There continues to be a *plethora* of different interpretations of Aquinas' conception of analogy and it is simply not possible here to go into the variety of these in depth. That differing interpretations reflect different metaphysical agendas is latent in Bernard Montagnes' expression of the diversity inherent in Thomistic thought,

> Chacune des grandes questions posées par une philosophie de l'être peut ainsi recevoir deux réponses entre lesquelles les thomistes se partagent. Mais les divergences qu'on rencontre à chaque fois ne sont ni fortuites ni dispersées, elles relèvent de la logique d'un système, quels que soient les noms des protagonistes ... Pour cela

---

[32] E. Przywara, *Polarity: A German Catholic's Interpretation of Religion*, 32.

deux voies se présentent, l'une consiste à découvrir l'unité des êtres dans les rapports de causalité qui les relient au premier d'entre eux, l'autre tente de réduire le multiple à l'un part voie conceptuelle, dans l'unité de l'idée d'être. Ces deux solutions, nous appellerons respectivement *métaphysique des degrés d'être* et *métaphysique de l'idée d'être*.[33]

The grounds of such a divergence between a metaphysic of degrees of being and a metaphysic of the concept of being are reflected in Mondin's break with the kind of approach exemplified by Phelan in his seminal book on the principle of analogy in Protestant and Catholic thought.[34] Here, Mondin highlights two opposing readings of Aquinas and introduces a new classification which may serve to suggest possible ways of moving beyond such divergences. Mondin's exposition constitutes a radical critique of Cajetan's systematisation of Aquinas' theory of analogy,[35] which is argued to have produced much of the confusion which has dogged this debate.[36]

Despite the inherent interest in investigating his careful and scholarly argumentation in detail, for our present purposes we shall simply refer to his conclusions concerning Aquinas' teaching in this area which he formulates in the following way, and which we quote at some length:

(1) The ontological ground of the analogy between God and other beings is the relation of efficient causality of these beings to God.

(2) Names applied to God and to other beings are predicated according to *analogy of one to another* [37] if they are names of absolute

---

[33] *La Doctrine de l'Analogie de l'Etre d'apres Saint Thomas D'Aquin*, Louvain, 1963, 162–4.

[34] Battista Mondin, *The Principle of Analogy in Protestant and Catholic Theology*, The Hague, 1963.

[35] Cf. Cardinal Cajetan's *The Analogy of Names* and *The Concept of Being* (Eng. trans and annotations by Bushinski and Koren), Duquesne, 1953.

[36] It may be noted that Mondin's work follows the lead given first of all by Etienne Gilson and continued by George P. Klubertanz in his book *St Thomas Aquinas on Analogy*, Chicago, 1960.

[37] Aquinas contrasts the analogy of one to another with the analogy of two to a third in the following way dealing with the latter first:

'The first is when one thing is predicated of two with respect to a third ("aliquid praedicatur de duobus per respectum ad aliquid tertium") thus being

perfections. In defining analogy of one to another Aquinas' constant
aim is to preserve God's absoluteness, pre-eminence and
transcendence. He condemns univocity, the analogy of two to a third,
and the analogy of many to one[38] because, by subjecting God to a
genus, they put Him on the same level as other finite things.[39] They
place Him under other categories and, therefore, annihilate His
uniqueness. It is a deep respect for God's absoluteness and uniqueness
that leads Aquinas to the doctrine of analogous predication of one to
another. This respect for God's pre-eminence also explains his
rejection of the analogy of mathematical (i.e. measurable) proportion.
But God's absoluteness and uniqueness are not to be saved at the
expense of other beings: their safeguard cannot be a mode of
predication which empties the name of its meaning when it is
predicated of finite beings. This is the danger of extrinsic attribution,
which in some respect is as pernicious as equivocity: it leads to
agnosticism either with regard to creatures or with regard to God.
Only the *analogy of one to another* does justice to the facts. According
to this mode of analogy the same absolute perfection is predicated
both of God and His creatures, but it is predicated *according to priority
and posteriority:*[40] the same perfection belongs to both of them but not

is predicated of quantity and quality with respect to substance. The other is when
a thing is predicated of two by reason of a relationship between these two ("aliquid
praedicatur de duobus per respectum unius ad alterum"): thus being is predicated
of substance and quantity. In the first kind of predication the two things must be
preceded by something to which each of them bears some relation: thus substance
has a respect to substance and quality; whereas in the second kind of predication
this is not necessary, but one of the two must precede the other.

Wherefore since nothing precedes God, but He precedes the creature, the
second kind of analogical predication is applicable to Him but not the first.' (*De
Potentia* 7, 7.) (Most of the quotations from Aquinas are taken from Mondin.)

[38] Here Aquinas provides the example of health: 'Thus with reference to one
health we say that an animal is healthy as the subject of health, medicine is healthy
as its cause, food as its preserver, urine as its sign.' (*Contra Gentiles* 1, 33.)

[39] Aquinas constantly sought to emphasise that God cannot be subsumed
under a class concept. 'Deus non est in genere .'

[40] 'What is predicated of some things according to priority and posteriority is
certainly not predicated univocally. For the prior is included in the definition of
the posterior, as substance is included in the definition of accident as an accident
is a being ... Now nothing is predicated of God and creatures as though they were
in the same order, but, rather, according to priority and posteriority. For all
things are predicated of God essentially. For God is called being as being entity
itself, and He is called good as being goodness itself. But in other beings
predications are made by participation, as Socrates is said to be a man, not
because he is humanity itself, but because he possesses humanity. It is impossible,

in the same way. Analogy of one to another is fit for theological discourse since, on one hand, it safeguards God's absoluteness and uniqueness and, on the other hand, does not destroy the ontological consistence of finite beings.

(3) Names of mixed perfections[41] are predicated of God according to metaphorical analogy.

(4) Names of absolute perfections[42] applied to beings of different species without any relation to God are predicated according to the analogy of proper proportionality.[43]

Although Cajetan's interpretation of Aquinas was adopted almost universally for centuries, Suárez, with whose conclusions Mondin wishes largely to identify, was one thinker who stood against the stream of thought and opposed this classification. This he did for two reasons.

(1) With respect to the analogy of proper proportionality, Suárez did not believe that Aquinas taught any such doctrine

in which the analogous name is predicated properly and intrinsically of all the analogates. Every true analogy of proportionality includes an element of metaphor and of impropriety, just as 'smiling' is said of a meadow through metaphorical reference. It is for this reason that Aquinas refuses to recognise any analogy of proportionality between God and creatures. For, 'being' and all the other names of absolute perfections are predicated properly and intrinsically of both of them. Therefore Cajetan is wrong in giving such prominence to the analogy of proportionality.[44]

(2) Suárez believed that besides an analogy of extrinsic attribution, Aquinas teaches an analogy of intrinsic attribution, that is, 'an analogy where the denominating form exists intrinsically in both (or all) the terms, in one absolutely and in the other or others relatively, through intrinsic relation to the former'.[45] Mondin comments,

---

therefore, that anything be predicated univocally of God and other things.' (*Contra Gentiles* 1, 32.)

[41] For example, 'God is Father'.

[42] For example, 'God is good'.

[43] Mondin, op. cit., 34–5. The footnotes are by way of clarification and have been added by myself.

[44] Ibid., 41.

[45] Ibid.

This kind of analogy is frequently illustrated by Aquinas through the predication of 'being' of substance and accident. Whereas substance is being in the primary and absolute sense, accident is not designated 'being' by extrinsic denomination from the being of substance but from its own proper and intrinsic being. The analogy between God and creatures is of the intrinsic attribution type. Therefore Cajetan is wrong in leaving out intrinsic attribution from his classification of analogy.[46]

Mondin concurs, therefore, with the conclusions of Suárez, asserting that the Cajetanist classification is wrong since it does not take account of Aquinas' primary type of analogy as it is used in theological statements, namely, **the analogy of one to another according to priority and posteriority** ('Analogia unius ad alterum per prius et posterius').

Cajetan identifies this form of analogy with either analogy of attribution or analogy of proportionality. The former is wrong because it does not take account of Aquinas' distinction between two different ways of designating a thing in its relation to another.[47] The latter is wrong because it fails to express that Aquinas bases the analogy of one to another on **direct (analogical) similarity** rather than **similarity of relations.**

Finally, in and through all this he fails to grasp Aquinas' motive in assigning an exclusive position to analogy of one to another in theology. 'Analogy of proportionality does not indicate either the causal nexus between God and creatures or God's priority over His creatures.'[48] Both of these are integral to Aquinas' interpretation of analogy in theology.

To summarise our conclusions to this point, the traditional understanding of the theological use of analogy was one which took the analogy of proper proportionality as providing the 'grammar' of theological statement where it predicated attributes of God. The appeal of this form of analogy was that it seemed to side-step the dangers of anthropomorphism by asserting that when we predicate a quality of God we are not

[46] Ibid.
[47] That is, he does not do justice to Aquinas' distinction between what was later termed 'intrinsic' and 'extrinsic' attribution.
[48] Mondin, op. cit., 50.

making a direct, intrinsic attribution, but rather making an analogical statement about the similarity of relations between humankind's possession of that attribute and God's. However, this approach raises several problems.

First, the predication of a similarity of relations risks anthropomorphism *no less* than the straightforward predication of a simple attribute. All that it does is *transfer* the similarity from a) the **quality** to b) the **subject's** *relation* **to the quality.** Indeed, unless the relationship between the qualities predicated of the divine and human is also involved (e.g. between human *goodness* and divine *goodness*) then there is no reason why another predicated quality cannot be asserted. For example, what is actually being stated may not be substantially different from the statement that there is an analogical proportionality between God's relation to divine goodness and the relation of human beings to human knowledge!

Second, the statement 'God is good' is logically far removed from the assertion 'God is to God's Goodness in a manner (proportionally) analogically similar to humankind's relation to its goodness.' These two statements affirm, quite simply, two utterly different things! Whereas the latter statement is making a claim about the proportionalities between two sets of *relationships* – relationships which may have the same proportionality given completely different predicates – the former is making the statement that God is good and thus predicates goodness of God *directly* and *intrinsically.*

The whole point of the debate is to ground the fact that one is deliberately using the *same* word and concept when one asserts that a particular woman or man is good as when one is asserting that God is good. Such a statement is not, in the first instance, making an assertion about a similarity of relations at all. Indeed, if the one kind of statement could automatically be translated into the other, then the statement 'God is good and Mother Theresa is good' could be interpreted as making the same kind of point as the very different statement 'God is good and Mother Theresa is European.' That is, one would be doing no more than affirming an analogical similarity between two proportional relationships, in this case, between God and

God's goodness and between Mother Theresa and her Europeanness. The shift of reference from one kind of predicate (goodness) to another (the predicated relationship of the subject to a primary predicate) does nothing to lessen the threat of anthropomorphism. It simply translates one analogical statement into a different one – one over which the risk of anthropomorphism continues to hang.[49]

In other words, the traditional interpretation of Aquinas purports to explain a feature, the nature of which it was never the concern of the theory of analogy to address.

Third, this interpretation fails to reflect a central element in Aquinas' theory of analogy – one which, he believed, must be central to any approach which did not fall to the charge of anthropomorphism. This is simply that intrinsic to the statement 'God is good and humankind is good' are the underlying presuppositions that a) the quality of goodness belongs primarily to God, and b) it can only be predicated of humankind in a secondary and derivative sense. Both these elements he regarded as essential, for example, with respect to the analogical (intrinsic) predication of the term 'good' of God.

For Aquinas, clarity on such matters is of critical importance if we are to predicate validly of God attributes which are used in everyday parlance of and by human beings in such a way that we both a) mean what we say, and b) avoid falling foul of anthropomorphism. These requirements are met by Aquinas, Mondin argues, solely by virtue of his advocating what Suárez later referred to as 'the analogy of intrinsic attribution'.

A New Classification of Aquinas' Modes of Analogy[50]

As a result of his analysis of the text of Aquinas and his critique of the problems inherent in the traditional exposition of analogy, both as interpretations of Aquinas and as offering a

[49] It may be added here that any hypostatisation of relations that is thinly veiled within this form of analogy will commit one to an infinite regress if one seeks to escape anthropomorphism by making the same kind of move a second time with recourse to the relation of the two subjects to their respective relationships.

[50] Mondin, op. cit., 51–3.

solution to the problem of human talk about God, Mondin offers a new and concise classification of types of analogy.

The distinctions he draws are between the following types of attribution:

(1) (a) the analogy of intrinsic denomination 'formally' based on a relation of efficient causality between the analogates – the *analogy of intrinsic attribution.* E.g. substance is being, God is being and man is being;

(1) (b) the analogy of intrinsic denomination based not on a relation of efficient causality but on a similarity of relations – the *analogy of proper proportionality.* E.g. the flight of an angel is to an angel as the flight of a bird is to a bird;

(2) (a) the analogy of extrinsic denomination according to proper signification – the *analogy of extrinsic attribution.* E.g. Peter is healthy and food is healthy;

(2) (b) the analogy of extrinsic denomination according to improper or metaphorical signification – the *analogy of improper proportionality or analogy of metaphorical proportionality.* E.g. Achilles is a lion and that beast is a lion;

(1) encompasses judgements which are analogous because of a variation in the meaning of the predicated attribute;

(2) encompasses judgements which are analogous because of a variation in the meaning of the copula 'is'.

Ontological Presuppositions

The most helpful aspect of Mondin's analysis and classification is the extent to which it exposes the underlying world-view or cosmology operative in (and integral to) this conception of analogy. As Mondin explains, intrinsic attribution requires

a real similarity between analogates and that this similarity is based on a relation of efficient causality ... For instance, we may know that an omelette has been prepared by the Chinese Chiang, but this fact gives us no assurance that the omelette is Chinese. We may have this assurance only if we can appeal to the principle of the likeness between cause and effect. Only if the Scholastic principle *omne agens agit simile sibi* (every agent acts in a way similar to itself) is valid are we justified in believing that there is something Chinese about the food. The possibility of analogy of intrinsic attribution rests, then, on the validity of the principle of likeness between cause and effect.[51]

His complaint about the Cajetanists was that this key principle undergirding Aquinas' entire theory of analogy was lost.[52] The whole thrust of Mondin's analysis is to show that the roots of the Thomistic doctrine of analogy are to be found in a cosmological principle – a principle of universal (as this includes the divine realm) similarity between agents and that which they cause to exist or produce.

This interpretation clearly echoes some of the findings of Hampus Lyttkens' earlier, massive volume on *The Analogy between God and the World* at the end of which he writes, 'Our conclusion will accordingly be that, on the grounds of the natural equipment of man bearing some likeness to God and of the likeness of creation to God, St Thomas holds that man has a natural way to a knowledge of God which, although deficient, is nevertheless true.'[53]

On this interpretation, however, two serious and closely related problems arise here for the Thomist position – of which Mondin neither offers any discussion nor even seems to be aware. First, if the principle *omne agens agit simile sibi* is applied to God and God's relation to the created order, then God is apparently being subsumed under a kind of generic

---

[51] Ibid., 67.

[52] 'Cajetan and Cajetanists (like Phelan) do not recognise intrinsic attribution. This forces them to turn analogies of natures into analogies of relations. For instance, if wisdom is predicated of God and man, according to the Cajetanists, wisdom is not predicated of both of them because in their natures there is some similarity with respect to wisdom, but because the relations Wisdom-God and wisdom-man are similar. But is this what we intend to say when we attribute wisdom of both God and man?' (Ibid., 69.) 'Intrinsic attribution explicitly signifies the similarity between the primary and secondary analogate. The secondary analogate is an imperfect imitation of the primary with respect to the property caused by the primary in the secondary analogate. Intrinsic attribution implicitly expresses also that the relation of the analogous property to the secondary analogate is an imperfect imitation of the relation of the same property to the primary analogate.' (Ibid., 70.)

[53] *The Analogy between God and the World: An Investigation of its Background and Interpretation of its Use by Thomas of Aquino*, Uppsala, 1953, 480–1.

category, namely the class of 'agents' to whom it applies universally that their actions bear some likeness to themselves. The question emerges whether there is not a concealed form of analogy of two to a third, or many to one, of precisely the kind that, on Mondin's account, Aquinas rejected. Second, this argument operates on the basis of the supposition that there is some kind of empirical necessity here which is so all-pervasive that it includes God. This is an argument not from probability but from necessity. Given that the argument is of the form 'All agents are such that ...' rather than 'It would seem probable that all agents may be of such a kind that ...', there is a directly perceived universal necessity which is relied on to undergird the very possibility of God-talk. Put simply, the argument involves projecting on to God a conception of agency formed in the context of – and deriving from – finite, human experience, and doing so in a manner that subsumes God under a common category with respect to whose members certain rules must apply. Both of these moves or presuppositions clearly require extensive justification, both theological and, indeed, philosophical. It is difficult to see how David Hume's criticisms of Aquinas' cosmological and teleological proofs for the existence of God may be avoided as rendering an insurmountable critique of this kind of move.

In his *Dialogues Concerning Natural Religion* Hume criticised any form of (teleological) argument which ran as follows: as a house implies the existence of an architect and a watch the existence of a watchmaker, so the universe involves the existence of God.[54] Even if one could establish that the universe, despite its elements of apparent purposelessness and disorder, was ultimately ordered, and further that this order could not be the result of a chance or random succession of events, then this still does not establish the existence of an Ultimate and Infinite God, but at most the existence of some kind of universe-maker. It fails to establish the existence of an Absolute (divine) Universe-maker. If we are to project anthropomorphic models or formulas rooted in human

---

[54] For a useful analysis of Hume's arguments here see John Hick, *Philosophy of Religion*, New Jersey, 1963, 25–6.

experience on to the Being of God then the Transcendence and Pre-eminence of God which Aquinas was so eager to safeguard is put at risk. By the same form of reasoning we cannot ground human talk about God in a principle of the form 'every agent acts in a manner similar to itself' where such a principle is grounded in a conception of the world rooted in human observations operative within that world.[55] A cosmology which sees God as forming part of a whole characterised by such principles (and which are in turn, therefore, the product of human speculation) cannot do justice to the God who is deemed to be Infinite and Transcendent – let alone, as traditional Thomism requires, Absolute.

The point at issue here is expressed with clarity by Barth in Volume Three, Part 3 of his *Church Dogmatics*. He writes:

> If the term *causa* is to be applied legitimately, it must be clearly understood that it is not a master-concept to which both God and the creature are subject, nor is it a common denominator to which they may both be reduced. *Causa* is not a genus, of which the divine and creaturely *causa* can then be described as species. When we speak about the being of God and that of the creature, we are not dealing with two species of the one genus being. When we speak about the divine nature and the human nature of Christ, we are not dealing with two species of the one genus nature. And so, too, in this case.[56]

Clearly, Barth is using the Thomist principle *Deus non est in genere* against the Thomist approach as we have found it to have been redefined by Mondin some decades after Barth wrote this. It is puzzling that although Mondin offers an extensive discussion of Barth's doctrine of analogy, as is discussed later in this chapter, Mondin never engaged with this central critique that Barth offers of the approach that Mondin endorses. Despite his criticisms, Barth goes on nevertheless to affirm, by way of a distinction between what he

---

[55] This must be the case even taking into account the careful qualifications built into the *analogia unius ad alterum per prius et posterius* which seek to bypass the problems of anthropomorphism.

[56] *C.D.* 3. 3, 102.

terms an *analogia operationis* and an *analogia entis*, the important insights that are apparent in Mondin's argumentation if undermined by his conclusions.

> It is true, of course, that although there is no identity of the divine and creaturely operation or *causare*, there is a similarity, a correspondence, a comparableness, an analogy. In theology we can and should speak about similarity and therefore analogy when we find likeness and unlikeness between two quantities: a certain likeness which is compromised by a great unlikeness; or a certain unlikeness which is always relativised and qualified by a certain existent likeness. The great unlikeness of the work of God in face of that of the creature consists in the fact that as the work of the Creator in the preservation and overruling of the creature the work of God takes the form of an absolute positing, a form which can never be proper to the work of the creature. But at the same time the divine work in relation to the creature also has the form of a conditioning, determining and altering of that which already exists. And inasmuch as the conditioning of another also belongs to creaturely activity, there is a certain similarity between the divine and the creaturely work. In view of this likeness and unlikeness, unlikeness and likeness, we can and should speak of a similarity, a comparableness, and therefore an analogy between the divine activity and the human. We have to speak of an *analogia operationis*, just as elsewhere we can speak of an *analogia relationis*.
>
> But the concept *causa* does not merely describe activities, but acting subjects. And between the two subjects as such there is neither likeness nor similarity, but utter unlikeness. We cannot deduce from the fact that both subjects are *causa* the further fact that they both fall under the one master-concept *causa*; that they may both be reduced to that one common denominator; that they are both species belonging to the one genus. On the contrary, they cannot even be compared.[57]

The paragraph which follows shows the significance of engaging in this debate for the purposes of our argument as it concerns the use of the term 'person' of God and humanity.[58] He continues,

[57] Ibid., 102–3.

[58] It is interesting to note the similarity between Barth's use of the notion of likeness in unlikeness and that of Przywara (in his book, *Polarity*), who similarly emphasises the being like and unlike. The latter, however, refers to the fact that 'the Deity and the creation are in "being" like and unlike, i.e. analogous to one another... (32).' However, it becomes clear as the discussion continues that this

Indeed, it would be a mistake to try to compare them simply because they are both *causa*. In the same way it would be a mistake to argue as follows. The Creator exists and has being no less than the creature. Therefore although the being of the Creator and that of the creature are unlike, in some respects they are like and therefore similar. There is therefore an *analogia entis* between God and the creature. And it would be a really serious mistake if we were to adopt this argument. Jesus Christ has a divine nature and a human. Therefore although the two natures are unlike, they are also alike and similar. There is therefore an *analogia naturae* between God and man, And to that extent we can speak of a master-concept, a common denominator, a genus (nature) which comprises both God and man. This is the type of mistake which we have to avoid at this point. This is the deduction which we have to recognise as false and therefore illegitimate.[59]

The validity of this kind of argumentation for establishing false means of approaching semantic continuity is not in doubt in my view, and this is critical here in assessing the Thomist *analogia entis*. As to whether this argument may be used against the adoption of the term 'person' for describing the members of the Trinity, this will be discussed more specifically later on in the context of further analysis of the function of theological language.

There appears still to be one potential form of defence of Aquinas' argument as it features in Mondin's classification. If it were to be asserted that the principle *omne agens agit simile sibi* applies to both God and the human context in the light of some free divine ordination of the state of affairs that gives rise to this, then the principle could be argued to be one with which one can work with impunity. That is because there could then be argued to be ordained warrant for affirming such an attribute or class concept of both God and humanity.

---

unity of 'being' underlies that like–unlike distinction and this is where he and Barth head in different directions. Przywara writes, 'For the *analogia entis* knits all that is creaturely into a total likeness to Deity, and yet to such a likeness as in its ultimate essence is in ... a condition of the tool in the hand of the artificer' (33). This underlies his further claim that 'Catholicism becomes possible as the unification of all forms of piety ... (33)!'

[59] *C. D.* 3. 3, 103.

If this were the case then there would have to be some 'free Self-giving to be described in this way' on the part of God. Clearly, however, no such conclusion could be read out of the created order and then used to think theologically in the light of the created order without, at worst, engendering a vicious circularity or, at best, serious internal incoherence.

For Barth, however, not only the content but the very fact of revelation suggests a divine ratification of the *non-parallelism* between the divine and human natures and the attendant *non-parallelism* between the different contexts in which the term 'cause' might be used. This suggests that our theological semantics may not operate by appealing to such a principle of likeness conceived in these terms. To the extent that Aquinas does not address the issues here sufficiently his undergirding of God-talk requires greater warrant.

What is clear is that if a principle of likeness is to function as an ontological principle sustaining God-talk, then we must not run together two very different forms of 'likeness': namely, a) that which is supposed to exist universally between agents and their effects, and b) that likeness (which is actually identity) which exists between God and his free Self-revelation to humankind in the Word. Much of the *analogia entis* debate has revolved around the attempt to interpret the latter 'likeness' in a supposedly more foundational likeness conceived in terms of the former.

As the argument progresses, we shall suggest that the very justification of God-talk requires a more sophisticated concept of the act of God and a more dynamic conception of the divine Being than the arguments to which Mondin has referred us in Aquinas suggest. This is something which we shall be looking not only to Karl Barth but also to Eberhard Jüngel to supply and which the philosophies of language offered by Wittgenstein and the Hintikkas may help to define further.

Barth's Doctrine of the Analogy of Faith

Following his analysis and reclassification of Aquinas' interpretation of analogy Mondin goes on to offer an assessment of Barth's arguments from a Neo-Thomist perspective. As explained earlier, Mondin's critique from the perspective of a Thomist advocate of the *analogia entis* will provide the context for our assessment of Barth's views. It is our belief that this should prove a concise means, first, of focusing specifically and precisely on what Barth *was* and *was not* attempting to do in his theological exposition of analogy and, second, of outlining the ways which remain open to us in exploring the nature of theological description.

Mondin opens his discussion of Barth's approach by stating that Barth refused to engage in a philosophical discussion of the problem of analogy, interpreting the problem of theological language, rather, as a theological problem.[60] The whole direction of Mondin's subsequent exposition and critique reposes on this initial characterisation of what Barth is doing. This is a widespread assumption which clearly encourages one to ask about the underlying definitions of philosophy and theology. What is plain is that Barth refuses to determine the nature of the free Self-giving of God to be spoken of *independently of* the event of God's actually giving of himself to be spoken in and through the Logos and by the Spirit. This does not constitute a refusal to engage in a philosophical discussion unless philosophical discussions must *necessarily* be uninformed by 'givens' – and this is clearly not the case in serious philosophical enquiry. The point is that Barth refuses to establish *a priori* as foundational any particular set of parameters in terms of which the nature of God-talk – its meaning, function and capacity to refer – requires to be understood. Moreover, he refuses to acknowledge *in advance* that any particular set of theses requires to be interpreted as an *a priori*, necessary condition of God-talk. As we suggested in chapter 1, this refusal is not grounded in the conclusions of

[60] '(Barth) believes that natural theology is necessarily a false theology and that any philosophical solution of the problem of theological language must be also false.' (Mondin, op. cit., 149.) Although it is not our concern here to discuss the nature of philosophy, the accuracy of this comment hangs not least upon the extent to which one is committed to an interpretation of the philosophical enterprise in *a priorist* terms which would be difficult to defend in contemporary philosophical circles.

some Humean critique of the possibilities of God-talk. Rather, it is grounded in the fact that obedience demands that we resolve these issues out of the facticity of God's givenness to be spoken of. To go behind this in order to establish some necessary form which any such spokenness is required to possess is a form of disobedience and, therefore, a *de facto* rejection of God's initiative in instigating and requiring God-talk in and through a reconciliatory commandeering of human language – a commandeering of human language, moreover, into which we cannot validly introduce the kind of form–content dichotomies implied by Mondin's comment.

Barth's affirmations would suggest, moreover, that it is futile to endorse a distinction between theology and philosophy here unless philosophy is unable to engage objectively with the empirically or factually given. A theologically adequate statement should not be a philosophically unsound statement (and vice versa) unless philosophy sets itself up as a religion and, thereby, makes claims that are beyond its remit. The question how theological terms refer to God is not decided, therefore, by abstract, human speculation, but lies with the manner in which God has chosen to give himself to be spoken of in Christ. And this suggests that God is spoken and wills to be spoken *out of, in the light of* and *by virtue of* God's gracious Self-gift in Christ. Our language is, therefore, 'chosen' by God in this and as such possesses warrant. This does not mean, of course, that human talk of the divine ceases to be analogical. Rather, it means that the grounds of the analogical extension of terms must both be established by God and be seen within the Body of Christ to have that divine endorsement. This would mean that they must be seen to be consistent with, to repose on and to serve the reality of God in the Word made flesh.

For Barth, analogical reference is grounded, therefore, in what we have seen to be the triune structure of revelation where God is the Revealer, the Revelation and the Revealedness and where the referential relation is carried within this dynamic. It is, therefore, God's Self-gift in the incarnation which provides the ontological ground of analogy.

Mondin goes on to argue that Barth strongly emphasises that 'the being of God cannot be compared with that of humankind',[61] and that, consequently, Barth vigorously refutes any form of *analogia entis*, any 'correspondence' or 'similarity of being'.[62] While it is indeed the case that Barth states that 'There is not a correspondence and similarity of being, an *analogia entis*', and that 'The being of God cannot be compared with that of man' – a point, incidentally, implied in a slightly inconsistent comment by Przywara[63] – we must also be clear as to what Barth means when he says this. He is arguing *a posteriori* out of the givenness of revelation which he interprets as suggesting that it is inappropriate to assume a unity of essence which includes the Father, Son and Holy Spirit on the one hand and the being of created (contingent) and alienated humanity on the other. The human subject is indeed created in the image of God, but the very limitation implicit in the term 'image' suggests that there is not a continuity of being but rather the opposite.

> If the humanity of Jesus is the image of God, this means that it is only indirectly and not directly identical with God. It belongs intrinsically to the creaturely world, to the cosmos. Hence it does not belong to the inner sphere of the essence, but to the outer sphere of the work of God ... In it we have to do with God and man rather than God and God. There is a real difference in this respect.'[64]

The *essential* difference between the divine and the human is reflected in Barth's emphasis that, 'There is total sovereignty and grace on the part of God, but total dependence and need on the part of man.'[65] However, it must also be stressed that Barth is equally concerned to break with any foundationally conceived, dialectical affirmation of an infinite qualitative difference between God and humanity – as any such universal negation is equally illegitimate theologically if it lacks explicit, theological warrant!

[61] *C. D.* 3. 2, 220.
[62] Ibid.
[63] Przywara writes, 'Deity is He who is beyond all comparison the ever Greater.' (*Polarity*, 33.) This having been said, the whole grammar of his discussion implies a principle of comparability!
[64] *C. D.* 3. 2, 219.
[65] Ibid.

The Implications of the New Covenant for the Analogy Debate

The thrust of Barth's arguments may be expressed in another way which finds support, Barth believes, in the scriptural notion of the New Covenant. The conception of the human creature as the image of God may not be taken to imply that there has been a replication or duplication in humanity of the divine Being, since the biblical material in no way suggests that God enters into alliance with a 'second God' in his eternal (and unilateral) covenant with man as revealed in Jesus Christ. Nor does man become a 'second God' when he takes part in this covenant and is delivered by this Deliverer. The covenant between God and humankind is not to be seen as a reciprocal relationship, in other words – it is not an event to be conceived in synergistic terms as taking place between ontological equivalents. It is this central and irreducible *difference* between the divine and the human which stands at the heart of God's covenant purposes in the incarnation, which, Barth believes, the presupposion of uninterrupted continuity of being (as implied by an *analogia entis*) fails to take seriously.

Throughout Part 1 of Volume Four of the *Church Dogmatics* Barth stresses the covenantal nature of any *correspondence* between God's purposes and humanity's. To paraphrase the relevant section of his argument: even the very finest persons cannot place themselves and their work, as this includes their language and semantic frameworks, in the service of the work of God, or make it a declaration of God's work and therefore a good work. When a human work becomes a declaration of God's work it is because God's own work has assumed this special form.

It is in these terms that Barth interprets biblical references to good human works. Such good works are the human participation by grace in God's making himself known in a very special way to particular men and women. That is, God's work declares and attests itself and makes itself known to them in such a manner that they are pressed into its service, empowered for it and given a willingness and readiness to take part themselves in its declaration. The work of God which has taken place *for* these as for all humanity also takes place *in* them, he argues, in the form of this illumination, with the result that as the people they are they have a share in it – only as its witnesses, but *as such* a real share. The history of the covenant, whose acting Subject is God, takes place in its relationship to them in such a way that their personal history, whose subjects they themselves are, can no longer be alien or neutral in its relationship to the covenant but actually *corresponds* to it. Correspondence of the human with the divine is grounded, therefore, in a form of human participation in a dynamic which recognises God as Subject. The argument clearly integrates with Barth's conception of revelation in the first volume of his *Church Dogmatics*, but it also opens the way for a more holistic understanding of communion and the participative base of semantic mediation (itself the *ekstasis* of communion) which *is* 'revelation', properly understood.

What is made absolutely clear is that 'goodness' is not, theologically speaking, some innate, static attribute which is imaged in or possessed by the created order and its semantic forms and constructs. Good God-talk, as good works in general, speaks of the dynamic presence of the One who alone is Good and whose Goodness is to be defined in terms of his unconditional, loving faithfulness to humanity grounded in eternity. Any presence of 'goodness' in humanity and consequently of a correspondence between human and divine goodness is to be understood in terms of the dynamic presence of God picking up, involving and transforming humanity in such a way that a 'corresponding' takes place, but also in such a way that this is solely affirmable in so far as we are affirming the transforming covenantal *presence* of God in, with and for humanity. Theologically speaking, therefore, divine Goodness is not defined in terms of a static quality which is innately reflected (albeit analogically) in human creatures constituting some static, human goodness. Again, as Jung Young Lee emphasises,[66] it is the *dynamic* nature of Barth's theological

[66] See our discussion below.

ontology that underlies his invariably careful expression of any 'correspondence' between the human and divine realms and it is this *dynamic* understanding of the divine Triunity that, as the *Church Dogmatics* progresses, is interpreted as constituting the grounds of any intrinsic correlation between that which is truly 'good' in the human context, on the one hand, and the Goodness of God, on the other. This is essentially a 'creative' correspondence testifying to God's dynamic presence rather than some 'created', static (and hence 'receptically' conceived) correspondence grounded in the *creatio originalis* and drawn upon either by exemplarist notions of *vestigia Dei* or by causal notions of a necessary analogical likeness between an Agent and the *extrinsic* products of its agency.

The *Analogia Fidei* as *Analogia per Prius et Posterius* and *Unius ad Alterum*

When, in Volume One of his *Church Dogmatics*, Barth sets out to critique the *analogia entis*, he admits the following grain of truth in Thomas Aquinas' conception of analogy. 'In rejecting the Thomist *analogia entis* we affirm the other idea of Thomas in which, for that matter, one might discern the content of truth in even the so-called *analogia entis: quum igitur christiana fides hominem de Deo ... instruit ... fit in homine quaedam divinae sapientiae similitudo* (Thomas Aquinas, *S. C. Gent.*, II, 2).'[67] In and through faith men and women are brought to participate in the divine wisdom in a manner which provides grounds for speaking of a correspondence. The condition of this, however, is clearly faith and, despite the 'content of truth' to which Barth has referred, it is the epistemic significance of faith that constitutes, at least in his mind, the primary difference between the Thomist approach and his own. Faith is, therefore, the decisive concept in the debate concerning the grounds for the applicability of our language to God.

So what does Barth mean by 'faith' in this context? To enquire into faith is to enquire into the 'knowability of the

---

[67] *C. D.* 1. 1, 239 (*K. D.* 1. 1, 252).

Word of God'. This knowability is given in the event of faith, and as such 'is not a possibility which man for his part brings to real knowledge, nor is it a possibility which in real knowledge accrues to man from some source as an enrichment of his existence'.[68] Rather, it has its absolute and unconditional beginning in God's Word independently of the inborn or acquired characteristics and possibilities of the human being. As such, faith 'never lives from or by anything other than the Word'.[69] And he adds

> We cannot establish it if, as it were, we turn our backs on God's Word and contemplate ourselves, finding in ourselves an openness, a positive or at least a negative point of contact for God's Word. We can establish it only as we stand fast in faith and its knowledge, i.e., as we turn away from ourselves and turn our eyes or rather our ears to the Word of God. As we hear it, we have the possibility of hearing it. Hence we do not affirm our own possibility but its reality, which we cannot do except as we stand fast.[70]

Consequently, faith is interpreted as the acknowledgement of God's Word, which is brought into force not by any human act and experience but 'by the Word of God acknowledged'. As real acknowledgement it leads us to make the positive claim that in faith humanity has real cognitive experience of the Word of God. Consequently, 'no *finitum non capax infiniti*, no *peccator non capax verbi divini,* can now prevent us from taking this statement seriously with all that it involves'.[71] Integral to this faith, there is the conviction that God is and must be spoken of. The Word is to be proclaimed, and this constitutes a linguistic and semantic enterprise involving the given facets of social and human experience and intercourse.

What Barth is suggesting here is that in faith there is given, by grace, a form of participative knowing, a knowing which is inseparable from the functioning of language, such that there is a warrant or, rather, a compulsion to attribute to God all

[68] *C. D.* 1. 1, 236 (*K. D.* 1. 1, 249).
[69] Ibid.
[70] *C. D.* 1. 1, 236–7 (*K. D.* 1. 1, 249).
[71] *C. D.* 1. 1, 238 (*K. D.* 1. 1, 250).

that which the experience of the Word of God drives us to affirm. As he suggests in Volume Two (Part 1),

> To the question how we come to know God by means of our thinking and language, we must give the answer that of ourselves we do not come to know Him, that, on the contrary, this happens only as the grace of the revelation of God comes to us and therefore to the means of our thinking and language, adopting us and them, pardoning, saving, protecting and making good.[72]

Far from any *sacrificium intellectus* or *fides quia absurdum*, what is affirmed in and through this process (as it is grounded in the divine initiative) is profoundly rational, objective and, indeed, 'scientific' – scientific, that is, to the extent that what is being affirmed is radically demanded by the nature of the object of the enquiry. The analogical attribution inherent in the God-talk emerging from it is ontologically grounded in the Being of God which is and is given *in* the Word. And, as Barth insists, the profoundly real and ontologically grounded knowledge that is given here 'surpasses' ('transcends' in the Bromiley–Torrance translation) and 'provisionalises' or 'circumscribes' (lit. 'brackets') the principle of the incapacity of the *finitum* or the *homo peccator* ('er überholt ihn, er klammert ihn ein')[73].

For Mondin, Barth's advocacy of the analogy of faith reflects an irrationalist, anti-philosophical bent. That this tends at best in the direction of an over-simplification is made clear from studying precisely the passage in *Church Dogmatics* Volume Two (Part 1), to which Mondin appeals ironically in support of his interpretation of Barth. It falls within a section on the knowability of God in which it is clear that Barth has no interest in *a priori* rejections of 'natural theology', let alone 'philosophy'. What does concern Barth is where foundationalist approaches to the reference and warrant of God-talk (and that includes those forms of philosophy which engage in God-

[72] *C. D.* 2. 1, 223.
[73] *K. D.* 1. 1, 250.

talk by making claims that go beyond the remit or warrant of philosophical enquiry) reflect a failure to think obediently and scientifically out of God's active and dynamic Self-giving for thought and speech. The section summary runs:

> The possibility of the knowledge of God springs from God, in that He is Himself the truth and He gives Himself to man in His Word by the Holy Spirit to be known as the truth. It springs from man, in that, in the Son of God by the Holy Spirit, he becomes an object of the divine good-pleasure and therefore participates in the truth of God.[74]

There then follows a discussion of the issue that concerns Thomism, namely the question of the possibility of the knowability of God by the human mind or expressibility of God in human language. Put quite simply, there is a consistent refusal in Barth to deal with the potentiality question in advance of the actuality question – a feature that many would argue to be more philosophically sound than its converse. As Wittgenstein stressed, affirming in effect the primacy of the retrospective over the prospective, philosophers must 'look and see'!

> To ask about the 'knowability' of God is to ask about the possibility on the basis of which God is known. It is to look back from the knowledge of God and to ask about the presuppositions and conditions on the basis of which it comes about that God is known. Only in this way, only with the backward look, is it possible to ask about the knowability of God in the Church's doctrine of God. We come to it from 'the knowledge of God in its fulfilment'. It is from there that we go on to ask about the knowability [Barth could have said 'speakability'] of God.

He then adds, 'The type of thinking which wants to begin with the question of the knowability of God and then to pass on from that point to the question of the fulfilment of the knowledge of God is not grateful but grasping, not obedient but self-autonomous.'[75]

---

[74] *C. D.* 2. 1, 63.
[75] Ibid.

Clearly, Barth's approach to the speakability question relates to his fundamental insistence, spelled out from the very beginning of the *Church Dogmatics*, that theology, or rather dogmatic theology, is the 'self-examination of the Christian Church in respect of the content of its distinctive talk about God'.[76] It is not, and must not become, simply the result of human speculation of a kind which refuses to allow its own abilities, capacities and conclusions to be informed *foundationally* by the specific activity of God in revelation – such that they become less than obedient, less than scientific and lacking in the theological warrant that is the Word. Barth could easily have added that such an approach must *a fortiori* be philosophically weak! Barth's interest in broaching the question of the speakability of God is one that concerns at its core the nature of theological obedience before a divine dynamic, whereas Mondin's concerns relate to the ratification of our innate human capacity and potential. The real dilemma for the 'Barthian' theologian here takes us back to the intrinsicity–extrinsicity issue raised in chapter 2. There is no way in which one can demonstrate the apodeictic force or nature of the demand for methodological obedience from a standpoint *extrinsic* to the Word of God – from a standpoint, that is, that does not fall 'under' the Word of God. And, as has already been perhaps too extensively rehearsed in our discussion, this is *not* an insistence that reposes on premises demonstrable on *a priori* grounds.

Of particular significance for our discussion here is the way in which Barth's emphasis on obedience in God-talk chimes with Aquinas' emphasis on the principle *per prius et posterius* in theological analogy. In Volume Four Barth writes, 'Obedience implies an above and a below, a *prius* and a *posterius*, a superior and a junior and subordinate.'[77] Barth's option for the *analogia fidei* stems not from any fideistic antipathy toward reason, but precisely from his concern that *at no point* must we forsake the theological principle *per prius et posterius*. In sum, the whole

[76] *C. D.* 1. 1, 11 (*K. D.* 1. 1, 10).
[77] *C. D.* 4. 1, 195.

thrust of his interpretation of analogy and emphasis on obedience derives from his concern that we uphold the principle that Mondin so stresses as one of the pillars of Aquinas' interpretation of God-talk! It is not surprising, therefore, that Barth's insistence should, at least on the surface, exhibit some similarity to Przywara's insistence that the revelation dynamic must invariably be seen to be *'from above downwards'* (his italics) and not 'from below upwards'.[78] What is *further* clear is that Barth's argument is also conditioned throughout by his determination to think in terms of Aquinas' other principle, namely that theological predication must be *unius ad alterum* rather than *duorum ad tertium*. Barth's stress on the singularity of the event of revelation and his defining of this in terms of the identification of the Content of Revelation with the Being of the Revealer seems to be the most fundamental and, indeed, primordial means of fulfilling this criterion possible.[79]

In other words, Barth's concern with the methodological import of 'obedience' which features so strongly throughout his *Church Dogmatics*, as in his critiques both of German 'Culture Protestantism' and of Brunner's 'natural theology', can be seen to reflect precisely those methodological concerns which, as Mondin emphasises so strongly, stand at the very heart of Aquinas' exposition.

Barth's determination to be methodologically 'obedient' leads him later in his *Church Dogmatics* to the controversial

---

[78] Przywara writes, 'God is neither the inner unity of the creaturely, nor can any form of unity of the creaturely count as an instance of Him. He is the Creator, and in so far all the contents of revelation and modes of revelation (whether natural or supernatural) combine in one, as ultimately revelations made in creaturely mode. Yet He is the essentially super-creaturely Creator, and therefore this unity which is achieved is not "from below upwards", i.e. in human reckoning "attainable", but only *"from above downwards"*, i.e. *"to be received"* as from His free revelation of Himself which is ever open.' (*Polarity*, 34.)

[79] In other words, Barth is consistent in his concern to avoid *a priori* decisions grounded in *generic* modes of thought. To utilise the form of argument that runs 'If an object is to be predicated of which belongs to the *genus* of the divine, then this can only be the case given the following conditions ...' is a repudiation of what Aquinas himself is seeking to emphasise in affirming his *unius ad alterum* principle.

view that this obedience finds its correlate and indeed its grounds in a *prius et posterius* in the inner life of God.

> We have not only not to deny but actually to affirm and understand as essential to the being of God the offensive fact that there is in God Himself an above and a below, a *prius* and a *posterius*, a superiority and a subordination. And our present concern is with what is apparently the most offensive fact of all, that there is a below, a *posterius*, a subordination, that it belongs to the inner life of God that there should take place within it obedience.[80]

It is in and through the 'becoming' that stems from this that we have the means of being faithful not only to the theologically sound principle of the *prius et posterius* but also, in the most radical way, to that of the *unius ad alterum* in God-talk where there can be a consistent freedom from subtle and underlying forms of 'generic' assumption – such as we find in the *omne agens* principle. It is also precisely here that we see the extent to which the dynamics of reconciliation and those underlying the 'correspondence' of theological statements with the divine are integrally bound up with each other.[81]

The emphasis on grace and the 'covenantal' nature of obedience echoes Barth's earlier insistence on the significance for the analogy debate of the Lutheran doctrine of justification.

---

[80] *C. D.* 4. 1, 200–1.

[81] The implications of Barth's comments on reconciliation for a 'dynamic' interpretation of theological language do not need to be spelled out, 'In the work of the reconciliation of the world with God the inward divine relationship between the One who rules and commands in majesty and the One who obeys in humility is identical with the very different relationship between God and one of His creatures, a man. God goes into the far country for this to happen, He becomes what He had not previously been, He takes into unity with His divine being a quite different, a creaturely and indeed a sinful being. To do this He empties Himself, He humbles Himself. But, as in His action as Creator, He does not do it apart from its basis in His own being, in His own inner life. He does not do it without any correspondence to, but as the strangely logical final continuation of, the history in which He is God. He does not need to deny, let alone abandon and leave behind or even diminish His Godhead to do this ...' (*C. D.* 4. 1, 203.)

It is significant how much more strongly Barth stresses the intra-divine relationship in this context – a dimension which, as we have suggested, is lacking from his interpretation of revelation and the Trinity in the first volume of his *Church Dogmatics* as it was moulded by his revelation model.

This was the grounds of Barth's critique of Quenstedt, who, in Barth's view, failed to appreciate that any *attributio* which interprets the creature as 'an analogue of God' in any way at all must have 'something to do with the grace of God'.[82] When Quenstedt suggests an *analogia attributionis intrinsecae* between God and humanity, Barth suggests, 'If he had thought of the grace of revelation, if in this place, too, this Lutheran had remembered the Lutheran doctrine of the forgiveness of sins by grace alone, he would undoubtedly have decided terminologically for the concept of an *attributio extrinseca*.'[83] The point which Barth is seeking to make here is clear – despite the fact that it is considerably less than obvious that it is, as Barth thinks, the *analogy of extrinsic attribution* which articulates best what Barth actually intends and, indeed, requires to say! The analogy of extrinsic attribution, unless understood very differently from its traditional definition, has arguably no theological use whatsoever. It fails to allow for the 'realised eschatological' element that is integral to the semantic function of theological language within the Body of Christ. Consequently, it cannot allow for that semantic shifting of our concepts and conceptualities that is integral to reconciled participation in the life of Christ and, therefore, to all forms of theological 'correspondence' – not least that corresponding that, this side of the *eschaton*, is 'through a mirror darkly' and solely by the grace of God which is God's life amongst us in Christ and our participation in it by the Spirit.

What emerges with unambiguous clarity from this whole discussion is that the question of the attribution of 'personhood' to the members of the Trinity concerns, for Barth, quite simply the obedient and *a posteriori* consideration of the (contingent) propriety of this affirmation and not any *pre*-supposed 'intrinsic' ontological continuity between the notion's divine and human 'domains'.[84]

---

[82] *C.D.* 2.1, 239. Barth is referring to Quenstedt's *Theol. Did. Pol.*, 1685, c. 8, sect. 2, qu. 1.

[83] Ibid.

[84] It is amusing to observe how John Baillie, in his discussion of 'Analogy and Symbol' in *The Sense of the Presence of God* (Gifford Lectures 1961–2, London, 1962,

Is the *Analogia Entis* Necessarily Incompatible with the *Analogia Fidei*?

One feature of Barth's discussion that is rarely acknowledged is that Barth makes it quite clear that it is eminently possible to interpret the *analogia entis* in such a way that there are no theological reasons for rejecting it whatsoever. As we shall see, his unhappiness with certain accounts of the *analogia entis* relates to its being conceived as a metaphysical principle which demands a theological methodology interpreted in *a priorist* terms thus giving theologians the right, as it were, to go behind the back of, or look away from, the reconciling event of God's Self-revelation in Christ when making affirmations concerning the nature, purposes and intentions of God. To appreciate the precise nature of Barth's views we must turn to his engagement, in *Church Dogmatics* Volume Two, Part 1, with the Roman Catholic theologian Gottlieb Söhngen, with whom Barth enjoyed some particularly constructive interaction and dialogue.

Söhngen insists that knowledge of the Being of God must not be superordinated but subordinated to the knowledge of the activity of God. This has the effect, Barth sees, of subordinating the *analogia entis* to the *analogia fidei*. In and through faith – itself the product of the Being-in-act of God – the Being-in-act of God is apprehended and spoken of.

Following the quotation of an important section from the article by Söhngen,[85] Barth goes on to use him to argue:

---

121), tries to utilise Barth's emphasis on the priority of the divine in order to affirm his own idealist approach to theological semantics. He writes, 'Dr Barth speaks truly when he says that God alone is properly and adequately to be called Father, and that it is in no figurative sense that we so call him. The divine is always prior. The ideal is always *a priori.*' What he fails to appreciate is the tension between his two last sentences unless one operates with a highly optimistic conception of an innate, intrinsic accessibility of human knowing to the divine realm. He might have emphasised that if the divine is always prior then our theological ideas (*noiai*) must be interpreted in *a posteriori* terms. Nothing makes this clearer than Jesus' emphasis on the semantic *discontinuity* of the two realms of meaning in his discussion of the use of the term 'Father' in Matthew 23:9.

[85] 'Pulchra et altissimae theologiae utilis est philosophia Aristotelis, si non secundum mentem humani auctoris, sed secundum mentem Verbi est ens ut qualitas, quomodo metaphysicus ens et qualitatem intelligit et de hac re loquitur,

a) that if action follows being and metaphysicians strive to trace activities back to their entitative foundations, this very procedure suggests that epistemologically '*esse sequitur operari* – the knowledge of being follows the knowledge of activity';[86]

b) that there is no degree in which humankind can 'sense the existence and mode of being of a self-disclosure of God. The self-disclosure of God can itself be known only in this self-disclosure.'[87]

Therefore, Barth concludes (citing sections from Söhngen's argument), '"the *analogia fidei* is *sanans et elevans analogia entis*". But that means, by Jesus Christ: "*Verbum divinum assumens humanam naturam est nostra analogia fidei assumens analogiam entis.*" (p. 208).'

Operating within this perspective Barth is more than happy to support an *analogia entis* in so far as this refers to a participation of the Word in humanity whereby we have a 'real participation of being in Him and by Him'. As Söhngen himself puts it, this participation in being is 'not a gracious participation in God by reason of a purely human ability for participation, but a truly human participation in God by reason only of the divine power of grace'.[88] There should be no opposition, therefore, between the *participatio fidei* and the *participatio entis* properly understood.[89]

The central issues which can now be seen to characterise Barth's concerns are:

a) the refusal to operate with a static notion of God or the divine substance or nature defined with recourse to an act-exclusive conception of Being. (It is inappropriate to postulate

---

sed secundum veram analogiam entis ut qualitatis concipitur et haec analogia entis est sub mensura fidei. (Quoted in C. D. 2. 1, 82 from 'Analogia fidei', *Catholica*, 1934, 136.)

[86] Quoted by Barth from the aforementioned article (198).

[87] Quoting p. 204.

[88] Ibid., 134f.

[89] The *participatio fidei* is, perhaps, better described as participation by the *grace* of God which is also discerned or recognised through the grace of God by the form of (rational) perception which is faith and which is brought about in us in and through the creative and reconciling activity of the Holy Spirit.

Lessing's 'big ugly ditch' when we are seeking to articulate the doctrine of God!);

b) the *a posteriori* (the *per posterius*) nature of reverent theological description – which is the epistemological side of the same coin, since each of these principles involves the other; and

c) the freedom of God must be acknowledged at the formal, methodological and epistemological levels – and not merely as an attribute to be 'recognised' at the secondary, 'material' level. The *actual* freedom of God has ramifications *vis-à-vis* the ground or warrant for God-talk – it is a component in the analogy debate.[90] Again, this issue is expressed supremely well by Söhngen whose approach Barth endorses in the following statement: 'For the Word of God must always be the sovereign Subject in every living movement of faith, which is always its own movement because it is carried by its substance and in that substance it has the inward constructive power consistent with its essence'.[91]

It is noteworthy that Barth does not appear here to be averse to the use of a 'philosophical'[92] approach which integrates with the conclusions flowing from a theological analysis of

---

[90] This is reflected in Barth's reference to the *analogia fidei* in his section (*C. D.* 2. 1) on 'The Being of God in Freedom', where he writes,

Christology, therefore, must always constitute the basis and criterion for the apprehension and interpretation of the freedom of God in his immanence. The legitimacy of every theory concerning the relationship of God and man or God and the world can be tested by considering whether it can be understood also in Jesus Christ. Is it capable of adaptation to the fundamental insights of the Church concerning the person and work of Jesus Christ – the *analogia fidei*? ... If we appeal to God and His freedom, in the last resort, directly or indirectly, we can expound and elucidate only this one theme. (320.)

[91] '*Analogia fidei*', *Catholica*, 1934, 136 (cited by Barth, *C. D.* 2. 1, 82).

[92] Use of the word in this context is always going to be dubious as it implies that there is a valid alternative to theological argumentation that functions prescriptively but exists in advance of *a posteriori* claims. It is not clear that this should be described as 'philosophy' more than what might be termed philosophical theology which engages analytically and critically with *a posteriori* claims. Philosophy of science no longer operates with the long out-dated (Kantian) rubric that suggests that reason can 'off its own bat' determine the bounds and possibilities of scientific investigation.

God-talk and its warrant. This suggests that the following conclusions at which Mondin arrives (and which exemplify a great deal of similar misrepresentation of Barth's position[93]), although partially accurate, are also partially false and overstated:

[93] E.g. In the concluding chapter of his small and very superficial book *Karl Barth: Theologian* (London, 1983), John Bowden endorses David Ford's assertion (from 'Conclusion: Assessing Barth' in *Karl Barth – Studies of his Theological Methods* (ed. Stephen Sykes, Oxford, 1979) that Barth's 'tendency is to restrict two-way influence and communication rather than engage in this and try to work out its appropriate form. The result is that, instead of offering a way of handling the manifold mutual interpenetration of theology, comparative religion, psychology, philosophy and the natural sciences, his rigid boundaries simplify the picture by excluding much relevant material' (196).

It is, however, Richard Roberts, in his recent book, *A Theology on Its Way? Essays on Karl Barth*, Edinburgh, 1991, who attacks Barth most strongly with the charge of isolationism – a charge concerning which Bruce Marshall rightly comments, 'No criticism of Barth is more common than this one, multiple versions of which have been proposed since the first volume of the Church Dogmatics appeared' (*J. T. S.*, 44, 1993, 455). Roberts argues that on Barth's account God 'denies, subverts, and supersedes the reality of the mundane (51). And Barth's interpretation of time and eternity leads to 'the effective encapsulation of revelation in its own time [77] leading to his denying that God can have any contact with the 'shared realities of human existence'.

It is difficult to deny that anyone who reads Barth is tempted to want to critique him from a perspective which wishes to see a massive integrating system conceived as one statement which will correlate with, and engage in dialogical interaction with, all that is going on in the other sciences. The various sciences (of which theology would be one) could then be interpreted as serving together to articulate God's purposes for the world. As such theology would be seen not to be 'self-enclosed' (Roberts) and every form of human enterprise could be seen as providing 'points of connection'. However, such a picture assumes a great deal about the nature of the theological task, its methods and epistemology and it is all too easy to be seduced by a facile model of theology conceived as simply one science among others and its conclusions as just one set of conclusions among others. The whole point of Barth's argument is that the 'object' and *modus operandi* of theology is unique and specific to its object precisely because its Object is radically unique and specific. It is such that we cannot assume *a priori* the self-contained and 'transcending' validity of the conclusions of other disciplines – disciplines which do not think in terms of the free Self-revelation of God and of his ultimate purposes for the created order.

If the general assumption is that Barth was not interested in integrating his theological conclusions with the interpretation of social issues then that would be a travesty. As a theologian he was supremely involved in matters relating to the *polis* – believing that theology should be pursued with the Bible in one hand and

The object of philosophy is abstract; the object of theology is concrete: the concrete, historical Word of God. The object of philosophy is within man's power; the object of theology is not: it is freely given by God ... There is no continuity between faith and reason, philosophy and theology, natural and supernatural, man and God.[94]

We may acknowledge that Barth is indeed sceptical about the capacity of some supposed human faculty of reason to establish theological truth 'off its own bat'. It reflects his sense of the epistemic incapacity of fallen creaturehood that he refuses to go either with Tillich, on the one hand, in interpreting the divine–human relation in terms of 'correlation' where a symbol 'participates in the reality which it signifies',[95] or with traditional Roman interpretations of an *analogia entis*, on the other hand, where these are grounded in a metaphysic of being which commits one to an ultimate and foundational continuity between the divine and the 'natural' or human order. However, his carefully nuanced discussion of these issues is certainly not grounded in a foundational assertion of human impotence at the rational, epistemic, semantic, symbolic, or any other level. Rather, it is essentially concerned to establish that it is theologically inappropriate to operate in terms of an 'idea of being in which God and man are always comprehended together, even if their relationship to being is quite different, and even if they have a quite different part in being'. To argue that in so far as the human being is a being, the human creature 'is able to

---

the newspaper in the other. And as his writing on Mozart would suggest, he can be almost too enthusiastic in his discussion of the relationship between theology and certain areas of the arts!

Unfortunately, one suspects that what Bowden and Roberts (and Ford?) are after is a multiplicity of theological 'roots' – roots of the kind that, as Barth observes, too often take the form of Trojan horses joyfully brought into the midst of the Body of Christ. (See chapter 4 below.)

[94] Mondin, op. cit., 150.

[95] Cf., for example, Paul Tillich, 'Theology and Symbolism' in *Religious Symbolism*, ed. F. E. Johnson, New York, 1955, 107–16; 'Religious Symbol and our Knowledge of God', *The Christian Scholar*, 38 (1955), 189–97 (both cited in Mondin). Cf. also A. I. C. Heron's critical evaluation of Tillich's thought in *A Century of Protestant Theology*, Cambridge, 1980, 136–44 (esp. 140–1).

know a being as such' and that therefore, 'in principle he is able to know all being, even God as the incomparably real being' and that 'Therefore if God is, and if we cannot deny His being, or on the other hand, our own being and that of creation, necessarily we must affirm His knowability apart from His revelation', is, for Barth, theologically invalid. What demands to be emphasised, therefore, is that when Barth is rejecting the notion of the *analogia entis* it is the approach summarised in this way (and which he sees as characterising Roman Catholic thought as it is expressed in its official teaching) that Barth is rejecting.[96] Absolutely no faith–reason dualism or dichotomy is either intended in, or implied by, his discussion!

If Söhngen's exposition of the *analogia entis* were what the *Magisterium* intended Barth would have been willing, it appears, to align himself with it.[97]

There is, therefore, no *necessary* conflict between philosophy and theology. Indeed, theology and philosophy must always go together, since all theology must have a philosophical form.[98] The important point is that we guard against allowing preconceived philosophical forms to smuggle in content or material foreign to the reality under investigation. Within the Christian faith and the theology which emerges from it, the Word must not be subjected to human presuppositions, but human presuppositions must be subjected to the Word. Mondin is, therefore, essentially correct when he suggests that, in Barth's view, 'Theology is never responsible for its statements to any philosophy; it is responsible only to God in Jesus Christ.'[99]

---

[96] *C. D.* 2. 1, 82–3.

[97] Referring to Söhngen's summary of his position, Barth comments, 'If this is the Roman Catholic doctrine of *analogia entis*, then naturally I must withdraw my earlier statement that I regard the *analogia entis* as "the invention of the anti-Christ". And if this is what that doctrine has to say to our thesis, then we can only observe that there is every justification for the warning that participation in being is grounded in the grace of God and therefore in faith, and that substance and actuality must be brought into this right relationship.' (*C. D.* 2. 1, 82.)

[98] I agree with Mondin's interpretation of Barth here (150).

[99] *The Principle of Analogy*, 151.

Mondin's Critique of Barth's Interpretation of Theological Attribution[100]

The *Analogia Fidei*, the Question of 'Being' and the Epistemologically Absurd

Traditionally, theological expression has utilised a whole variety of different kinds of terms in contexts where these are used both of God and of humanity – e.g. eye, mouth, being and spirit, not to mention 'person'. Clearly, it is believed that we know what we mean not only when we use them in relation to the creaturely realm, but also when we use them with respect to God. Both Barth and Mondin agree that there is here neither univocity (since there is no parity between humankind and God) nor equivocity (since this would make all knowledge of God impossible). Analogy is, therefore, in the view of both theologians, the legitimate and correct interpretation of theological discourse.[101]

To the extent that God-talk emanates from a divinely initiated dynamic which is thus a 'language-claiming event' involving a necessary, yet derivative, phatic acknowledgement on the part of human beings, a theory of analogy is unavoidable, not because it is imposed by humankind but because it is chosen and affirmed by God: 'Pressed by the true revelation of God, we are pushed to use the word "analogy".'[102] As Mondin rightly points out in discussing this facet of Barth's position, the relationship posited in God's true revelation attracts the word analogy to itself, and compels us to use it. Accordingly, analogy is not a deification of man and his word. By declaring that analogy is the correct interpretation of theological discourse we are not placing our trust in anything immanent in us or in this word. The necessity of analogy is,

---

[100] The following section is an attempt to engage specifically with Mondin's critique of Barth. I have chosen to do this not only because such an influential critique requires a fairly detailed response, but as a means of clarifying further the key issues which require to be taken into consideration for the purposes of the wider concerns of this book.

[101] *C. D.* 2. 1, 223–5.

[102] *C. D.* 2. 1, 226.

therefore, a factual one – the result of our being driven or compelled by God's free revelation to engage in God-talk. It may be argued, therefore, that it is freely established by God quite independently of whether or not it is prescribed by a metaphysic of being.

For Barth, this suggests that it is inappropriate to appeal, in our interpretation of theological reference, to some cosmological conception of created reality conceived independently of the full Self-revelation of God in the One by whom and for whom all things were created. If we are to base our understanding of God on some notion of analogical 'likeness' between the Creator and the created order (which, as Lyttkens, Mondin, Klubertanz[103] and others have argued,[104] is the essential emphasis in the metaphysics which underlies the Thomistic interpretation of analogy), Barth believes it to be both unnecessary and unwarranted not to begin with the one in whom we see the Father, who is uniquely in the likeness of God as the one in whom we have the fullness of the Godhead dwelling bodily.

Mondin points out quite correctly here that analogical 'predication'[105] on this model implies a theological semantics which is entirely different not only from the *analogia entis*, but from a Tillichian interpretation of symbol based on a correlation between finite and infinite – one might add that Soskice's account of the metaphorical nature of 'reality depiction' in theology would be ruled out here owing to implications of an underlying correlation, albeit one that is metaphorically conceived. By contrast, the *analogia fidei* is grounded on the unilateral (*unius ad alterum!*) relation between God and the creature given by grace in the Second Adam, in the New Covenant. Any interpretation of the semantics of

---

[103] E.g. 'St Thomas often uses the language of likeness (*similitudo*) to describe the analogy between God and creatures.' (*St Thomas Aquinas on Analogy*, George P. Klubertanz, Chicago, 1960, 48.)

[104] Cf. von Balthasar's carefully nuanced discussion of Barth's engagement with the 'likeness' issue in 'Analogie and Dialektik', *Divus Thomas* 22, 2 (1944), 171–216.

[105] The word 'affirmation' rather than 'predication' is clearly preferable in this context!

theological expression interpreted in terms of metaphorical reality 'depiction' would require to be grounded in a prior God–humanward dynamic which involves a more participative and dynamic conception of analogical affirmation than the semantics of metaphorical depiction (which is more 'ocular' in conception and arguably, therefore, more static).

Unfortunately, however, Mondin is guilty of a serious misinterpretation of Barth's exposition of the *analogia fidei*, one that does not help bridge the gulf between their underlying theological semantics. He writes of Barth's alternative that, 'It differs from analogy, inasmuch as analogy admits the possibility of a true interpretation of theological language also outside Revelation. This is denied by *analogia fidei*.'[106] However, the *analogia entis* which Barth rejects, far from merely 'admitting the possibility of a true interpretation of theological language *also outside* revelation' (my italics), generally insists on the necessary possibility of the true interpretation of theological language *prior* to the interpretation of revelation – and where it is suggested that this is a necessary condition of the *rationality* of God-talk! It is the *a priori* determination that the meaning of terms *may not* undergo any form of semantic shift in its theological context of meaning that is the problem for Barth.

Second, when Barth insists on the necessity of the *analogia fidei*, he is not interested in the *a priori* rejection of possibilities, he is, rather, committed to being obedient to *a posteriori* theological *obligations*. To the extent that this is the case, it may (and I feel should) be suggested that the real openness to 'being' is found in Barth since *he* may be argued to be the one who, as a matter of fact, takes 'being' seriously. For Barth, to take 'being' seriously is to allow our approach to be determined by what actually *is* or *takes place* rather than to approach 'being' by determining in advance what must actually be '*of necessity*' – where this 'necessity' is defined not logically or rationally (in the light of the nature of reality) but

---

[106] Mondin, op. cit., 153.

rationalistically. Barth's conception of the theological dynamics of analogical affirmation is his alternative to operating with a metaphysic or concept of 'being' (be it what Bernard Montagnes refers to as either a 'métaphysique des degrés d'être' or a 'métaphysique de l'idée d'être')[107] where these latter may not necessarily be prescribed (or should we say 'post-scribed') by the demands of 'being' itself namely, that which *actually* and *objectively is*!

With greater accuracy of interpretation than attends other facets of his interpretation of Barth, Mondin outlines four reasons as to why Barth interprets human language as having the God-given power to speak about God:[108]

1. God creates language first for Himself. Our words are not our property but God's. However, God places them at our disposal. For example, the words 'father' and 'son' do not first and properly have their truth in our thought and language. God is *the* Father and *the* Son. When God authorises and commands us in God's revelation to make use of our views, concepts and words, God is not doing something inappropriate – God takes to Himself something that belongs originally and appropriately to God.

2. Humankind can extend its language to God because God has already used human language of Himself. So humankind can apply, for example, the terms 'reason', 'speaking', 'hearing' and 'understanding' to God because God has already claimed these words for Himself and humankind cannot abandon them unless it wishes to take up a stand somewhere other than where the Word of God is heard.

3. Humankind can extend its language to God because the meaning of its language is first and fully realised only in God.

4. Humankind can extend its language to God because it has been sanctified by Christ and the Church.

Whereas the above is a reasonable[109] systematisation of part of Barth's argument, his description and assessment of its

---

[107] *La Doctrine de l'Analogie de l'Etre d'apres Saint Thomas D'Aquin*, 162–4.

[108] Mondin, op. cit., 156–7. I have taken the liberty of altering Mondin's terminology here into its inclusive forms simply because the quotation is such a lengthy one and so many of the terms used may be deemed to be 'exclusive'.

[109] Clearly, Barth would have been unlikely to have used the phrase reiterated throughout Mondin's summary 'Humankind can extend its language to God

context in Barth is considerably less adequate. Mondin asserts that for Barth the mystery and the ambiguity of theological language derives from what he quotes Barth as terming the 'contradiction between form and content'.[110] This he supports with a non-existent reference (p. 466ff., G. T. Thomson translation)! There is no reference on these pages to any such theme, although it may be said that elsewhere Barth *does* speak of 'the distinction, nay opposition, between form and content'.[111] This is not the same. To quote the original, Barth writes, 'Eine Aufhebung des Unterschiedes, ja Gegensatzes von Gestalt and Gehalt vermögen wir nicht zu vollziehen.'[112] This is very different from the kind of contradiction ('Widerspruch') which would commit one to 'faith' due to the absurdity of its object (whatever such a 'faith' might be), and which Mondin suggests may be involved by Barth's position.

What Barth clearly wishes to stress here is that we cannot operate in terms of a natural harmonisation or innate compatibility between the divine Word to humanity and the created order such that, whereas we hear the 'God with us' spoken to us by means of the secular form through which it is spoken, this 'means' may actually cease to be a 'means' and be supposed to speak this Word *itself*, that is, by itself and of itself. The natural world may not be assumed to communicate God's Word by some means that is intrinsically and in itself in harmony with the message and, furthermore, perceived demonstrably or intuitively to be so. There is a real tension and differentiation between the evil, the injustice, the suffering and pain of the cross (what Alan Lewis, for example, has referred to as the rupture of meaning and discontinuity involved by it[113]) and God's Word to humanity in and through

because ...' as it has a somewhat Pelagian ring to it. *We* do not extend our language to God, rather, as Jüngel makes clear, our language is commandeered by God. In other words, the revelation event includes the semantic extension of our language in and through a dynamic that is irreducibly *trinitarian* and which is initiated and realised by *God*.

[110] Mondin, op. cit., 158.

[111] G. T. Thomson translation of *Church Dogmatics*, 1. 1, 200.

[112] *K. D.* 1. 1, 182.

[113] 'The Burial of God: Rupture and Resumption as the Story of Salvation', *S. J. T.* 40 (1987), no. 3.

it – and yet the two cannot be separated. The message of the cross is foolishness to the Greeks, a stumbling-block to the Jews. If it were not so then there would be a collapsing of God's message into the event of innocent suffering in such a way that there could be no message of hope.

On the basis, however, of his confused rendering of Barth on this point, Mondin goes on to argue

> the category of form–content is exposed to the danger of exaggerating God's transcendence. And it seems to us that Barth has not been able to escape entirely this danger. He usually stresses so much the worldliness of the human form, its reality and evidence both in the case of the Word of the Bible and of the human person Jesus, that the divine Word and the divine Person is absolutely hidden. This is not inconsistent with Barth's basic principle of the *Sola Fides*. But the *credo* here risks becoming only a *credo quia absurdum*.[114]

This reflects a serious failure to understand Barth. To suggest (on the basis of a misquotation) that a) he advocates an 'absolute' hiddenness; b) that this meshes with the form of perception that is *sola fides*, and that, therefore, c) his thought is heading in the direction of a *credo quia absurdum* points to a degree of hermeneutical failure which is not uncommon but which is deeply frustrating.

The context of Barth's discussion of the form–content opposition is an exposition of the divine *unveiling* for our knowing – precisely the opposite of an absolute hiddenness which demands faith in the absurd. There is an absolute giving-to-be-known but in conditions which involve, at one level, (precisely by virtue of their unveiling), a form that actually, necessarily and simultaneously 'veils' that which is given to be known – where 'veils' clearly does not mean 'conceals absolutely' but functions metaphorically to allow an emphatic assertion that there is a giving-to-be-known through, and *by means of,* this veiling. A paradox of the kind discussed and brought out by Barth in his discussion here commits one in no respect whatsoever to the kind of logical absurdity that Mondin's innuendoes suggest.

---

[114] Mondin, op. cit., 159.

Indeed, that precisely the opposite is defensibly the case may be illustrated by recourse to a simple example which helps to illustrate (analogically) that veiling can be the very condition of cognitive perceptions resulting in truth claims which are far from absurd. The example is of a context where an *unveiling* would immediately suggest that the same true claim would indeed involve blind faith. If one were to witness a helium balloon rise into the clouds, one would be entitled to suggest (given the further, prior perception of its non-flammability) that the outer skin of the balloon concealed helium. This would naturally involve a degree of cognitive faith in a variety of *a posteriori* theorems and derivative scientific principles which supported this conviction. The observer, however, may be entitled to claim to know thereby that the outer layer of the balloon did conceal helium. If it were suggested that rational certainty required an absolute 'unveiling' of the helium such that it be no longer in any respect 'hidden' from view, and that this was requisite if its presence were to be identified without absurdity, one would be left with a scenario in which one lacked, as a result, the most straightforward means of affirming its presence. We are not suggesting that there is a direct parallelism here with God's presence – this would be to commit oneself to a most unsatisfactory form of Apollinarianism! Rather, we are suggesting that the kinds of conditions on which Mondin seems to rely for his argument to work may be shown by analogy to fail to operate in certain contexts in the physical world. Veiling of one kind or another may be seen in a variety of different cases to be the condition of the revelation of something's being and identity. The observer's desire to unveil the gas in order to confirm its presence without absurdity would be based on the presupposition that the gas was identifiable in certain predetermined ways and that its presence was confirmable by certain means, all of which were inappropriate to the nature of the gas and the conditions of our capacity to confirm its presence. To act on this desire would be irrational and unscientific.

Clearly, the same point could perhaps be made by rather less simplistic analogies in the area of subatomic physics, although the profoundest and most directly analogical discussion of 'veiling' for the purpose of revealing is to be found in Søren Kierkegaard's *Philosophical Fragments* and his 'poetic' tale of the love of the king for the peasant girl.

An important qualification, however, needs to be borne in mind here – lest attempted refutations with recourse to analogies become a ratification of a Mondinian *vestigium Dei!* As Barth comments in Volume Four, 'we cannot really know Jesus Christ without realising ... the inadequacy of all analogies to His own becoming and being'.[115]

The Dynamic of Cognitive Reference

When expounding the inseparability of form and content for Barth, Mondin writes,

> Its content, the thing signified, is divine; its form, the mode of signification, is human. Theological language considered in its form is always and only human language. But its content is the *concretissimum*, God in God's own Reality. Humankind is incapable of arriving at a separation of the form from the content and at an isolation of the divine meaning hidden under the human form. Not even faith can do this for faith is precisely to hear 'the divine content of the Word of God, although absolutely nothing but worldly form is discernible by us.[116]

Barth does indeed insist that a clear distinction must be made between form and content in theological expression and that neither a separation nor an identification is possible. What this gives rise to, however, far from being a logically absurd human enterprise, is a profoundly cognitive enterprise (some, indeed, would say *too* epistemically oriented, as I have mentioned above), but one where this cognitivity reposes on the free grace of God.

> Invariably, then, faith is acknowledgement of our limit and acknowledgement of the mystery of God's Word, acknowledgement of the fact that our hearing is bound to God Himself, who now leads

---

[115] *C. D.* 4. 2, 58.

[116] The quotation cited here is taken from *C. D.* 1. 1 (G. T. Thompson translation, Edinburgh, 1936), 201. Mondin, op. cit., 158.

us through form to content and now from content back to form, and either way to Himself, not giving Himself in either case into our hands but keeping us in His hands.'[117]

What should be clear from this is that it is inappropriate to suggest that the twofoldness here involves any absolute hiddenness.

> It might seem surprising that the movement of faith, or rather the movement of God's Word which faith can only follow, is described so explicitly as twofold. This is not done in the interests of a scheme but because the matter described leaves us no option. It is especially true that what is at issue in faith is to pierce, or to see to be pierced, the concealment in which God speaks to us in proclamation, in the Bible and in Christ Himself, and thus to see and hear that the very concealment of God is his true and real revealing.[118]

Again, the epistemic and cognitive acknowledgement of God's Word – and where God *is* God's Word – consequent upon a dynamic divine revealing is not a hiddenness requiring a *fides quia absurdum*. Accordingly, the form–content distinction functions precisely to emphasise the *cognitive* nature of this divine revealing and not the opposite.

In his famous essay, 'Über Sinn und Bedeutung', Gottlob Frege interpreted the sense ('Sinn') of a term as the mode of designation of its reference ('Bedeutung').[119] In Fregean terms one might suggest that for Barth God establishes himself ('takes place') as the *dynamic* reference ('Bedeutung') of the term in such a way that its normal, everyday, specifically human sense ('Sinn') may come to penetrate to a deeper reference in a manner which transforms and conditions anew

---

[117] *C. D.* 1. 1, 176 (*K. D.* 1. 1, 183).

[118] *C. D.* 1. 1, 176–7 (*K. D.* 1. 1, 184).

[119] Cf. Gottlob Frege, 'On Sense and Reference', in P. Geach and M. Black (eds.), *Translations from the Philosophical Writings of Gottlob Frege*, Oxford, 1952, 56–78.

This is not to imply that an actual reference is assured. Frege writes, 'The expression "the least rapidly convergent series" has a sense; but it is known to have no reference, since for every given convergent series, another convergent, but less rapidly convergent, series can be found. In grasping a sense, one is not certainly assured of a reference' (58).

its sense. That is, a semantic shift is generated by which the reference becomes the mode of the (re)designation of the sense! This is what Jüngel conceives as the *commandeering* of language. What should be clear is that the divine 'becoming' here means that the sense and scope of the reference of the relevant terms is not to be conceived as static or as predetermined by prior rules of use.

In the light of Wittgenstein's insight that the meaning of a term is its use and the manner of its use is prescribed by the whole context in which it occurs, one might say that, for Barth, the whole context of the use of language is moulded by the concrete content which God gives to the reference of this language in the particular context of its use, that is, in the Church. What is of essential significance here is that this content cannot be separated from the human context of its use – even by faith.

In other words, two facets underlying theological reference require to be stressed.

a) God gives us neither abstract concepts nor a-historical ideas, but himself in an intensely personal act in space-time and this Self-gift may neither be translated nor transmuted into products of the human mind as abstracted ideas, or truths. Nor may it be divorced from history and the concrete and personal life of the Church. What is given remains *God* without any divine reduction. The divine mystery is not lost.

b) At the same time, however, God is truly *given* in human form in a manner which involves a semantic shift or reconstruction and which presupposes the Body of Christ (and, in particular, the early community of disciples and apostles, not to mention the Old Testament writers) as the 'hinge'[120] integrating the two dimensions not in a fixed but in a flexible and dynamic way.

It may be observed that a) and b) reflect the epistemic implications of the *anhypostasia* and the *enhypostasia* respectively.

In contradistinction to Mondin's assessment, it could well be argued that it is precisely Barth's integrative articulation of

[120] This is a term borrowed from T. F. Torrance.

the form–content distinction on the one hand and the theological dynamic which underlies it on the other which points to Barth's primary accomplishment in his discussion of the grounds of analogical affirmation. These two central emphases in Barth's discussion correspond to his affirmation of the two-way divine 'movement' on the one hand and his framing of the human task as participative 'acknowledgement' on the other.

Mondin's Interpretation of the *Analogia Fidei*

Mondin summarises Barth's formulation of the *analogia fidei* by way of the following three theses (which I have placed in quotation marks).[121] It is immediately significant that two of these are framed in negative terms and the other framed in terms of a conditional qualification. Barth's own expression of his theology, by contrast, is essentially affirmative. The 'No' always stems from and finds its force in the 'Yes'.[122] If Barth himself were to have defined the ground of God-talk and its form in terms of a series of theses, one suspects these would have been in the affirmative – although the critics of Barth have been quick to translate his theological affirmatives into anthropocentric negatives. I shall seek to offer alternative (and rather less concise) theses which serve not to quote but to interpret Barth in interaction with and in contra-position to Mondin.

---

[121] Mondin, op. cit., 159–64.

[122] Cf. Jüngel's discussion of this *vis-à-vis* the Barmen Declaration in *Mit Frieden Staat zu Machen* (Eng. trans. by Bruce Hamill and A. J. Torrance entitled *Christ, Justice and Peace*, Edinburgh, 1992). Jüngel comments that, 'the Barmen Declaration had something much more important to say than a mere "No". It had firstly and above all to say "Yes" to the one whom alone one can trust unconditionally, both in life and in death. It had first and above all to give positive expression to what evangelical truth is … The "No" has no independent meaning. It depends completely on the "Yes". It can only be heard when the "Yes" is heard. The fact that this "Yes" is not a clever little theological invention, but rather a confession of the "Yes" which is spoken by God and which has become event in Jesus Christ, is brought to expression in the Barmen Declaration in that each thesis begins with God's Word itself – with a text from Holy Scripture.' (10–12.)

1. 'Human reason alone is unable to conceive any true concept of God.'[123]

Barth would wish to begin in the affirmative. The knowledge of God involves an act of acknowledgement involving all our capacities and where God is the ground of this as the Revealer, Revelation and Revealedness, as the *Agent*, the Personal and Dynamic *Content* and the Active *Condition* of this event.

To seek to define our concept of God with recourse to human capacities and abilities defined *a priori* and in advance of this event (*ante factum*) becomes a *de facto* and *post factum* denial of this event and involves a formal repudiation of the divine freedom at the material level.

2. 'Analogous concepts of God are made possible only by Revelation.'[124]

The event of revelation not only obliges but compels human beings to acknowledge the Being and nature of God as God *is* eternally and antecedently in himself and as this is revealed in the event of God's Self-gift. This acknowledgement involves analogical affirmation grounded in the commandeering and claiming of human language in and through the event of revelation itself.

3. 'Analogous concepts do not express God openly but only hiddenly.'[125]

God alone expresses God, not analogous concepts *per se*. God expresses God in an event whereby faith is provided which may pierce the concealment in which God speaks to humankind in proclamation, in the Bible and in Christ himself. In and through this the very concealment of God may be seen and heard to be his true and real revealing.[126] This event appropriates in a transforming initiative our linguistic forms of expression, the whole complexity of the terminologies involved together with the rules of use integral to these. Far

---

[123] Mondin, op. cit., 159.
[124] Mondin, op. cit., 161.
[125] Mondin, op. cit., 163.
[126] Cf. *C. D.* 1. 1, 177 (*K. D.* 1. 1, 184–5).

from being a static form of 'reality depiction' this is a dynamic event which stimulates the metaphorical and analogical usage of terms and which serves to transform or bring about shifts in the rules of use of the relevant semantic concepts. This event of semantic transformation is inseparable from the life of the Body of Christ.

Toward a Theological Ontology of Communion

Barth's exposition of analogy suggests a new framework in terms of which we might understand the analogy between human and divine existence – one which is radically different from that of traditional Thomism. This should be examined briefly before consideration of the specific analogies which stem from the person of Christ as the incarnate **Word** of God to humankind.

1. A central affirmation throughout the history of the Christian Church has been the scriptural one that women and men are created 'in the image of God'. The *imago Dei* has been widely interpreted as denoting some capacity in the human being which in turn is interpreted as providing the point of departure for articulating knowledge of God.[127] For Barth, however, the *imago Dei* does *not* refer to some particular quality, capacity or capability which humankind possesses. Human beings are an image of God *as human beings*. 'Human beings would not be human if they were not an image of God. A man or woman is an image of God inasmuch as he or she is human.'[128]

Barth's interpretation here relates to his perception that men and women were not created as independently existing, self-contained individuals with static and definable essences. The covenant, as it provides the key to the interpretation of God's purposes in creation, establishes that men and women are to be conceived as relational beings and that their true being, in its *irreducible* particularity, is to be discovered in the

---

[127]The 'faculty of reason' or the 'moral conscience' have widely been considered prime candidates for this role.

[128] *C. D.* 3. 1, 207.

fullness of communion with God. As such their being mirrors God's purposes in salvation-history as this defines living in truth within the complexity of human relationships.[129] This form of personal being *is* the image of God in humankind and as such it is not something which humankind possesses. It denotes nothing less than what the person *is* in truth. The image of God in humankind is particularly manifest, Barth affirms, in the I–Thou relationship – where the human I–Thou is to be conceived as an image of the divine I–Thou. This is not an analogy of being, as traditionally understood, but an **analogy of relation** (*analogia relationis*) – 'as the addressing I in the divine nature is related to the addressed divine Thou ... so also in human existence the I is related to the Thou, man to woman'.[130]

The similarity consists therefore in the correspondence between the I–Thou relationship of Father and Son, and the I–Thou relationship of man and woman, which he takes to provide the profoundest expression of interpersonal relationship in the human realm.[131] The dissimilarity is most noticeable in the fact that in the human realm this takes place between different individuals; in God, on the contrary, it takes place within the same, unique *Individuum*.[132]

2. In Barth there are at least three areas of 'similarity' or 'correspondence' involving Christ to which we must also draw

[129] 'That real man is determined by God for life with God has its inviolable correspondence in the fact that his creaturely being is a being in encounter – between I and Thou, man and woman. It is human in this encounter, and in this humanity it is a likeness of the being of its Creator and a being in hope in Him.' (*C. D.* 3. 2, 203.)

[130] Ibid., 220.

[131] Dietrich Bonhoeffer echoes this when he writes, 'The likeness, the analogy of man to God, is not *analogia entis* but *analogia relationis*. This means that even the relation between man and God is not a part of man; it is not a capacity, a possibility, or a structure of his being but a given, set relationship ...' *Creation and Fall*, London, 1959, 37.

[132] As Professor Jung Young Lee emphasises in his exposition of Barth, 'In spite of the similarity of correspondence between human and divine encounter, the divine I-Thou is quite different from the human I–Thou. The I–Thou relationship in God takes place in the one and unique individual, while the I–Thou in man takes place in two different individuals, the man and woman.' ('Karl Barth's Use of Analogy in his *Church Dogmatics*', *S. J. T.* 22 no. 2 (1969), 144.)

attention here. These may be regarded as 'continuities in discontinuity' – analogical parallelisms which constitute the 'hinge' of the divine–human communion at the focal-point of 'salvation-history' and in the covenant relationship which is the *telos* of the creative purposes which stem from the eternal love of God. Mondin correctly articulates three distinct analogies here, although it is plain that none of these can be stated adequately without reference to the others.

a) There is the analogy between Christ and God. The relationship which God established in Jesus with humankind is not foreign to God in that this new relationship serves to image the mutual love inherent in God. In God's inner life there is thus the prototype of the I–Thou relationship of which Christ's relation to humankind is an image.

> If 'God for man' is the eternal covenant revealed and effective in time in the humanity of Jesus, in this decision of the Creator for the creature there arises a relationship which is not alien to the Creator, to God as God, but we might almost say appropriate and natural to Him. God repeats in this relationship *ad extra* a relationship proper to Himself in His inner divine essence. Entering into this relationship, He makes a copy of Himself. Even in His inner divine being there is relationship.[133]

b) There is the analogy between Christ's humanity and his divinity. Barth maintains that between Christ's humanity and his divinity there is not only parallelism, but an inner agreement. Moreover, the correspondence and similarity between the two is not merely factual but 'essential'. 'The humanity of Jesus is not merely the repetition and reflection of His divinity, or of God's controlling will; it is the repetition and reflection of God Himself, no more and no less. It is the image of God, the *imago Dei*.'[134]

He writes,

> there is a factual, a materially necessary, and supremely, as the origin of the factual and materially necessary, an inner divine correspondence

---

[133] *C. D.* 3. 2, 218.
[134] *C. D.* 3. 2, 219.

and similarity between the being of the man Jesus for God and His being for His fellows. This correspondence and similarity consists in the fact that the man Jesus in His being for man repeats and reflects the inner being or essence of God and this confirms His being for God.[135]

c) There is an analogy between humanity in general and Christ's humanity. This he construes in terms of the analogy of relation which portrays the *Grundform* or 'secret' of humanity, i.e. the I–Thou relation: as Jesus is for God or for humanity, human beings are for other human beings. Jesus embodies as human the secret of humanity in general, which is our free and glad being with others, co-humanity.[136]

The argument (and its theologically *a posteriori* nature) is reflected quite clearly when he writes in Volume Three, Part 2:

> In the light of the Word of God and on the presupposition of the given divine reality of revelation, i.e., of the humanity of the man Jesus, we have been speaking about the creaturely essence of man, human nature. On this basis, we could not say anything other or less of man than that by nature he is determined for his fellow-man, to be with him gladly. It would be inadmissible to describe man as a being to which this determination does not radically belong but is alien. A being to which it was alien would be different by nature from the man Jesus. If man were a being of this kind, we should either have to say that only the man Jesus was real man as God created him, or that Jesus was not a real man at all, but a being of a different order. If, however,

---

[135] *C. D.* 3. 2, 219. Again, he writes, 'The correspondence and similarity of the two relationships consists in the fact that the freedom in which God posits Himself as the Father, is posited by Himself as the Son and confirms Himself as the Holy Ghost, is the same freedom as that in which He is the Creator of man, in which man may be His creature, and in which the Creator–creature relationship is established by the Creator. We can also put it in this way. The correspondence and similarity of the two relationships consists in the fact that the eternal love in which God *as* the Father loves the Son, and *as* the Son loves the Father, and in which God *as* the Father is loved by the Son and *as* the Son by the Father, is also the love which is addressed by God to man. The humanity of Jesus, His fellow-humanity, His being for man as the *direct correlative* of His being for God, indicates, attests and reveals this correspondence and similarity ... it *follows* the essence, the inner being of God.' (Italics mine.) (*C. D.* 3. 2, 220.)

[136] Ibid., 273.

there is similarity as well as dissimilarity between him and us, to His being for others there must correspond as at least a minimum on our side the fact that our human being is at root a free being *with* others. This is what we have maintained as the secret of humanity.[137]

By using the word *with* as opposed to *for*, Barth is anticipating the point John Zizioulas will make when he suggests that personal *ekstasis* requires our being reborn from above. It reflects ecclesial rather than biological existence. Barth can be seen here making the connection between the human form of *being for* the other (which is redeemed humanity) and *being with* the other, which describes the form of our natural, biological existence. Clearly, the 'being with' can take the form of a 'being against'.[138]

The manner in which these three aspects of what is essentially a single, analogical relation articulating the form of divine–human atonement all coinhere is reflected powerfully in Barth's analysis of chapter 17 of John's Gospel, where he explores what he refers to as the 'full correspondence and similarity' which characterises 'the relationship between God and man represented within the creaturely world, as a history played out in the cosmos, in the man Jesus, in His fellow-humanity, in His relationship to His disciples'. This correspondence, he suggests, is grounded in the 'glory' of the 'original, the relationship within the divine being, the inner divine co-existence, co-inherence and reciprocity'. What we might term the *substance* of this analogy lies in the fact that 'the relationship of Jesus to the disciples is not original, but an exact copy of the relationship in which He stands to the Father and the Father to Him'.[139] He concludes,

> Thus the divine original creates for itself a copy in the creaturely world. The Father and the Son are reflected in the man Jesus. There could be no plainer reference to the *analogia relationis* and therefore

---

[137] Ibid., 274.
[138] It might be said that this parallels at the personal level the kind of distinction Heidegger made between *Zuhandenheit* and *Vorhandenheit*.
[139] *C. D.* 3. 2, 220.

the *imago Dei* in the most central, i.e., the christological sense of the term.[140]

In sum, Barth insists, like Aquinas, that at the very heart of the Christian faith there is to be found an *analogia* – an *analogia* which, as in Aquinas, denotes correspondence and similarity in disparity.[141] The parallels between them, however, do not stop there! This *analogia* is *unius ad alterum* – in Barth, the *unius ad alterum* element is reflected, as we have suggested, in his emphasis on the *a posteriori* nature of theological attribution as this is involved by that theological obedience which **is precisely** the recognition of the *prius-posterius* ordering grounded in 'the prior relationship of the Father to the Son and the Son to the Father, of God to Himself'.[142] If Barth's *analogia* is to be described as an *analogia relationis* and not as an *analogia entis*, then Mondin's systematisation of Aquinas would suggest that Aquinas' conception of analogy ought *not* to be described as an *analogia entis*, but rather an *analogia causae* or *analogia causalitatis*.

The thrust of our argument here is quite simple. One does not need Söhngen's discussion to clarify that, properly speaking, there is no more reason for Aquinas' theory of analogy to be described as an *analogia entis* than for Barth's! Which form of analogy is more ontologically fundamental is addressed by the question whether the Being of God is to be conceived first in causal terms or more fundamentally in terms of the triune interrelations.

Unfortunately, it seems Barth failed to appreciate the full ramifications of his own position. This failure derives from a confusion illustrated, for example, when he argues that 'for all the disparity ... there is a correspondence and similarity between the two relationships. This is not a correspondence and similarity of being, an *analogia entis*. The Being of God cannot be compared with that of man.' Clearly, we would argue that the *analogia entis*, properly defined, does not

[140] *C. D.* 3. 2, 221.
[141] *C. D.* 3. 2, 219–20.
[142] *C. D.* 3. 2, 220.

require this kind of comparability any more than an *analogia relationis*–as is reflected *precisely* in Barth's use of the metaphor of image in this context. He continues,

> But it is not a question of this twofold being. It is a question of the relationship within the being of God on the one side and between the being of God and that of man on the other. Between these two relationships as such – and it is in this sense that the second is the image of the first – there is correspondence and similarity. There is an *analogia relationis.*[143]

Here, it seems, Barth falls foul of precisely the same confusion discussed earlier and which is found in those who interpret theological analogy as an analogy of proper proportionality believing, thereby, that they escape anthropomorphism. It is not clear why correspondence between relationships is relevantly different from correspondences between 'beings' or 'attributes' – especially if we are not to dichotomise between being and act or being and being-in-relation. Barth's statement seems to commit him to precisely the same kind of error which he refuted in his critique of the *analogia entis.*

The weakness in Barth's argument here, which, as we shall suggest, is similar to that reflected in his opting for *Seinsweise* as opposed to *Person*, is his refusal to lay claim to the fact that 'being' may be given theological reinterpretation in dynamic, relational and personal terms. There is no need, therefore, to be as suspicious as Barth was of the terms 'being' or, indeed, 'person'.

Moreover, it seems almost perverse to shy away from an analogy of *being* in favour of an analogy of *relations* while, at the same time – when referring to the intra-trinitarian relations – opting precisely for the term 'being' (*Seins*-weise) in place of a term that denotes an essentially relational reality, namely 'person'. Barth's two decisions would seem to want to cancel each other out!

The kind of theological apperception for which Barth strove required an insistence on a relational reinterpretation

[143] Ibid.

of 'being' as also of 'personhood' when used to interpret the intra-trinitarian life. This end was not served by departing from these terms in these two central areas. This only involved the 'dis-integration' of a sorely needed *unified* and *a posteriori* theory of the relationship between the divine and contingent orders.

Given that the use of neither term commits one to any 'parity' across the 'gulf', it is difficult to see why Barth failed to appreciate their potential for bringing out the participative *koinonia* which is God's intention for the created order (conceived in protological and eschatological terms) as this is grounded in the divine Triunity.

To summarise, there are at least three ways in which the theological ontology of the analogy of faith expounded by Barth differed from the Thomist conception of the *analogia entis* with its underlying cosmology – all of which would seem to be served more effectively by a creative synthesis of the *analogia entis* (redefined), the *analogia relationis* (carefully defined) and the *analogia fidei* (or, rather, *analogia gratia*).

First, Barth's analogy of faith served to obviate any attempted universalisation of a principle of causality or *a priori* (that is, programmatically or rationalistically conceived) metaphysic of being in the light of which human beings then engage in the 'projective' predication of qualities of God. The traditional Thomist account of the *analogia entis* has tended to stand in danger of failing to take seriously the revealed distinction between God and humankind by reducing it to a quantitative difference, to a difference of degree. It thus risks bringing God and humankind together under the same (metaphysical) category of being, namely an 'idea' or a 'genus' in which God and humankind are comprehended together – an *analogia duorum ad tertium*. Barth insisted that theology take due cognisance of the fact that ontological 'at-one-ment' between God and humanity was not a 'given' but something realised by the grace of God and realised fully only in the *eschaton*.

Second, it allowed the priority of God over humanity to be reflected not only in defining the form of analogical predication, but in its material content. It interpreted theological statement in a radically *per prius et posterius* and *unius ad alterum* manner not only in formal ways but also at the material level. It interpreted God as free.

The *analogia entis* was perceived by Barth as instituting an inversion of the divine–human relationship. Instead of operating from God's Word to humankind as this defines the nature, character and presuppositions of the human–divine relationship, the *analogia entis* started with humankind in an attempt to define the structural form and semantic conditions for theological predication. As such it side-stepped God's dynamic Self-accommodation to humankind in an attempt on the part of the human to elevate its language and conceptuality to God. As one commentator puts it, 'The *analogia entis* reverses the direction of Divine-human encounter ... Thus it is a counterpole to grace which moves downward.'[144]

There was an underlying concern here in Barth (as has been noted in previous chapters) to safeguard the freedom, transcendence and grace of God and obviate forms of what may be termed 'naturalist' semantics, 'naturalist' epistemology and 'naturalist' ontology where one risks making an idol of some natural construct – operating in the light of some deified, 'religious' product of the alienated (*echthros*) human mind.

Third, the analogy of faith was perceived by Barth as allowing an analogy of relations which challenged the more static, model of (pseudo-logical) relations reflected in the traditional analogy of proportionality. Barth's *analogia relationis* sought to bring into a dynamic correlation relations of the divine to the divine (the Father and Son) and relations of the human to the human. In this way it pointed to a relational foundation which lay not in the supposition of proportionalities

---

[144] J. Y. Lee, 'Karl Barth's Use of Analogy in his *Church Dogmatics*', *S. J. T.* 22 no. 2 (1969), 136. Lee also provides two additional 'ground motives' leading to Barth's rejection of the *analogia entis*. First, 'the *analogia entis* assumes man's receptiveness to God's revelation apart from God's grace. Thus it conceives that the knowledge of God is capable in natural man *prior to* and *apart from* God's encounter.' Furthermore, 'the *analogia entis* makes out of the "He" an "It" and of the "Becoming" a "Being". God, who is static and impersonal, is quite contrary to our God, who is always personal and dynamic in His relation to man.'

confirmed speculatively from within the created order but rather in terms of 'personal' interrelations affirmed concretely of the One who participates in the eternal communion of the Godhead and who also creatively *realises* this in the created order as the dynamic and 'koinonial' *vinculum* between the sphere of intra-divine communion and that of inter-human mutuality.

The Contrast between the Two Approaches

Professor Jung Young Lee has argued that the essential difference between the ontologies underlying the *analogia entis* (in terms of which we might describe the approach of St Thomas Aquinas) and the *analogia fidei* is the contrast between a 'static ontology' and an 'active ontology'. Barth conceives of analogy 'in terms of a dynamic relationship rather than in terms of static being. According to him, a being becomes actual in that it is active ... Everything, even God, man and the world, must be conceived in terms of this dynamic and active relationship.'[145]

One might say that in Aquinas we find the philosophical mind struggling with a problem, 'How can our human language refer to that Being on which the entire realm of human existence is contingent?' The question is then answered in terms of this very principle of contingency essential to which is believed to be the further principle *omne agens agit simile sibi.* In Karl Barth we have the church theologian who is describing the role theological language plays in the context of the dynamic communion between God and humankind revealed and established in the human world by the creative initiative of the triune God – an initiative perceived (*on theological grounds*) as exposing the impropriety of any 'speculative' or 'metaphysical' approach to the problem or, indeed, even of any 'speculative' definition of the nature of the problem.

At one level, therefore, we find ourselves dealing with a confrontation between two 'cosmologies'. The first is characterised by 'universal' principles of causal agency and contingency constituting a cosmology whose focus is the

[145] Ibid., 146.

ultimate agency of the Absolute Agent. The second stems from insight into the Being of God deriving from God's unique Word to humanity in Christ – an event which is perceived to show that the heart of the divine purpose for the universe is not a static and necessary metaphysical principle but the mutual and dynamic intra-relations of the communion of the Trinity.

This having been said, we must guard against a potential misconstrual of Aquinas here. A serious misconception would be displayed if Aquinas were interpreted as advocating either an impersonal or, indeed, mechanistic ontology as the grounds of analogical predication. He was supremely aware of the diversity of 'causes' which can operate in the natural world (and the highly 'personal' nature, for example, of final causes). His advocacy of the principle *omne agens agit simile sibi* is not, therefore, necessarily incompatible with a personal conception of the metaphysical network of relations under-lying God-talk. What was not clarified is the significance for God-talk of the network of relations which impacts on the created order in Christ and the Spirit and which is one of free communion, to be distinguished, therefore, from that singular form of 'relation' with the created order which is causal agency.

At another level, the methodological confrontation is reflected in the fact that, on the first, our language can refer to the ineffable God on the basis of a principle discerned from the created order suggesting that our human language can 'refer' to the Transcendent. In terms of the second our language can refer (lit. 'carry back') to God because God actively elects to refer our language back to himself in such a way that God's ultimate purposes are made known in space-time in and through an event of communion through which our language and terminology are moulded and transformed such that they might serve to create and sustain communion and semantic 'atonement' between the creaturely Body of Christ and the Transcendent and Ineffable Triunity. The 'carrying back' of the semantic function of our terms, the referring of our conceptualities, is part of the 'carrying back' of humanity into full participation in the triune Life. Reference is by grace.

Patristic Parallels[146]

Barth's approach may too easily appear to be an attempt to provide a post-Humean, post-Enlightenment model of theological attribution which side-steps Hume's critique of 'natural religion' on the one hand and, to some extent, the Kantian critique of the powers and possibilities of human reason with regard to the knowledge of God on the other. In suggesting that this is certainly not the motivating force behind Barth's discussion (as is clear, not least, from his debates with Brunner), it is relevant to note the continuity between Barth's conception of the grounding of analogy in the Trinity and Athanasius' conception of the ana-logic of theological terms. In his article 'The Logic and Analogic of Biblical and Theological Statements in the Greek Fathers', T. F. Torrance expounds the interpretation of the grounds of theological statement inherent in the thought of Athanasius and Cyril of Alexandria as follows:

> The Incarnation means that God has really given himself and communicated himself in his eternal Word to mankind (*sic*). It is out of that Word and in accordance with the way which that Word has taken in the Incarnation that genuine theological statements are made. They are genuine statements in so far as they *derive from* that Word and *refer back* to it: that is their essential *ana-logic*. Theological thinking is thinking of and on the ground of a given Reality ... What God is to us in Jesus Christ he really is antecedently and eternally in himself - that is the ana-logical reference.[147]

---

[146] For an impressive account of the extensive parallels with Barth's own work, the influences on him and also his misinterpretations of patristic theology I would again refer the reader to E. P. Meijering, *Von den Kirchenvätern zu Karl Barth*, Amsterdam, 1993. For his discussion of the distinction between Barth's approach and the Arian debate cf. 60f. and 66f. Meijering does not go as far as T. F. Torrance (see footnote below) in drawing out the epistemological and semantic significance of the *homoousion* – although he seems to be aware of the discussion (cf. 85).

[147] T. F. Torrance, *Theology in Reconstruction*, London, 1965, 36. This conception is reflected in the Nicene Creed where it is asserted that the Son is 'of one being with the Father', *homoousios to patri*. As Torrance comments further, '... the actual hinge of meaning and apprehension is the Incarnation and in the Incarnation the identity between the Being of Christ and the Being of God – that is, the *homoousion*. Apart from the *homoousion* there is no real connection between our human knowing and speaking of God, and God himself in his own reality and

It is here that the distinction between *theological* statements and *mythological* statements becomes particularly relevant. Without an ontological grounding of analogical affirmations concerning the Being and nature of God, theological statements cannot be distinguished from mythological statements, that is, statements projected non-cognitively and groundlessly (i.e. without *logos* or *ratio*) on to the Ineffable and Unknowable at a point where intellectual honesty would require an attitude of open agnosticism. Again, T. F. Torrance refers to Athanasius' distinction between *muthologein* which is *kat'epinoian* and *theologein* which is *kata dianoian*.[148] The former derives from human speculation independently of God's concrete and specific Self-accommodation and as such, as Athanasius perceives, has no real and ultimate validity or justification. The latter is grounded in the Being of God as God gives himself to be known '*kata physin* and *alethos*'[149] in space and time in the person of the Word of God and by the Spirit – and where crucially the *homoousion* is affirmed of both the Word and the Spirit, as his letters to Serapion make so clear. This provided in Athanasius' mind the sole, possible ground of knowledge of the ineffable God.

Alasdair Heron summarises the key epistemological issues here between Athanasius and Arius in a way that, at least in one respect, comes close to expressing something of Barth's fears concerning the proponents of the *analogia entis* – namely that it risks replacing reverent theological description with anthropological projection.

> If one takes seriously Arius' conception of the divine being, it is hard to see how anyone could know anything about God at all. By a curious irony, on which Athanasius was not slow to remark, Arius seemed to possess a good deal of privileged information. But where had he got it from? Athanasius was in no doubt about the source: the Arians had

nature. Hence in formulating the *homoousion* the fathers were penetrating down into the depth of the divine logic of grace, and tracing its reference or ana-logic back to its source in the eternal Logos in the Being of God.' (39–40.)

[148] Cf. T. F. Torrance, op. cit., 35 and 48, and also his exposition of the theology of Athanasius in his book *Theology in Reconciliation*, London, 1965.

[149] *Theology in Reconstruction*, 35.

fabricated this concept of the divine being out of their own minds, thus making their own intellects the measure of ultimate reality and assigning to Christ, the Word made flesh, the place which their minds could make for him.[150]

This reflects the extent to which consideration of the possibility and validity of talk about God is governed ultimately by the ontology or cosmology underlying our theological statements. It is not surprising that Eberhard Jüngel's comments contrasting Barth and Bultmann should parallel comments that Torrance makes comparing Athanasius and Arius.[151] In *Gottes Sein ist im Werden*, Jüngel argues,

> Paradoxical as it may sound, the doctrine of the Trinity in Barth's theology (1932) has the same function as the programme of demythologising in the theology of Rudolf Bultmann. ... If we understand Bultmann's programme as the concern for appropriate speech about God (and therewith about man) and if we view the fulfilment of this concern as a concern not to objectify God or let him be objectified as an It or He ... then we shall not fail to recognise a conspicuous parallelism to the significance which Barth attributes (and gives) to the doctrine of the Trinity.[152]

He then goes on to argue that, 'the doctrine of the Trinity, according to Barth, has precisely the task of comprehending the 'subject of revelation' as the subject' that 'remains *indissolubly* subject'.[153]

It is also interesting to note a certain parallelism between the development in Barth's thought and that of Athanasius. There is clearly an Apollinarian tendency in Barth's revelation model in Volume One of the *Church Dogmatics*. Just as Athanasius' weakness in his *De Incarnatione* was his failure to give sufficiently explicit theological weighting to the humanity of Christ, this may be seen also to have been Barth's weakness

---

[150] 'Homoousios with the Father' in *The Incarnation*, ed. T. F. Torrance, Edinburgh, 1981, 70.

[151] Cf. also A. I. C. Heron's parallel critique of 'modern Arianism in Britain' as exemplified in the advocacy of demythologisation of the doctrine of the incarnation by the authors of the book *The Myth of God Incarnate* (1977), ibid., 75.

[152] Eng. trans., *The Doctrine of the Trinity*, 21–2.

[153] Ibid., 22–3.

in his earlier thought. What Barth's early interpretation of revelation required to expound with much greater depth was what Athanasius was to emphasise so impressively in 'Discourse Two' (as also in Discourses One and Four) of his *Four Discourses against the Arians*, namely the *priesthood* of the Logos. The epistemic and semantic implications of Christ's *priesthood* constitute the primordial condition of humanity's participative communion with God to the extent that this includes our epistemic capacities in a creative and re-creative act.

The *Vestigia Dei* Question Revisited

It is necessary for us to return now to the question presented at the start of this chapter, concerning whether and how we may conceive of the grounds of a unified interpretation of the Being of God and of the created order. As we suggested, this question is essential if we are to consider any continuity conceived in personal (or personalistic) terms between the communion of the Trinity and contexts of human communion either within or outwith the Body of Christ.

Prior to our patristic 'aside' we hinted that this matter concerns the question of an 'atonement' between God and humanity, and it would seem that the event of the 'at-one-ment' has epistemic and methodological implications which take a different form from, (a) that of a unified ontology conceived as a human project, on the one hand, and (b) those accompanying approaches which operate from the postulation of an absolute disjunction (or disassociation), on the other. A proper theological emphasis on epistemic atonement conceived in participative terms, and as this includes semantic atonement, may be seen to contrast with the epistemologically motivated drive toward unification at the ontological level, on the one hand, or a postulated, prior ontological bifurcation, on the other. The issue here relates to what may be described (in the light of our patristic aside) as the possibility of what one might term, if somewhat clumsily, a 'Logontology' stemming from the given 'Logontic' impetus to theology (as opposed to *noetic* or *ontic*). If theology operates from such a *Logontic* ground which is not conceived as belonging either to some predetermined ontic set of 'beings' participating in 'being' (and quantified therefore in terms of a prior ontology) or noetic set of concepts (conceived with appeal to a foundationalist epistemology), then this allows the subject of revelation to remain 'indissolubly subject' (Jüngel) in the theological enterprise. The first question is whether this does not offer a *via tertia* between what Zizioulas has described as the classical alternatives of ontological monism on the one hand and a Gnostic dualism ('the Gnostic gulf between God and the world') on the other.[154] The second question is, however, whether the approach prescribed by this allows for the kind of semantic continuity between the divine and human realms which means theology and the Christian faith can 'make sense'.

The notion of *vestigia Dei* may be seen here as representing the 'ontologically monistic' drive on the part of Western theology to offer a unified interpretation which integrates the divine and human realms. This it does by suggesting a correlation and connection between created forms and the Being and nature of God, but it does so with recourse to clusters of (triadic) metaphors suggesting 'traces' or 'reflections' or 'echoes' – or, indeed, in the case of the weight–number–measure triad, intra-categorial analogical 'parallels'. Such triads, as Barth points out, may be picked from a whole variety of domains – nature, culture, history, religion and the human soul.[155] Which particular metaphor is implied depends on the nature of the particular *vestigium* to which reference is being made. Some examples, notably the spring, stream and lake triad, would appear to be illustrations rather than arguments for a vestigial connection. Where the concept is used to denote some form of integral connection, the concept itself leaves open the question as to whether these 'traces' are necessarily embedded (as suggested by the Thomistic principle of the necessary similarity between effects

---

[154] *Being as Communion*, New York, 1985, 16ff.
[155] *C. D.* 1. 1, 336–8 (*K. D.* 1. 1, 355–7).

and their agent) or deliberately 'inscribed'[156] into the created order as Calvin suggested.[157]

Barth's discussion reflects his perception that the central question for theological language concerns whether we can operate in the light of the assumption of a *vestigium Dei* immanent in created forms of conceptuality, thought and semantic expression. Such *vestigia* may be conceived either as direct traces in the created world of human conceptuality and thought forms, or as an indirect and derivative possibility stemming from the fact that theological language emerges from reference to the material world or, more precisely, non-conceptual created reality. He writes, 'one may say that the problem at issue is that of theological language, which even though it can only be the language of the world, must still believe at root, cost what it will, that contrary to the natural capabilities of this language it can and should speak of God's revelation in this language as theological language.'[158]

It is particularly pertinent to this discussion that Barth chose to examine this question immediately prior to his discussion

---

[156] There is no need to go into the ramifications raised by the suggestion that if they are inscribed then this implies a prior inscribability – and hence an inherent natural potential on the part of the created order. Our response to this kind of question should be clear from what has been said earlier.

[157] The *opus Dei* (or the *opificium Dei*) has impressed on it the signs of the workmanship of its *Opifex*: 'on each of His works He has inscribed unmistakable marks of His glory'. (*Institutes of Christian Religion*, 1. v. 1 (*C.R.* II, 41).) This is a free act on the part of God. As T. H. L. Parker comments on Calvin's exposition, 'Thus, in creating the universe God made it a representation of Himself. This He did freely; He need not have left these marks upon His work. For they are not like the adventitious evidences that enable us to "date" or "place" a poem or concerto ... the *certae notae* are deliberately inscribed by God upon His workmanship for the purpose of making Himself known to men.' (*The Doctrine of the Knowledge of God*, Edinburgh, 1952, 18-19.) What is more, given its divinely-bestowed, created capacities the human mind *would* have been able, therefore, to come to knowledge of God from the created order '*si integer stetisset Adam*'. (*Inst.*, 1. ii. 1 (*C.R.* II, 34).) However, as Barth points out in *Nein!*, this phrase is definitive in the understanding of the early chapters of the *Institutio*. (Cf. Parker, 27.)

[158] *C. D.* 1. 1, 341 (*K. D.* 1. 1, 360). Also, *C. D.* 1. 1, 344 (*K. D.* 1. 1, 364): '... we have also indicated its basis [i.e. that of the hunt for *vestigia trinitatis*] in the problem of theological language'.

of triune personhood. And it is necessary, although not for this reason alone, to examine Barth's arguments before going on to evaluate his discussion of triune personhood.

What is the essential thrust of Barth's concerns? The primary question which one may expect to be asked concerns the theoretical plausibility of the notion of the *vestigium Dei.* Barth is not concerned with any *a priori* investigation as to whether there may or could be 'something in it'. His preferred question is not the theoretical one as to whether or not there may be such traces – indeed, he asks 'Why should there not be something in it?' For Barth 'the only question is what'.[159] In other words, we should simply 'look and see', and give theological consideration to the merits of any such claim and any underlying assumptions to which it is committed.

The issues raised here are interpreted by Barth as leading us to the heart of the question about the nature of theological semantics. For this reason we must quote him at some length:

> Theology and the Church, and even the Bible itself, speak no other language than that of this world which is shaped in form and content by the creaturely nature of the world and also conditioned by the limitations of humanity: the language in which man as he is, as sinful and corrupt man, wrestles with the world as it encounters him and as he sees and tries to understand it. (Die Sprache, **in der** der Mensch, wie er nun einmal ist … sich mit der Welt, wie sie ihm begegnet und wie er sie sieht und zu verstehen vermag, auseinanderzusetzen versucht.)[160] The Bible, the Church and theology undoubtedly speak this language on the presupposition that there might be something in it, namely, that in this language God's revelation might be referred to, witness might be given, God's Word might be proclaimed, dogma might be formulated and declared. The only question is whether this possibility is to be understood as that of the language and consequently of the world or man, or whether it is to be regarded as a venture which is, as it were, ascribed to the language, and consequently to the world or man, from without, so that it is not really the possibility of the language, the world, or man, but the possibility of revelation, if in the form of concepts and ideas that exist elsewhere and independently,

---

[159] *C. D.* 1. 1, 339 (*K. D.* 1. 1, 358).
[160] *K. D.* 358 (bold print mine).

in correspondence with the created world and the capacity of man as he attempts an understanding of this world, we really come to speak of revelation and therefore of the Trinity, of the remission of sins and eternal life, i.e., of things for which man's speech as such has no aptitude whatever. Now it cannot be said that the discoverers of *vestigia trinitatis* have made this distinction.[161]

Two features of Barth's argument are of crucial importance for our discussion. First, he sees language as that from within which man wrestles in order to 'attempt an understanding of this world'. He does not operate on the assumption of some prior non-semantically-mediated thought to which words are simply attached. Barth's semantics are not incompatible with the Hintikkas' notion of language as universal medium[162] – that language mediates the world to us and is thus the place of our engagement with it. This will be seen to be significant on account of the substantial implications here for the redefinition of analogy. Second, Barth is concerned to obviate the belief that theological expression is grounded in the 'correspondence' ('Entsprechung') between language on the one hand and the created world and human capacities on the other, and that there is an inherent capacity for correspondence on the part of these with the triune being of God. This suggests that Barth is not 'referentialist' in his interpretation of meaning, that is, he would not interpret the referential capacity of terms (analogical or otherwise) as constitutive of their meaning.

In contraposition to views which assume some kind of vestigial capacity, he wishes to affirm that 'the true *vestigium trinitatis* is the form assumed by God in revelation'.[163] Yet again, Barth's concern is with divine freedom on the one hand (which means that if there is a 'correspondence' it will be a *corresponding*), and with preserving a dynamic interpretation of God on the other (which means further that such a corresponding will be a dynamic and 'act-ual'

---

[161] *C. D.* 1. 1, 339 (*K. D.* 1. 1, 358–9).
[162] Merrill B. and Jaakko Hintikka, *Investigating Wittgenstein*, Oxford, 1986
[163] *C. D.* 1. 1, 339 (*K. D.* 1. 1, 359).

corresponding where God is freely identifying himself with what we might call the 'correspondent' – a 'correspondent' which is only such in so far as it is given to be, and actively sustained in its being as 'correspondent' by God).

Earlier we referred to Jung Young Lee's discussion of Barth's conception of analogy and its essentially dynamic character. The same applies here in that any static notion of a trace which does not fully reflect (or, worse, which excludes) a proper recognition of the fact that such semantic participation on the part of any facet of the created order in the divine life must be by way of the dynamic and free Being-in-act of God, may not be considered a 'trace' or reflection of the divine life – it cannot reflect or 'correspond' in any way with the God who is *essentially* free, who must be interpreted as Lord in His revelation and whose Being *is* in his free act. If a *vestigium* is a *vestigium Dei*, then these essential features of God *should* be held forth in and through the respective *vestigium.*

It poses no surprise, therefore, that, for Barth, we are brought back to his 'realisation that the true *vestigium trinitatis* is the form assumed by God in revelation'.[164] The trace, echo, reflection and parallels of the divine nature are to be found in God's free and dynamic presence in the person of Christ and the revealed Word. Here we have reflected, although never 'captured', the free and dynamic presence of God.

Arguing that for the Fathers true apprehension of the *vestigium trinitatis* was only on the presupposition of reve-lation, *trinitate posita*, he suggests that the original intention had been not so much to find *vestigia trinitatis in creatura* as *vestigia creaturae in trinitate*. In other words, the concern was not so much an 'apologetic' one as a 'polemical' one, not so much an attempt to demonstrate the possibility of revelation in the world of human reason, but to establish the actual possibilities of the world of human reason as the scene of revelation. They were not, in other words, trying to explain the Trinity by the world, but rather trying to explain the world

[164] Ibid.

by the Trinity in order to be able to speak about the Trinity in this world. Their approach was an expression of the confidence that the Trinity can reflect itself in things. Their various 'more or less felicitous discoveries of *vestigia* were an expression of this confidence, not of confidence in the capacity of reason for revelation but of confidence in the power of revelation over reason'.[165]

The real danger of this kind of approach, however, is the risk that will always attend such an enterprise, namely that of a subtle reversal in which we find

> polemics becoming apologetics, the attempt to fashion theological language becoming a surrender of theological language in favour of some alien speech, the assumed and asserted intelligibility of revelation becoming an original commensurability of reason with revelation, the synthetic 'God into the world' becoming an analytic 'God in the world,' the claiming of the world by revelation becoming a claiming of revelation by the world, and the discovered intimation becoming a self-conceived proof.[166]

Barth's concern about the dangers of introducing, by way of the notion of the *vestigia*,' the idea of a second root of the doctrine of the Trinity' immediately raises the question again of the risk of an ontology of personhood underlying the semantics of the term 'person' in such a way that this notion becomes just such a second root in a manner which undermines at the semantic level the free, specific and concrete particularity of God and, therefore, undermines the possibility of the radical redefinition of the notion *for the sake of personhood*, that is, for the sake of the fulfilment of 'personhood' in a manner which crucially *transcends* the conceptual potential of a prior (and *ergo* pre-conditioning) 'personalist' apperception. The question that emerges, therefore, concerns whether the immanence of personal communion is best served by an approach informed by the *predication* of personhood of the members of the Trinity to the extent that this may lead to the endorsement precisely of a second root conceived

---

[165] *C. D.* 1. 1, 341 (*K. D.* 1. 1, 360).
[166] *C. D.* 1. 1, 341 (*K. D.* 1. 1, 361).

anthropologically. This would involve a consequent reversal of the theological order and the risk of a second root becoming a second *root* which assumes equal or, indeed, primary importance. It is precisely this which (as we shall argue in chapter 4) is witnessed in LaCugna's theology, if not ultimately in that of Zizioulas. And, as we shall suggest, this threatens to eclipse a proper *theological* conception of precisely those dynamics central to the trinitarian realisation of personal communion.

The need for obviating such methodological confusion is expressed by Daniel Hardy when he argues (albeit in unnecessarily 'impersonal' language), the 'self-determination of God' generates an 'information density' with which we are presented in the second person of the Trinity. This places us under a 'pressure of interpretation', a pressure which 'demands the differentiation of God from the sum of the domains of the world'.[167] The pressure of interpretation must always be from Christ as the 'information density' of the Trinity to the sum of other domains. This essential obligation in the order of theological interpretation can subtly be circumvented if an ontology accompanies a term predicated of God or any aspect of God.

Colin Gunton has spoken of 'a series of concentric circles' concentrated on the centre, namely, 'the personal act of divine self-revelation which is Jesus Christ',[168] and, in his recent book on revelation, he writes, 'There are varieties of mediation, but there is one Lord. When we speak of revelation, we are speaking first of all of Jesus Christ, who thus forms the focus of all that we have to say. The centre of our attention is the glory of God in the face of Jesus Christ ...'[169]

The issue at stake here concerns whether *vestigia Dei* do not risk subverting this 'pressure' of interpretation, 'concentricity' or 'focus of mediation' to the extent that the conceptions of Triunity which may supposedly be found in the world (be it in

---

[167] 'Christ and Creation', in *The Incarnation*, ed. T. F. Torrance, Edinburgh, 1981, 105.

[168] The Warfield Lectures, Princeton Theological Seminary, 1993 (unpublished manuscript), 58.

[169] *A Brief Theology of Revelation: The 1993 Warfield Lectures*, Edinburgh, 1995, 125.

either logical, mathematical or indeed personal relations) may fail to take seriously the 'godness' of the One whom Holy Scripture calls God. To take Gunton's metaphor further, if there are other circles of mediation generating waves from other centres, be they conceptual, ontological, metaphysical, semantic, or epistemological, these will generate cross-currents which threaten to undermine the concentricity demanded by the Logos. The effect may be the generation of dissonance and a confused patterning of thought unless some means is produced to show an intrinsic consonance between the relevant *foci.* If this is to be done, the immediate question is: with reference to which centre or focus are the relevant consonances to be defined? This brings us back to the central, and quite straightforward, issue underlying the entire debate. If we deny the fundamental *singularity* of this source of 'pressure' or concentricity, then we cannot avoid finding ourselves struggling with the regress of an infinite series of 'third man' questionings which, if they are not to be resolved in the trinitarian event of the revelation of the Logos, will ultimately find a thoroughly unsatisfactory and Cartesian resolution in the singularity which characterises the mind of the human subject. We revert to the *muthologein kat'epinoian* of the Arian position.

Barth challenges the concept of *vestigia trinitatis* by asking: 'did it not fail what it was meant to prove, and if that was not perceived, did it not really lead away from what it was meant to prove? Was not the proof of the Trinity along these lines bound to lead logically to a denial of the trinitarian God of Holy Scriptures because it proved and put in His place a God constituted *totaliter aliter*?'[170] Citing examples that are topical in contemporary interreligious dialogue, he refers not only to the Babylonian triads but also to the Brahman Trimurti which he interprets as formulations of a triply membered world-principle. Again, the question that emerges is: does all that is found here by way of a triadic godhead deserve to be called 'God'? Or is the focus simply an arbitrary human affinity for the number three?

[170] *C. D.* 1. 1, 342 (*K. D.* 1. 1, 361).

That this denotes, for Barth, the essential and underlying weakness of the traditional form of analogy is made clear from the following statement he makes concerning Keckermann:

> when Keckermann ... could venture to say: *quam est necessarium, hominem esse rationalem ... tam est necessarium in Dei essentia tres esse personas,* the way was prepared for this reversal. Could it be avoided once this *quam ... tam* was attempted?'[171]

If St Thomas' own qualifications of analogical statements (namely that they be *unius ad alterum* and *per prius et posterius*) sought to guard against precisely such an *Umkehrung*, the question is left open as to whether Western thought as a whole has been as careful. As is witnessed in so many different debates, the desire for an anthropocentric *Umkehrung* is the most fundamental temptation with which Western theology has had to struggle and with which it must still continue to wrestle.

Interpretation *versus* Illustration

The intention of our interpretation of Karl Barth so far has been to argue that it is Barth, rather than those who would stand in the Thomist tradition generally, who takes seriously Aquinas' central principles of theological affirmation, namely that it be *unius ad alterum* and *per prius et posterius*. Barth's fear of the reversal which is too easily introduced by the 'finders of the *vestigia trinitatis*' quite simply reflects his adherence to these methodological affirmations. What Barth fears was precisely what Aquinas also set out to oppose, namely, an approach to theological affirmation which is *per posterius et prius* as this stems from an *analogia duorum ad tertium* – the supposed analogical attribution of the number three, for example, to both the Trinity and some humanly designated *vestigium trinitatis* where the controlling determinant too easily becomes *the number three*.

The related refusal to assume ontological parallelisms between the divine and created orders means that Barth also

---

[171] *C. D.* 1. 1, 343.

insists on a radical distinction between interpretation and illustration. This he explains as follows: 'Interpretation means saying *the same thing* in other words. Illustration means saying the same thing *in other words.*'[172] Clearly, what is intended in this slightly abstruse expression of the distinction is that the latter involves conceptual parallelisms (thus reducing theological affirmation to conceptual expression) whereas the former is testimony to one reality with which there are no parallelisms but which may be articulated (or, rather, which may articulate itself) in a whole variety of different ways. It is precisely this dynamic which must characterise the theological enterprise.

That the question here yet again reflects the issue pointed out by Jung Young Lee, namely that central for Barth is the dynamism at the heart of his semantic ontology, is reflected in Barth's comment that in illustration 'We no longer trust revelation in respect of its self-evidential force' ('hinsichtlich ihrer eigenen Beweiskraft').[173] There is a 'commandeering' of language on the part of revelation in and through which God actively conditions (reconciles) the 'sense' of the terms involved.

Eberhard Jüngel stresses this powerfully, speaking of the *gain* to theological language of this revelational dynamic – the alternative to which could only be a *loss* to revelation. Relating this to Barth's concerns with regard to the pursuit of *vestigia trinitatis*, he writes,

> The problem of making such an attempt to speak theological language consists in the fact that this language 'can only be the language of the world' which, however, 'must ... at root always speak *contrary* to the natural capacity of this language, must speak of God's revelation *in* this language as *theological* language.' (*C.D.* 1.1, 341.) Revelation cannot be brought to speech 'by a possibility of logical construction' (346). In Barth's sense that would be just an *analogia entis*. But the language in which the revelation shall be able to come to speech must, 'as it were, be commandeered' (340) by revelation. Where such

---

[172] *C. D.* 1. 1, 345 (*K. D.* 1. 1, 364).
[173] Ibid.

commandeering of the language by revelation for revelation becomes event, then there is a gain to language. It consists in the fact that God as God comes to speech. Over against this, in the reverse case, one would have to speak of a loss of revelation if revelation is commandeered by language on the pattern of the *analogia entis per analogiam nominum*. This loss consists in the fact that God does not come to speech as God but as *nomen*. The antithesis of *analogia entis* and *analogia fidei* can accordingly be so characterised: *analogia entis* (*nominum*) leads to a loss of revelation; *analogia fidei* leads to a gain to language, to the possibility of theological speech about God.[174]

The appropriate relationship between revelation and language, as Jüngel endorses it, is to be conceived as *interpretation* where the 'interpretation of revelation by language is an event in which language is "commandeered" by revelation ... the interpretation of revelation is thus an act of daring which is "*demanded* of language from outside it" (339)'.[175] But to speak of an act of daring is clearly insufficient! Consequently, Jüngel adds, 'At the same time, however, this demand on language will have to be understood in such a way that revelation grants *courage* to speak of God, so that interpretation is possible.' If this courage were to be construed as a self-willed human act, if the compulsion were a human impulsiveness, the *per prius et posterius* would be displaced and the 'dynamism' would be one that was less than theological. Rather, 'the revelation of God itself is the enabling of the interpretation of revelation'.[176] The *compulsion* in the event of the interpretation of revelation (to which we referred earlier in this chapter) must clearly be explained in terms of the agency of the Holy Spirit and the divine dynamic constitutive of the Body of Christ. When this is acknowledged as involving or necessitating (as it must) a form of semantic participation as the *sine qua non* of this event, this makes it even more difficult to draw distinct lines between the dynamic at the heart of proclamation and the dynamic which is the very ground of theological interpretation. In other words, in the

---

[174] *The Doctrine of the Trinity*, 11–12.
[175] Ibid., 13.
[176] Ibid., 15.

final analysis it is not as easy as one might think to distinguish between the two 'forms of life' which constitute theological articulation and proclamation.

One final comment requires to be made here which is pertinent to the interpretation of the Triunity with recourse to the concept of the person. The dynamic which is constitutive of the whole semantic process of theological affirmation involves an open-endedness in the meaning of terms, a creativity which (as we shall explore further in the discussion of metaphor) expands and enriches language opening up new horizons in the interpretative (and hence revelatory) event. With great profundity, Jüngel takes Barth's argument still further, maintaining that,

> Interpretation protects the sameness of revelation in that it brings revelation (and only this) as revelation to speech. But where also language (*nomina*) as revelation is brought to speech along with revelation, revelation is no longer protected as revelation *and* language no longer as language. *Therefore every loss of revelation is at the same time a loss of language.* When language itself aims to be revelation it loses itself as language. But where revelation commandeers language, *the word of God* takes place. The word of God brings language to its true essence.[177]

What emerges from this debate is that 'a hermeneutic which inquires after the self-interpretation of God is in essence something different from the Aristotelian hermeneutic of signification'. The former takes more seriously the 'nature' of language, its own life and validity, its function, possibilities and potentiality, than the more static interpretation of the meanings of theological terms reflected in the traditional analogical debates where the meaning of terms was conceived in terms of some innate and inert referential capacity.

Later on we shall return to the question how seriously Barth took this potential (the potential for the dynamic enrichment of the 'language of the world') as a matter of fact in trinitarian affirmation by allowing for the extension of language which

[177] Ibid., 13–14.

is so integral to a proper understanding of the participation of the human in the divine and which, as we shall suggest, is of such profound significance for the integration of theology and theological anthropology that is demanded by the Christian concept of *koinonia*.

Does Barth escape all Forms of *Vestigia Trinitatis* and Illustration?

In chapter two we referred to Barth's adoption of certain grammatical metaphors in his exposition of the doctrine of the Trinity. We referred to his talk of a 'threefold sense' ('dreifacher Sinn') to the statement 'God reveals Himself as Lord', such that when we speak of the Trinity we are saying the same thing 'three times in three indissolubly different ways'. In this context we discussed his metaphorical appropriation of the notions *Wiederholung* and *Doppelgänger* and his exposition of the Trinity in terms of the threefold Revealer, Revelation and Revealedness. In the light of this the question requires to be asked whether Barth himself can obviate the charge of engaging in 'illustration' by recourse to models of grammatical form – the logical structure, that is, of what Rowan Williams describes as his 'expressive view of language' and 'linear model of God's trinitarian utterance'. Do we not find here subliminal *vestigia trinitatis*?

Barth was aware that this accusation might be made of at least part of his discussion. With remarkable honesty and humility he comments,

> we have to realise that when ... we sought to arrange the biblical concept of revelation under the aspects of veiling, unveiling and impartation we came remarkably close to the fatal Augustinian argument and in no sense safeguarded ourselves against the suspicion that we, too, might be using an illustration and playing a little game with a supposed *vestigium trinitatis* (that could perhaps be traced back to the little sentence 'I show myself'). In this respect did not we, too, let ourselves be buttressed, strengthened and confirmed by something other than revelation, namely, by a possibility of logical construction? In the last resort was it the Bible that spoke to us or only this possibility? Did we find the root of the doctrine of the Trinity in revelation or ultimately only this other root? We wanted to find the

root of the doctrine in revelation, not another root … But if anyone were to bring against us the charge that the real issue for us too was the other root, we could never accuse him of malice, for even with the best will in the world we could not completely or unequivocally escape the appearance that this might be so. It is as well to be clear about all this.[178]

What would appear to emerge from this is that, although there is a distinction to be made between an approach that understands itself as illustrating theological truth and that which is committed to serving the self-evidential dynamic of revelation in an act of interpretation, *it will not always be easy to delineate decisive boundaries between the two.* As Wittgenstein's 'family resemblance' argument establishes, it is possible to make clear *distinctions* and they can be distinctions of fundamental importance despite the fact that clear *boundaries* may not be drawn. The entire language event, not least the act of interpretation, is simultaneously both compromised and enriched by recourse to the pluriform, attendant associations, histories and metaphorical allusions bound up with the use of terms. Consequently, there is an inescapable 'illustrative' dimension to the whole project of theological interpretation and expression. To adopt a category from the thought of Michael Polanyi here, the fundamental issue here may be said to concern whether the illustrative dimension plays a *focal* role (i.e. is 'attended to') or a *subliminal* one (i.e. is 'distended from'). In the latter case, illustrative elements are malleable such that they may function benignly given proper epistemic objectivity – the commandeering and reconciling Self-interpretation of God. The deliberate 'focal'

---

[178] *C. D.* 1. 1, 346 (*K. D.* 1. 1, 365). See also his discussion of 'Trinity in Unity', where he says of God, 'He is the beginning without which there is no middle and no end, the middle which can be only on the basis of the beginning and without which there is no end, and the end which is based wholly and utterly on the beginning. He is the speaker without whom there is no word or meaning, the word which is the word of the speaker and the bearer of his meaning, and the meaning which is the meaning of both the speaker and his word.' And then he adds, 'But let us stay clear of the zone of *vestigia trinitatis* on which we are already trespassing.' (*C. D.* 1. 1, 364; *K. D.* 1. 1, 384.)

use of illustration, however, is risk-laden and carries subliminal consequences which can be considerably less than benign.

Vestigia Creaturae in Trinitate and Triune Personhood

A great deal has been said about the dangers of a) an ontology which seeks to bridge the distinctions between the divine and the human; b) a semantics which does not take seriously the distinction and the ordering inherent in the 'informing' of our theological language, and c) the risks of operating in terms of parallelisms and correspondences between the created realm and that of the Creator. For these reasons we appealed to Eberhard Jüngel to help in the delineation of various parallel distinctions which require to be made as, for example, a) that between essentially 'static' views of the nature of semantic reference and an appreciation of the dynamic commandeering of our language with an associated shifting in the meanings of terms and where all this, as Jüngel suggests, is intrinsic to the revelation event, and b) the distinction between the Pelagian act of illustration and the theological event of interpretation. On strictly *a posteriori* grounds we emphasised the discontinuity between our alienated and created thought forms and the dynamic reality of God, and we mentioned some of the methodological, epistemological and semantic implications of this.

However, on similar *a posteriori* grounds it is also necessary to affirm positively the radical and dynamic *continuity* between the divine and the human that is the event of Christ. To fail to admit this (for example, by virtue of affirming or postulating some infinite qualitative gulf between the divine and the human ... or, indeed, for any other reason) is to repudiate the revelation event itself. This means, as Barth suggests but does not expand, that it is indeed appropriate to speak of a *vestigium creaturae in trinitate* with respect to the trinitarian event of Self-revelation. God's Self-identification in Christ, within the created order, commits us to, indeed *demands* of us, the affirmation that the created order, to the extent that it is integral to this event, is indeed taken into the event of the triune Being of God with us.

The (logically) *post factum* implication of this is that if we are to speak of God it will be by virtue of God's creating and sustaining, by the Spirit, an essential *continuity* here in such a way that our affirmation of the personhood of Christ becomes at one and the same time the affirmation of the second person of the Triunity. There is, as it were, a drawing up or referring of our language (perceived now to reflect the Trinity) into the communion constitutive of God in and through our being brought to participate in it, in and through the Body of Christ. In this way our language can consequently, or rather 'sub-sequently' be used within the created realm in redeeming, reconciling ways that both serve and also reflect our free participation in the divine Triunity. What is implied here is what one might term a *creative continuity* which involves a semantic continuity grounded in a divine dynamic which takes the form of the redemptive commandeering of our terms and grammar to the extent that in Christ's 'becoming' our language or semantic thought forms 'become' integral to the reconciling and atoning dimension of the Christ event. As we shall see in our final chapter, this means that it is not only appropriate but also necessary to acknowledge the Wittgensteinian inclusion of language in the concept of 'world' when interpreting Paul's statement that God was in Christ reconciling the (language) *world* unto himself.

This suggests that the distinction between *literal* and *analogical* theological statements does *not* refer in the first instance to some presupposed, metaphysical gulf between God and humanity but, rather, to the *eschatological* tension between the Kingdom which is, on the one hand, *quodammodo praesens* and yet, on the other, *quodammodo absens*. This distinction only makes sense, of course, in the light of God's free decision to *be* with us in Christ. When Barth suggests a preference, therefore, for the analogy of 'extrinsic attribution' over the analogy of 'intrinsic attribution', he risks denying (paradoxically) the realised eschatological element and the very divine dynamic of revelation that he was so keen to affirm! Taken to its logical conclusion this is as problematic as the, at times, stark contrast he makes between the *analogia relationis* and the *analogia entis*.

The dynamic continuity involved here clearly does not mean, however, that we are justified in assuming statically conceived 'natural' continuities. Jesus' teaching in the Matthean account expresses the issue here with remarkable clarity. 'But you are not to be called "Rabbi", for you have only one Master and you are all brothers. And do not call anyone on earth "father", for you have one Father, and he is in heaven. Nor are you to be called "teacher", for you have one Teacher, the Christ ...'[179] It may be suggested that the midrash here exaggerates a point for the purpose of emphasis and that there was no serious suggestion that the terms 'father' or 'teacher' should no longer be used in any other context by Jesus' followers. What it *does* bring out, however, is the extent to which the use of such terms involves a discontinuity. This discontinuity denotes the semantic shift that is brought about by God's Self-revelation and the consequent liberation of these terms for new depths of meaning within the theological context – new depths of meaning which also apply in the anthropological context, as is implied by the verses which follow relating to our becoming servants, the full meaning of which is redefined by Jesus on the cross. 'The greatest among you will be your servant.'[180] What we come across at various points here are theologically obligatory (and non-private) forms of 'semantic inversion'! The 'dynamic' of this semantic inversion, moreover, is actually *intrinsic* to God's triune 'becoming'.

It is often the case, paradoxically, that the tighter the signification of the terminology used in everyday life (the more constrained, that is, the family resemblances associated with a term), the greater its potential for metaphorical extension and transformation – and so much the greater also its metaphorical capacity for 'reality depiction', to use Soskice's term.[181] The issues raised here will be explored further in the

---

[179] Mt. 23:8–10 (*New International Version*).
[180] Verse 11.
[181] As will be suggested later on, I prefer the rather more clumsy expression 'doxological, reality-participation'!

final chapter. Suffice to say, the term *Person*, we shall suggest, may be seen to be an example of the kind of term which, when used of God, serves the commandeering of language by revelation in particularly effective ways – in rather more effective ways, that is, than Barth's preferred term *Seinsweise*, whose somewhat indeterminate and amorphous nature undermines the semantic dynamic of revelation (as also the communion integral to it) and, worse, threatens to open the door to the wrong kind of subsuming of the divine within quasi-neutral, *pre-determined* conceptual classes. It will be suggested that such a move exemplifies a failure fully to appreciate the creative commandeering of language which revelation involves and which constitutes the divine dynamic ('anhypostatic' and 'enhypostatic') which is essential and, indeed, *intrinsic* to theological description at every level.

4

Triune Personhood

Karl Barth

In a chapter entitled 'The One and the Three' in his book *The Triune Identity*, Robert W. Jenson writes of Barth that he 'perceives the difference between the Hellenic quest for God ... and the gospel's proclamation that Jesus is God's quest for us ... more rigorously than any before him'.[1] It is this insight that Barth uses 'as the sole motor of trinitarian discourse'.[2]

Jenson goes on to emphasise that Barth's key statement that '*God* reveals Himself. He reveals Himself *through Himself*. He reveals *Himself*[3] serves as an essential defence against both subordinationism and modalism.[4] This is the case because the answer to all three of revelation's questions is quite simply *God*. Over and against subordinationism, there is no possibility of any answer referring to anything less than God, and over and against modalism there is no possibility of the three implied questions being amalgamated into one, since if this were the case 'the real God would remain behind revelation and we would be back on our quest'.[5] In sum, Barth's formulation of the triune structure of revelation is essential to

---

[1] Jenson adds here in brackets 'except Luther?'

[2] 'The entire doctrine of the Trinity ... is but the specification of which God it is that *can* so reveal himself as in fact happens with Christ.' (*The Triune Identity*, Philadelphia, 1982, 137.)

[3] Quoted by Jenson, ibid.

[4] Cf. *C. D.* 1. 1, 350–1 (*K. D.* 1. 1, 369–70). Here we see Barth's concern to insist on the divine unity in a manner that leaves no room either for modalism or subordinationism – or for any form of 'modern naturalism', pantheism or other influential contemporary form of 'religion'.

[5] Ibid.

213

the Gospel's alternative to religion conceived as a vain human quest for God.

Without a doctrine of a triplicity which simultaneously stresses the absolute identity of God's being in and through this triplicity, there is no grounding to the 'good news' of God's taking to himself precisely that same humanity that cannot approach him by its own efforts – since it would neither know who God is nor how to approach him. It is this perception which, at least in Jenson's view, leads to Barth's emphasis on the identity of God's Being as the revealer with God's Being as the revelation.[6] If the facticity of revelation – and not merely its content – if its very form involves a doctrine of the Trinity, is it this identity of Being which is to be the ground of the doctrine of the Triunity?

As we discussed in chapter 2, Barth articulates this unity of identity with recourse to the metaphor of a *Wiederholung*.[7] It is important to appreciate that Barth's emphasis on unity in the doctrine of God does not derive from any idealisation of mathematical or numerical oneness (as this has characterised much Western philosophy of religion), nor the idealisation of a principle of simplicity (as may be suggested by Richard Swinburne's utilisation of the dictum *simplex sigillum veri* – rightly criticised by Alvin Plantinga). Rather, his concern with unity is essentially – at least in intention – a concern with *identity*. When we meet God's revelation, or are met by the revelation of God, we are met not by part of God, nor by instantiations of the divine, but with the *Person* of God, the identical divine Subject in his singular totality. In other words, Barth's governing concern here is precisely that which leads him to affirm that what God is toward us he *is* eternally and antecedently in himself – 'God is action and relatedness

---

[6] In Barth's words, 'If the *tropos apokalupseos* is really a different one from the *tropos huparxeos* and if the *huparxis* is the real being of God, then this means that God in His revelation is not really God.' (*C. D.* 1. 1, 353; *K. D.* 1. 1, 372.)

[7] Concerning the 'triple repetition' involved here, Jenson adds, 'Only by this repetition is God so present to us that we can in no way get past him, and just this inescapability is his lordship, that is, his deity.' (Op. cit., 138.)

antecedently in himself.'[8] When God meets us we are met by God as he is in himself.

Barth's concern that the unity of God is perceived and interpreted in *a posteriori* terms and that there is no *a priorism* of numerical unity in the doctrine of God is reflected in his comment concerning the metaphor of repetition or reiteration, 'As the doctrine of the *repetitio aeternitatis in aeternitate* the doctrine of the Trinity confirms the knowledge of the unity of God, but not any knowledge of any unity of any God.'[9] The unity of which he speaks must be that demanded by the identity or nature of the object given to be spoken of and to be proclaimed.[10]

But there is a great deal more that requires to be said if Barth is to take the debate further by filling out his doctrine of God's Triunity *materially* in a manner that articulates the relationship between this 'singular' divine identity-in-reiteration and the intra-divine relations which, as the Gospel bears witness, are open for human participation in and through Christ. The question that will require to be asked here is whether Jenson's comment that Barth's contribution to the 'required new trinitarian analysis is not so great as might be expected ...'.[11] For all Barth sought to pick the eyes out of the traditional definitions of the divine Triunity, the

---

[8] Ibid. This is reflected in Barth's perception that the doctrine of the threeness of God is to be interpreted as referring not to 'three instances of one deity' but 'three events of one deity' (Jenson).

[9] *C. D.* 1. 1, 353 (*K. D.* 1. 1, 373).

[10] Any appeal of the numerical 'one' is as trivial and irrelevant to the doctrine of the Trinity as the numerical 'three'. As Gunton comments concerning the 'famous and futile quest for analogies of the Trinity in the created world', their 'weakness is their employment as attempts to illustrate the divine Trinity: the world is used to throw light on God, rather than the other way round, so that attention falls on irrelevancies like the number three rather than on the personal nature of the triune God' (*Persons, Divine and Human*, ed. Christoph Schwöbel and Colin E. Gunton, Edinburgh, 1991, 55). Precisely the same can happen with the number one but in a slightly less obvious manner due to the inherent appeal of the number one, namely the appeal of simplicity – the tacit assumption that *simplex sigillum veri* (Swinburne). No such appeal attaches to the number three!

[11] Jenson, op. cit., 138. That it is my judgement that Jenson's own solution is problematic for similar reasons should become clear.

question one is required to ask is whether he did enough to explore the nature of the triune communion in a manner that binds together the other central doctrines of the faith and, further still, whether facets of his own approach do not reverberate against such an outworking.

Moltmann has argued that Barth 'uses a non-trinitarian concept of the unity of the one God – that is to say, the concept of the identical subject'.[12] Given LaCugna's emphasis (prior to her exploration of triune personhood) that 'theological reflection on the nature of God is inseparable from [the] theology of grace, theological anthropology, christology, pneumatology, and ecclesiology',[13] what is required to be established in dialogue with Barth and in critical assessment of his thought is whether he has provided a sufficiently integrative interpretation of the relations of the divine Triunity to establish, as is necessary, the essential grammar of these other doctrines whose compass extends beyond that of the doctrine of revelation.

The One and the Three in Barth

Barth's discussion of the unity of the Trinity, 'Unity in Trinity', is comparatively brief and, significantly, *precedes* his discussion 'Trinity in Unity'. What soon becomes clear is that for Barth the Trinity is the name of *a* ('eines') single being ('Einzigen'), that is, the name 'of the one and only Willer and Doer whom the Bible calls God'.[14] Consequently, the 'presupposition and goal of the church' with respect to the doctrine of the Trinity is 'the doctrine of the unity of God, of the divine *monarchia* ...'[15]

The controlling theme throughout Barth's discussion is his equation of the Lordship of God with the essence of God and, therefore, with what the Church has referred to as God's

---

[12] *The Trinity and the Kingdom of God: The Doctrine of God* (Eng. trans. by Margaret Kohl), London, 1981, 144.
[13] Catherine Mowry LaCugna, *God for Us: The Trinity and Christian Life*, New York, 1991, 231.
[14] *C. D.* 1. 1, 348 (*K. D.* 1. 1, 368).
[15] *C. D.* 1. 1, 349 (*K. D.* 1. 1, 368).

deitas, the divine *ousia, essentia, natura* and *substantia.*[16] The
God who addresses us, be it as Yahweh dwelling on Sinai, or
the Father and Son as they are distinguished in the New
Testament, is to be conceived, therefore, as a single Thou,
'who meets man's I and unites Himself to this I as the
indissoluble Subject and thereby and therein reveals Himself
to him as his God'.[17] There is no sense, therefore, in which the
Christian faith has three objects. 'Three objects of faith would
mean three gods. But the so-called "persons" in God are in no
sense three gods.'[18] At the same time, Barth is also concerned
to stress the personal nature of the divine unity, in that
threeness is not in any sense a 'threeness of essence', it is a
threefold repetition of the single divine person.[19]

To summarise the structure of his argument in Barth's own
words, therefore,

> The triunity of God does not mean threefold deity either in the sense
> of a plurality of gods or in the sense of the existence of a plurality of
> individuals or parts within the one Godhead ... The idea we are
> excluding is that of a mere unity of kind or a mere collective unity,
> and the truth we are emphasising is that of the numerical unity of the
> essence of the 'persons', when in the first instance we employ the
> concept of repetition to denote the 'persons'. It is as well to note at
> this early stage that what we to-day call the 'personality'
> ('Persönlichkeit') of God belongs to the one unique essence of God
> which the doctrine of the Trinity does not seek to triple but rather to
> recognise in its simplicity.[20]

But what Barth now requires to explain is whether his
solution does not open the door to risks of a different kind
from subordinationism or modalism but which may also have

[16] Cf. *C. D.* 1. 1, 349–51. 'The concept of equality of essence or substance
(*homoousia, consubstantialis*) in the Father, Son and Spirit is thus at every point to
be understood also and primarily in the sense of identity of substance. Identity
of substance implies the equality of substance of "the persons".' (351).

[17] This forms part of the bold-print précis at the top of the chapter, *C. D.* 1. 1,
348 (*K. D.* 1. 1, 367).

[18] *C. D.* 1. 1, 349 (*K. D.* 1. 1, 369).

[19] 'The name of Father, Son and Spirit means that God is the one God in
threefold repetition ...' *C. D.* 1. 1, 350; (*C. D.* 1.1, *K. D.* 1. 1, 369.)

[20] *C. D.* 1. 1, 350 (*K. D.* 1. 1, 370).

damaging consequences, not least for integrating the theologies of revelation and communion.

Barth's comparatively brief discussion is heavily oriented throughout, as one might expect, around metaphors relating to the divine Lordship (which is the section's controlling motif), and those of God's meeting or encountering humankind. These concern: a) the 'meeting' ('entgegentreten') of the divine Thou and the human I; b) the 'binding' ('verbinden') of the divine Thou and the human I; c) God's indissoluble subjectivity; and d) the 'singularity' of God – which is arguably a metaphor given its various and diverse rules of use in the human context.[21] And, as we have already mentioned, the term 'Trinity' is conceived accordingly as the 'name' of a ('eines') single being.[22]

Although metaphors of the kind listed have a place of enormous importance and prominence in Scripture, such a

---

[21] Two qualifications in Barth's favour must be made here.

1) First, he is quite clear when discussing 'Trinity in Unity' that 'The unity of God confirmed in the doctrine of the Trinity is not to be confused with singularity or isolation. ... Singularity and isolation are limitations necessarily connected with the concept of numerical unity in general. The numerical unity of the revealed God does not have these limitations.' (*C. D.* 1. 1, 354; *K. D.* 1. 1, 373.) Clearly, Barth is aware that there is a risk of projecting too literal a conception of singularity on to God and subsuming God under some numerical class concept – something which I believe he does not sufficiently avoid. He is also fully aware of the distinction between unity and singularity and that we do not base our conception of divine unity on some preconceived concept of divine singularity. However, it is not clear that he is completely consistent here as his conception of the divine singularity does seem to influence his development of the notion of Triunity.

b) Second, Barth is also clear that the numerical concepts are used of God metaphorically. 'It is true of numerical concepts in the doctrine of the Trinity generally that *haec sancta trinitas, quae unus et verus est Deus, nec recedit a numero, nec capitur numero ... In divinis significant (termini numerales) illa de quibus dicuntur*, they are to be understood metaphorically, they do not posit quantity in God, and in the last resort they merely imply negations.' (*C. D.* 1. 1, 354.) Barth is correct in suggesting, of course, that they do not posit quantity in God, but there is a reality-depicting dimension to their metaphorical use that clearly transcends the merely negative. Perhaps if Barth had seen this he might have been happier with a use of threeness, i.e. with respect to divine personhood, which would have had a more constructive referential capacity than his understanding of metaphor may have allowed!

[22] *C. D.* 1. 1, 348 (*K. D.* 1. 1, 368)

list is one-sided and far from comprehensive. The question immediately arises as to whether a rather more complex 'braiding' of metaphors is not necessary to articulate the dynamic Reality of God as he embraces humankind and re-presents humanity, in and through the revelation event, to himself and in himself in a manner which is considerably more complex and open than may be suggested by his 'meeting' us as Lord or 'binding' us to himself as Lord in an exercise of the divine freedom.

The literalism, moreover, in Barth's talk of 'singularity' generates a tension. This is reflected in his bold print thesis or précis at the start of the chapter. He wishes to stress first that the God who reveals himself according to Scripture is One in three distinctive ('eigentümlichen') modes of being subsisting in their mutual relations ('in ihren Beziehungen untereinander bestehenden Seinsweisen'): Father, Son and Holy Spirit. However, he also wishes to insist, 'It is thus that He is the Lord, i.e., the Thou who meets man's I and unites Himself to this I as the indissoluble Subject and thereby and therein reveals Himself to him as his God.'[23]

At the very least we are presented with a straining of compatibility between the notions of distinctive mutual relations and the customary 'grammar' associated with the divine 'Thou' or 'I'. This requires some explanation, if not resolution, as the tension here is not of the kind which serves positively some form of metaphorical depiction or articulation of reality. Further to this, Barth's reference to the Trinity as 'the name of a single being' comes closer than is helpful to using the term 'single' in a manner which threatens to subsume God within a class of 'single beings' – that is, where singularity is conceived with reference to its application within our own sphere of existence and where the principles of individuation are the 'particularising' dimensions of space and time. The question that immediately emerges is why there is no consideration of the possibility that reference may be made to what Peter Brunner refers to as a 'divine "we"'? He writes, 'The wonder of God's inner trinitarian life is that the

---

[23] Ibid.

numerically single personal "I" of the one being that God is ...
has his being only in the true community of a personal
"we"'.... The basic meaning of the begetting of the Son is that
God posits community in himself.[24]

What Barth's conception of unity fails to take due cognisance
of is the extent to which the New Testament accounts make it
difficult to avoid affirming that God is a Thou to himself and
an I in relation to himself, and that this eternal mutuality is
opened to the world so that we are brought into communion
within the union not of *a* 'we' but of *the* one, eternal and
primordial We – 'The Father and I (i.e. "we") are one.' There
is, after all, a substantial grammatical difference between a)
'The Father and I are one', and b) 'The Father and I are
single' – or, indeed, as Barth's conception of identity would
suggest might be said, 'The Father and I is/am one.' Greater
argumentation is required if Barth is to interpret the doctrine
of the Trinity in such a way that there is no distinction to be
made between the singular identity implied by the phrase 'I
am' and that being affirmed by the sentence 'The Father and
I are one'. The notion of God as an indissoluble, single subject
is not required by Christian monotheism[25] (from which we
would certainly not wish to depart) and fails of itself to allow
sufficiently for the kind of distinctions which require to be
made here.

That Barth is at least notionally aware of the issue here
(even if he fails consistently to work through the implications
of it) *may* be implied by a comment in the section entitled
'Trinity in Unity'.

[24] Unpublished Heidelberg Lectures, Autumn, 1954 (quoted in Jenson, op.
cit., 147).

[25] For a detailed discussion of the extent to which the doctrine of the Trinity is
the positive condition for a consistent monotheism, cf. W. Pannenberg, 'Die
Subjektivität Gottes und die Trinitätslehre', *Kerygma und Dogma*, 23, 1977.
   Barth is unambiguously clear throughout his discussion (*C.D.* 1. 1, 351ff.) in
a way that Karl Rahner *may* not be, that monotheism stresses divine unity – and
not what we might term a 'monadic' conception of God. The doctrine of the
Trinity and monotheism are thus two sides of the same coin. Cf. Rahner's
derogatory reference to the 'mere monotheism' of many Christians in *The Trinity*
(Eng. trans. by Joseph Donceel), London, 1970, 10–11.

He writes,

> The unity of God confirmed in the doctrine of the Trinity is not to be confused with singularity or isolation ('Einzelheit oder Einsamkeit') ... Singularity and isolation are limitations necessarily connected with the concept of numerical unity in general. The numerical unity of the revealed God does not have these limitations.[26]

However, in the light of his ensuing explanation it becomes clear that what Barth is seeking to offset is primarily what one might term the *external* risks of singularity, namely the apparent requirement and precondition that singularity be defined with respect to the existence of other extrinsic beings. He writes,

> God is One, but not in such a way that as such He needs a Second and then a Third in order to be One, nor as though He were alone and had to do without a counterpart, and therefore again ... not as though he could not exist without the world and man ... In Himself these limits of what we otherwise regard as unity are already set aside. In Himself His unity is neither singularity nor isolation.[27]

Intimations of Barth's Interpretation of Personhood

It is precisely here that Barth introduces the whole question of triune personhood, and he does so in a context which suggests that clarification requires an appeal to the distinction between *Deus ad extra* and *Deus ad intra*. Whereas it is often suggested that there is a modalist tinge in Barth reflected here,[28] we would argue that, although the outcome may echo certain features of modalism, the essential problem is a different one. It concerns at root *an inadequate integration of the enhypostatic movement* represented by the incarnation – and, in particular, the vicarious and priestly roles of Christ –

---

[26] *C. D.* 1. 1, 354 (*K. D.* 1. 1, 373).
[27] Ibid.
[28] E. P. Meijering, for example, writes, 'Schliesslich rückt Barths Betonung der Einheit in der Dreiheit und seine Ersetzung des Wortes "Person" durch Seinsweise in die Nähe des Sabellianismus ...' (*Von den Kirchenvätern zu Karl Barth*, Amsterdam, 1993, 57.)

with the doctrine of the Trinity. This relates to a further failure to offer a sufficient integration of this dynamic with an affirmation of the identity of the immanent and economic Trinities. The principle of integrity, which, as we have seen, Barth is so keen to affirm (i.e. the *a posteriori* perception of the integrity of the divine Being as this is intrinsic to the event of revelation), requires that *what God is eternally and antecedently in himself he is toward us* and *what God is toward us he is eternally and antecedently in himself.* Therefore, where God is deemed to have his being *in se* as a mutuality of love, what God is *in se* he is *ex se* in such a manner that this becomes the very ground of our participation in God – God recreates us (i.e. we are 'reborn from above', as Zizioulas will be seen to emphasise) in order to be taken to participate in the 'mutuality' of the intra-divine communion (*theosis*).

This has substantial ramifications not least for the doctrine of communal or participatory knowing and, therefore, for the doctrine of revelation itself. What Rowan Williams described as a formulation of the Trinity in terms of an expressive view of language fails to take sufficient account of the extent to which theological knowledge (what Barth holds to derive from the context of the divine address in revelation) emerges in the context of communal participation where one is brought to participate in the 'being addressed' of the One who is addressed for us and in the one response of the One who makes the 'once and for all' valid response to this address on our behalf. Attributing to the Holy Spirit the role or function of Revealedness is insufficient. The vicarious faithfulness – as this includes faith – of Christ (so critical to Paul's argument concerning justification, if faith is not to be conceived as a work) and the continuing priesthood of Christ (as interpreted by the author of the Epistle to the Hebrews), conceived in terms of its enhypostatic dynamic, requires to be taken into account here. This is essential if the grace of the triune God is to be conceived in terms of the full 'vitality' of its perichoretic energy, that is, as denoting the two-way movement grounded in the mutuality intrinsic to the Triunity and opened to humanity in the revelation event. The movement here is one which involves a simultaneous 'ebb and flow' and resulting 'energetic congruence' (Hardy[29]), a dynamic personal co-presence, that is, which takes the form of a simultaneous and participative drawing and meeting, a vicarious presenting of the human person to the Father and the Father to the human person in and through Christ by the Spirit. And it is in and through this that humanity is presented with 'God for us', where this 'for us' takes the form of a personal 'taking of our place', an event in which the Triunity is perichoretically present 'in us' – where this communion becomes *'intrinsic'* to us to the extent that we are 'in Christ' and he in us. It is this dynamic which stands at the heart of the Lord's Supper and which is a considerably richer one than may be communicated with recourse to a unidirectional model of singular address by an irreducibly singular subject. It is also one that is essential in an adequately integrative doctrine of revelation.

What requires in particular to be emphasised with regard to the nature of revelation is that it takes the 'mind of Christ' to know the Father – no one knows the Father except the Son and those to whom the Son gives to know him.[30] When the Son reveals the Father to a person this revealing is considerably more than the heuristic bridging of an epistemic gap by way of a 'revealedness' which is identified with the Spirit. The event requires to be explained in more radically personal categories. We are taken to share in the Son's personal communion with the Father in and through the personal agency of the Spirit. Theologically this should be interpreted as an ecclesial event in which the eucharist is inseparable from the proclamation of the Word. The epistemic communication that takes place is simply one dimension of the communion into which we are reconciled to participate. Furthermore, the revelation event is provisional, incomplete, through a mirror darkly. It is fully 'realised' in the Son alone and only open to us, therefore, to the extent that the agency of the Spirit recreates us for participation *en Christo.* Revelation, or what I

---

[29] Cf. Dan Hardy and his use of the poetry of Michael O'Siadhail (*The Chosen Garden*, Dublin, 1989), in 'The Spirit of God in Creation and Reconciliation', in *Christ and Context*, ed. Hilary Regan and Alan J. Torrance, Edinburgh, 1993.

[30] Cf. Mt. 11:27 and Jn. 17:25.

would prefer to term 'epistemic atonement', is thus an event of provisional, participatory communion within the intra-divine communion. The revelation event, so central to Barth's exposition in the first volume of the *Church Dogmatics*, requires us to take more account of these elements than he did – or, indeed, could have done, given the extent to which his whole discussion is locked into certain metaphors and conditioned by too literalistic an interpretation of them.

Seeing the need for a more relational interpretation of the Trinity than Barth expounds in the first volume, Robert Jenson attempts to advance the discussion by offering further explication of the trinitarian nature of the divine agency. This he does with recourse to what he terms 'ten "notions" and eight "relations"'. He writes,

> if we take the relations in pairs, using the active relations for the Father and the Spirit and not duplicating, we get: the Father gives and intends, the Spirit frees and witnesses, Jesus is intended and is witnessed to. And interpreting each pair personally, we get: the Father gives and intends = is Subject; Jesus is intended and is witnessed to = is Object; the Spirit frees and witnesses = is Spirit.[31]

Unfortunately, despite a) Jenson's accurate perception of the need to introduce a more dynamic interpretation of triune agency and what we might call a richer 'braiding' of the intra-divine dynamics, and b) his success in offering a profounder characterisation of the agency of the Spirit in this context than Barth offers, it is our view that his own solution is also inadequate. This is because it further compounds Barth's failure to interpret the vicarious subjectivity of the Son in relation to the Father. There is a whole dimension to the 'Subjectivity' of the person of the Son which cannot be reduced to the agency of the Spirit. Again, the weakness would appear to be that Jenson's account, like Barth's, is preoccupied with the divine intention *vis-à-vis* witness, i.e. *revelation* rather than *worship*, and fails to appreciate the extent to which one can only arrive at an appropriate interpretation of the former in the light of the latter where

[31] Jenson, op. cit., 148.

worship is interpreted as the gift of free participation in the glory of God or, more fully, the gift of participating by the Spirit in the Son's communion with the Father.[32] Revelation does not denote a form of knowledge that 'confronts' God as its 'object'. Rather, it is personal knowledge of a kind that is participatory and emerges within the context of worship, in and through the creativity of the divine communion and through the (indwelt) economy of the Spirit.

Barth's Discussion of Trinitarian Personhood

It is in the context of this question as to whether Barth succeeded in Volume One in offering an adequately integrated conception of the mutuality intrinsic within the Trinity that we return to the central question of our study, namely, how far we should or should not refer to the 'members' of the Trinity as 'persons'.[33]

We must now assess Barth's own arguments in this regard – although we do this in complete endorsement of Barth's comment that 'At this point, not only we but without exception all who have studied this matter before us enter upon the most difficult section in the investigation.'[34]

---

[32] Particularly relevant to this are Colin Gunton's comments, 'Through his humanity the risen Christ is present in and with the church in order that as God he may lift the community into the presence of the Father. The matter can, and must, also be understood pneumatologically. The church is the true church at worship insofar as – only, but really insofar as – the Spirit ever and again constitutes the community of believers as the church by bringing them into the life of God through the Son. Theology does not therefore begin in abstract observation ...' (*The Promise of Trinitarian Theology*, Edinburgh, 1991, 5.)

[33] Hopefully, it should be clear in the light of our discussion above that without such a basis theological anthropology can never be adequately theological and grace will ultimately collapse into law – the human–Godward dimension is left to the non-divine human subject and as such becomes something which it is incumbent upon humanity to offer.

[34] *C. D.* 1. 1, 355 (*K. D.* 1. 1, 374). Barth is also profoundly humble about his attempts to address the problems. At the end of his discussion he speaks of the 'menacing proximity of theological error', commenting, 'We, too, are unable to avoid the fact that every step of ours in this field is exposed to danger, whether the threat comes from the tritheistic heresy or the modalist heresy, or whether there be on either side suspicion of the opposite error. We, too, are unable to take a middle course in such a way that every misunderstanding is ruled out and our orthodoxy is unequivocally assured ...' (*C. D.* 1. 1, 368; *K. D.* 1. 1, 388.)

For the purposes of evaluation several features of Barth's discussion are particularly relevant.

1) The Manner in which Barth introduces his Discussion The discussion is introduced by posing the question:

> Under what common term are these three [Father, Son and Spirit] to be understood? What are these three – apart from the fact that all together as well as each individually they are the one true God? What is the common principle of their being, now as Father, now as Son and now as Spirit?[35]

If the term 'person' is to be appropriate, it is assumed, it must denote some kind of 'general referent' or common denominator. Its warrant would thus be some quality, facet or entity which should necessarily be present in all contexts of the term's use. In other words, there is an Aristotelian tinge to his 'categorial' way of posing the question. But does this not risk misjudging the propriety or otherwise of the use of any term for the following reasons?

a) The term might 'mean' something slightly different in the case of each 'member' of the Trinity – that the term may perhaps denote what Wittgenstein has termed 'family resemblances' between the various applications of the terms rather than some identically shared core, common facet.[36] It is not necessarily the case that the term 'person' applies to the Father in precisely the same way that it applies to the Holy Spirit, for example.[37]

---

[35] *C. D.* 1. 1, 355 (*K. D.* 1. 1, 374).

[36] Barth may recognise this when he comments, 'The situation would be hopeless if it were our task here to say what is really meant by "person" in the doctrine of the Trinity.' (*C. D.* 1. 1, 355; *K. D.* 1. 1, 375.) Or again, 'To the question: *quid tres?* i.e. what is the *nomen generale* or general concept for Father, Son and Spirit, no real answer can be given, *quia excedit supereminentia divinitatis usitati eloquii facultatem.*' (*C. D.* 1. 1, 355–6; *K. D.* 1. 1, 375.)

[37] For a methodical analysis and survey of this issue see Heribert Mühlen's *Der Heilige Geist als Person: In der Trinität, bei der Inkarnation und im Gnadenbund,* Münster, 1963. It is interesting to note that despite extensive analysis of the debate concerning the nature and definition of the term 'person' throughout the history of thought, there is no discussion or response to Barth's exposition of these matters in this book!

b) The term's capacity to effect, on the one hand, the denotation of a concrete referent while, on the other, communicating a radical open-endedness with respect to the being of the referent may be exactly what makes it an appropriate term to use.

c) The theological use of the term may be argued to be such that the event of its referring involves the denotation of its referent *precisely* in such a way that the referent is defined in terms of its relations and, therefore, the being of that to which (or 'those to whom') it is related. Unless this potentiality is itself to be regarded as a common property, the very strength of the term 'person' may be excluded by precisely the question Barth is asking.

2) The Negative Orientation   The discussion throughout is characterised by an eagerness to avoid various perceived risks. Indeed, the appeal of the term *Seinsweise* is more a negative one than a positive one, namely its perceived neutrality, rather than its capacity to denote positively something of the ontology of the Triunity.

The primary areas of concern over the word *Person* operative in his mind are the following:

a) His first concern with the term person is its historical connection with the term *prosopon*, which implies the arbitrary or temporary assumption of a 'face' or appearance by God. This, he argues, would involve a form of 'Sabellianism' where the 'persons' are conceived as manifestations of a hidden *quartum quid*.[38]

b) His second area of concern relates to the conception of the person as a *hypostasis*. When hypostasis is translated into Latin, it becomes *substantia*, in the sense of *natura* or *essentia*. To interpret the members of the Trinity in terms of these connotations may lead to, or be perceived as implying, a latent tritheism.

---

[38] As mentioned above in chapter 2, Barth may not have understood properly the patristic critique of Sabellianism. Cf. Meijering's discussion in *Von den Kirchenvätern zu Karl Barth*, 57.

The reference to the three divine persons certainly means something very different from a juxtaposition like that of three human persons, and for this reason, that a juxtaposition of human persons denotes a separateness of being (*diversitas essentiae*) which is completely excluded in God ...[39]

This concern is reiterated later on, when he comments on Anselm:

> Anselm had against the term *persona* the soundly based objection that *omnes plures personae sic subsistunt separatim ab invicem, ut tot necesse sit esse substantias, quot sint personae.* This is true of human persons but it is not true of the divine persons. Hence he, too, will speak of *personae* only *indigentia nominis proprie convenientis* ...[40]

The meaning of the term 'hypostasis' cannot be discussed in any great depth here, other than to say that Zizioulas is just one example of a person who expounds its radical compatibility with the notion of *ekstasis* in such a way that to talk of three personal hypostases does *not* involve reference to a separateness existing between three ontologically circumscribable or 'monadic' beings.

Barth's arguments here are puzzling at other levels, too. First, his argument might also be used with respect to the trinitarian names, 'Father' and 'Son'. Two 'persons' of the Trinity, if we are to follow the non-theological currency of these terms, could be argued to imply precisely such an individuation, i.e. one which involved no less a 'separation' of being or 'juxtaposition' than he is suggesting is implied by the term 'person'. But there is a second and more significant question we have for Barth. The metaphorical thrust of the New Testament language here would suggest that Christian *koinonia*, without in any way undermining the particularity that attends personhood, suggests a union and communion which is very different from a 'discrete separateness of beings' *even at the anthropological level*. The nature and form of the Church conceived as the Body of Christ, for example, seeks to

---

[39] *C. D.* 1. 1, 355 (*K. D.* 1. 1, 375).
[40] *C. D.* 1. 1, 356 (*K. D.* 1. 1, 375–6).

redefine human personhood as irreducibly constituted by what is an intrinsic, i.e. *ontological,* union and communion. Are we to reject the term of human beings, too, in this context?

This is a topic to which we shall return. Suffice to say that if, as we have argued in the previous chapter, there *may be* a place for an *analogia entis,* interpreted along the lines of Söhngen's arguments, then this would seem to suggest that the Body of Christ constitutes the primary context for the creative commandeering of language – a commandeering grounded in a continuity established by God which is, therefore, *from* the divine *to* the human and which is to be found in that divine communion present with us in and through the human Jesus as the one who grounds, sustains and constitutes the Body of Christ. Given a) the potential for the redefinition of the language of personhood within such a context and the establishment of its intrinsic connection with the language of union and communion; b) the correlation of this conceptuality with that of the *analogia relationis,* and c) the resonations with the terms 'Father' and 'Son', not to mention the New Testament language of the Spirit, as these denote that union and communion constitutive of God as also of the Body of Christ, it seems puzzling that Barth was not less inclined to reject this terminology and was as influenced as he was by the perceived determination of the term's reference by the 'natural' world! The opportunity, not least, for the integrating of theology, ecclesiology and theological anthropology was surely immense – and served considerably less adequately by the term *Seinsweise.*

c) A further danger perceived by Barth is that of undermining divine transcendence. Barth endorses J. Gerhard's reference to a 'magnum imo infinitum discrimen'[41] between the divine and human persons, and much of the tenor of Barth's discussion suggests a fear on his part of a subtle anthropomorphism usurping the exposition of the Trinity in such a way that the integrity of the revelation event

---

[41] *C. D.* 1. 1, 357 (*K. D.* 1. 1, 377).

is put at risk. To offset this danger, however, he appeals to the inconceivability and ineffability of the divine nature which, unless carefully interpreted in *a posteriori* terms, similarly risks undermining precisely this same dynamic.

> The more the distinction of persons is regarded as taking place in and grounded in the divine essence itself, the more conceivable [see footnote] in fact becomes the inconceivability of this distinction; the distinction participates in the inconceivability of the divine essence, which would not be the essence of the revealed God if it were conceivable, i.e., apprehensible in the categories of *usitatum eloquium.* Hence neither *persona* nor any other term can perform the service of making this distinction really conceivable.[42]

In support of this Barth quotes Augustine's statement 'Verius enim cogitatur Deus quam dicitur et verius est, quam cogitatur' and Anselm's reference to the 'ineffabilis pluralitas' of the 'tres nescio quid'.

It is clear that there are appropriate concerns reflected in Barth's discussion. Clearly, all our formulations and conceptualities must indeed recognise the divine freedom and transcendence. However, there is a tendency to interpret the very necessary 'theological open-endedness' of the conceptuality that we use in referring to the Being of God in terms of questionable conceptions of theological reverence and divine ineffability on the one hand (which can too easily take the form of a false modesty inspired by certain pseudo-philosophical demands which are inappropriate in the face of revelation), or of the 'inconceivability of the divine essence' on the other. In other words, a proper theological reverence in the face of revelation may commit us to make affirmations, by way of the commandeered function of terms, such that it is precisely the refusal to use the language of the created order that is irreverent and arrogant. Secondly, certain forms of affirming the inconceivability of the divine essence may amount, in the face of the communion event that constitutes revelation, to a disobedient refusal to think that which is given

---

[42] *C. D.* 1. 1, 356 (*K. D.* 1. 1, 375). There is here a mistake in the Bromiley edition which translates *begreiflicher* as 'inconceivable'!

to be expressed cognitively! Here we would agree strongly
with Eberhard Jüngel's refutation of approaches that adopt
an attitude of resignation before God conceived as the
Unthinkable. The Unthinkability of God (as it derives from
the insights of John 1:18a) should lead, rather, to the
determination to think 'decisively' – 'Decisively, in that in
view of this very truth it must emphasise fully that God himself
has made himself accessible: ... the only Son, who is in the
bosom of the Father, he has made him known. (John 1:18b).'[43]
There is still more that may be said in this regard.

First, we must point out that it is not as easy to distinguish
between the thinkable and the sayable as Barth (with the help of
Augustine) seems to suggest in the above discussion – especially
when we are referring to God.[44] As Jüngel argues so effectively:

> [W]e can regard the word 'God' as a 'note of the presence of a thing'
> whereby we have not yet arrived at any agreement about the relation
> between presence and absence. Accordingly, the 'signified thing' (*res
> significata*) signalized through this word, God himself, is not the
> question at all 'in the usual sense of a content distinct from the word
> itself' – a sort of speechless thing that has to be brought into the
> language by being named, that is, designated by a vocable. ... On the
> contrary, it is here a question of God himself as Word.' That which the
> word 'God' signalizes can be found only in the word, more precisely,
> in the fact that certain words confront a person in a way at least
> hermeneutically comparable to the experience of invective.[45]

Jüngel's point here may be argued to apply precisely to the
term 'person' used of the members of the Trinity. Barth's

---

[43] *God as the Mystery of the World* (Eng. trans. by Darrell Guder, Grand Rapids,
1983), 9. It should be added that I am not implying that Barth is not fully aware
of this issue generally in his theology. It is rather that in this context he falls back
on argumentation that is not justified by the general thrust of his theology.

[44] In Jüngel's words, 'We must carefully consider whether words really are
always mere representatives of something else which itself is wordless.' (Ibid., 10.)
We might also comment, however, that although Jüngel frames his discussion of
the thinkability of God in terms of a discussion of theological language and
although he makes use of Wittgenstein (ibid., 7), his discussion in the
'Introduction' to *God as the Mystery of the World* tends to suggest too easy a
distinction between the thinkable and the sayable.

[45] Ibid., 11.

discussion is framed as if the challenge is to name a 'speechless thing ... that has to be brought into the language by being named, that is, designated by a vocable ...' The term for which he opts is thus a term which is as cognitively neutral as possible. As such it seems that Barth underestimates the extent to which the language of *Seinsweise* risks sterilising rather than communicating an appreciation of the dynamic, perichoretic and participative presence of the Triunity. It is inappropriate, not least in theology, to dissociate the meaning of a word from its ('performative') effect, its conditioning of the apperception of the theological community.[46] A false conditioning is a false communication and thus a semantic distortion.[47] Diluting language which communicates divine 'communing' into that which communicates mere 'being' can have that effect!

The tenor of Wittgenstein's insights in his *Philosophical Investigations* is that what cannot be said cannot be thought, and that what is thought is couched in the language usage and skills in making distinctions of a public domain *into which* we are born and *in the context of which* our processes of conceptualisation develop and emerge. We must, therefore, be clear about what we are suggesting when we say that what is thought may be truer than what may be said – and truth, of course, should be conceived as a function or property of statements in the public domain, rather than of inexpressible (semantically unformulatable) thoughts.

It is, of course, essential to avoid an opposite nominalist extreme here. However, neither an incipient semantic

---

[46] 'Performatives' function not to describe or report, their utterance is rather a form of action. Austin provides the following examples: "'I do (...take this woman to be my lawful wedded wife)" – as uttered in the course of the marriage ceremony ... "I name this ship the *Queen Elizabeth*" – as uttered when smashing the bottle against the stern ... "I bet you sixpence it will rain tomorrow."' (J. L. Austin, *How to Do Things with Words*, Oxford, 1962, 5.)

[47] This is not to deny that it may be the case that Barth believes the term 'person' may have a misguided, performative functionality by conjuring up a mistaken conception of the way God is. However, the functionality of the alternative has a sterilising effect on the way we conceive of the divine dynamic. It is not clear that Barth fully appreciated that.

docetism on the one hand nor an esoteric interpretation of meaning and truth on the other are acceptable alternatives. This is because they fail to take seriously a) God's commandeering of our language together with the concrete implications of that, and b) the semantic implications of revelation within the communion of the Body of Christ, namely, that God is 'communally thought and spoken', or, should we say, 'spoken and thought' in a manner that is true to God's remaining free and 'personal', and in such a way that his Reality may never be reduced to the truth of propositions.

Second, Barth's reference to the inconceivability of the divine essence in defence of a degree of agnosticism *vis-à-vis* the articulation of the trinitarian distinctions here is puzzling. His concern to obviate modalism is an attempt to clarify that there is no inscrutable essence behind God revealed as Trinity. This reflects his eagerness to affirm the divine integrity in revelation – that what God is toward us he is eternally and antecedently in himself. Without suggesting against Barth that God may be reduced to human thought, all this would suggest that 'inconceivability' for the natural mind should not be appealed to too quickly as a criterion in the choice of terms unless it denotes an *a posteriori* 'not to be conceived'. And it is far from clear that that is what is demanded of us by John 17, for example – namely that the Father and Son must *not* be conceived as 'persons' in communion.

Third, Barth's emphasis on the evils of what we might term 'foundationalism' (epistemological, methodological, semantic or ontological *a priorism*) and his determination to engage in theological affirmation in *a posteriori* ways mean that genuine reverence and awe (as opposed to the 'false modesty' referred to above) is such that we must *not* say that God's Eternal Being is not given to be thought or spoken of in certain respects when God *is* toward us in a manner that requires of us the 'daring' to speak of God. In other words, Barth is, arguably, being internally inconsistent when he appeals here to a non-revelation-oriented *via negativa* when faced with articulating distinctions expressed in and through the biblical witness in irreducibly 'personal' terms (e.g. Father and Son) and metaphors (cf. the endless references to the purposive agency of the Spirit). These words would appear to endorse a network of semantic rules and regulations which mean that, as these words are commandeered, so the associated language-games and networks of associations are also 'commandeered'. The term 'person' belongs to these.

What Barth is, of course, absolutely *correct* to warn against is a literalism or nominalism on the other side which implies non-analogical parallelisms between the human and the divine which a) are not driven and commandeered by the revelation event and the participative life of the Church, which b) fail to accept the open-endedness of theological conceptuality, and which c) suppose that conceptual deductions can be made in the divine realm on the basis of the naturalistic use of the same terminology in the human context. None of these matters, however, should preclude the use of the term 'person' any more than they should preclude the use of the terms 'Father', 'Son' and 'Spirit' (or, for that matter, *Seinsweise*).[48] It is interesting to note that Barth's argumentation *vis-à-vis* the term 'person' parallels, in certain respects, contemporary feminist objections to trinitarian language in its totality!

d) A fourth area of nervousness for Barth (one which has already been met with in his discussion of the perceived separateness of persons in 2b above) results from his genetic investigation of the semantics of the term 'person' stemming from Augustine through to idealist thought, and concerns weaknesses in the use of the term as it has developed, and continues to function, in philosophical anthropology. One prime concern for Barth is the manner in which the history of thought, as exemplified in the writing of Boethius (*Persona est naturae rationabilis individua substantia*) and Aquinas, has interpreted personhood as denoting individuation – 'an essence existing in and for itself, separate in its existence from others'. Barth makes mention of St Thomas' wrestling with the concept with reference to the members of the Trinity and

---

[48] These arguments are not primarily intended to be negative arguments against the use of the term *Seinsweise*, but rather arguments which seek to negate the arguments against the use, indeed, 'decisive' claiming of the term 'person'.

redefining it to denote simply the element of incommuni-
cability (that is, the element of individuation). This he applies
to the members of the Trinity in such a way that no plurality
of substance is implied. The *personae* of the Trinity are therefore
described by Aquinas as *res subsistentes in divina natura.* In a
critical section of his discussion Barth makes it clear that he is
not happy with Aquinas' interpretation of the *res subsistentes*
which are, in Barth's summary, 'nothing but *relationes,*
intradivine relations'.[49] He adds,

> we can hardly feel convinced that even a comparative aptness – there
> can be no question of any other – in the use of the concept of person
> has been explained by Thomas in such a way that we are forced to
> abandon the reservations in relation to it for which appeal can always
> be made to Augustine and Anselm. If Thomas has provided a true
> explanation, within the bounds of the possible, for what the three
> involve in triunity, he has done this, *not in the form of an interpretation
> of the concept of person, but by means of the concept of relations.*[50]

Barth chooses, therefore, to align himself rather more
closely with the tradition of Augustine and Anselm at this
point owing, perhaps, to a lack of appreciation of the benefits
to be accrued from the term's being redefined and filled out
theologically (in the light of a proper integration of the
immanent and economic Trinities – and therefore the intra-
divine relations) in such a manner as to synthesise the notion
of *hypostasis,* as this involves 'particularity' (Gunton) or the
element of *incommunicabilitas* (Aquinas) on the one hand and
that of relation on the other – what Zizioulas will conceive as
the *ekstasis* of the personal *hypostasis.*[51]

A central concern of Barth is to avoid tritheism which, he
fears, may be encouraged by the utilisation of the term

---

[49] *C. D.* 1. 1, 357, ('nichts Anderes als *relationes,* innergöttliche Beziehungen,'
K. D. 1. 1, 376).

[50] *C. D.* 1. 1, 357, italics mine (*K. D.* 1. 1, 377).

[51] As LaCugna puts it, 'Barth's view is a hybrid of the Latin theology of the
Trinity in which the one divine substance exists in three persons, and the idea of
God as Absolute Subject who exists under the aspects of self-differentiation and
self-recollection.' (*God for Us,* 252.)

'person' given modern developments in the use of the term.[52] The widespread influence of the concept of personality (*Persönlichkeit*) which emerged in nineteenth-century anthropology and the emphasis on self-consciousness or self-awareness (*Selbstbewußtsein*), both of which are now popularly associated with the concept, are perceived to complicate matters here. Consequently, he dismisses Richard Grützmacher's (as, indeed, Melanchthon's[53]) attempt to ascribe a separate I-centre with a separate consciousness, will and content to the trinitarian persons. The suggestion that we have three absolute personalities 'working side by side and together' is too close, he believes, to the tritheistic concept of three manikins (*marmousets*) which Calvin rightly rejected long ago. Indeed, Barth finds it understandable that, in the face of this option, Neo-Protestant thought should choose to seek refuge in the alternative Sabellian option where there was advocated an 'economic' Trinity of revelation with God remaining in the background as absolute personality. This option, however, is no better, leading, as it does, to the widely held doctrine of a Quaternity – which effectively posits three manikins as three of the four![54]

The question to which Barth finds himself returning throughout his discussion concerns whether there is sufficient warrant simply to reiterate the traditional term, as some scholastic theology continues to do, and elucidate it as if nothing had changed since the Middle Ages – that is, as if the definition produced by Boethius still continued to be 'relevant and intelligible'.

The obvious riposte to be made here is that these issues apply not simply to the term 'person', but to a very great deal of the terminology – theological and ecclesiastical – that

---

[52] *C. D.* 1. 1, 357 (*K. D.* 1. 1, 377).

[53] Barth regards Melanchthon's comments that 'Persona est subsistens vivum, individuum, intelligens, incommunicabile, non sustentatum ab alio' as suspicious, especially when he suggests that the divine persons are 'tres subsistentes … distincti seu singulares intelligentes …', savouring too much of tritheism. (*C. D.* 1. 1, 358; *K. D.* 1. 1, 377.)

[54] Cf. *C. D.* 1. 1, 358 (*K. D.* 1. 1, 378).

Barth uses and would endorse. The everyday usage of the traditional terms 'Father' and 'Son' may also be argued to suggest precisely the same kind of individuation which Barth fears. When used of different subjects, they suggest a plurality of personalities as also of self-consciousnesses, wills and intelligences. To be more topical, however, feminist theologians are arguing forcefully in the contemporary climate that the 'traditional' language of Fatherhood is also now dated and inappropriate in an egalitarian and 'sexually inclusive' modern world. As the early Church saw, applying all such terms to God requires a revision within the theological context or a demythologisation to remove the sexuality and individuality associated with the terms. In other words, the arguments which Barth is using could be used even more forcefully (and are so used by feminist theologians such as Sallie McFague, Rosemary Radford Ruether and Elisabeth Schüssler Fiorenza) in support of a departure from the trinitarian 'names' *in toto* – names which are clearly intended to serve a referential function (albeit analogical-metaphorical) which is cognitive and 'reality depictive', yet where this involves a dramatic shift in the rules of use which characterise their ordinary usage. Barth shows no desire to do this.

It may also be added that in the present context the 'sexually-inclusive' term 'person' may, indeed, make it easier to defend the trinitarian terminology by re-enforcing the inclusive grammar of the doctrine. Moreover, if we can show how the term 'person' is commandeered for analogical usage in the theological context, the manner in which the terms 'Father' and 'Son' function becomes that much clearer. The feminist argument for a functionalist revision of the trinitarian language (where Father, Son and Holy Spirit are replaced by Creator, Redeemer and Sustainer/Giver of Life,[55] for example) is strengthened if the trinitarian members are described as essentially *Seinsweisen* rather than *Personen*, for

---

[55] This pseudo-trinitarian (indeed, anti-trinitarian) formula is now used extensively in worship throughout the United States, Canada and Australasia in Catholic and Protestant worship.

the simple reason that the term *Seinsweisen* opens the door to functionalist interpretations in a way that the term *Personen* does not.[56]

3) The Underlying Material Concerns   However, it is the material issues in Barth's argument which are obvious throughout this section that concern us most deeply. In chapter 2 we suggested that his conception of the form and structure of revelation conditions his doctrine of the Triunity. That this serves to influence his non-advocacy of the term 'person' becomes clear in the following quotation and its influence on the course of the discussion.

> In view of the history of the term person in the doctrine of the Trinity one may well ask whether dogmatics is wise to continue using it in this connexion. It belongs to another locus, to the doctrine of God proper, and to this as a derivation from the doctrine of the Trinity. For it follows from the trinitarian understanding of the God revealed in Scripture that this one God is to be understood ... as the Lord ... as an I existing in and for itself with its own thought and will. This is how He meets us in His revelation. This is how He is thrice God as Father, Son and Spirit.[57]

As we argued earlier, Barth's commitment to interpreting God as the singular 'I' – an 'I' that meets us three times – is integral to his decision that the term 'person' does not belong to the locus of the doctrine of the Trinity.

What is revealing here is the distinction he introduces between the 'doctrine of the Trinity' and 'the doctrine of God proper'. Although he would suggest that the use of the term 'person' of God derives from the doctrine of the Trinity, all that we have read seems to suggest that the influence is in the

---

[56] I would admit that these considerations are perhaps more tactical than theological. The fact that term *x* makes it easier to present a certain error than if we were to opt for term *y* is not in itself sufficient theological argument for choosing term *y*. Having said that, it is also the case that Barth's own arguments are tactical in that they are influenced by consideration of the cultural associations with the term 'person' which were in operation when he was writing. I would certainly not criticise him for taking this into account!

[57] *C. D.* 1. 1, 358–9 (*K. D.* 1. 1, 378).

other direction, that it is his doctrine of God as the sole
Subject of revelation that determines that the term 'person'
should not be used of the trinitarian members. It is far from
clear that it is an *a posteriori* consideration of the triune
interrelations that leads him to his interpreting 'the doctrine
of God proper' in terms of 'the concept of the identical
subject'![58]

Although Barth does suggest that his concern is not to seek
to dispose of the term *Person*,[59] he also confirms that the only
reason the term is still used is because there is an absence of
a better concept with which to replace it. His underlying
distancing of himself from the term becomes more obvious,
moreover, when he suggests we should apply it 'only in the
sense of a practical abbreviation and as a reminder of the
historical continuity of the problem'.[60]

4) Barth's Use of the Term *Seinsweise*   Barth's positive
reasoning in using the term *Seinsweise* is quite simple and
concerns his analysis of what he interprets to be the biblical
concept of revelation. This he conceives, however,
independently of the whole biblical testimony to the intra-
divine communion as the ground of God's reconciling Self-
giving for epistemic communion.[61] In other words, it seems at
this point that Barth risks failing to be true to the *content* of
biblical revelation through his concern with the biblical
concept of revelation. Whatever the case, his analysis suggests
that 'the one God, i.e. the one Lord, the one personal God, is
what he is not just in one mode but ... in the mode of the
Father, in the mode of the Son, and in the mode of the Holy
Ghost'.[62] Barth is keen to emphasise the threeness as ways of

[58] Barth's argumentation here adds support to Moltmann's comment that
'Barth uses the doctrine of the Trinity in order to secure the sovereignty of God
in his rule.' (*The Trinity and the Kingdom of God.*)

[59] 'We have no cause to want to outlaw the concept of person or to put it out
of circulation.' (*C. D.* 1. 1, 359; *K. D.* 1. 1, 379.)

[60] *C. D.* 1. 1, 359 (*K. D.* 1. 1, 379).

[61] He comments 'we appeal in support simply to the result of our analysis of the
biblical concept of revelation ...' (*C. D.* 1. 1, 359; *K. D.* 1. 1, 379.)

[62] *C. D.* 1. 1, 359 (*K. D.* 1. 1, 379).

being, yet without threatening the absolute oneness of the divine essence (*Wesen*).[63] The term *Seinsweise* serves this by way of affirming that there *are* three ways of *being*, ways of subsisting, that is, of possessing this one essence, and this term does so without implying either a duplication or a quadruplication – something which Barth suggests is involved, for example, by Thomas' phrase 'relatio ut res subsistens in natura divina' (*Summa Theologica* 1, qu. 30, art. 1c).[64] The terms *res* and *natura*, Barth believes, imply different subjects of divinity.[65] And fear of this kind of mistake clearly added momentum to his decision to expound the triune relations in terms of the category of *Seinsweisen* and his consequent use of the metaphor of reiteration.[66]

As we have seen, Barth saw *Seinsweise* as a more neutral, and therefore safer, term than *Person*, in that it would appear to carry less baggage with it. However, the implications of his move and the notion of the Singular Divine Person or Subject implied by it are certainly not perceived as neutral by Barth's critics. For example, LaCugna believes that, despite the fact that Barth rejects the notion of a discrete I-centre applied to God, he was not 'entirely able to resist using it'. She continues, 'The only difference is that the divine essence, not the three divine persons, is made the referent of this self-consciousness.' Exactly the same mistake applies to Rahner as well, she suggests. Consequently, she concludes that 'The one self-conscious Subject thus subsists or exists under three modalities' and that 'In the end neither Barth nor Rahner was able to break away entirely from the Cartesian starting-point'.[67]

---

[63] The foundational importance for Barth is reflected not only in various comments he makes but also his use of quotations from, for example, Scheeben and Bartmann.

[64] Quoted by Barth, *C. D.* 1. 1, 365 (*K. D.* 1. 1, 385).

[65] *C. D.* 1. 1, 366 (*K. D.* 1. 1, 386).

[66] Although Thomas seems less nervous about describing the members of the Trinity as 'persons', his argumentation has the effect of displacing the problem (and making it worse) by the utilisation of an Aristotelian (and therefore less than personal) conception of substance with respect to the divine unity.

[67] *God for Us*, 254.

Even if LaCugna's comments apply largely to the more extreme expressions of Barth's position in Volume One, and despite the fact that Barth's arguments are ambiguous, there is more than an element of truth to her criticism. His professed concern to express by the term *Seinsweise* 'relatively better and more simply and clearly the same thing as is meant by "person"' thinly veils the influence on Barth's thinking of the conception of God as singular Subject.[68]

It is also argued in this respect (for example, by Moltmann – albeit rather too sweepingly) that a connection is to be found here between the conception of God as singular Subject and the sovereignty motif which may be argued to require much more extensive redefinition than it receives as Barth uses it with respect to the dynamic of revelation. In Moltmann's words, 'The revelation of God's sovereignty is nothing other than the assertion of his divine subjectivity or "I-ness", i.e. God's "personality".'[69] And, further still, 'Barth's particular interest in the doctrine of the Trinity is 'for the sake of securing the sovereignty of God ...'[70] It would appear, however, that this latter comment overstates the case, since the sustained and careful nature of Barth's discussion suggests that his foundational concern (albeit not always consistent) is to articulate *a posteriori* the dynamics of the Gospel as it interprets itself in the Scriptures. Barth is not ostensibly interested in using the doctrine of the Trinity *in order to secure* any specific theological notion or tenet! What must be acknowledged is that the cross and the dynamics of communion may require a more nuanced conception of divine sovereignty than features in Barth's conception of the divine Lordship in the event of revelation.

---

[68] *C. D.* 1. 1, 359 (*K. D.* 1. 1, 379).

[69] *The Trinity and the Kingdom of God*, 141. This connects with another comment made by LaCugna, 'Despite his emphasis on the divine persons as modes of God's being, Barth's view is quite different from the way Greek theology understands the relationship between personhood and being. For Barth, the essence of God is uni-personal. The God who 'distributes' the divine essence in three modes of being is the Sovereign Subject.' (*God for Us*, 252.)

[70] Moltmann, ibid., 141.

5) A Hint of Idealism?   It seems that Karl Barth took over the term *Seinsweise* from I. A. Dorner, whom he admired,[71] and who influenced his thinking.[72] The use of this expression in Dorner exemplifies a particular form of the idealist conception of God as absolute, divine personality. He writes,

> In the trinitarian processes of the life and spirit of God, absolute personality is the eternally present result; so the self-conscious God, who desires and possesses himself, is also present in such a way in each of the divine distinctions that these – which would not in themselves and individually be personal – yet participate in the One of the divine personality, each in its own way. But as the absolute divine personality is the single constitution of the three divine modes of being (*Seinsweisen*) which participate in it and has its understanding in them, as they have theirs in it, so this same divine personality which, in its ultimate relationship and according to its nature, is holy love, is also the single constitution and the highest power of all divine characteristics.[73]

The tenor and content of this quotation add some plausibility to the suggestion made, not least by Moltmann, that the shaping of Barth's discussion in the first volume of the *Church Dogmatics* was influenced by philosophical idealism.[74]

---

[71] Dorner is one of those to whose influence he attributed the rise of the 'new golden age' which dogmatics enjoyed prior to the Roman Catholic revival last century. Cf. *C. D.* 1. 1 , 276 (*K. D.* 1. 1, 293).

[72] Cf. T. F. Torrance, *Karl Barth: Biblical and Evangelical Theologian*, Edinburgh, 1990, 10. Although I am not aware of Barth's attributing his use of the term *Seinsweise* to any particular source, Jürgen Moltmann is almost certainly correct when he comments that 'Barth took over the concept of "modes of being" from Dorner.' (*The Trinity and the Kingdom of God*, 241, n. 21.)

[73] *System der christlichen Glaubenslehre*, 1, Berlin 1879, §32, 430. This quotation is cited in Moltmann, op. cit. 241, n. 21.

[74] Cf. the comparison and discussion of the similarity of Barth's and Hegel's doctrine of the Trinity by L. Oeing-Hanhoff, 'Hegel's Trinitätslehre' in *Theologische Quartalschrift*, 159 (1979), 287-303 (cited by Moltmann).

See also Richard Roberts' essay, 'Barth on Time' (in Stephen Sykes (ed.), *Karl Barth —Studies of his Theological Methods*, Oxford, 1979, chapter 4, where he outlines some parallels between Barth and Hegelian idealism (cf. particularly 93–6). This essay is reproduced in Roberts' recent book *A Theology on Its Way? Essays on Karl Barth*, Edinburgh, 1991. This contains a further essay entitled 'The Ideal and the Real', in which he discusses similar issues in greater detail.

If, as we have suggested, Barth took over the *Seinsweise* notion
from Dorner, it is not unrealistic, given the idealist influence
on Dorner's exposition of the doctrine of God, to suggest that
Barth may have taken over (subliminally even if not
intentionally) rather more than merely the word. In a section
entitled 'Trinitarian Monarchy: Karl Barth', which argues
that Barth is indeed influenced by the idealist conception of
the absolute subject or personality, Moltmann writes:

> The primordial image of the 'absolute subject' in heaven corresponds
> to the modern perception of human subjectivity as regards nature
> and history; and the personal God in eternity corresponds to the
> bourgeois culture of personality. It is the absolute personality of God
> that makes man a person … For these historical reasons it is quite
> understandable that the early church's trinitarian formula: *una
> substantia – tres personae* should now be replaced by the formula: one
> divine subject in three different modes of being. The modern
> bourgeois concept of personality and subject seems to make traditional
> talk about the three Persons of the Trinity impossible. But if the
> subjectivity of acting and receiving is transferred from the three
> divine Persons to the one divine subject, then the three Persons are
> bound to be degraded to modes of being, or modes of subsistence of
> the one identical subject.[75]

Referring to rather later developments in the history of
idealism than LaCugna identifies with Barth's doctrine of
God,[76] Moltmann goes on to point to modern German
idealism's responsibility for the interpretation of the divine
monas as the absolute, *identical subject*, suggesting this leads to
Barth's primordial stress on self-revelation and his implicit
use of idealism's 'reflection logic'. He comments, 'Barth's
Idealist heritage finally betrays itself in the use of the reflection
structure to secure God's subjectivity, sovereignty, selfhood
and personality.'[77] 'If instead of thinking of God deistically as

[75] Moltman, op. cit., 139.
[76] Ibid., 139–44. It must be said that, in my judgement, Moltmann's critique is
undermined by his too frequent use of emotive terms like 'bourgeois' applied in
pejorative ways. There is a journalistic gloss to his writing here that risks taking
the place of careful argumentation.
[77] Ibid., 142.

substance, we think of him theistically as subject, then this triadic process of reflection is intellectually necessary. It is through self-distinction and self-recollection that God shows himself to be the absolute subject.'[78] Indeed, it is this 'reflection logic' which, Moltmann believes, is revealed in Barth's decision to begin not with the God who reveals himself (the Father) but with the concrete and specific revelation who is the Son (the 'Godhead Jesus Christ'). And it is also to this influence that Moltmann traces Barth's under-characterisation of the doctrine of the Spirit[79] – 'The God who reveals himself in three modes of being can no longer display subjectivity in his state-of-revelation, the Holy Spirit.'[80]

On a wider scale, Rowan Williams suggests that a 'kinship with Hegel' on the part of Barth is evident in the 'similarity of pattern' between Barth's concept of the Word and Hegel's pan-unity of 'Absolute Spirit, the one and universal self-

---

[78] Ibid.

[79] Cf. Thomas Smail's critique of Barth in *The Giving Gift: The Holy Spirit in Person*, London, 1988, 43. Smail sees Barth as failing adequately to challenge the marginalisation of the doctrine of the Holy Spirit in Western theology. This, he suggests, is why Berkhof can quote 'so trinitarian a theologian as Karl Barth to support his own binitarian position. He quotes Barth as saying that the Spirit "is not other than the presence and action of Jesus Christ himself: his stretched out arm; he himself in the power of his resurrection".' Smail continues by admitting that 'There are other more genuinely trinitarian strands in Barth's doctrine of the Spirit, yet in his later theology there is a growing tendency to regard the Spirit as simply the way in which the risen Christ goes on acting in the Church. This brings him very near in practice to Berkhof's binitarian position, even if he would have rejected it formally in the name of a fully trinitarian understanding of the being of God' (43).

Such an interpretation finds some endorsement, and much fuller explanation, in A. I. C. Heron's *The Holy Spirit*, London, 1983, where he comments that Barth 'is especially critical of the concept of divine "persons", preferring the other ancient term "mode of being". Further, the "mode of being" of the Spirit as the event of the divine self-relating tends to reduce simply to the presence and action of the Father or of Christ. Consistently with this, he strenuously defends the *filioque* on quite traditional Western grounds' (167). We might add that the fact that Heron immediately goes on to discuss Hendrikus Berkhof and the influence of Barth on his account suggests that Smail's critique may well have been influenced by Heron's analysis!

[80] Ibid.

thinking thought'.[81] And Horst Pöhlmann further suggests that there are strong parallels between Barth's *Aktualismus* and the dynamic conception of Being that characterises Hegelianism. Thus, he suggests, Hegel's influence can be seen to be reflected in Barth's refutation of the *analogia entis*, which is motivated, Pöhlmann argues, by Barth's refutation of the dichotomy between being and act. He comments, 'Was Barth einmal von Hegels Gottesanschauung schreibt, gilt auch von seinem eigenen Gottesbegriff: "Gott ist nur Gott in seinem göttlichen Tun." Gott ist reines Geschehen. – Aber nicht nur Gott, sondern auch der Mensch ist, was er ist, in actu.'[82]

Clearly, the implications of this analysis certainly chime with the thrust of our own argument that the *Seinsweise* concept underplays the notion of the free and specific agency of the Spirit just as it underplays the notion of a mutuality of relations between the Father and the Son – a weakness that becomes rather more obviously manifest in Karl Rahner's exposition of the doctrine of the Trinity, which, as Moltmann rightly points out, is so similar to Barth's.[83]

There are, however, at least four forms of reply which might be given to suggestions that Barth's interpretation was shaped by idealism.

First, Barth's decision to begin not with the Father as Revealer but with the givenness of Revelation in Christ, to interpret the Spirit as the condition of the perception of this Revelation and to interpret the Father (the Revealer) in the light of this does not solely lend itself to being interpreted in terms of the subliminal appeal of the reflection logic of German idealism. It may also be interpreted in terms of the

---

[81] Rowan Williams, 'Barth on the Triune God' in Stephen Sykes (ed.), *Karl Barth – Studies of his Theological Methods*, 188. David Ford also suggests a closeness of Barth to Hegel in his concept of rationality. Cf., 'Conclusion: Assessing Barth' in op. cit., 196.

[82] Horst Georg Pöhlmann, *Analogia entis oder Analogia fidei?, Die Frage der Analogie bei Karl Barth*, Göttingen, 1965, 117.

[83] 'Karl Rahner developed his doctrine of the Trinity with an astonishing similarity to Barth and almost the same presuppositions.' (*The Trinity and the Kingdom of God*, 144.)

influence on Barth of Athanasian orthodoxy and the affirmation of the *homoousion* with respect both to the Son and to the Spirit. This is not to say it *must* be interpreted this way, but there would seem to be strong evidence to suggest that the thrust of this approach, including the perceived monarchian element here, is most effectively interpreted in the light of patristic influences.[84]

Second, Barth himself is fully aware of the 'reflection logic' of which Moltmann speaks in German idealism, and his own comments here are particularly relevant.

a) First, referring to Schelling's triad of subject, object and subject-object, and to Hegel's 'in itself' of the subjective spirit as thesis, 'for itself' of the objective spirit as antithesis, and 'in and for itself' of the absolute spirit as synthesis, he comments, 'We may quietly state that these very climaxes of Idealist philosophy would be quite unthinkable except against the background of Christian dogmatics even if they were not just new variations on Augustine's proof of the Trinity.'[85] In other words, the triadic dynamics represented by idealist philosophy may, he suggests, be traced to the Augustinian *vestigia trinitatis*. This means that if a Christian theologian appears to reflect such a dynamic in his or her exposition of the doctrine of the Trinity, it may be because *both* were influenced by the same *theological* source – although, again, Barth has no desire to align his own formulation with the Augustinian *vestigia trinitatis*!

b) Second, Barth then distances himself from precisely the interpretation Moltmann would later place on his interpretation of the Trinity by commenting, 'It is clear that the logico-grammatical scheme of subject, object and predicate would also belong to this context *if it were our real key to the doctrine of the Trinity.*'[86] Claude Welch also anticipated this kind of critique in 1952, and argued, 'The relations of origin, or processions, are not here part of a rationalistic or quasi-

---

[84] For an extended discussion of (and, indeed, emphasis on) the influence of Athanasian doctrine of the *homoousion* on Barth, see T. F. Torrance, *Karl Barth: Biblical and Evangelical Theologian*, 165–77.

[85] *C. D.* 1. 1, 338 (*K. D.* 1. 1, 357).

[86] Ibid. (italics mine).

rationalistic deduction of the doctrine of the Trinity (as in Anselm or Hegel).'[87] A rather profounder discussion of the question at issue by Wolfhart Pannenberg, however, suggests that there are certain parallels which commit both to similar forms of critique.[88] In sum, the manner in which Barth conceived of the logic of revelation means that the suggested parallels between Hegel's treatment and Barth's, even if they reflect different intentions and are given a different kind of warrant, may not be ignored. How useful such an observation is, however, for an evaluation of Barth's doctrine of the Trinity remains open to question.

Third, with reference to the above comments of Williams and Pöhlmann – particularly the latter – parallelisms can clearly be drawn between the dynamic understanding of reality that characterises both Hegelian emphases on the one hand, and the dynamic conception of God and the all-pervasive reality of the Logos articulated in Barth on the other. Moreover, it is clear that both hold to the impropriety of a dichotomy between Being and act. But to suggest, as Pöhlmann does, that Barth is committed to the view that 'Alles ist dynamisch ... Alles ist Tat',[89] on account of Barth's endorsement of an 'actualistic ontology'[90] or an actualistic pan-unity, falls short of the mark, in our view, since it fails to appreciate that Barth simply is not concerned with the establishment of any such ontology. If the articulation of the One discerned to be *Immanuel* suggests that we cannot divorce act from Being, the divine Being from the divine presence, even if the influence of Hegel was to help him in his articulation of this fact, Barth cannot on that ground be argued to have been seeking to establish or advocate a pan-actualist[91] or pan-logicist ontology any more than an ontology

---

[87] Claude Welch, *The Trinity in Contemporary Theology*, London, 1953, 197.

[88] 'Die Subjektivität und die Trinitätslehre: Ein Beitrag zur Beziehung zwischen Karl Barth und der Philosophie Hegels', *Kerygma und Dogma* 23 (1977), 25–40, see especially 36.

[89] Pöhlmann, op. cit., 117.

[90] Ibid., 119.

[91] 'Man kann deshalb ohne Übertreibung von einem Panaktualismus Barths sprechen.' (Ibid., 117.)

of divine communication or, indeed, of communion. The simple reason for this concerns Barth's commitment to the distinction between *theology* and *ontology* and his refutation of any *universal* (*pan*) ontology which subsumes both God and humanity within the domain of its principles as theologically and methodologically indefensible.

Fourth, with respect to Moltmann, his criticism of Barth requires to be seen from the perspective of his own theological agenda. It cannot be our concern to discuss Moltmann's doctrine of the Trinity in any depth here, but it is certainly worth noting Moltmann's own suggestions as to how the doctrine – and in particular his notion of trinitarian personhood – should be developed. Moltmann's own determination to move away from affirming the identity of the Revealer and the Revelation, the slightly individualistic nuances in his interpretation of trinitarian personhood and his advocacy of his 'social Trinity' which interprets the Trinity as 'community', mean that he is arguing from a standpoint which may be argued to be sailing too close to tritheism.[92] Moreover, his discussion throughout reflects a projection of anthropological categories into God and the generic (non-analogical) application of the terms 'person', 'social' and 'community' to both the divine and human realms which warrant considerably more discussion than he seems to realise he should devote to them.[93] By contrast, Barth investigated

---

[92] It is interesting to observe that Moltmann felt obliged to produce a self-defence on this score! Cf. J. Moltmann, 'The Unity of the Triune God', with responses by J. B. Cobb, S. B. Thistlethwaite and J. Meyendorff, *St Vladimir's Theological Quarterly* 28, 1984. Moltmann's use of Joachim of Fiore's doctrine of the Kingdom (see 203–9) and the three forms of the Kingdom identified with the Father, Son and Spirit serve, in my opinion, to introduce flagrant confusion into the debate. One is reminded of Barth's warning 'It would be pagan mythology to present the work of God in the form of a dramatic entry and exit of now one and now another of the divine persons ... or of totally individualised powers ...'. (*C. D.* 1. 1, 374; *K. D.* 1. 1, 394.)

[93] Cf. Moltmann's discussion of the 'sociality of the divine persons' (198) in the Trinity. This gives rise to a doctrine of the Trinity which 'compels us to develop social personalism or personal socialism' (199). Another conception which Moltmann uses generically of human and divine relationships and which also savours of tritheism is that of *community*. In my view it is not helpful to articulate the intra-divine communion in terms of the category of *community* for the simple

the semantic and analogical issues with detailed argumentation and a degree of *a posteriori* reverence which we do not meet in Moltmann. The tendency in Moltmann is for his theology to be shaped by a prior personalist, indeed socio-political, ontology.[94]

Unfortunately, the various elements of truth and insight throughout Moltmann's analysis are frequently undermined by the somewhat extravagant, broad-brush and impressionistic nature of some of his criticism and accusation-by-innuendo. For example, in the section which constitutes a critique of Barth's 'trinitarian monarchianism', he suggests that 'viewed theologically this [the modern degrading of the three Persons to modes of being of the one identical subject] is a late triumph for the Sabellian modalism which the Church condemned. The result would be to transfer the subjectivity of

reason that community does not communicate adequately the loving *union* intrinsic to the divine Triunity and of which inter-personal communion at the human level (let alone community) is a mere reflection across a gulf.

[94] I certainly do not wish to suggest that there are no social or political ramifications of a proper doctrine of the Trinity. That there are very substantial socio-political implications is beyond all doubt! However, there is ground for concern if the terms 'social' and 'community' are used generically in such a manner that divine ratification or endorsement is assumed for policies identified with the adjective 'socialist'. Leonardo Boff is one example of a theologian who may be seen to push the implications of a rich and profoundly insightful exposition of the Trinity too far in this direction. This is reflected in what he describes as 'the best formula to represent the Christian God', namely, 'Three Persons and a single communion and a single trinitarian community.' (*Trinity and Society*, Eng. trans. by Paul Burns, Maryknoll, 1988, 133.) The extent of Moltmann's influence on his argumentation becomes clear when, in arguing that 'Societies with a socialist regime are founded on a right principle' (150), he makes reference to Moltmann's statement that 'Only a Christian community that is whole, united and unifying, free of dominion and oppression, and only a humanity that is whole, united and unifying, free of class domination and dictatorial oppression, can claim to respect the trinitarian God ... This is a world in which human beings hold everything in common and share everything, except their personal characteristics.' (151 – the quotation from Moltmann is cited from his 'Inviting Unity', *Concilium* 177 (1985), 50–8.) For a critical evaluation of liberation theology in the light of the doctrine of the Trinity see my chapter entitled 'The Theology of Liberation in Latin America', in *Different Gospels*, ed. Andrew Walker, London, 1988, 183-205. For explicit discussion of the relationship between theological and political statement see my 'introduction' to Eberhard Jüngel's *Christ, Justice and Peace* (Eng. trans. of *Mit Frieden Staat zu Machen* by Bruce Hamill and A. J. Torrance), Edinburgh, 1992.

action to a deity concealed "behind" the three Persons.' Although he suggests that these are only 'dangers' of which we have to be aware if these ideas are taken to their conclusions, he makes no attempt to confirm that Barth rejected in detail precisely such modalist notions and discussed at length the dangers of the notion of a deity existing 'behind' the three Persons. As we have seen, Barth believed such an approach involved either a quaternity or a denial that God *is identical with* the *Seinsweisen* and thus a collapsing of the very notion of revelation.[95]

Further still (and relating to the idealist charge), Moltmann's statement in this section that in 1927 'Barth developed the doctrine of the Trinity out of the logic of the concept of God's self-revelation'[96] is hard to reconcile with Barth's own extended repudiation of what he terms the 'serious or mocking charge' (made by less than 'attentive or sympathetic' readers) that in the earlier edition of the first volume of the *Church Dogmatics* he was using the logic of the sentence 'God speaks' to form the grounds or rationale of his doctrine of the Trinity.[97] It is not

[95] When Moltmann goes on to speak vaguely of the risk of a 'monotheism only fortuitously connected with Christianity in any way, a general transcendentality and a vague human religiosity which would simply swallow up the particular identity of the Christian faith', it seems quite irresponsible that he should be discussing these risks within a section which is ostensibly or supposed to be discussing problems attending Karl Barth's doctrine of God. As Robert Jenson would confirm, few are as opposed to this as strongly as Karl Barth and few operated a doctrine of God so clearly designed to obviate such risks!

[96] *The Trinity and the Kingdom of God*, 140.

[97] 'In the first edition of this book (p. 127) I referred to these three questions and then continued with the words: "Logically they are quite simply questions about the subject, predicate and object of the short statement: 'God speaks', *'Deus dixit.'*" On various sides these words have been taken amiss. The serious or mocking charge has been brought against me that here is a grammatical and rationalistic proof of the Trinity, so that I am doing the very thing I attack elsewhere, namely deriving the mysteries of revelation from the data of a generally discernible truth ... Naturally, it is not my thought then, nor is it now, that the truth of the dogma of the Trinity can be derived from the general truth of such a formula ...' Such a formulation of the doctrine of the Trinity 'can be called rationalistic, however, only when we can show that the use is not controlled by the question of dogma, i.e., by subordination to Scripture, but by something else, most probably by the principles of some philosophy.' *C. D.* 1. 1, 296 (*K. D.* 1. 1, 312).

clear that Barth ever, even in his early work, *consciously* 'developed the Trinity *out of* the logic of the concept of revelation'[98] despite the fact that his formulation may have been, as we have suggested, (subliminally) over-influenced by his interpretation of the grammatical structure of revelation in the biblical witness.

6) The Divine Threeness, Modalism and the Question of the Mutuality of the *Seinsweisen*   When Barth comes to discuss the question of the interconnections of the *Seinsweisen*, his interpretation seems devoid of suggestions that there is a dynamic mutuality in relating and interrelating between the particular *hypostases* – a feature which, although it does not in itself involve modalism, may suggest, at first sight, that Barth is closer to the dangers of this than he might wish to admit. His revelation model would appear to lead to more weight being given in this part of his discussion to the mutually related *functionalities* of the *Seinsweisen* than to any essentially relational dynamism of the Triunity. To say this is not, however, to accuse Barth, as flatly as LaCugna does, of a 'form of modalism' (although she is not so quick to accuse him of Sabellianism[99] – a direction in which Meijering suggests Barth is indeed edging the doctrine[100]).

Against such a direct accusation of modalism, unless it is explained more carefully than LaCugna succeeds in doing, it can be argued that it fails to take due cognisance of the features of Barth's thought which we discussed earlier and which receive further discussion below, namely a) his abso-

---

[98] Moltmann, op. cit., 141 (italics mine).

[99] Cf. *God for Us*, 252. Here LaCugna refers to Barth's suggestion that 'person' be replaced by 'modes of being', as his operating 'within the presuppositions of critical philosophy since he regarded God as one personal subject who exists in three modes of revelation, as Father, Son, and Spirit'. She concludes, 'The result is a form of modalism; whether this modalism is Sabellian could be debated.'

[100] Prior to his conclusion that Barth does push us closer to Sabellianism (see footnote above), Meijering comments 'Der Begriff der "Seinsweise" könnte an sich der sabellianischen Interpretation der Trinität näher kommen ...' (*Von den Kirchenvätern zu Karl Barth*, 54.) However, he also refers us to Barth's own rejection of the term *prosopon* as evidence of Barth's own desire to obviate any latent Sabellianism in the terminology used of the Trinity.

lute identification of God with the three *Seinsweisen* in their particularity – a feature of the divine which he emphasises as being 'irremovable' and 'ineffaceable', and b) his categorical repudiation of a quaternity or of any move to subordinate the *Seinsweisen*, insisting that either of these collapse the very grounds of, and impetus for, God-talk.

One final facet which we have not mentioned of the appeal for Barth of the term *Seinsweise* is relevant here. It lies in the perceived capacity of this notion to pick up on and, indeed, to reconcile a variety of different but related conceptions prominent within the Christian tradition – most of which sought to establish the doctrine of the Trinity against the threat of modalism while also seeking to retain the fundamental unity of essence in God. Traditional terms such as, for example, *hypostasis* (as used by the Eastern Church), *tropos huparxeos* (*modus entitativus*–Quenstedt), *modus entis* (Wollebius), *modus subsistendi* (Burmann) and *subsistentia* (Calvin) are all taken by Barth to communicate something to the characterisation of the *nescio quid*. *Seinsweise*, he believes, serves to capture the essential core of a series of concepts and of the theological definitions of the concept of the person which have been provided throughout the history of trinitarian thought.

Taken in this way, the term succeeds, Barth believed, in denoting the following emphases essential for the debate:

> In all three modes of being God is the one God both in Himself and in relation to the world and man. But this one God is God three times in different ways, so different that it is only in this threefold difference that He is God, so different that this difference, this being in these three modes of being, is absolutely essential to Him, so different, then, that this difference is irremovable.[101]

Despite, therefore, the apparent vagueness of the term, for Barth there is no possibility of coalescence or dissolution of any or all of these three into one. They are ontologically essential to the divine Being in and through their differentiation. The threeness is grounded in the 'one essence of the revealed God' and as such is, to repeat, 'irremovable'

---

[101] *C. D.* 1. 1, 360 (*K. D.* 1. 1, 380).

('unaufhebbare') and 'ineffaceable' ('unverwischbare') and thus essential to it. Barth believes these factors are preserved by the term *Seinsweise* in such a way that the various and difficult extraneous associations which he sees as relating to the term *Person* are avoided.

However, Barth also wishes to insist that the members of the Trinity are very much more than mere *Seinsweisen*. They are distinctive modes of being whose way of being is a *proprie subsistens* characterised by an essential *incommunicabilitas*. Whatever we might add by way of specification, there will always be a 'more than' with respect to any attempt to characterise the *Seinsweisen* for the simple reason that the 'more than' will necessarily project toward the *natura divina* – 'the one undifferentiated essence with which Father, Son and Spirit are, of course, identical'.[102] To the extent that they are qualifications of the divine essence in which they all share and with which they are identical, there cannot be any stipulation of the natures of the *Seinsweisen* which is not infinitely 'more than ...' and transcendentally open-ended in this respect. Ultimately, they are qualifications of the divine Being, particular, specific and unchangeable modes of it which none the less participate in the perfection of the divine essence.

The force of Barth's slightly convoluted argument here amounts to little more than that *Seinsweise* may be a useful and safe word to appeal to when we are engaged in the task of explaining why the term *Person* is used rather than any other.

We have already pointed out the extent to which Barth's doctrine of God is influenced by an 'expressivist' model of divine communication. This same revelation model may be seen to apply also in his critical discussion of the threeness of the divine modes of being.[103] What immediately strikes the

---

[102] *C. D.* 1. 1, 361 (*K. D.* 1. 1, 381).

[103] E.g. 'we can and must say now that formal distinctions in the three modes of being – that which makes them *modes* of being – can indeed be derived from the concept of revelation.' *C. D.* 1. 1, 363. See also footnote below and our discussion in chapter 2.

reader is the extent to which the threeness, rather than being characterised in the light of the primordial or ontologically primitive intra-divine communion between the Father and Son in the Spirit, is expounded with reference to a triplicity or ternary (*Ternar*) of functions, activities and analogical 'themes' which he deems to reflect threeness while affirming the simultaneous, perichoretic qualification that 'in His essence' all aspects must be affirmed to be 'indistinguishably one'.[104] In general his treatment in this section would seem to contrast in emphasis with one which focuses on the irreducible mutuality of relations of communion[105] essential to the three in their incommunicable distinctness and as they constitute the communion which is ontologically intrinsic to God.

The question that we must ask is how far Barth's conception of the unity in difference of the *Seinsweisen* contrasts ultimately with the kind of oneness in diversity characteristic of the *sumploke eidon* in terms of which Plato, in the *Symposium*, expounds the final or ultimate unity of the forms and where participation is conceived as 'essential' union.[106] There is absolutely no conceptual or ontological connection between the Greek interpretation of participation conceived as *methexis*

---

[104] This is clear from Barth's continual references in his treatise on the Trinity to his 'analysis of the concept of revelation'. The orientation of his thinking is summarised when he writes: 'The threeness of the one God as we have met it in our analysis of the concept of revelation, the threeness of revealer, revelation and being revealed, the threeness of God's holiness, mercy and love, the threeness of the God of Good Friday, Easter and Whitsunday, the threeness of God the Creator, God the Reconciler and God the Redeemer – all this can and should … draw our attention and serve as a pointer to the problem of the threeness of God.' (*C. D.* 1. 1, 361–2; *K. D.* 1. 1, 381.)

[105] I say 'relations of communion' to reflect what Zizioulas refers to as loving *ekstasis*, which is very different from relations of *origin* which Barth *does* discuss, but which is rather different, i.e. not in itself a form of 'relating' but one of ontological *grounding* or *ordering*, that is, *taxis*.

[106] It is relevant to this question of a possible parallelism to suggest that Plato does not fall foul of a 'third man argument' in his conception of the *sumploke eidon*. The union of the forms is not by virtue of an extrinsic relationship or an extrinsic *tertium datum* which would itself require a form and where this would constitute an infinite regress. There is a basal givenness in Plato which may be defined as a kind of eternal *perichoresis* or *immanentia*. This having been said, what Plato is referring to could never be described as a *koinonia*.

and the New Testament interpretation of participation as *koinonia*! And it is with this question in mind that we must look both at his discussion of the divine Triunity and his interpretation of *perichoresis*. Does Barth's model of God's 'threefold Self-communication' (the phrase which Moltmann uses to denote Rahner's doctrine of God) lead, as it would in Rahner, to a denial of mutuality within the Trinity?

The affirmation of 'Triunity', Barth suggests, reflects the twofold perception that first, 'for those who hear and see revelation in the Bible the Father, Son and Spirit, or however we name the three elements in the biblical revelation, come together in the knowledge and concept of the one God'. Second, 'we see on the other side how for them the source and goal of this knowledge and concept are never a sterile one but are rather the three, whatever we call them. In practice the concept of triunity is the movement of these two thoughts.'[107] Barth's explanation refers to the unity of the Father, Son and Spirit as a oneness of essence ('Das Wesen Gottes ist ja eines'[108]). However, he also speaks of 'fellowship' ('Gemeinschaft') and 'a definite participation ("eine bestimmte Teilnahme")' of each mode of being in the other modes of being, and, indeed, since the modes of being are in fact identical with the relations of origin, a complete participation of each mode of being in the other modes of being',[109] where this participation is to be conceived as a 'co-presence' ('Mitgegenwart') of the modes of being in each other. This he explains with reference to the doctrine of the *perichoresis* – or *circuminsessio*[110] – where 'the divine modes of being mutually condition and permeate one another so completely that one is always in the other two and the other two in the one'. He then adds, 'Sometimes this has been

[107] *C. D.* 1. 1, 369 (*K. D.* 1. 1, 389).

[108] *K. D.* 1. 1, 390.

[109] *C. D.* 1. 1, 370 (*K. D.* 1. 1, 390).

[110] It must be pointed out that Barth rejects the (now popular) conception of a cyclical dynamics associated with the term *perichoresis,* preferring its Latin translation as *circuminsessio* – what he terms a 'dwelling in one another, immanentia, inexistentia' (*C. D.* 1. 1, 370; *K. D.* 1. 1, 390) – rather than *circumincessio.*

grounded more in the unity of the divine essence ("Wesen") and sometimes more in the relations of origin as such. Both approaches are right and both are ultimately saying the same thing.'[111] None of the modes of being would be what it is 'without its co-existence with the others ... none exists as a special individual' and 'all three "in-exist" ("inexistieren") or exist only in concert as modes of being of the one God and Lord who posits Himself from eternity to eternity'.[112] Barth regards the doctrine of *perichoresis* as 'an important form of the dialectic needed to work out the concept of "triunity"'. The question we are left with is whether it should be conceived dialectically or, rather, dynamically in terms of the category of communion. Despite Barth's occasional association of the notions of *perichoresis*, communion and modes of being,[113] he fails to ground his exposition in Volume One in anything like as dynamic a conception of the perichoretic communion of the Trinity as is to be found, for example, in the writings of John Zizioulas and others from the Eastern tradition.

In stark contrast to the concept of oneness of being underlying Plato's theory of *methexis*, the very different notion of participation identified by the New Testament as *koinonia* should commit us to an irreducibly relational conceptuality denoting a radically interpersonal overlapping or inter-penetration of being, where this is conceived in such a way that the personal hypostases are fully realised in this and not in any way subsumed by it. Theologically speaking, *koinonia* designates a union in God which is such in its transcendent realisation that it can also be spoken of as an *intra*-personal (in addition to *inter*-personal) communion intrinsic to the being of the one, eternal God. In other words, it allows us to speak

---

[111] Ibid.

[112] *C. D.* 1. 1, 370 (*K. D.* 1. 1, 371).

[113] In his section entitled 'The Eternal Father', Barth refers to the unity of the Trinity *ad extra*, arguing that 'the unity of their work is to be understood as the communion of the three modes of being along the lines of the doctrine of "perichoresis", according to which all three, without forfeiture or mutual dissolution of independence, reciprocally interpenetrate each other and inexist in one another.' (*C. D.* 1. 1, 396; *K. D.* 1. 1, 417.)

simultaneously of the person (singular) of God and the persons (plural) of the Trinity. This dynamic in God is such that the question as to which is more fundamental between union or communion is inappropriate and fundamentally anthropomorphic or, indeed, cosmo-morphic – deriving, that is, from a failure to think out of the unique form which the divine communion takes *ad extra*. As Moltmann argues quite rightly, 'The unity of God is to be found in the triunity of the Father, the Son and the Holy Spirit. It neither precedes that nor follows it.'[114] He also writes, 'The concept of person must ... in itself contain the concept of unitedness or at-oneness, just as, conversely, the concept of God's at-oneness must in itself contain the concept of three Persons.'[115]

It is from within this perspective that the irrelevance of the 'chicken and egg' questions which have so haunted the history of Christian thought becomes clear – questions, that is, of the form: does the concept of communion presuppose the prior concept of being or essence? Is unity of being or essence more fundamental than union in communion? Or should we rather define both the oneness of God and the cause of divinity in terms of the person of the Father conceived as the *fons deitatis* or *arche* – a question to which we return below in our discussion of Zizioulas?

There is not the space here even to begin to discuss the history of these debates. Suffice to say that an *a posteriori* theology, as Barth sought to provide, which thinks *out of* the primordial nature of the triune communion that is to be identified with God and which does not project foreign categories of divine subjectivity on to the Trinity, should not lead to those kinds of debate which have so divided East and

---

[114] *The Trinity and the Kingdom of God*, 190. Earlier in the same book he writes, 'The unitedness, the at-oneness, of the triunity is already given with the fellowship of the Father, the Son and the Spirit. It therefore does not need to be additionally secured by a particular doctrine about the unity of the divine substance, or by the special doctrine of the one divine lordship.' (150.)

[115] Ibid., 150. Although I am happy with the main thrust of this statement, I am not happy with some of Moltmann's terminology here! The notions of union and communion are clearly preferable to those of unitedness and at-oneness, which are too individualistic and hence err in the direction of tritheism.

West. It is our view, therefore, that if Barth's discussion had integrated more effectively the notions of *koinonia* and 'essence' or 'being', this would have opened the door to a conception of the divine economy which involved a richer integration of communion and communication, a participative 'worship model' in interaction with his 'revelation model', and an exposition of the Triunity of revelation in terms of the *mutuality* of the divine communion. A more unambiguous affirmation of the primordial nature of the intra-personal communion of the Trinity than he offers would have exposed as vacuous any attempt to determine ultimate origins or ontological grounds in terms of a) monist or static notions of divine substance or essence, or b) monadic, Cartesian conceptions of a divine ego or 'subject of consciousness' – both of which appear to influence to some degree sections of Barth's exposition.

A doctrine of the Trinity which takes seriously the mutuality of loving communion opened up for humanity in Christ by the Spirit suggests the ultimate identification of the source of being and the communion of the Triunity.[116] The communion of God is in no sense to be conceived as a qualification of a more foundational category of 'being' or 'substance'.[117] The triune communion characterises Reality (Being) at the most fundamental level – it is that in which we live and move and have our being. The communion of the Trinity as such constitutes the *arche* and *telos* of all that is. It provides the hermeneutical criterion of all that has existence (of good as well as evil) and compels us to conceive and reinterpret Being in terms of divine personhood and the ultimacy of the intra-divine personal communion. That the critical controls on the understanding of this would have to remain radically

---

[116] Cf. Moltmann's notion of the 'open Trinity' in *The Trinity and the Kingdom of God, passim.*

[117] If subatomic physics has disposed of the myth that at the most basic level we must posit some primordial substance to be conceived as the ground and postulate of the notion of relations, trinitarian theology has (analogically!) suggested precisely this at the theological and cosmological levels!

theological (and therefore *a posteriori*) and not anthropological is expressed in Barth's emphatic reminder, 'This is the unique divine trinity in the unique divine unity.'[118]

Nothing less, therefore, than the most fundamental ontological and cosmological issues are at stake here in the debate concerning the mutuality and communion which characterises the Triunity. Lack of clarity here has ramifications for the whole of theology – not least the nature–grace debate and the doctrines of creation, reconciliation and the covenant as these are irreducibly bound up with the doctrine of God. Consequently, consideration of Barth's revelation model and the manner in which he approaches the notion of triune personhood raises issues of the most fundamental importance for theology in its totality!

Two important issues must be borne in mind in a final assessment of Barth.

1) First, there is a tension in Barth's thought. He is ambiguous and the attempt to formulate a consistent critique is continuously met by comments he makes which seek to counterbalance weaker arguments he may have used elsewhere. This is particularly true in his continual reminders of the need to interpret the *Seinsweisen* in relational terms. He seems to endorse a whole series of attempts throughout the history of thought to emphasise the fundamental importance of the relations in denoting the trinitarian modes of being.[119] Precisely what he means, however, is not always clear. The term 'relation' can refer to logical relations, the ordering of things, the ontological co-ordinates of a thing or a facet of something conceived with respect to something else. It may refer to genealogical connections, mutual conditions, causal, 'aitial' or ontological grounds. The concept in each of these cases is radically different from that unique and specific redefinition of the term 'relation' denoted when reference is

---

[118] *C. D.* 1. 1, 364.
[119] Cf. *K. D.* 1. 1, 384–6.

made to the dynamic mutuality of the inner communion between the Father and the Son in the Spirit.[120]

A brief modification of Barth's own definition of the 'persons' of the Trinity may serve to clarify the point. He concludes his discussion by suggesting that 'at the point where earlier dogmatics and even modern Roman Catholic dogmatics speak of persons we prefer to call the Father, Son and Spirit in God the three distinctive modes of being of the one God subsisting ("bestehenden") in their relationships [Barth uses the word "Beziehung" rather than "Verhältnis" here] one with another'.[121] By the term '*bestehenden*' Barth is referring to the Latin word *subsistens*. What we would suggest is required here is an integration of *sub-sistens* (*hypo-stasis*) and *ek-sistens* (*ek-stasis*) in a manner that removed the ambiguity of the word *Beziehung*. The thrust of our suggestion is that the use of the term 'person' within the context of careful theological definition and a suitably *a posteriori* rendering of the semantics of the term would serve much more effectively to communicate a sense of the dynamics intrinsic to the intra-divine love and communion. Moreover, it would also lead to a closer integration of this with the vicarious humanity and priesthood of Christ as these form the very grammar of the Gospel.

2) Second, no particular word is sacrosanct and there is, therefore, no warrant for any *absolutisation* of the use of any term – not least the term 'person'.[122]

---

[120] The very ambiguity of the term *Relativität* which Barth uses (*K. D.* 1. 1, 386) in connection with the term *Relation* illustrates this point. There is a need for some clarity in distinguishing between 'relativity' and 'relatedness'.

[121] *C. D.* 1. 1, 366 (*K. D.* 1. 1, 386).

[122] Analogous statements and reminders may be made concerning the use of the term 'person' to the following comments Alasdair Heron makes with respect to the term *homoousios*. 'Homoousios belongs with the theologian's toolbox; it is part of his terminology, in itself dogmatic rather than kerygmatic in character. There it has its place and its abiding validity. But what really matters is to grasp what it means – that in Christ God himself has come among us, identified himself in solidarity with us, and claimed us as his own. The key to the Gospel is not the word *homoousios*, but the Word made flesh ...', ('*Homoousios* with the Father' in *The Incarnation*, ed. T. F. Torrance, Edinburgh, 1981, 76.)

What is to be stressed here is not any particular concept but the dynamic Reality which the doctrine of the Trinity seeks to serve. *Non sermoni res, sed rei sermo subiectus,* as Barth reminds us. However, as will also become clear from further discussion of Eberhard Jüngel and the Hintikkas, the realities of human existence, the social semantics of divine communication and the integration of language and thought are such that the *res* and *sermo* actually participate in each other in the revelation event in such a way that the language of God-talk ceases to be extrinsic to the revelation event itself. Human participation in that event includes the language of proclamation, and theological language must integrate with the participative event. In other words, the dynamic Reality which the doctrine of the Trinity seeks to serve actually 'takes place' in and through the event of articulation of that reality. Human thought, expression, speech and the form of semantic sociality that theological enquiry is may not be separated from each other. Any attempt to do so can only be seriously distortive. The terminology of God-talk is not separate from, and must therefore reflect, the participative nature of the event of revelation. The 'quasi-performative' or 'success' element in proclamation and the articulative nature of theology are radically intermeshed.

Our prime concern in this examination of Barth's discussion of the propriety or otherwise of the terms *Seinsweise* and *Person* concerns the extent to which Barth has allowed the issues to be adjudicated with recourse to a 'revelation model' which inadequately expresses the dynamic relations of mutual love within the Triunity on the one hand and which fails to integrate with an adequate conception of semantic participation (as this is constitutive of human thought and understanding) on the other. A doxological model which balanced metaphors of 'address' and 'meeting' with those equally important New Testament notions of *koinonia,* communion and participatory being and worship could have addressed these concerns much more adequately. Moreover, any residual influence of the 'infinite gulf' of his earlier dialectical theology would have been tempered further as he would have been forced to emphasise the 'actual' in Christ as opposed to the necessary (albeit 'given') conditions of possibility *vis-à-vis* the knowledge of God and God-talk.

Karl Rahner and John Zizioulas: Two Contrasting Expositions of Triunity

Karl Rahner

In his contribution to *Mysterium Salutis, Grundriss heilsgeschichtlicher Dogmatik. Vol. 2,* entitled 'Der dreifaltige Gott als transzendenter Urgrund der Heilsgeschichte', Karl Rahner sets the scene for his discussion of the doctrine of the Trinity by objecting to the failure on the part of Christians to integrate the doctrine of the Trinity with their interpretation and living of life.[123] He comments that 'despite their orthodox confession of the Trinity, Christians are, in their practical life, almost mere monotheists', and that 'should the doctrine of the Trinity have to be dropped as false, the major part of religious literature could well remain virtually unchanged'.[124]

---

[123] Eberhard Jüngel endorses fully Rahner's comment here. Cf. *God as the Mystery of the World,* 371. Quoting Rahner on this issue, he adds, 'Perhaps the end of theism had to begin to dawn in order to disclose the existential relevance of a doctrine of the Trinity which must be grounded and explicated anew.'

Our primary concern in this discussion is to explore the integration of the doctrine of the Trinity (*ad intra* and not merely *ad extra*) and human being. This is not done by translating the doctrine into practical (moral) implications but rather by exploring the dynamic of worship as this is all-inclusive of the human person as he or she is liberated for participation, and taken to participate in, the triune life of God.

[124] *The Trinity* (Eng. trans., by Joseph Donceel, of cited article), London, 1970, 10-11. Also, 'the treatise on the Trinity occupies a rather isolated position in the total dogmatic system ... Its function in the whole dogmatic construction is not clearly perceived.' (14). Later on (39), he emphasises the 'abstract impractical character' which is so frequent in treatises on the Trinity.

There is no question that this is how the doctrine is widely conceived. Immanuel Kant writes, 'From the doctrine of the Trinity, taken literally, nothing whatsoever can be gained for practical purposes...' (*Der Streit der Fakultäten*, Ph. B. 252, 33, quoted in Moltmann, *The Trinity and the Kingdom of God*, 6). Kant believed that it would remain equally irrelevant for practical living whether we had to worship three or ten persons in the deity. (Moltmann, op. cit., 6).

The concern behind Rahner's slightly puzzling, indeed misleading, use of the term 'monotheist' in this profoundly pertinent observation,[125] is first to focus on the uniqueness of each of the hypostases and, second, to open the way to a fuller appreciation of the ontological relations proper to each respective 'person' in relation to humanity.[126] The grounds of the 'monotheistic' weakness, Rahner believes, are bound up with the Western dichotomy between the treatises *De Deo Uno* and *De Deo Trino,* where the former has been too concerned with what might be termed 'the one divinity' of God, addressing God's essence and its unicity at the cost of an adequate theological or ontological analysis of the unity of the divine persons. 'The separation of the two treatises here and the sequence in which they are explained' probably derives, he suggests, 'from the Augustinian–Western conception of the Trinity' which begins with the one God, the one divine essence as a whole, and only *afterwards* interprets God as three persons[127] – a criticism echoed in Colin Gunton's devastating critique of the influence of Augustine on Western theology.[128] The medieval Latin Church's emphasis on the

R. Seeberg also observed, as Jüngel points out, that a practical unitarianism emerged in part as the result of the enclosure of the doctrine of the Trinity within the immanent life of God and that therefore the doctrine of the Trinity 'needs another theoretical foundation than the old one.' (R. Seeberg, *Zum dogmatischen Verständnis der Trinitätslehre,* 1908, 5, quoted in Eberhard Jüngel, *God as the Mystery of the World,* 370.

[125] As Pannenberg comments, 'The doctrine of the Trinity, in the sense of patristic theology particularly, must be understood as the Christian form of monotheism. It must actually be interpreted as the positive condition for a consistent monotheism.' (W. Pannenberg, 'Die Subjektivität Gottes und die Trinitätslehre', *Kerygma und Dogma* 23, (1977), 39, n. 34) Barth also stresses that 'With the doctrine of the Trinity, we step on to the soil of Christian monotheism.' (*C. D.* 1. 1, 354; *K. D.* 1. 1, 374.) (Both cited in Moltmann, *The Trinity and the Kingdom of God,* 241, n. 22).

[126] Cf. Rahner, *The Trinity,* 11–15.

[127] Ibid., 17.

[128] 'Augustine, the Trinity and the Theological Crisis of the West', *S. J. T.* 43, 33–58. Professor Gunton argues that Augustine simply does not have the 'conceptual equipment' to avoid a 'collapse' into the kinds of weaknesses exemplified by Eunomianism, modalism and, indeed, Arianism. (58). Consequently, his influence on the West has not always been a constructive one with respect to the doctrine of God.

unicity of the divine essence integrated with this with the result that the treatise becomes, as Rahner sees it, 'quite philosophical and abstract and refers hardly at all to salvation history'. Its concern with the necessary metaphysical properties of God means that it fails adequately to address 'God as experienced in salvation history in his free relations to his creatures'.[129]

It is Rahner's intention to break with both the dichotomy to which we have drawn attention and also the formal doctrines of a 'Trinity which is absolutely locked within itself'[130] in an attempt to proffer a coherent integration of the treatises 'On the One God' and 'On the Trinity', to try and redress the *a priorisms* inherent in the doctrine of God characteristic of Western theology.[131] Rejecting the 'isolation' of the treatise of the Trinity, he argues 'There *must* be a connection between Trinity and man.'[132] The key to this is to be found in the two-way identity statement: 'The "economic" Trinity is the "immanent" Trinity and the "immanent" Trinity is the "economic" Trinity.'[133] Two features of Rahner's argumentation are immediately significant. He insists that: 1) a proper interpretation of grace sees it as the 'self-communication of God (not primarily as "created grace") in Christ and in his Spirit'; and 2) 'there is at least *one* "mission", *one* presence in the world, *one* reality of salvation history which is not merely appropriated to some divine person, but which is proper to

---

[129] Rahner, op. cit., 17–18.

[130] Ibid., 18. Cf. 'The isolation of the treatise of the Trinity *has* to be wrong.' (21.)

[131] We must mention that Rahner's alternative to *a priori* deduction is not what he describes as 'a merely *a posteriori* gathering of random facts'. Rather, he opts for what he calls a 'middle way', namely, 'the recognition of what is experienced aposteriorily as transcendentally necessary, because it has to be, because it cannot be mere facticity, whatever the reasons from which this necessity may be inferred.' (Ibid., 100, fn. 18.) 'Necessity' is always problematic especially if it is used, as Rahner would wish, of the transcendental. Is it really the case that humankind can determine at the level of the transcendent that a truth is a 'necessary' one, as opposed to one that is freely and purposively intended by God?

[132] Ibid., 21.

[133] Ibid., 22.

him. ... There has occurred in salvation history something which can be predicated only of one divine person.'[134]

This commits Rahner to a break with scholastic notions of the divine essence and involves a) his moving away from the notion of 'created grace' to interpret grace as the dynamic of God's personal involvement with humanity; b) his emphasis on the 'integrity' of the divine identity in salvation (i.e. what God *is toward us* is God as he really *is* and vice versa), and c) his emphasis, which is involved by this, on distinctive appropriation.[135] These facets set the scene for an integration of a theology of divine communion – where God is interpreted in a more dynamic and onto-relational manner – and a participative anthropology.[136]

Significant here also is his repudiation of the view that '"hypostasis" in God is a univocal concept with respect to the three divine persons'. If this were to be the case, he argues, then 'there would no longer be any connection between "mission" and the intra-trinitarian life'.[137] As Rahner appreciates, acknowledging the non-univocality of the application of the term 'person' with respect to the persons of the Trinity is critical for a proper grasp of the analogical and non-generic manner in which the term 'person' is used in this context. He adds, 'We should keep in mind that the ways in which each person is a person are so different that they allow

---

[134] Ibid., 22–3.

[135] See his discussion 'Common Activity "ad extra" and Appropriation', 76 ff.

[136] There is insufficient space to do more than comment here that it is a matter of enormous puzzlement that Rahner believed he could integrate his insights here with his 'transcendental anthropology' – something which Fergus Kerr has shown to be incompatible with his use of Heidegger. ('Rahner Retrospective III: Transcendence or Finitude', *New Blackfriars* 62 (September 1981), 370–9.) Rahner's Kantian approach to anthropology witnessed in *Geist im Welt*, which he wrote early in his career (his doctoral thesis), and the transcendentalism on which his exposition of Christian theology, which he wrote at the end of his life, is grounded, both seem to be arguably incompatible and, at the very least, made superfluous by the implications of his identification of the immanent and economic Trinities!

[137] Rahner, op. cit., 30.

of only a *very loosely* analogical concept of person, as *equally* applicable to the three persons.'[138]

What Rahner (like Barth) fails fully to appreciate, however, is the extent to which the term 'person', interpreted theologically, has *unique* potential to sustain precisely the necessary 'looseness' to which he refers – something which John Zizioulas grasps much more fully in his discussion of human capacity and incapacity and his consequent refusal to interpret personhood with recourse to determinable boundaries. Like Barth, Rahner was concerned with what the various 'persons' might be argued to possess in common. What he too fails to appreciate is the unique potential of the term 'person' to denote the essential *incommunicabilitas*, distinctness and specificity of each 'member' of the Trinity while retaining the open-endedness and conceptual 'fluidity' necessary if the irreducibly and uniquely *relational* nature of this kind of reality is not to be undermined. An appropriately theological interpretation of the notion 'person' communicates precisely that what it is referring to is something very different from an essence or commonality, namely an onto-relational 'identity' which requires to be interpreted with specific reference to its own unique framework of interrelations. It is not clear that *Subsistenzweise* is any more successful in communicating this dynamic than *Seinsweise*.

Several central propositions affirmed by Karl Rahner are pertinent to our discussion, namely:

1) that a) each of the trinitarian persons is 'personal and particular'; and b) this personal particularity is reflected in the communication of each person;[139]

2) with respect to any real distinctions present in what is communicated by God, to the extent that there is a real distinction there 'for us', 'then God must "in himself" carry

---

[138] Ibid., 29.

[139] He writes, 'each one of the three divine persons communicates himself to man in gratuitous grace in his own personal particularity and diversity.' (Ibid., 34–5.)

this distinction'.[140] He states unambiguously, therefore, '*Economic* Sabellianism is false.'[141] And he also affirms that the '"threefoldness" of God's relation to us in Christ's order of grace is already the reality of God as it is in itself: a three-personal one';[142]

3) that 'this self-communication of the persons occurs ... according to, and in virtue of, their mutual relations',[143] and that the eternal relation between the Father and the Son is a welcoming each other in love, a drawing and returning to each other;

4) that 'That which is communicated is the triune personal God', such that the free, gratuitous bestowal that is God's self-utterance and 'self-donation' 'occurs only in the intra-divine manner of the two communications of the divine essence by the Father to the Son and the Spirit';[144]

5) that the Self-communication of God remains sovereign and incomprehensible and continues to dwell – even as it is received – in its uncontrollable and incomprehensible originality;

6) that God's trinitarian communication is the ontological ground of the life of humanity under grace;[145] and

7) that proper, human self-understanding is irreducibly bound up with the perception of the Trinity.[146]

There is a great deal in Rahner's discussion that echoes similar themes in Barth's discussion. The above list of

---

[140] Ibid., 36 note 34. Later on in the discussion he repeats his insistence that the 'distinctions of "God for us" are also those of "God in himself"'. (44.)

[141] Ibid., 38.

[142] Ibid.

[143] Ibid., 35.

[144] Ibid., 35–6.

[145] Ibid., 35.

[146] He writes, 'When a true statement about the Trinity is correctly understood and translated into our life, the correctly understood theory points quite naturally towards real life, as lived in faith and in grace, in which the mystery of the triune God himself holds sway and which is not simply constituted by its conceptual objectification.' (Ibid., 48.) Or, again, 'Man understands himself only when he has realized that he is the one to whom God communicates himself' (47).

affirmations should make that obvious. Both theologians, moreover, shared similar fears. These find expression in the influence which three factors have on Rahner's discussion, namely: 1) a determination to avoid treating the persons as separate centres of consciousness;[147] 2) a profound awareness of the danger of operating from a tritheistic starting-point; and 3) a concern not to regard the term 'person' as sacrosanct, as if it could not be improved upon – this he stresses despite his full appreciation of the central role the term has played in the tradition of orthodox trinitarian theology.

Like Barth before him, Rahner's fundamental emphasis focuses on divine Self-communication which serves as the central, determining theme in his exposition of the Trinity. At various points the influence of Barth's exposition of the Trinity in terms of the structure of revelation becomes clear and he comes close to interpreting the unity of the Father, Son and Spirit in terms of the integration of the Revealer, the Revelation and the Revealedness – a parallelism which expresses most effectively the 'intrinsicity' (which we described in chapter two) integral to the revelation event, but less constructive when seeking to articulate the nature of the divine communion.[148] Despite the apparent replacing of the

---

[147] Cf. ibid., 56, 75 and 106. For example, he comments, 'it is evident that the element of consciousness, which nowadays and from long ago is almost spontaneously connected with the concept, does not belong to it in our context ...' (75), or, again, 'Whatever would mean three "subjectivities" must be carefully kept away from the concept of person in the present context' (75–6), and, finally, 'when *today we* speak of person in the plural, we think almost necessarily, because of the modern meaning of the word, of several spiritual centers of activity, of several subjectivities and liberties. But there are not three of these in God ...' (106).

[148] Rahner continually emphasises God's Self-communication, referring to it as 'the self-communication which wills itself absolutely and creates the possibility of its acceptance *and this acceptance itself...*' (ibid., 97–8, italics mine). Also, he writes, 'the human personal subject is the addressee who is, of his very nature, demanded by the divine self-communication, which creates him as the condition of its own possibility' (91). Unless the creativity here refers exclusively to *creatio originalis*, then this may also be seen to involve the intrinsicity which we have discussed. Rahner is not saying that the human being is created to be the free and creative co-condition of the event of communication!

Spirit with divine causality there is a Barthian nuance in his statement, 'The Son is first ... the self-communication of the Father to the world in such a way that in the Son he is radically *there* and that his self-communication entails, as an effect produced by itself, its radical acceptance.'[149]

Despite the suggestion of an entailment here, Rahner is simultaneously nervous of promoting a doctrine of the Trinity which commits him (by way of a triune logic – or transcendental onto-logic – of the divine Self-communication) to a deterministic anthropology. The event of the divine Self-communication, he emphasises, is a liberative act and the divine Self-communication elicits an 'answer of *free* love in man's decision'. In order for this to be the case, he argues, the Self-communication 'must render such an answer possible, make room for it ...'[150] This it does by constituting the consummation of the being of the human subject – 'it must open the field of transcendence or even contain transcendence within itself as its own moment'.[151]

This statement (and in particular the qualification, 'or even') constitutes a remarkable move for Rahner in that it suggests a *dynamic* conception of the bestowal and creation of epistemic conditions within the human subject in the process of the divine Self-communication – where this takes place in and through the trinitarian event as it involves the particular *hypostasis* of the Son. This should mean, as we suggested earlier, a radical revision of the kind of approach witnessed in

---

[149] Ibid., 63. Or again, 'what we call "Holy Spirit", God (hence the Father) really communicates himself ... he produces this self-communication in us and maintains it by himself. Hence the "Spirit" must be God himself' (67). However, Rahner is also, like Barth, aware of the dangers of an invalid form of 'deduction' of the Trinity. When discussing the innerly-related moments of the 'Son' and the 'Spirit' in the divine Self-communication, he comments in a footnote, 'It does not claim to deduce them [the Son and the Spirit] from our mere concept of a self-communication of God which we might perhaps abstractly construct ...' Yet, he adds, 'There is a strange overlapping of experience and insight in transcendental necessity. Even that which is known only through factual experience may occasionally be recognized as necessary: thus, in the present case, the two moments of a freely posited reality, as belonging necessarily together' (85).

[150] Ibid., 96.

[151] Ibid., 97.

Rahner's earlier expositions of his 'transcendental anthropology' which suggest that the conditions of the awareness of God are anthropologically demonstrable in advance of the revelation event.[152] This is not, however, what we find in his later work *Foundations of Christian Faith* (1976).[153] How far Rahner is foundationally committed to the repudiation of mediating created hypostases remains, at best, an open question for there he commences his whole systematic, theological exposition by analysing the nature of 'the hearer of the message',[154] 'transcendental experience',[155] 'man as transcendent being'[156] and 'personhood' as the 'presupposition of the Christian message'.[157] Despite his suggestion that if God is not the given there is no Self-gift on the part of God and that what would be communicated would be something other than God's Self,[158] he leaves himself open to being interpreted as believing that the 'hearer of the message' has an innate capacity to aspire to the transcendent whether there is a specific and particular act of Self-bestowal on the part of God

---

[152] That Rahner is aware of the *a posteriori* and *de facto* obligations of the revelation event is suggested by his comment that 'as the self-communication must be understood as absolutely willed by God it must carry its acceptance with it. If we are not to downgrade this communication to the level of a human *a priori* and *thus do away with it* the acceptance must be brought about by the self-communicating God himself.' (Ibid., 97 – italics mine.)

It may be added that John Zizioulas sees Rahner as exemplifying the school that emphasises humanity's natural (transcendental) capacity for God. Cf. 'On Human Capacity and Incapacity, A Theological Exploration of Personhood', *S. J. T.* 28 (1975), 405.

[153] *Foundations of Christian Faith: An introduction to the idea of Christianity* (Eng. trans. by William Dych), London, 1978.

[154] This is the title of chapter one of *Foundations of Christian Faith*.

[155] E.g. ibid., 20. In chapter one he writes of the human subject, 'In the fact that he experiences his finiteness radically, he reaches beyond this finiteness and experiences himself as a transcendent being, as spirit.' (32.) Again, he argues that 'being constituted as transcendental subject, he is in the presence of being as mystery ...' (42). It is difficult to understand how Rahner feels he can combine these facets of his anthropology with a Heideggerian talk of the *existentiell* constitution of *Dasein*, although he refers throughout to the *existentiell* as opposed to the existential.

[156] The title of chapter one, section 3.

[157] The title of chapter one, section 2, subsection 1.

[158] Cf. ibid., 101 *et passim*.

or not! Moreover, given his unambiguous assertion that 'the structure of the subject itself is an *a priori*',[159] Rahner seems less than committed to the question of any such Self-bestowal's involving the transformation of the *subjective* conditions of the 'hearing' of the message.

Why this is significant is that what is at issue here is the distinction between a participatory anthropology grounded in the irreducibly trinitarian dynamic of grace and a transcendental anthropology grounded in an analysis of human nature and the postulation of some universal and 'essential openness'.[160] These two alternatives point to the kind of distinction between cosmologies to which we referred in chapter 2. The former involves precisely the kind of radical revision in the interpretation of being that is required if we are to break with the disjunction between the treatises *De Deo Uno* and *De Deo Trino*, as Rahner so strongly advocates.

However, the extent to which Rahner has fully and consistently broken with this and thus moved into the kind of personal and 'relational' or onto-relational approach which is required is best judged in the light of his discussion of triune personhood. It is to this that we now turn more specifically.

When we make use of the concept of 'person' the following must apply:

a) the concept must not serve to generalise that which is absolutely unique.[161] What is really common to Father, Son and Spirit is 'precisely the one and only Godhead';[162]

b) the divine persons may not be enumerated in the same manner that applies to other kinds of distinct entities. Whereas

---

[159] Ibid., 'Introduction', 19.

[160] Ibid., 19ff.

[161] Again, one wonders whether this is consistent with *Foundations of Christian Faith* where his exposition 'Man as Person and Subject' (chapter 1, 26ff.) is presupposed by his later exposition 'God as Person' (chapter 2, 71ff.). His argument leaves it open as to which is *prius* and which is *posterius* – at the methodological level, at least – and whether there is not a latently generic presupposition in operation at the material level.

[162] Ibid., 104.

individuals in another context may, he suggests, be 'added up', this is not the case of the triune persons;[163]

c) the reference of the term to God is not the same as elsewhere – it has a 'linguistic usage which exists nowhere else';[164]

d) the meaning of the phrase 'three persons', when used of the Trinity, is derived 'subsequent to' our experience of salvation-history; here, it should be added, Rahner perpetuates a confusion sustained throughout his study by suggesting the generalisation is a 'logical explanation' where what he means at best is 'deriving from an analysis of that experience which is God's Self-communication';[165]

e) it serves to counter modalistic understandings; and

f) it does not suggest a mutual love within the Trinity. He writes, 'there is properly no mutual love between Father and Son, for this would presuppose two acts'.[166] This reiterates the implications of his earlier statement: 'Hence within the Trinity there is no reciprocal "Thou".'[167]

---

[163] See the analysis above of Barth's discussion of numericity.

[164] Ibid., 105.

[165] Cf. ibid., 53, where he writes, 'By a logical explanation of a statement about a certain state of affairs, I mean an explanation which makes the statement in question clear, that is, more precise ... To put it roughly: the logical explanation explains by making more precise; it does not use one state of affairs to explain another one. Hence all the concepts used to explain that statement can be derived from it.' He distinguishes such an explanation from an ontic explanation which 'is one that takes into account another state of affairs, in such a way that this helps us to understand what is to be explained'. What Rahner terms a 'logical explanation' would be much better described as an ontological explanation which interprets something in the light of its own specific reality and grounds. In the context of the term 'person' used of the Trinity, the explanation of any particular use of the term requires onto-relational exposition where the reality is interpreted in its own essential relations to the other persons of the Trinity. The expression 'logical explanation' completely fails to communicate this!

[166] Ibid., 106. This stands in stark contrast with, for example, Colin Gunton's recent exposition of the doctrine of the Trinity in which he states that 'in eternity Father, Son and Spirit share a dynamic mutual reciprocity, interpenetration and interanimation'. *The One, the Three and the Many*, Cambridge, 1993, 163.)

[167] Rahner, op. cit., 76. This is also implied by his preference for St Thomas' concept of the person (*subsistens distinctum in natura rationali*) over that of Richard of St Victor (cf. 104, footnote 25.)

Rahner concludes that the term 'person' may best be explained and correctly interpreted as 'distinct modes of subsisting' ('Subsistenzweisen').

> The one self-communication of the one God occurs in three different manners of given-ness, in which the one God is given concretely for us in himself ... God is the concrete God in each one of these manners of given-ness – which, of course, refer to each other relatively, without modalistically coinciding. If we translate this in terms of 'immanent' Trinity, we may say: the one God subsists in three distinct manners of subsisting.[168]

Rahner sees this as better, simpler and more in harmony with the traditional language of theology and the Church than Karl Barth's phrase – moreover, it reiterates what St Thomas sought to affirm in his definition of 'person'.

LaCugna suggests that 'subsisting' is more concrete than Barth's 'being'.[169] However, given a) that *Sein* in Barth does not mean 'essence'; b) that Barth's fuller definition is 'eigentumliche Seinsweise', and c) Barth's very extensive argumentation which sets out to offset the dangers of modalism and essentialism and to insist on the distinctiveness of the *Seinsweisen*, it is hard to accept that this is the case.

It may well be argued that the term *Subsistenzweise*, appeals to a theology which has not liberated itself from a dichotomy between the divine essence and the divine Being as is reflected in Thomas *and* in certain features of Rahner's discussion.[170] This, indeed, clearly underlies his failure to countenance mutuality and reciprocity between the persons.[171]

---

[168] Ibid., 109.

[169] *God for Us*, 253.

[170] Cf. for example, his statements with respect to the 'persons' of the Trinity: 'the manner of subsisting is distinct through its relative opposition to another one; it is real through its identity with the divine essence' or, again, 'the one and same divine essence subsists in each of the three divine manners of subsisting'. (Op. cit., 114.)

[171] Rahner's definition of the concept of 'person' is a profoundly individualistic one and one which has little to do with the modern concept of person, as Moltmann points out in *The Trinity and the Kingdom of God*, 145. A similar

By contrast, Eberhard Jüngel is, in our view, profoundly right to insist, as he does, that it is impossible to offer a proper reworking of the doctrine of the Trinity in the light of the 'passion history of God' before we have exposed and broken from the 'aporia of the traditional doctrine of God'. The aporia of which he speaks is the separation from each other of the essence and existence of God.

> The God who is love is totally identical with his essence in his existence. His existence is his essence. That is precisely what the doctrine of the Trinity formulates. It does this by thinking of the essence of God, which is love, as an essence constituted by relations and by thinking of the relations which constitute God's essence as the divine essence.[172]

Rahner's Interpretation of Triune 'Personhood' Although we would be eager to endorse several of the points made by Rahner with respect to the use of the term 'person' of God, it is on point (f) above (the question of mutuality and reciprocity within the Trinity) that we must focus in our evaluation of Rahner's understanding of the divine Triunity. This is because it serves in many ways to make explicit the weaknesses of the 'revelation model' when it allows a 'linear' (Williams) interpretation of the structure of communication (with what Rahner determines as a 'logical analysis' of necessary transcendental conditions) to condition theology, rather than a theological and thus *onto-relationally conceived* interpretation of the inclusive communion of God opened to us in Christ by the Spirit. In Rahner we see made explicit the (often implicit) tendencies which underlie Karl Barth's interpretation.

argument is to be found in Bantle's profound critique of Rahner, 'Person und Personenbegriff in der Trinitätslehre Karl Rahners', *Münchner Theol. Zeitschrift* 30 (1979), 11–24. He concludes 'Karl Rahners Interpretation des in die Formulierung des Trinitätsdogmas eingegangen Personbegriffs kann nicht befriedigen. Sie ist weder vom Schriftbefund noch vom Personverständnis der Kappadozier, des Leontios von Byzanz, des Boethius und des Thomas von Aquin gedeckt und geht, insofern sie den modernen Personbegriff als etwas durch und durch anderes ansieht als den Personbegriff der Alten, von einer falschen Voraussetzung aus.'
[172] *God as the Mystery of the World*, 371.

The connection between his (linear) 'revelation model' and the denial of mutual and reciprocal relations within the Trinity is quite clear in the text, in that the statement that there is properly no *mutual* love between the Father and the Son follows directly his insistence that 'there is only *one* self-utterance of the Father, the Logos. The Logos is not the one who utters, but the one who is uttered.'[173] The same connection is made clear in his earlier statement that 'there is no reciprocal Thou'. The sentence that follows it runs, 'The Son is the Father's self-utterance which should not in its turn be conceived as "uttering", and the Spirit is the "gift" which does not give in its turn.' What we have is a formulation of the Triunity with recourse to two (mixed) metaphors which relate to the form of the logico-grammatical relations between the various constituents of a sentence of the following kind: *the utterer utters the (non-giving, i.e. passive) gift of his self-utterance.*

The question has to be raised as to whether the uttering and giving metaphors conceived in terms of their transitive logic – *and where this formal structure functions as a third, attendant, subliminal metaphor* – have not taken on a life of their own, thereby controlling his articulation of the form of the divine Triunity. This was something which Barth sought to avoid – hence his vigorous denial that he was offering a grammatical proof of the doctrine of the Trinity. One has to ask whether the Triunity is not in danger of being reduced to the *form* of a rather individualistically conceived event of divine Self-expression.[174] Indeed, it is not difficult to read much of what

---

[173] *The Trinity*, 106.

[174] Cf. LaCugna's comment that Rahner (like Barth) was not entirely able to resist making use of the Cartesian conception of a person as a discrete self-consciousness but in such a way that it is 'the divine essence, not the three divine persons which are made the referent of this self-consciousness'. (*God for Us*, 254.) Her summary continues: 'The one self-conscious Subject is made the referent of this self-consciousness.' This means that, in the final analysis, rather than Karl Rahner's discussion succeeding in its attempt, as T. F. Torrance puts it, to bring about a 'rapprochement between the understanding of Latins and Greeks, of Western and Eastern Christians ...' ('Toward an Ecumenical Consensus on the Trinity', *Theologische Zeitschrift* 31 (1975), 337), he seems, as LaCugna suggests, 'to vacillate between the perspective of Greek theology which emphasizes God the Father as origin and Latin theology which emphasizes the threefoldness of the divine nature.' (*God for Us*, 254.)

Rahner writes concerning the common activity *ad extra*, the appropriations and the processions (the originality of the Father, the generated utterance which is the Son and the passive/active spirational dynamic of the Spirit[175]) and even circumincession (which he refers to as 'the mutual inexistence of the three persons') in precisely these terms.

Rahner's denial of the mutual loving and reciprocal personal address within the Triunity raises the question as to how seriously he is committed *in practice* to the two-way identification of the immanent and economic Trinities and what the hypostatic union specifically involves with respect to the unique *hypostasis* of the Son. Can we not – or, rather, must we not – 'prescind' from the hypostatic union to a mutuality of love and a relationship characterised by a reciprocal Thou which is integral to the intra-divine life? Moreover, are Rahner's conclusions that 'Jn. 17:21; Gal. 4:6; Rom. 8:15 presuppose a creaturely starting-point for the "Thou" addressed to the Father'[176] genuinely *a posteriori* ones? Or is it the case that his conception of the dictates of his transcendental necessity (interpreted in the light of his 'logical' analysis) legitimates dichotomies between the immanent and economic Being of the Son and/or within the hypostatic union? If the three New Testament verses mentioned above (and the many more which they exemplify) are to be attributed to the human creature 'Jesus' or some creaturely hypostasis of the Spirit, but not to the second or third persons of the Trinity, how can he avoid suggesting that the human Jesus might have addressed a creaturely Thou to the Son? Rahner's statement (in which he has been argued to have been 'misled by a rational analysis of merely inter-human connections'[177]) commits him to a docetic interpretation of the humanity of Jesus in a manner that severs his own identification of the immanent and economic Trinities from the human Jesus. This has the effect of emptying into 'mere abstractions the New Testament

[175] Rahner, op. cit., 78.
[176] Ibid., 76.
[177] T. F. Torrance, 'Toward an Ecumenical Consensus, 344.

revelation which speaks of a mutual knowing and loving between the Father and the Son, the Son and the Father, which is clearly not limited to the economic inhomination of the Son'.[178] As a result, Rahner's identification of the immanent and economic Trinities risks becoming abstract and theologically impotent formalism of precisely the kind that he set out to avoid.[179] Moreover, it would seem to suggest further a duplication of the economies – a divine economy and a creaturely 'economy' of the economy of the Son. What is clear is that Rahner could not insist on an identification of these, which leaves one asking whether any such creaturely 'economy' is an economy at all. Put another way, the prayer life of Jesus becomes, at best, peripheral to the incarnational event and incidental (or coincidental?) to his being 'Immanuel'.

The problem here is reflected in the anthropological implications of Rahner's conception of God's Self-giving communication. This is a Self-giving for the purpose of human loving and knowing of God and the Truth, but it is not a Self-giving as part of God's communal purposes – and where the communion of the Body of Christ extends from the economic activity of the Trinity so that the new humanity might be brought to participate in the intra-divine communion of God. LaCugna has commented that the key to Rahner's theology of the Self-communicating God is that 'God gives us God's *self*, not a "share" in divine life.'[180] Although we are in complete agreement with this comment, LaCugna herself fails to appreciate sufficiently the extent to which this connects with the relationship between the *Deus ad extra* and *Deus ad intra* – despite the fact that she senses problems with Rahner's account here, suggesting there is a need for a revision of Rahner's exposition of the Trinity which addresses whether

---

[178] Ibid.

[179] In other words, T. F. Torrance's statement that Karl Rahner's 'basic approach ... has the effect of making the Economic Trinity the norm for all our thought and speech about God' is, we would argue, threatened by his denials here. (Cf. 'Toward an Ecumenical Consensus', 337.)

[180] *God for Us*, 236, footnote 22.

'there are two "levels" to the Trinity, one *ad intra*, the other *ad extra*'.[181] The issue being touched on in this comment might have been put more plainly. The substantial question concerns whether Rahner's identification of the immanent and economic Trinities is not merely an analysis of the transcendentally necessary 'logic' (and modalities) of the *Deus ad extra* alone – interpreted independently of the *Deus ad intra*, which I am assuming to mean 'God in his relations toward himself'. In other words, Rahner (in common with much modern trinitarian theology) fails to work out the implications for his two-way identification of the immanent and economic Trinities of the distinction between the *Deus ad intra* and *Deus ad extra*, and vice versa. Consequently, he fails to appreciate the profoundly important distinction which requires to be made between the meaning of the word 'immanent' on the one hand, and the expression *Deus ad intra* on the other. This leads to a devaluation of the fundamentally important intersection, overlapping or, indeed, *concentricity* of the *Deus ad intra* and the divine economy. The divine dealings with humankind find realisation and consummation in God's relations to himself interpreted in a trinitarian way. And it is here and here alone that we come to understand the New Testament meaning of participation as *koinonia* in utter contrast to *methexis*.

A more radical identification of the immanent and economic Trinities would interpret the *Deus ad intra* in such a way that the incarnationally open life of prayer, worship and communion as this involves the Father, the Son and the Spirit was seen both to present to us (*economically*), but also to take us by grace to participate in, the eternal communion of the Trinity *ad intra*.[182]

[181] Ibid., 'Introduction', 13.

[182] First, it is difficult to see how this is not the necessary outcome of an identification if the 'persons' of the Trinity are not to be defined in a manner that includes their relations – unless the mutual relating is denied at the level of the economic. This is, of course, what Rahner seems to be doing given his reference to the 'creaturely' nature of the mutuality.

Second, I am making a similar point here to that which T. F. Torrance seems to be making in his comment on Rahner's formal identification first of the

One aspect of the confusion here relates to the term 'immanent', which is a theologically weak term implying a static conception of God 'as he remains in himself'. The phrase *Deus ad intra* is a much healthier one, in that it implies that God, conceived independently of his relations toward that which is not God, still remains a relational being. In other words, the Latin *ad* allows itself to be interpreted in more dynamic terms than does the alternative combination of the Latin terms *in* and *manere*![183] Consequently, we would suggest that the most healthy ontological distinction is between *Deus ad intra* and *Deus ad extra* where reference to the divine economy may be made with respect to both. The culmination of the divine mission (*ad extra*) will be participation in the divine life (*ad intra*), and the ground and impetus of the mission *ad extra* is the eternal dynamic *ad intra*. Consequently, the apotheosis of the divine *telos* requires to be defined with respect to the economic Trinity *ad intra*. This is not an

Economic and the Immanent and then vice versa: 'Most of his discussion appears to relate to the second part of that axiom, the Trinity *ad intra* is the Trinity *ad extra*; but much more attention must be given to the first half of the axiom, the Trinity *ad extra* is the Trinity *ad intra*.' ('Toward an Ecumenical Consensus', 349.) One might add, however, that T. F. Torrance's statement here is a shade ambiguous given that there is not always a clear directionality in identity statements in the English language – thinking about such statements can engender a *Gestalt* switch!

[183] It may be noted that Moltmann also expresses qualms concerning the notion of the 'immanent Trinity', although his discussion of the problem is rather imprecise and wide-ranging. He writes, 'The notion of an immanent Trinity in which God is simply by himself, without the love which communicates salvation, brings an arbitrary element into the concept of God which means a break-up of the Christian concept. Consequently this idea safeguards neither God's liberty nor the grace of salvation. It introduces a contradiction into the relationship between the immanent and the economic Trinity: the God who loves the world does not correspond to the God who suffices for himself.' (*The Trinity and the Kingdom of God*, 151.)

In private conversation, T. F. Torrance suggests what might seem to be a 'more neutral' option where we refer to the 'immanent Trinity' as the 'ontological Trinity'. However, one senses a slightly Calvinist risk here of implying that *Deus ad extra* is not the concern of ontology. For this reason I prefer his further suggestion that 'inherent' or 'intrinsic' might be used. To the extent that intrinsicity easily includes a dynamic conception of relations and has no 'monadic' connotations, the term 'intrinsic' Trinity may have advantages over the expression 'immanent Trinity'.

identification, as it only takes place in the light of the divine freedom and, therefore, presupposes both an ontologically prior (and, indeed, from the human perspective historically prior) movement *ad extra* and also a radical distinction – though not disjunction – between the divine and the human. A related point to this is particularly well made by Christopher Kaiser when commenting on Augustine. He writes, 'the complete dissociation of [the] eternal intra-trinitarian relations from ordinary human relations forced him into a rather static concept of deity, on the one hand, and an individualistic concept of humanity, on the other'.[184] Precisely this applies, in the final analysis, to Rahner owing to his failure to take to their radical conclusions those theological principles so emphasised by him at the start of his treatise on the Trinity.

The Theology of the Cross and the Question of Divine Unity   It is in the theology of the cross, however, that the central theological issues here become particularly clear – as also in the theology of worship and the sacraments. As Jüngel notes, it is only when there is a proper two-way identification of the ontological and economic Trinities (Jüngel uses the terms 'immanent' and 'economic') that there is made possible a theology of the Crucified One. It is also here that theology stands to be liberated, in Jüngel's words, from the traditional overemphasis on the 'absolute unity of divine activity outwardly'. This certainly does not mean that what is being advocated is a disunity of the divine economy. Rather, it means that there is an openness in theology to the theologically unanticipatable and inconceivable openness of the life of God in such a way that theology can take seriously the notion of the divine union and communion without either reducing it to, or replacing it with, *a priori* conceptions (or metaphysical dogmas) of a unity of essence.

In attempting a radical theological redefinition of the Trinity which breaks with the traditional Western approach to

---

[184] Christopher B. Kaiser, *The Doctrine of God. An Historical Survey,* London, 1982, 81. (Quoted in Gunton, *The Promise of Trinitarian Theology,* 95.)

unity, Jüngel presents us with a particular challenge with respect to the theology of the cross. In his words, the interpretation of the immanent Trinity as a statement of the divine self-relatedness, 'collides with the word of the cross which states that God gave up his beloved Son for us all ...' It is precisely here, however, that the key to a theological reinterpretation of unity within the Trinity is to be found. That is because it is here and here alone that we discover the irreducibly trinitarian meaning of the statement 'God is love.' And it is as we discover this that we may begin to understand the extent to which this involves an appreciation of the integration at the deepest level of the divine self-relatedness and selflessness as these characterise the communion of the intra-divine life. Few expound this with greater depth than Eberhard Jüngel, and we quote him here at some length:

> But the very essence of love would be mistaken if one were to play off the self-relatedness and the selflessness of God against each other. That is as little possible as the (often attempted) opposition of 'immanent' and 'economic' Trinity. The essence of love would also be mistaken if the attempt were made to think of God's self-relatedness and selflessness, or God's inner-divine love and his love of man, or of the 'immanent' and the 'economic' Trinity as *paradox*. In love, selflessness and self-relatedness do not contradict each other ... Rather, self-relatedness and selflessness *correspond* to each other in such a way that here, as we have already shown, the basic structure of evangelical talk about God is to be applied *mutatis mutandis;* we must speak of a still greater selflessness in a very great, a properly great self-relatedness. A 'still greater selflessness in the midst of a very great and justifiably great self-relatedness' is nothing other than a self-relationship which in freedom goes beyond itself, overflows itself, and gives itself away. It is pure overflow, overflowing being for the sake of another and only then for the sake of itself. That is love. And that is the God who is love: the one who always heightens and expands his own being in such great self-relatedness still more selfless and *thus* overflowing.[185]

Redefining Triune Personhood   The outcome of this is that the doctrine of the Trinity demands a conception of the

---

[185] *God as the Mystery of the World*, 369.

282   *Persons in Communion*

triune persons which integrates their distinctness and particularity, on the one hand, and their radical union and communion, on the other. This requires to be done in a manner which obviates reference to Aristotelian categories of essence, as these have haunted Western theology, on the one hand, and Platonic models of a transcendental union, on the other, since both of these fail to communicate the dynamic unique to communion and defined with recourse to that singular 'love' which is witnessed in and through the separation and rupture of the cross. Heribert Mühlen's observation seems pertinent to this, 'The differentness of the divine persons, to the extent that they are persons ... is so great, that it cannot be conceived as any greater, whereas their unity ... is so intensive that it cannot be conceived of as any more intensive.'[186] And Eberhard Jüngel's reference to the dynamic of selflessness and self-relatedness serves to point to the grammar of personal communion as we are met by it in the theology of the cross – a communion that compels us to speak, in *a posteriori* terms, of a) the absolute uniqueness and distinctness of the second person of the Godhead; of b) the radically perichoretic union and communion of God fully present in the Crucified One, and finally of c) the identity of the intra-divine relations with the divine economy. Furthermore, it does so in a way that obviates another danger. This is that the rupture which the cross represents is overwhelmed or 'harmonised' by way of the kind of prior 'ontology of communion' which suggests that the immanent Trinity expresses itself in the economic Trinity but that the events of the divine economy only 'selectively' present us with the immanent Being of God – and where the principles of selection are determined by our prior definitions of the category of communion.

This is a weakness which we shall meet in the theology of John Zizioulas, despite what we shall argue to be his profoundly

---

[186] *Die Veränderlichkeit Gottes als Horizont einer zukünftigen altkirchlichen Christologie* Münster, 1969, 25, quoted in Eberhard Jüngel, *Gott als Geheimnis der Welt*, Tubingen, 1982, 371.

useful contribution to the redefinition of the concept of person in the context of the criteria we have determined.

John Zizioulas

The writings of John Zizioulas offer an incisive exploration of the ontology of triune personhood carried out in such a way as to integrate our understandings of being and communion on the one hand, and divine and human personhood on the other.

Zizioulas' early essay, 'On Human Capacity and Incapacity: A Theological Exploration of Personhood,'[187] sets out to explore the implications of the uncircumscribability of human capacity and, therefore, of human personhood. The person is unique in that she or he is characterised by an irreducible *uncontainability* within definable limits, that is, the person 'goes beyond his actual state in a movement of transcendence of the actual human limitations'.[188] The very nature of the person is such that it may not be described with reference to traditional, Western, 'static' conceptions of 'substance', 'qualities' and 'essence'. Neither can the person be defined by reference to innate capacities or incapacities – his model of 'transcendence' is conceived in profoundly different terms from those of Karl Rahner's transcendental anthropology.

Zizioulas continues by suggesting a definition of personhood which (implicitly) involves internal warrant for his using the notion both of God and of humanity. By saying that the very essence of the person is such that rigid or static notions of capacity and incapacity do not apply, he defines a person such that what we might term the 'fixities' which denote or determine that which is essentially 'finite' are bypassed in the definition. The definition is radically open-ended and defined not in terms of internal features or qualities but in terms of relationships – where relating is not in any way conceived as a 'constriction' or limitation of nature but precisely the opposite. And it is this that underlies his statement later in the

[187] *S. J. T.* 28 (1975), 401–8.
[188] Ibid., 401.

same article, that the notion 'Person', properly understood, is 'perhaps the only notion that can be applied to God without the danger of anthropomorphism'.[189]

So how is personhood to be understood? Negatively, human personhood

> should not be understood in terms of 'personality', i.e. of a complex of natural, psychological or moral qualities which are in some sense 'possessed' by or 'contained' in the human *Individuum*. On the contrary, being a person is basically different from being an individual or 'personality' in that the person can not be conceived in itself as a static entity, but only as it *relates to*.[190]

Consequently,

> personhood implies the 'openness of being', and even more than that, the *ek-stasis* of being, i.e. a movement towards communion which leads to a transcendence of the boundaries of the 'self' and thus to *freedom*.[191]

This means that

> in contrast to the partiality of the individual which is subject to addition and combination, the person in its ek-static character reveals its being in a *catholic*, i.e. integral and undivided, way, and thus in its being ek-static it becomes *hypostatic*, i.e. the bearer of its nature in its totality.[192]

Ekstasis and *hypostasis* are affirmed, therefore, to be the two basic 'aspects' of personhood.

Conceiving of being as personal in this way means that first, being cannot be contained or divided and, second, that the mode of its existence, its hypostasis, is absolutely unique and unrepeatable.

The introductory sections of Zizioulas' book, *Being as Communion*, constitute a kind of sociology of knowledge

---

[189] Ibid., 420.
[190] Ibid., 407–8.
[191] Ibid., 408.
[192] Ibid.

seeking to trace through the history of ideas the differing influences on Western and Eastern conceptions of God, ontology and personhood. Roman thought, he suggests, with its fundamentally legal, organisational and social bent, concerned itself with the structure of human relationships, the ability to form associations, to enter into contracts, to establish *collegia* and to constitute and organise life in a state. However, it did not concern itself with ontology and with 'the *being* of man'. The Roman conception of personhood failed adequately to progress beyond the original concept of *persona* as *prosopon* or *prosopeion*, that is, with the theatrical nuances of the word and its associations with theatrical masks and the roles of actors in plays.[193] In short, the Western philosophical and theological mentality is perceived to have failed to penetrate beyond a) the coalescence of *persona* with *prosopeion* (as interpreted by the ancient Greeks), and b) static conceptions of substance moulding an ontology which failed to represent the irreducibly relational nature of persons. The result is the failure in the West to grasp the ontological originality of personhood and the consequent, irreducible relationality of being.

The salvation of ontology from static models of substance and its redefinition in personal terms is traced by Zizioulas to the marriage of Christianity with its biblical tradition and the Greek interest in ontology. The coming together of these two traditions led in the Greek Fathers to an event of revolutionary import, namely, the emergence of the 'concept of the person with its absolute and ontological content' – a development that has constituted an underappreciated and undervalued[194] philosophical landmark in the history of ideas. This 'revolution in Greek philosophy' took the form of 'the identification of the "hypostasis" with the "person"',[195] and was the direct result

---

[193] For a discussion of the etymology of the word 'persona', see M. Nédoncelle, 'Prosopon et persona dans l'antiquité classique', *Revue des sciences religieuses* 22 (1948), 277–99 (cited in Zizioulas, *Being as Communion: Studies in Personhood and the Church*, New York, 1985, 33)

[194] The 'revolutionary significance' of these in the development of Greek thought seems to have escaped the attention of the history of philosophy ...' Zizioulas, *Being as Communion*, 39.

[195] Ibid., 36.

of the Cappadocian concern 'to give ontological expression to its faith in the Triune God', to 'develop a solution to the trinitarian problems ...'[196] The essential grammar of this move was that the term 'hypostasis' was 'dissociated from that of *ousia* and became identified with that of *prosopon*'.[197] The result was the admission of a relational term (*prosopon*) into ontology and the drawing of an ontological category (*hypostasis*) into the relational categories of existence. The culmination of this process was the identification of being and communion. 'To be and to be in relation become identical.'[198]

The ontological significance of this was that the notion of personhood became the essential ontological concept. Two central discoveries characterised this. First, 'The person is no longer an adjunct to a being, a category which we add to a concrete entity once we have first verified its ontological hypostasis. It is itself the hypostasis of the being.' And, second, 'Entities no longer trace their being to being itself – that is, being is not an absolute category in itself – but to the person, to precisely that which constitutes being, that is, enables entities to be entities.'[199] Zizioulas sums this up by saying,

> In other words from an adjunct to a being (a kind of mask) the person becomes the being itself and is simultaneously – a most significant point – *the constitutive element* (the 'principle' or 'cause') of beings'.[200]

Two alternative ontologies characterised the influences on Greek thought at that time. These were, on the one hand, monism (he argues that ancient Greek ontology was fundamentally monistic[201]) and, on the other, Gnostic dualism. What Zizioulas describes as two critically important 'leavenings' served to deliver patristic thought from these two influences. These were:

a) the repudiation of 'the ontological absoluteness of cosmological necessity' by way of the biblical doctrine of

[196] Ibid., 87.
[197] Ibid.
[198] Ibid., 88.
[199] Ibid., 39.
[200] Ibid.
[201] Ibid., 16.

creatio ex nihilo, by making the existence of the world, existent things, a 'product of freedom' such that the being of 'the world became free from necessity';[202] and

b) the identification of God with the person – 'the being of God Himself was identified with the person'.[203]

Implications of the Greek Identification of 'hypostasis' and 'person'   The identification of 'hypostasis' and 'person' was, Zizioulas argues, a move of profound significance for the formulation of the doctrine of the Trinity and there are three reasons for this.

First, it enabled a formulation which obviated the dangers associated with the trinitarian use of the term 'hypostasis', namely a) Platonic conceptions of the union of God and the world, and b) the tritheistic dangers that emerge if there is to be an identification of 'hypostasis' with substance.

Second, the emergent concept of personhood provided theology with conceptual tools which helped it, on the one hand, to avoid Sabellianism by giving 'ontological content to each person of the Holy Trinity' and, on the other, to safeguard its essential 'biblical principles', namely: 'monotheism and the absolute ontological independence of God in relation to the world'.[204]

Third, it led to an integrated conception of the life of God and that of the Church. If, as Zizioulas suggests, 'The ecclesial experience of the Fathers played a decisive role in breaking ontological monism and avoiding the "gulf" between God and

---

[202] Ibid., 39–40.

[203] Ibid., 40 'This "leavening" was effected through the disputes of the Holy Trinity, mainly through the theology of the Cappadocian Fathers and above all by St Basil.'

Running through Zizioulas' exposition here is the underlying question as to how far the divine persons should not be conceived, to adopt a phrase from Alasdair Heron, 'in *supra*-personal rather than merely personal terms' (*The Holy Spirit*, 174). Zizioulas' easy adoption of the same term without exposing the need for some distinction leaves one with a degree of uneasiness. His reply to any such unease might well be that it is the result of thinking in Western terms, that is, in terms of the category of 'capacity'.

[204] Ibid., 37.

the world',[205] the result was an integrated conception of the communion of God and human participation in the life of God which gave ontological grounds to ecclesial being and the eucharistic experience. 'The life of the eucharist is the life of God Himself ... the life of communion with God, such as exists within the Trinity and is actualized within the members of the eucharistic community.'[206] The consequence of this is the profoundly important point that 'Knowledge and communion are identical.'[207] It is here that we see the profound strength of Zizioulas' approach to trinitarian description over against that of Rahner. Divine communication in the context of faith is an event of communion and demands to be conceived, therefore, in terms of participation within the communion (and hence within the 'mutuality') of the triune life.[208]

In sum, for Zizioulas the task of the formulation and expression of the union and communion of the Trinity and of the integration of the doctrine of the Trinity with human existence was both initiated and served by the Greek Fathers' furnishing theology with the category of the person.

There is, however, a more questionable side to Zizioulas' discussion, in particular his endorsement of certain facets of the trinitarian theology of the Cappadocian divines – facets which are arguably in tension with the primary insights he extrapolates from patristic thought.

He writes – and I quote him here at some length:

> Among the Greek Fathers the unity of God, the one God, and the ontological 'principle' or 'cause' of the being and life of God does not consist in the one substance of God but in the *hypostasis*, that is, *the person of the Father*. The one God is not the one substance but the Father, who is the 'cause' both of the generation of the Son and of the

---

[205] Ibid., 16.
[206] Ibid., 81.
[207] Ibid.
[208] A ramification of this will be that there is an irreducible 'sacramental' ground to that participative knowing (by acquaintance and not merely by description) presupposed by theological articulation.

procession of the Spirit. Consequently, the ontological 'principle' of God is traced back, once again, to the person. Thus when we say that God 'is', we do not bind the personal freedom of God – the being of God is not an ontological 'necessity' of a simple 'reality' for God – but we ascribe the being of God to His personal freedom. In a more analytical way this means that God, as Father and not as substance, perpetually confirms through 'being' His free will to exist'.[209]

Zizioulas' eagerness to explain the unity of God in a manner which obviates recourse to 'being' or *ousia*[210] leads him to endorse the Cappadocian interpretation of unity in terms of the singular personhood of the Father. This fails to take proper cognisance of the ontological significance of the union integral to the divine communion and involves projecting a causal ordering into the Godhead. As I shall argue below, what promises to be a theological cosmology begins to smack of a cosmological theology!

He continues,

> If God exists, He exists because the Father exists, that is, He who out of love freely begets the Son and brings forth the Spirit. Thus God as person – as the hypostasis of the Father – makes the one divine substance to be that which it is: the one God ...

This means that 'the personal existence of God (the Father) constitutes His substance, makes it hypostases. The being of God is identified with the person.' He continues, 'What therefore is important in trinitarian theology is that God "exists" on account of a person, the Father, and not on account of a substance.'[211]

Two fundamental issues are raised by the sections I have quoted.

First, Zizioulas consistently argues that it was contemplation of the doctrine of the Trinity and the ecclesial or eucharistic experience of the Church which gave rise to the notion of personhood and initiated the revolution in the history of

---

[209] Ibid., 41.
[210] His dismissal of the concept of *ousia* seems to reflect his reading it in the light of the Western conception of *substantia*.
[211] Ibid., 41–2.

ideas. However, in his exposition of the Trinity as we have it here, one wonders whether the tail is not in danger of wagging the dog – that is, whether a foundational(ist) ontology of personhood together with attendant notions of personal freedom, creativity and, in particular, causality do not threaten to become the driving force (or 'critical control') in his exposition of the doctrine of God. One wonders if the words 'a person' in his statement 'God exists on account of a person' betray an overly generic utilisation and elevation of the notion. Zizioulas may wish to defend himself against this charge by reiterating his view that the notion 'person' is distinct, even unique, perhaps, in that it possesses the capacity to be used across an infinitely broad spectrum.[212] There remains, however, the suspicion that his exposition of the Trinity is, perhaps, over-conditioned at points by a 'personalist' ontology.[213] At the same time, however, it must also be said that his revision of trinitarian expression by way of the category of 'person' stands to breathe new life into the Western debates by revising radically the traditionally static conceptualities that have done such damage to the doctrine of God. In short, it is also the case that profoundly liberating ways forward are offered by his central theses.

Our second concern, intimated above, relates to his endorsement of the Cappadocian projection of causal notions into the internal life of God. This would seem to be potentially damaging to his identification of being and communion. The Father, he argues, is the 'cause' of the divine substance – its being and unity. The hypostases of the Son and the Spirit are, as such, contingent and derivative. This suggests that the Son (as also the Spirit) is that 'than which something greater can be conceived', and that the personhood of the Son is

---

[212] As I have pointed out above, he argues that the notion is 'perhaps' uniquely suited to be attributed to the divine without the risk of anthropomorphism.

[213] In a similar vein, his particularly interesting discussions of 'presence', 'presence-in-absence' and 'transcendence' may also be criticised theologically for having been conditioned too much by existentialist influences on his thought.

profoundly different from that of the Father. This has the effect of reducing the unity of the Godhead to the personal singularity of the Father. The thrust of these arguments suggests a failure to interpret the Oneness of God in the Light of the free communion and mutuality of God. An *a posteriori* ontology of intra-divine communion risks being subsumed by a cosmological category of causality.[214] In his book *The Trinitarian Faith*, T. F. Torrance argues strongly against this facet of Cappadocian thought. The arguments he uses are relevant to our discussion at this point:

> The Cappadocian rebuttal of the charge that their differentiation between three *hupostaseis*, with their distinct modes of existence, implied three ultimate divine Principles (*archai*), and their attempt to secure the oneness (*henosis*) of the Godhead by referring the three Persons to a single Principle (*arche*) or Cause (*aitia*) in the Father, were made at the expense of a damaging distinction between the Deity of the Father as wholly underived or 'uncaused', and the Deity of the Son and of the Spirit as eternally derived or 'caused'. Moreover, in differentiating the Persons of the Holy Trinity they cast the internal relations between the Father, the Son and the Holy Spirit into the consecutive structure of a causal series or a 'chain' of dependence 'through the Son', instead of conceiving of them more, like Athanasius, in terms of their coinherent and undivided wholeness, in which each Person is 'whole of the whole'.[215]

A whole series of questions results from Zizioulas' utilisation of this Cappadocian approach. For example, how does this causal series or chain of contingency in God integrate with the eucharistic experience that Zizioulas perceives as the context of trinitarian articulation? Second, what does this causally conceived hierarchical conception of the triune communion suggest about the mirroring of the divine life in the ecclesial communion – given his emphasis on the Christian community

---

[214] To suggest that this approach characterised the theology of the 'Greek Fathers' generally, as Zizioulas implies (op. cit., 40), misrepresents the diversity of views on this matter in patristic thought.

[215] *The Trinitarian Faith*, Edinburgh, 1988, 238.

as the *imago Dei*?[216] Or, third, given Zizioulas' insistence that in patristic thought 'the *arche* of the world was transposed to the sphere of freedom,'[217] is the freedom of the Father to be conceived as *qualitatively* distinct from that of the Son and Spirit? Does the ontological freedom of the *arche vis-à-vis* the hypostases of the Son and the Spirit parallel the cosmological freedom of the Father *vis-à-vis* the created order as a whole?

It is Zizioulas' contention that, despite the fact that 'It would be unthinkable to speak of the "one God" before speaking of the God who is "communion",[218] it is not only thinkable but necessary to speak ontologically of the one person before speaking of the God who is 'communion'. So, although he is eager to stress that 'The Holy Trinity is a primordial ontological concept and not a notion which is added to the divine substance or rather which follows it ...',[219] he is also eager to insist that 'this communion is not a relationship understood for its own sake ... Just like "substance", "communion" does not exist by itself: it is the Father who is the "cause" of it'[220] – and he goes on to endorse Rahner's interpretation of the Cappadocians in this regard.[221]

This, however, gives rise to further questions and concerns.

First, is he really being consistent with himself? If the Trinity derives from a causal act of the Father, is the 'concept' of the 'Holy Trinity' really being conceived as ontologically primordial? Does *the* exclusively primordial reality not actually become the person of the Father?

---

[216] Does it, as is suggested, warrant a hierarchical system of church order where the bishop is called 'father' as the *vestigium patris*?

[217] Zizioulas, op. cit., 39–40.

[218] Ibid., 17.

[219] Ibid.

[220] Ibid. This comment suggests that LaCugna is not entirely correct when she suggests that, for Zizioulas, 'love causes God to be who God is' (*God for Us*, 261). I am not aware of Zizioulas using the term 'cause' in precisely this way – the term is used not of love, nor of communion, but of the person of the Father.

[221] Zizioulas ibid., 88. LaCugna makes a similar generalisation: 'In Greek theology – and this difference [from Barth] is decisive – one specific hypostasis of God the Father is identified with the divine ousia and grounds the personhood of God.' (*God for Us*, 252.)

Second, Zizioulas commits theology by these means to 'a kind of subordination of the Son to the Father' – even though he might not be 'obliged to downgrade the *Logos* into something created'.[222] But this compels one to ask *why* he wishes to do this, given the extent to which the concept of communion is not one of *external* relations but of the communion of persons who have their being in *ekstasis* – and where the very concept of communion includes that of persons. Should this not mean that the intra-divine communion is not only a primordial concept but an eternal 'given', that is, ontologically primitive and original? Zizioulas insists that the 'thesis of the Cappadocians that introduced the concept of "cause" into the being of God assumed an incalculable importance' because, among other things, it obviated the view that the ultimate ontological category is a 'structure of communion existing by itself'.[223] Given that what is being referred to is not some contingent existent or mere 'structure' conceived as 'existing by itself', but nothing less than God, it seems to us that he fails to offer sufficiently compelling arguments as to why it should be of 'incalculable importance' that we do *not* conceive of the intra-divine communion of the Triunity as the ground of all that is, that is, as sufficient in itself and as indeed 'capable' of existing 'by itself'.

While agreeing strongly with Zizioulas that the West has everything to learn in these debates from the Greek Fathers, might not an integrated articulation of the eternal communion of the Trinity be served more effectively by drawing on a) Gregory Nazianzen's concept of a Trinity of hypostatic relations, b) Athanasius' doctrine of the reciprocal indwelling of the three hypostases, and c) Cyril of Alexandria's conception of the procession of the Spirit from the Father through the Son, where there is affirmed a 'doctrine of coinherence in the one identical being of God, according to which the Father, Son and Holy Spirit mutually indwell and contain one another,

---

[222] Zizioulas, ibid., 89.
[223] Ibid., 17–18.

while remaining what they are' – and where the notion of causal relations within the Trinity is thus rejected?[224] Such an approach would serve to safeguard two facets integral to the divine integrity in the open communion of the Self-revealing Triunity. First, 'what God is toward us in Christ and in the Spirit he is inherently and eternally in himself in the one being of the consubstantial Trinity' and, second, 'what he is intrinsically and indivisibly in his eternal Triunity he is toward us in the incarnation of his Son and in the mission of the Spirit'.[225]

In contrast to the notion of Basil and his brother Gregory that two hypostases derive their being from the being of the Father, it is Cyril's emphases which safeguard the ultimacy of personal communion over against monarchian conceptions of the ultimacy of the singular person whose being must ultimately be constituted by an event of causal self-hypostatisation given that the intra-divine relations of communion are derivative. To quote T. F. Torrance again,

> Cyril's conception of the interrelation of the three perfect, coequal, coeternal, enhypostatic Persons through their wholly reciprocal indwelling and containing of one another, in which they are inconfusedly united and inseparably distinguished, was very different, for it carried within it the combined notion of *mia ousia* and *mia arche*.[226]

When the Trinity is interpreted in this way the Monarchia is identified with the Triunity of God and affirmed with respect to God's external relations with the created order rather than (quasi-external!) relations internal to the Godhead.

---

[224] The quotation is taken from T. F. Torrance, *The Trinitarian Faith*, 338. This statement should perhaps be treated with some caution, as it can be argued that there *is* historical evidence in the Alexandrian tradition for the rejection of the importation of 'causal' thinking. Given that proviso, however, Torrance's comments place in question Zizioulas' claim that the Cappadocian position, as it affirmed 'the final assertion of ontology in God has to be attached not to the unique ousia of God but to the Father, that is, to a hypostasis or person', was 'characteristic of all the Greek Fathers' (*Being as Communion*, 88).

[225] Torrance, op. cit., 339.

[226] Ibid., 340.

It refers thus to God's free, creative and gracious initiative in bringing humankind to participate in the eternal and ontologically ultimate communion of the Triunity. And in this way it denotes the being-in-act of God as it 'takes place' in the economy of the divine love *toward us*.

Finally, we come to Zizioulas' profoundly creative ecclesial and anthropological insights. The potential of these insights for a creative integrating of the doctrine of God and theological anthropology is clearly enormous. It is precisely this potential, however, which obliges us to question one central feature of his anthropology as it concerns the interpretation of the cross and its significance for the doctrine of the Trinity.

As the subtitle of *Being as Communion* suggests,[227] there is a tight integration in Zizioulas of his anthropology and his ecclesiology. The first sentence of his book runs 'The Church is not simply an institution. She is a "mode of existence," *a way of being*.'[228] This he means in the most literal sense. The Church is not simply something with which beings become involved or occupy themselves, it is a way of being. He continues,

> In the first place, ecclesial being is bound to the very being of God. From the fact that a human being is a member of the Church, he becomes an 'image of God', he exists as God Himself exists, he takes on God's 'way of being'. This way of being is not a moral attainment, something that man *accomplishes*. It is a way of *relationship* with the world, with other people and with God, an event of *communion*, and that is why it cannot be realized as the achievement of an *individual*, but only as an *ecclesial* fact.[229]

The postulate of this for Zizioulas is the 'eternal survival' of the person and it is in these terms that soteriology finds its definition.

> The eternal survival of the person as a unique, unrepeatable and free 'hypostasis', as loving and being loved, constitutes the quintessence

---

[227] *Studies in Personhood and the Church.*
[228] Op. cit., 15.
[229] Ibid.

of salvation, the bringing of the Gospel to man. In the language of the Fathers this is called divinisation (*theosis*) which means participation not in the nature or substance of God, but in God's personal existence. The goal of salvation is that the personal life which is realised in God should also be realised on the level of human existence.[230]

Two questions are posed by what may appear to be a glossing over the boundaries between human being and divine being by way of what we might term an 'ontology of ecclesiality'. First, how far can such affirmations take account of the hard realities of suffering, alienation, and separation – not only through death, but as a result of physical, social, economic and other factors – of cerebral disintegration through age, mental handicap and so on? Are we not compelled to take these factors seriously as ontologically *constitutive* of personal, creaturely identity?

Second, does it allow us to describe as 'persons' human beings who have not experienced salvation, who may not have found, or been 'found by', this salvific communion, who may not be said to have been 'divinised' by being brought through eucharistic or ecclesial experience to participate (cognitively) in God's personal existence? When Jesus refers to 'the least of these', may he not be referring to individual human beings who do not have this 'capacity' or have not had the opportunity for such cognitive communion and yet who are loved by God *as persons*?

The Biological and Ecclesial Hypostases   These questions of biological constraint (our human finitude, conditioned-ness), alienation and mortality are responded to, in Zizioulas' system, by way of a distinction between two forms of existence, namely *the hypostasis of biological existence* and *the hypostasis of ecclesial existence*. This distinction he traces to Patristic theology's refusal to endorse a humanistic interpretation of the person.

---

[230] Ibid., 49–50.

1) The biological mode of existence (the hypostasis of biological existence) is 'constituted by a human being's conception and birth. Every man [*sic*] who comes into the world bears his or her "hypostasis" (mode of existence) which is not entirely unrelated to love: he is the product of a communion between two people.'[231] The biological constitution of the human hypostasis suffers radically from two features which 'destroy precisely that towards which the human hypostasis is thrusting, namely, the person'. The first is 'ontological necessity'. Our mode of being is inevitably bound to our natural instincts, to impulses which are 'necessary' and beyond the control of human freedom. We are, in other words, conditioned by our 'natures'. The second 'passion' (lit. 'something from which we suffer') is the 'passion' of individualism – the separation of the hypostases. This is identified ultimately with the last and greatest 'passion' of humankind, that is, with the disintegration of the hypostasis which is death. The body as conditioned, as individualising and as mortal hinders us from becoming persons, that is, from affirming ourselves as love and freedom.[232] The survival of the person, therefore, involves a transcendence of our biological constitution through ecclesial communion. This constitutes the very essence of salvation.

---

[231] Ibid., 50. Zizioulas sees erotic love as an astounding mystery of existence, concealing in the deepest act of communion a tendency towards an ek-static transcendence of individuality through creation.

[232] He writes, 'Death is the "natural" development of the biological hypostasis, the cession of "space" and "time" to other individual hypostases, the sealing of hypostasis as individuality. At the same time it is also the definitely tragic "self-negation" of its own hypostasis (dissolution and annihilation of the body and of individuality), which in its attempt to affirm itself as hypostasis discovers that finally its "nature" has led it along a false path towards death. The "failure" of nature, as it is expressed in the biological identity of man, reveals two things simultaneously. The first is that, contrary to the "assurance" of its biological drive, for the "hypostasis" to survive it must express itself as "ecstasy" – not sequentially but simultaneously, not first as being and then as person. The second is that this "failure" of the survival of the biological hypostasis is not the result of some acquired fault of a moral kind (a transgression), but of the very *constitutional make-up* of the hypostasis, that is, of the biological act of the perpetuation of the species.' (Ibid., 51–2.)

Fairness to Zizioulas requires that he be quoted here at some length:

> Man as a biological hypostasis is intrinsically a tragic figure. He is born as a result of an *ecstatic* fact – erotic love – but this fact is interwoven with a natural necessity and therefore lacks ontological freedom. He is born as a *hypostatic* fact, as a body, but this fact is interwoven with individuality and with death. By the same erotic act with which he tries to attain ecstasy he is led to individualism. His body is the tragic instrument which leads to communion with others, stretching out a hand, creating language, speech, conversation, art, kissing. But at the same time it is the 'mask' of hypocrisy, the fortress of individualism, the vehicle of the final separation, death. 'Wretched man that I am!' Who will deliver me from this body of death?' (Rom. 7: 24). The tragedy of the biological constitution of man's hypostasis does not lie in his not being a person because of it; it lies in his tending towards becoming a person through it and failing. Sin is precisely this failure. And sin is the tragic prerogative of the person alone.
>
> Consequently, for salvation to become possible, for the unsuccessful hypostasis to succeed, it is necessary that eros and the body, as expression of ecstasy and of the hypostasis of the person, should cease to be the bearers of death. Two things therefore appear to be indispensable: (a) that the two basic components of the biological hypostasis, eros and the body, should *not* be destroyed ...; and (b) that the constitutional make-up of the hypostasis should be changed – not that a moral change or improvement should be found but a kind of new birth for man. This means that although neither eros nor the body are abandoned, they nevertheless change their activity, adapt themselves to the new 'mode of existence' of the hypostasis, reject from this activity of theirs which is constitutive of the human hypostasis whatever creates the tragic element in man, and retain whatever makes the person to be love, freedom and life. This is precisely what constitutes that which I have called the 'hypostasis of ecclesial existence'.[233]

---

[233] Ibid., 52–3. Elsewhere Zizioulas describes sin as denoting the 'individualised and the individualising Adam in us' characterised by the desire to seize, dominate and possess being in such a way that the human ekstasis fails to be fulfilled in communion with God, in ecclesial participation within the Body of Christ. (Ibid., 107.)

2) The eternal survival of the person which is the essence of salvation is to be identified with the transforming of our biological constitution into a new mode of existence – the hypostasis of ecclesial existence. This is constituted by the new birth of the human being which Zizioulas identifies with baptism.

> Baptism as new birth is precisely an act constitutive of hypostasis. As the conception and birth of a man [*sic*] constitute his biological hypostasis, so baptism leads to a new mode of existence, to a regeneration (1 Peter 1:3, 23), and consequently to a new 'hypostasis'.[234]

This is what is meant by our being born 'anew' or 'from above' (John 3:3,7). It is precisely this possibility that patristic christology strives to proclaim as the good news.

> Christology, in the definitive form which the Fathers gave it, looks towards a single goal of purely existential significance, the goal of giving man the assurance that the quest for the person, not as a 'mask' or as a 'tragic figure', but as the authentic person, is not mythical or nostalgic but is a historical reality.

This means that Jesus Christ may be described as Saviour not because he introduces into the world some 'beautiful revelation', a 'sublime teaching' about the person, but 'because he realises in history *the very reality of the person* and makes it the basis and "hypostasis" of the person for every man'.[235]

Here we see the extent to which Zizioulas breaks with theological approaches operating from a 'revelation model' and consistently redefines the theological enterprise from the perspective of a 'communion model' – a model which sustains (and presupposes) a commonality of personhood between God and humanity. In doing this Zizioulas does a great deal to take theology beyond the obsession with epistemological concerns which has characterised so much

---

[234] Ibid., 53.
[235] Ibid., 54.

theology since the Enlightenment – even, as Colin Gunton suggests, Karl Barth's theology.[236]

Bonhoeffer accused Barth of revelational foundationalism – a 'positivism of revelation' – and it is has been suggested that this can lead to a form of isolationism. What we are required to ask of Zizioulas here is whether his account is not open to a parallel charge of operating an ontological 'positivism of communion' or 'personalist foundationalism' which fail to take seriously human continuity with society at large and the ontological implications of this – not least the fact that we cannot escape 'social sin' and our implication within it by having a new mode of existence bestowed on us as particular individuals.

It is important here to take cognisance of the full significance of the sacraments for his ontology. The ecclesial hypostasis is constituted by baptism into the community of the church, that is, 'from above', and it is further sustained by, and grounded in, the 'experience' of the eucharist which is also 'from above'. The 'from above' element, however, is not merely some *recreatio originalis*, that is, a transformation where God is postulated as the original cause or mover of a new, isolationist – and subsequently self-sustaining – state of enlightenment. Rather, it denotes the bestowal and sustenance of what he describes as the *'sacramental* or *eucharistic hypostasis'*.[237] This does not annihilate our 'sociality' – the givenness of our social connectedness in the natural order – but rather transforms it in and through the bestowal of an 'ecclesiality' the fulfilment and realisation of which is interpreted eschatologically.

Zizioulas' interpretation of the 'eucharist' is profoundly important here. He insists that 'the eucharist is first of all an assembly (*synaxis*), a community, a network of relations, in

---

[236] He writes, 'Karl Barth saw himself primarily as standing before the God made known – revealed – in Scripture, and as is well known, his preoccupation with revelation gave to his theology a strongly epistemic drive, which at the same time showed him to be working in some way in the context of, although also against, the Enlightenment.' *The Promise of Trinitarian Theology*, 4–5.

[237] Zizioulas, op. cit., 59.

which man "subsists" in a manner different from the biological as a member of a body which transcends every exclusiveness of a biological or social kind'.[238] The eucharist has 'as its object man's transcendence of his biological hypostasis and his becoming an authentic person ...'[239] To the extent that this takes place, 'every communicant is the whole Christ and the whole Church'.[240] Here we see what Zizioulas means by what he terms the 'catholicity' of a being.[241] Personhood is ultimately a transcendence beyond biological constraints which is conceived eschatologically and which takes place in such a way that there is a *perichoretic* communion of persons participating in the triune, personal life of God.

Critical Assessment Zizioulas' exposition of the distinction between biological and ecclesial hypostasis leaves open the extent to which the kind of transcendence 'beyond created existence'[242] does or does not include those 'persons' whose 'biological' constitution (either through immaturity, cerebral handicap or deterioration through old age) is such that this kind of cognitive transcendence is no longer possible. To this extent, one finds oneself compelled to ask on what basis such a person's eternal life and 'survival' depends? Is it the *ekstasis* of other persons or some past or potential cognitive *ekstasis* which provides the necessary condition of such 'survival'? The question also requires to be asked whether the distinction between the biological and ecclesial hypostases does not circumvent too easily the issues posed by the extent of human alienation – the distortive ravages of social exploitation, extreme poverty and personal tragedy. What is the meaning of the Gospel of grace for those of us who may not so easily be described as spiritual or ecclesial 'survivors' for the eternal domain of communion? The story of Jesus' life and death

---

[238] Ibid., 60.
[239] Ibid., 61.
[240] Ibid.
[241] Cf., for example, ibid., 106.
[242] Ibid., 170.

testifies to a divine immanence which is much more than an ek-static participation with people whose personhood is thus realised in an event of communion. An adequate account of the grace of God must speak of that 'unheard-of immanence: God's presence, incarnate and unseen, in that godless world, among its criminals and cripples, its villains and victims, beside whom and as whom Jesus lived and died and was interred'.[243]

This leads to our second question, which concerns whether the vicarious life and work of Christ risks being reduced, in terms of this kind of ontology, to its ek-static effect, that is, its creating and sustaining a dynamic of ecclesial communion, where its significance is limited to the ecclesial hypostases of those in whom the conditions of 'personhood' are thus realised. May not a new kind of 'limited atonement' be introduced here through a failure to appreciate the extent to which grace denotes a reconciling love and atoning which goes far beyond that sphere of personal transformation and subjective sanctification that is the Church? Moreover, does participation in Christ not mean sharing in the one who *alone* can realise and *has realised* personhood and realises it vicariously on behalf of those in whom it is *not* fulfilled this side of the *eschaton*? And is this not, moreover, the sole hope of the totality of alienated humanity – not only of those outside the Church, but of those within it too?

It is surely imperative that salvation remain a gift of grace, that is, the unconditional acceptance through the New Covenant in Christ of those whose lack of ability, whose weakness and/or alienation may mean they find no confidence in any new mode of existence conceived subjectively. Is this

---

[243] See Alan Lewis' penetrating discussion of the interrelationship between the cross and the doctrine of God in 'The Burial of God: Rupture and Resumption as the Story of Salvation', *S. J. T.* 40 (1987), no. 3, 351. Lewis reminds us, 'Mark has a Roman officer penetrate the *incognito* at the point of maximum ungodlikeness (15.39); but the Christian church has found all this a dangerous narrative, too difficult, often, to remember.'

not the essential message at the very heart of the eucharist? The focus of the eucharist must remain the good news of the unconditional acceptance of sinners in the person of the One who stands in their place and takes their judgement upon himself – and not merely a eucharistic experience confirming a new, 'subjective' or personal mode of existing.

But finally, and most importantly, the question to which we must now turn asks how far Zizioulas' ontology takes seriously the 'brokenness' of the cross – with which both Jüngel and Moltmann have sought to engage so powerfully. It is here that Alan Lewis finds the most serious weaknesses in Zizioulas' theological exposition. Lewis emphasises the need for an exposition of the Christian story which 'actually remembers and faithfully evokes the meaning of that story as first narrated'. He continues,

> Truly to remember the abrupt and final termination of his life, while knowing already that Jesus is the incarnate, risen Lord, is to follow a story which identifies God himself with a corpse. Once cross and resurrection comprise a single movement, its end visible from its beginning, the grave-shaped boundary which unites them prevents the relativising of either to the other. The death of Jesus is no mere prelude to his exaltation, any more than the raising puts an interpretative gloss upon his humiliation. Instead, the continuity of Easter with Good Friday shockingly insists that the powerful, resurrecting God has himself succumbed to godforsakenness and termination, and that only as the victim of death and godlessness will God secure a victory over them.

In Lewis' view, Zizioulas' ontology of communion contrasts with the theological emphases of Jüngel in that the former fails to take sufficiently seriously the 'rupture' to which the cross testifies. He comments,

> Zizioulas seems reluctant to acknowledge the death of Jesus as significant for God's being. For him the movement back from resurrection to incarnation indicates that, though no stranger 'to the conditions of biological existence', 'Christ escaped the necessity and the passions of nature'. When he rose from the dead 'the real hypostasis of Christ was proved to be not the biological one but the eschatological or trinitarian hypostasis' (p. 55). But how real is the

incarnation if Christ is held to have escaped biological necessity or 'the tragic aspect of the human person' because of his trinitarian personhood?[244]

This last point in Lewis' discussion directs us to the crucial theological issue in Zizioulas' exposition. Does his theological ontology of communion not begin to take on an *a priori* role, rather as we have suggested both Barth's and Rahner's appeal to the revelation model and its logical structure tended to do?

The result in Zizioulas is a docetic tendency to which Lewis again draws attention by picking up on Zizioulas' notion of the 'survival' of the human person – a concept which may owe more to Greek ontology than to the Christian doctrine of God's raising Jesus from the dead. Lewis adds to what he has stated above,

> A similar flirtation with docetism seems to affect Zizioulas' interpretation of the resurrection as 'the persistence, the survival of being', which makes the cross a failed attempt to suppress being (p. 108). This surely evades the finality and reality of the death of Jesus, presupposing an ontology in which God swamps non-being with the power of being, rather than receiving non-being into himself and thus going beyond it.[245]

Despite these weaknesses, the value of Zizioulas' contribution to the area of enquiry in which we are engaged remains very substantial indeed. Supremely important is his establishing the primacy of communion over revelation and affirmation of the integral relationship between truth and communion – 'the essential thing about a person lies precisely in his being a revelation of truth, not as "substance" or "nature" but as a "mode of existence"'.[246] Consequently, his

---

[244] Ibid., 350.

[245] Ibid.

[246] He continues, 'This profound perception of the Cappadocian Fathers shows that true knowledge is not a knowledge of the essence or the nature of things, but of how they are connected with the communion-event.' (*Being as Communion*, 106.) Unfortunately, despite the truth of this, he presents us here with an

discussion offers support for interpreting revelation in the context of a proper appreciation of the divine communion and human participation – theological and social – rather than the other way round.

Second, and related to this, he emphasises the importance of integrating sacramental and ecclesial participation and theological knowing, thereby integrating further (and in a manner that is anthropologically constructive) ecclesial communion, on the one hand, and divine communication or revelation, on the other.

Third, he offers a truly dynamic anthropology where the self is conceived as irreducibly open-ended and non-circumscribable. Consequently, his thought opens up a way through some of the traditional impasses between transcendental anthropologies on the one hand and anthropologies grounded in preconceived notions of human finitude and sinfulness on the other.

His creative and critical, cross-fertilising engagement with Boethian and Augustinian,[247] as also Cappadocian, approaches suggests the extent to which Barth and Rahner might have allowed their interpretations of personhood to have been revised by the doctrine of the Trinity in a manner that opened up the profound anthropological implications of the intra-divine communion and our being brought 'economically' to participate within it by the Spirit and in and through the priesthood of Christ.

Fourth, the integrative conceptions of divine personhood and of perichoretic, intra-divine communion which he offers provide a basis for a theology of participation which has enormous ramifications for the analogy debate – although he does not spell these out. The semantic implications of his theology of participation, of his analysis of capacity and incapacity, and of his relating communion and communication, personhood and truthfulness, serve to suggest profoundly

unnecessary either ... or ...! Knowledge of the nature of something should include knowledge of a thing's relations.

[247] Cf. 'On Human Capacity and Incapacity', 405–6.

constructive ways forward through the polarisation between the Protestant *analogia fidei* and the Roman *analogia entis* – ways that reflect the areas of commonality of insight shared by Barth and Söhngen in their eagerness to find dynamic, rather than static, models for the interpretation of theological language within the ecclesial context of revelation.

Conclusion: Moving Beyond Barth's Revelation Model

Doxological Participation

Our discussion as to whether we should ascribe the notion of personhood to the Father, Son and Holy Spirit has raised, *first*, questions of theological method, *second*, questions as to the manner in which terms refer to God and, *third*, questions about the nature of the divine Triunity. We have seen in our expositions not only of Barth but also of Rahner the extent to which their considerations as to whether or not to adopt the notion were bound up with their models of divine revelation or Self-communication. This served to have a negative influence on their evaluation of the appropriateness of the term. It was argued that the factors which influenced their approach betrayed weaknesses in their integration of the *intrinsic* trinitarian relations and the trinitarian relations *ad extra*. By contrast, and utilising theological insights derived from Zizioulas and Jüngel, we suggested that what was required was a more integrative theological model than the 'revelation model', and a more profound interpretation of the notion of personhood on the one hand and of the divine communion and intra-divine mutuality on the other.

Our intention, therefore, in this concluding chapter is threefold.

1) First, we shall attempt to suggest an alternative theological model which is potentially more integrative than Barth's 'revelation model'. However, in offering an alternative we shall seek to reflect some of the profound, indeed essential, methodological insights regarding the *a posteriori* nature of

theology and the epistemological and methodological significance of divine freedom so effectively expounded by Barth (as outlined in the opening chapter). Our alternative means of access to the doctrine of the Trinity may be seen to reflect a 'doxological model' which leads to a rather different conception of the divine Triunity by offering a) a closer integration of the *trinitas ad intra* and the divine economy – and thus greater emphasis on the grounds of human participation in the intra-divine life – and b) a more dynamic conception of personhood with respect to both the divine and also the human realms.

2) Second, we shall seek to show how an alternative 'doxological' or 'communion' model suggests a rather different approach to theological semantics. It requires, we shall argue, to be conceived in rather more fully participative terms than is implied in Barth's own revelation model.

3) Third, it will be suggested that some of Barth's own insights and concerns *vis-à-vis* the nature of analogy may be argued to find expression here in what we would term an *analogia communionis* – an analogy grounded in participative being and one which serves to integrate certain facets of the *analogia fidei* with others of the *analogia entis*. Such an *analogia communionis* would be grounded in a conception of triune personhood which, in contrast to the general thrust of Western thought (from which Söhngen fails adequately to move away), necessitates a primordial ontological synthesis of God's Being and act on the one hand and God's Being-in-communion on the other.

In the light of a discussion of the nature of metaphor in the theological context and the emphasis of Merrill and Jaakko Hintikka on language as 'universal medium', we shall seek to suggest that the use of the term 'person' stands to serve the participative context of theological description or reference most effectively – more effectively, that is, than either 'ways of being' or 'ways of subsisting'.[1] That the model outlined serves

---

[1] It is important to note that the debate does not concern the question of definition. As Alasdair Heron reminds us, 'In any discussion of the suitability of such terms as "person" or "hypostasis" in this connection, it must be kept in mind

the integration of theology and anthropology should, one
hopes, become clear, although this will not be developed
explicitly.[2]

that they were initially drawn into service to refer to rather than to define the
distinct identities of the Father, of Jesus Christ, or the Holy Spirit.' (*The Holy Spirit*,
London, 1983, 174.)

[2] This is something which I have sought to do to some degree elsewhere, in
critical dialogue with Neo-Kantian theological anthropology and the contemporary sociological critiques of 'narcissism' offered by Christopher Lasch. See
'The Self-Relation, Narcissism and the Gospel of Grace' *S. J. T.* 40 (1987),
481–510. In this article I discuss some of the philosophical and sociological issues
relating to conceiving of human personhood in radically 'relational' terms.
Space does not allow further discussion of these issues here and it is not, in my
view, *immediately* necessary for our particular concerns here to do so. However, it
is certainly significant to note Strawson's argument in *Individuals. An Essay in
Descriptive Metaphysics*, London, 1959, which serves to establish that the concept
of the person is a) logically primitive and not derivative; b) logically prior,
therefore, to the notion of individual consciousness, and c) an entity of which
both mental and material characteristics are predicated. Both Strawson's
arguments and those of Gilbert Ryle (most notably his discussion of the notion
of 'spirit' and rejection of the Cartesian notion of the 'ghost in the machine') are
significant for rejecting the forms of dualistic interpretation of the human
subject that undermine an adequate recognition of the irreducible relationality
of the self. Jan Rohls discusses precisely these issues with reference to Ryle and
Strawson in his article 'Die Persönlichkeit Gottes und die Trinitätslehre *Ev.
Theol.*, 1985 (March/April) 124–39, cf. in particular 130–1 – as does Adrian
Thatcher in *Truly a Person, Truly God*, London, 1990, cf. especially chapter 6, 'Jesus
– God in Person'. Colin Gunton moves beyond Rohls by pointing out, quite
rightly, the weakness of Strawson's book which is 'that of the mainstream debate
as a whole, as is suggested by the title ... *Individuals*'. Gunton continues, 'To treat
the person and the individual as the same thing – to define the person as an
individual – is to lose both person and individual.' (*The Promise of Trinitarian
Theology*, Edinburgh, 1991, 88.)

In his important book, *In Search of Humanity: A Theological and Philosophical
Approach*, London, 1982, John Macquarrie expands on Ryle's discussion of the
elusiveness of 'I' (cf. chapter 4, entitled 'Egoity'). This is important in order to help
establish the epistemic problems of a Cartesian starting-point and integrates very
effectively with Wittgenstein's semantically oriented critique of Cartesianism. This
again aids the project of conceiving of the person in 'relational' and non-solipsistic
terms. Taken together, therefore, the work of Gilbert Ryle at the epistemic level,
that of Strawson at the logical level, that of Wittgenstein at the semantic level and
that of Christopher Lasch at the sociological level (in his critique of narcissism) do
a great deal to encourage a radically different approach to selfhood than that which
has been moulded by the Cartesian influences on Western culture and theology.
It is especially in the context of these critiques of the *status quo* that Michael

The Doxological Model

Our exposition of a 'doxological model' of the theological enterprise will be couched in a critical dialogue with two leading contemporary theologians, both of whom have sought to stress, in the context of expositions of the doctrine of the Trinity, the fundamental significance of worship for theology. Our own interpretation of the nature of worship and the doxological 'grammar' of theology will be expounded in the context of this critical discussion.

Jürgen Moltmann

In *The Trinity and the Kingdom of God,* Jürgen Moltmann states that there is an integral connection between knowledge and participation.[3] Exploring the theological implications of this, he argues that there is an essential unity between theological knowing, theological participation and, also, *doxology.*[4] He then goes on to suggest that 'The assertions of the immanent Trinity about eternal life and the eternal relationships of the Triune God in himself have their *Sitz im Leben,* their situation in life, in the praise and worship of the church ...'[5] While the point which Moltmann makes here is a profoundly important one for our defining the very *structure* of the theological enterprise, his ensuing exposition proves disappointing as an exploration of the implications of this. Rather, it serves in certain respects to exemplify the Pelagian tendencies in so

Polanyi's analysis of the nature of the person and personal knowing can be seen to break new ground and open the door to 'post-critical' avenues of thought.

I can only mention what may be termed the deontological challenge to 'Cartesian' accounts as this concerns circularities stemming from the ultimate inaccessibility of, and impossibility of offering a final account of, one's own motivation. This ethical paradox is most effectively addressed by Luther's perception of the anthropological coherence of grace, and this I also discuss in the article cited above.

[3] Expounding the relationship between knowledge and participation (although the force of his discussion is lost in the English translation) Moltmann insists 'to know means to participate in the fullness of the divine life', op. cit., 152.

[4] Again, Moltmann's exposition lacks precision. He comments, 'the perceiving person participates in what he perceives, being transformed into the thing perceived through his wondering perception.' (Ibid.)

[5] Ibid., 152.

many supposedly theological considerations of the nature of doxology.[6]

This is reflected in two interrelated weaknesses in his discussion.

First, he assumes that worship is essentially something which *we* do and initiate – albeit by the Spirit and in the fellowship of Jesus.[7] As in his other writings, there is neither appreciation nor discussion of the significance of the mediatorial priesthood of Christ – that our worship is the *gift of participating, through the Spirit, in what Christ has done and is doing for us in his intercessions and communion with the Father.*[8] For Moltmann, worship is construed as a subjective, anthropological response to, or even consequence of, the human perception of the divine joy and, what is more fundamental for Moltmann, the divine *pathos* – God's sharing in our suffering in solidarity with us.[9]

Second, his rather Pelagian interpretation of worship results from a near collapse of the 'immanent' Trinity into the economic Trinity. This is due in part to his somewhat anthropomorphic 'chicken and egg' struggle over which comes first between the divine freedom and the divine love[10].

---

[6] This is reflected, in part, in the very manner in which he finishes this sentence – it ends with the doxological statement 'Glory be to the Father and to the Son and to the Holy Ghost', as if this served to represent a sufficiently doxological dynamic in his exposition!

[7] Jeremy Begbie makes a useful distinction between 'worship as task' and 'worship as gift'. Moltmann would deny that his theology suggests that worship should be conceived as a task but, without the conception of worship as a gift of participation in the priesthood of Christ, it is difficult to see how worship (given that it is an *obligatory* response) does not ultimately become a task – one that we cannot fulfil.

[8] This is an interpretation I owe to my father, James B. Torrance.

[9] His approach to the nature of worship (as human-centred) and its impetus are reflected in the following: 'The man or woman who suffers God in the fellowship of the crucified Jesus can also praise God in the fellowship of the Jesus who is risen. The theology of the cross becomes the theology of doxology.' (*The Trinity and the Kingdom of God*, London, 1981, 8.)

[10] 'This distinction between immanent and economic Trinity would be necessary if, in the concept of God, there were really only the alternative between liberty and necessity. But if God *is* love, then his liberty cannot consist of loving or of not loving.' (Ibid., 151). See also my reference to Moltmann's concerns about the immanent Trinity in chapter four.

But it is also brought about by his adoption of a form of panentheism that fails adequately to distinguish between God's time and created temporality.[11] Indeed, he seems to include God within a cosmology which exhibits what D. C. Williams terms the 'myth of passage'[12] – a feature shared with process theology.

The effect of this is to undermine the element of 'transcendence' that is intrinsic to doxological participation

---

[11] See Barth's discussion, 'The Eternity and Glory of God', *C. D.* 2. 1, especially 612–19. He writes, 'although God's eternity is not itself time it is as such the absolute basis of time, and therefore absolute readiness for it' (618). Again, 'the temporality of eternity may be described in detail as the pre-temporality, supra-temporality and post-temporality of eternity' (619). Barth's use of 'pre', 'supra' and 'post' here is clearly metaphorical, otherwise he would be committed to postulating a meta-time with respect to which God's time was 'pre' and 'post' with regard to created time. Any such postulation would commit him to an infinite regress. That this is an appropriate reading is warranted by his interpreting human time within the context of his theology of the divine constancy. As already mentioned, Richard Roberts offers a substantial critique of Barth's view of time in his essay, 'Barth on Time' (in Stephen Sykes (ed.), *Karl Barth – Studies of his Theological Methods*, Oxford, 1979, chapter 4). Roberts' pseudo-foundational dichotomy between being and act means that it is difficult to accept his critique as reflecting a sufficiently 'in depth' understanding of what Barth is seeking to do. Jüngel's interpretation in *The Doctrine of the Trinity: God's Being is in Becoming*, Edinburgh, 1976, is far more profound in this respect. Having said that, Roberts' discussion of the parallelisms between Barth and Hegel is certainly relevant.

[12] See 'The Myth of Passage', *The Journal of Philosophy* 48, no. 15, July 1951. For a critique of Moltmann's concept of time see my response to his paper 'Christ in Cosmic Context' in *Christ and Context*, ed. Hilary Regan and Alan J. Torrance, Edinburgh, 1993, chapter 7. (Moltmann's response to my critique is also published in the same volume.)

Moltmann seems to subsume God under an Augustinian conception of absolute time (cf. Augustine's *Confessions*, book 11, chapters 14–27, and Wittgenstein's devastating critique of this in *The Blue Book*). Moltmann's projection of created temporality on to God has led Geoffrey Bromiley to describe Moltmann's theology as a form of process theology. (For a critique of this kind of approach see Alan G. Padgett, 'God and Time: Toward a New Doctrine of Divine Timeless Eternity', *Religious Studies* 25, 209–15. He writes, 'Although we are in God's time (and thus God is in our time, too) God transcends time. He cannot be measured by our time ... God is timeless, then, when by "time" we mean the ordinary, Measured Time of our universe. ... God is relatively timeless, which means that he is not in any Measured Time' (214–15). The question which Padgett's discussion raises, however, is whether he is allowing his conception of eternity and of God's participation in time to be conditioned sufficiently by God's being toward us in Christ or, rather, by analytic determinations based on prior definitions of God and eternity.)

by effectively 'historicising' God, and thus 'cementing' God into the process of the human struggle.[13] By failing to interpret God's participation in the human struggle as a free *ekstasis*, albeit as an event in which God has his Being and which is in no sense 'arbitrary', Moltmann fails to appreciate the extent to which participation in God's intra-divine glory requires to be described as a participation on the part of the human person in the transcendent triune Life. Doxological participation is an event of *grace* – a concept which barely features in Moltmann's theology – and not, therefore, of any natural human response or innate capacity.[14] As such, worship may be described as an event of 'theopoietic' *koinonia*, which is both 'in Christ' and 'through the Spirit', and one, therefore, in which the Kingdom of God is 'in a manner' actually and freely *present* – and not merely future, as Moltmann seems to suggest.

These emphases are important if worship is not to be interpreted as *kata sarka*, that is, if we are to be liberated from Pelagian notions of worship for a proper conception of worship as a mediated gift of participating in the intra-divine communion wherein it is the one High Priest *alone* who offers that worship and 'worthship' that the unconditional grace of God unconditionally requires of us.[15] It is precisely the

---

[13] The word 'cemented' ('hineinzementiert') is the word Rahner uses in an interview published in Moltmann's *In der Geschichte der dreieinigen Gottes: Beiträge zur trinitarischen Theologie* (Munich, 1991, 170), to which Jürgen Moltmann writes a posthumous reply. Rahner uses it of his own 'cementing' into the 'horribleness' of the world and comments that Moltmann's theology of the death of God 'does not help me to escape from my mess and mix-up and despair if God is in the same predicament'. Detecting in Moltmann and others a 'projection into God of division, conflict, godlessness and death', he asks 'What use would that be to me as consolation in the true sense of the word?' (*History and the Triune God* (Eng. trans. by John Bowden), London, 1991, 122–3.)

[14] Cf. again Fergus Kerr's powerful critique of Karl Rahner's attempt to combine a transcendental anthropology with Heideggerian categories, 'Rahner Retrospective III: Transcendence or Finitude', *New Blackfriars* 62 (September, 1981), 370–9.

[15] It is important to note that 'worthship', as it denotes the form of communion with God required by God's grace, includes as integral to it 'epistemic truthfulness'. This is relevant for a proper appreciation of the integral connection between doxological participation and theological epistemology. It is also important here to appreciate that the latter is included in and grounded in the former and not the other way round.

theological insight that God's grace actually includes the provision of the very response demanded by it that distinguishes Christian worship from religious ritual. Christian worship becomes thus the free participation by the Spirit in something that God perfects on our behalf, whereas worship as religious ritual is a human task, namely one that ultimately can be little more than the vain attempt on the part of finite creatures to approach the 'Transcendent' (whatever they suppose this to mean) and offer some (equally supposedly) requisite attitude.

By contrast, Christian worship shares in a human–Godward movement that belongs to God and which takes place *within* the divine life. It is precisely into and within *this* that we are brought by the Spirit to participate as a gift of grace. It is this *enhypostatic* emphasis which liberates us from a model of participation conceived as a purely subjective – and, therefore, ultimately inexplicable – act on the part of those who are *echthroi te dianoia*.

Worship is not some valiant subjective response, therefore. It is a gift of grace which is realised vicariously in Christ and which is received and participated in by the Spirit. It speaks of a *theosis* or *theopoiesis* whose form and content are 'from above'. One might even suggest that it is more consistent *here* to speak of a *vestigium trinitatis*, in that the Father is the author of worship, the Son the worshipper and the Spirit the agent of worship (where the worship may be identified with the presence of the Spirit), than to speak of the structure of revelation as manifesting such a *vestigium*! Why? The reason is that this model of the theological structure of worship (as this may be conceived in terms of the inclusive economy of the Trinity *ad intra*) fulfils three criteria that Barth's revelation model fails adequately to meet.

a) It denotes more fully the open and inclusive communion of the Trinity.

b) It interprets the interrelations of the Trinity in more strongly communal (i.e. personal) rather than functional terms.[16]

---

[16] I should add that had Barth's 'revelation model' of Volume One been construed in terms of his trinitarian exposition of the theology of reconciliation as we find it in Volume Four, one doubts whether the weaknesses to which I am referring would have been present in this form.

c) It enables a fuller characterisation of the *agency* of the Spirit – that is, it avoids the reductive tendency implicit in Barth's identification of the Spirit as the 'Revealedness' which risks the interpretation of the Spirit as merely a passive or postulated epistemic condition.

Catherine Mowry LaCugna

LaCugna serves as another significant example of a contemporary, trinitarian theologian who emphasises the fundamental importance of the integration of doxology and theology.

Her appreciation of the historical relationship between credal and doxological formulation is reflected in her detailed historical analysis of these issues.[17] Making extensive use of Jungmann's masterly study, *The Place of Christ in Liturgical Prayer*,[18] she points out that 'the normal pattern of Christian prayer prior to the fourth century was to God through Christ, emphasising the high priestly role of Christ who in his humanity intercedes for us on our behalf'. She then goes on to reiterate Jungmann's observation that, following the debates over the *homoousion*, the fear of subordinationism led to a widespread emphasis on *triadike pistis* (trinitarian faith) conceived in such a way that 'the mediatorship of Christ as high priest in his humanity (*oikonomia*) fell more and more into the background'.[19] Indeed, by the end of the fifth century, as Jungmann suggests, there was little place for the mediatorial priesthood of Christ. Prayer was no longer *to* the Father *through* Christ *in* the Spirit and hence through the divine economy, but took the form simply of a glorification of the Trinity. As LaCugna rightly affirms, the motivation behind these developments was the fear of a subordination either of Christ or of the Spirit, that is, a fear of undermining the *homoousion* which was now the criterion of orthodoxy. The result of this was that the incarnation, and in particular the

---

[17] See chapter 4 of *God for Us*, New York, 1991, entitled 'Christian Prayer and Trinitarian Faith'.
[18] New York, 1965.
[19] *God for Us*, 125.

'enhypostatic' movement, was undermined in such a way that a gulf emerged between God and humanity and a proper trinitarian understanding of the grace of God was lost. We would add that the effect in the West would ultimately be the subordination of the doctrine of the Trinity and the move to monadic and deistic conceptions of God, with a loss of a due appreciation of the relevance of the Trinity.

Moreover, as the mediatorial place of Christ was lost sight of, LaCugna argues, 'the distinction between God and Christ became merely academic'. This led in turn to a situation where the 'veneration of the saints increased dramatically, since they in their humanity could provide the necessary bridge between us and God'. And, as she further observes, 'This last development coincided with the growing devotion to Mary.'[20]

As we have seen, Moltmann's attempt to overcome precisely this gulf as it emerged in Western thought can be traced to a) his doctrine of the divine pathos; b) a high doctrine of the continuity between the social Trinity and human sociality – what one might almost describe as denoting a socialist *analogia entis*! and c) the near reduction of the immanent Trinity into the economic where the Trinity *as a whole* is 'incarnated' into the historical process. This latter tendency is evident in his use of Joachim of Fiore with his 'triadic' interpretation of history and his translation (in precisely the opposite direction from Rudolf Bultmann) of the transcendent into the futural .

LaCugna's response to the gulf which she exposes shares a certain amount in common with Moltmann in the manner in which she uses the Trinity to model inclusive fellowship. Moreover, she also falls into a Pelagian tendency in her conception of salvation. The essential weakness in LaCugna's account can be traced, in our view, to her inability to appreciate the essential *evangelical* significance of the *homoousion*. This is reflected by her puzzling statement that the Nicene affirmation of Christ as *homoousios* with God 'created an obvious incommensurability with *oikonomia*, now identified specifically

---

[20] Ibid., 127. It is interesting that this comment should be made by a Roman Catholic theologian.

with the humanity of Christ'.[21] As a result, when she comes to draw her conclusions, in which she wishes to stress the close relationship between the Trinity, theology and doxology,[22] instead of endorsing a recovery of the divine economy as it involves the mediatorial priesthood of Christ, LaCugna supports a kind of realised – *and humanly realisable* – ontology of communion. The exposition of this reposes on her use of the metaphor of the 'Household', which, in turn, constitutes the controlling *motif* in her theology of the sacraments.

By simply endorsing the humanly-inclusive, trinitarian communion, rather than seriously thinking 'out of' it, that is, *in terms of* it, she is led to what tends to be a synergistic conception of human fellowship with the Trinity and, consequently, a somewhat deontological and utilitarian conception of the nature and function of worship and the sacraments. The essential nature of doxology she conceives in the following way: 'God is praised because of what God is doing, has done, will do on our behalf ... God is praised on the basis of God's self-revelation in Christ and the Spirit ...'[23] This means that for LaCugna – as was the case with Moltmann – worship is essentially something which *we do*, a task which we perform, in response to what *God has done and is doing*.[24] The sacraments function accordingly as a means of helping us in what we must *do* and *be*, that is, they 'empower us to live in right relationship with God, with ourselves, with others', and at their core is to be found the effecting of the 'ontological change' that gives rise to this. This change is not what she terms the 'scholastic' notion of an ontological change taking

---

[21] *God for Us*, 209.

[22] Her penultimate chapter is given that name.

[23] Ibid., 367. She adds, 'The vocation and freedom of the theologian derive from doxology, which is animated by the Spirit of God who speaks truthfully about God' (367–8).

[24] She concludes, 'theology in the mode of doxology is contemplative and speculative, as well as practically oriented'. 'Trinitarian theology is inherently doxological', therefore. 'Understood as a way of rendering praise to God, trinitarian theology of God reconnects spirituality with theology, orthodoxy with orthopraxis, the contemplative with the speculative, apophatic with kataphatic, the pastoral with the academic.' (Ibid., 368.)

place in the eucharist, it is not 'a change in substance but a personal transformation and renewal, and a new capacity for relationship, so that our true nature may be more perfectly *expressed*' (italics mine).[25] This applies not only to the eucharist but to the other 'primary sacrament', namely baptism, which is 'the sacramental and ontological act that transforms solitariness and separateness into communion'.[26]

The result of her approach is that, despite some important elements of truth and insight here, she fails to appreciate the full implications of what we might term the relationship between the *hypostasis* of the Trinity and its *ekstasis* in grace. The Trinity stands in danger of becoming, for LaCugna, essentially a social *Exemplar* in which we seek to participate by effecting worship and by inclusive forms of *praxis* as these are enabled through the subjective ontological change associated with sacramental experience.

The result is that worship and sacramental celebration is conceived in a rather 'ends-oriented' manner. Ethical transformation becomes a primary and direct goal of sacramental experience rather than a secondary (and *ergo* more, not less, effectively realised) consequence of the primary end of the sacraments, namely the discovery of our righteousness as it is 'included' by grace within the righteousness of God in Christ, and the liberation to live in the light of the fact that we have been made righteous in and through the vicarious faithfulness of Christ.

The result of the kind of theological approach adopted by LaCugna is reflected in the fact that her final emphases are on *orthodoxy* and *orthopraxis*.[27] The former, moreover, is conceived essentially as a means to the latter. It would appear to us, however, that she misses both *by a whisker* through her failure to perceive the precise nature of the dynamic of grace.[28] The event of grace does not stop where the free human response begins; it includes precisely that human response to the

---

[25] Ibid., 404.
[26] Ibid.
[27] Ibid., 383.
[28] And it should be pointed out that a miss is as good as a mile!

extent that the human response is completed on our behalf in Christ. Grace relates not only to the anhypostatic movement, but to the enhypostatic movement as well. Without appreciating this, one cannot grasp the profound anthropological (and psychological) significance of Luther's point that we do not *do* God's will until we *desire* to do God's will. This desire is given *en Christo* as we are brought to participate in *his* human life and live 'out of' the vicarious worship (as this includes the totality of human 'worthship') provided in him by the Spirit *on our behalf* – and where we are thereby recreated to live *out of* this event of grace in all its *objectivity.* It is as we find ourselves (*post factum*) subjectively caught up in this event of participation that the implications of God's covenant commitment to humanity are *subjectively* (and subliminally) realised in us such that there may be brought about, by grace, a reforming and transforming of our lives and apperceptions – where this is rooted in subjective desire, that is, a desiring that is given, a 'desire' that is not 'desired' in advance of its being realised in us.

LaCugna's concluding chapter is entitled 'Living Trinitarian Faith' and concerns 'The Practicality of the Doctrine of the Trinity' (the title of the first subsection). As such, it amounts to an exposition of Christian ethics as the expression of various forms of communion lived out and 'entered into' in the light of the divine monarchy who is the 'one origin, one principle, one rule'.[29] This leads to various insights into 'Trinitarian politics' and various forms of 'living God's life with one another' (living out the 'inclusive household') which she describes under the headings: 'ecclesial life', 'sacramental life', 'sexual life', 'Christian ethical life' and 'spiritual' life.

Consequently, her exploration of God's grace (conceived anhypostatically) is then translated into forms of 'praxis'. What is so obviously missing throughout this culmination of her exposition of the Trinity is nothing less than the ontology of 'communion' for which her entire *opus* intends to strive. There is an inability adequately to distinguish between the

[29] Ibid., 389.

subjective event of (sacramentally aided) communing and the *koinonia* that is the New Creation by grace and in Christ. Communion is not something into which we 'enter'[30] so much as something into which we are drawn by the Spirit. It is, moreover, neither a form of 'praxis' nor a mode of *doing*, but a dynamic in which we find ourselves. It is a mode of *being* (as Zizioulas sees), but one which is discovered *a posteriori* in and through the event of our participation within it. This discovery is identical with the event of discovering, by the Spirit, the communion completed *en Christo*. As such, it is a form of discovery which is unique in that it is 'performative' in its significance, that is, the discovery 'act-ually' (as this discovery is a divine act[31]) or ek-statically effects in us the subjective participation which it denotes objectively. This is precisely what underlies the 'I yet not I', the 'I live, nay, Christ lives in me' dynamic of the Christian life. And, as has been suggested above, the New Covenant actually realises in us (albeit incompletely) by the Spirit the obligations (which the Torah articulates) that are fulfilled in Christ. Now that we live by that faithfulness of Christ by which we are made righteous, we are brought to live 'out of' Christ by the Spirit in such a way that 'we are no longer under the supervision of the law'.[32] What is important to grasp here is that this is an *ontological* (christological) point which may not be reduced to or translated into a *deontological* one – not even by advocating an 'ethic' of communion.

Dr Douglas Campbell, the Pauline scholar, argues convincingly that in Paul's specific use of *pistis* in Romans and Galatians and his contrasting it with *ek ergon nomou* his intention is

> not at all to contrast different types of human motivation in salvation, but more probably to contrast a *christocentric* perspective with an

---

[30] This is the metaphor which she uses continually, for example: 'Entering into the life of God means entering in the deepest way possible in the economy, into the life of Jesus, into the life of the Spirit, into the life of others.' (Ibid., 382.)

[31] Cf. my discussion in chapter 2 about the intrinsicity which is essential to the revelation event. Precisely this same intrinsicity applies here!

[32] Gal. 3:25.

anthropocentric one. That is, Paul contrasts a dependence on Christ's faith and obedience as the ground of salvation, with any human-centred approach to salvation – *whatever form that might take!*[33]

Arguing that a *christocentric* understanding of *pistis* (which, he argues, is warranted by the syntax of the phrases *ek pisteos* and *dia tes pisteos* in Romans and Galatians[34]) challenges the profoundly mistaken emphasis that 'the condition for receiving the gospel's offer of eternal life is, pure and simple, and according to the apostle Paul himself, belief' or some Bultmannian faith. He continues,

> a christocentric understanding of *pistis* challenges this whole approach to the gospel, and its supposed presentation by Paul. A renewed emphasis on Christ's (and God's) faithfulness, shifts the initiative throughout the process, and the very fulfilment of salvation's conditions, back to God, and above all to God's work in Christ. Thus a covenantal rather than a contractual structure begins to emerge from Paul's letters ...[35]

The theological thrust of Paul's argumentation taken as a whole is that *pistis Christou* used with *dia* or *ek* refers to the faithfulness of Christ as this is to be identified with the faithfulness of God. Any faith or faithfulness we might have is the gift of participating in Christ's faith and faithfulness. It is in precisely these terms that Christ's faith and faithfulness 'makes possible our faith and faithfulness towards God'. It is thus the objective and vicarious 'faithfulness' of Christ that is proclaimed as the Gospel – it is on this that we are brought by

---

[33] 'The Crisis of Faith in Modern New Testament Scholarship' in *Religious Studies in Dialogue: Essays in honour of Albert Moore*, ed. Simon Rae and Peter Matheson, Otago, 1991, 172–3.

[34] 'The Meaning of Pistis and Nomos in Paul: A Linguistic and Structural Perspective', *J. B. L.*111.1 (1992), 91–103. See also his monograph, *The Rhetoric of Righteousness in Romans 3:21–26*, J. S. N. T. Supplement, Sheffield, 1992.

[35] 'Covenantal' denotes here an unconditional, unconditioned and unilateral promise (*diatheke*). This distinction is borrowed by Campbell from J. B. Torrance. Cf. J. B. Torrance, 'Covenant and Contract, a study of the theological background of worship in seventeenth-century Scotland', *S. J. T.* 23 (1970), 51–76; idem, 'The Contribution of McLeod Campbell to Scottish Theology', *S. J. T.* 26 (1973), 295–311.

the Spirit to repose, and not on any event of 'faith' on our part or, for that matter, any other form of communing conceived as a human self-act.

Properly interpreted, a Christian *theology* of communion, conceived in *a posteriori terms*, appreciates the extent to which the indicatives not only precede the imperatives but actually include their realisation objectively *en Christo*. Moreover, these imperatives must not be conceived as relating primarily to those (ethical) modes of living other than those which take the form of 'worship'. They include *both*, since no dichotomy can be drawn between the two – both denote 'being-in-communion' with God and humanity. Christian ethics concerns liturgy!

Is this to endorse antinomianism? This is the old, confused question (used against Paul) that inevitably emerges at this point. The answer should be plain! When people actually and joyfully believe, look to and repose on the fact that God in Christ freely completes on their behalf everything that could possibly be required of them and by the Spirit intercedes for them, they *will not* respond, in the face of and looking to the crucified Lord's word of grace to them, 'Good, now it doesn't matter what I do or how I behave!' Any such response could only derive from a loss of belief in and a failure to repose on Christ's vicarious faithfulness – something that is more likely to be encouraged by focusing on the imperatives of obligation or, worse, attempting to 'strengthen' them by making them conditions![36]

It is pertinent to this to notice an important parallelism between *Romans* and *Hebrews*. The central thrust of Romans is that we are made righteous through the faithfulness of Christ. Righteousness, the *dikaiomata tou nomou*, is therefore given in Christ and that is the grace of God. However, liturgical obligations were also outlined in the Torah, and the author of the *Epistle to the Hebrews* addresses the question of the obligations of the covenant *vis-à-vis* worship referring to the *dikaiomata latreias* (Heb. 9:1). Here we find the parallel argument that *these* are fulfilled in Christ who is the one true High Priest of

---

[36] Cf. Gal. 3:17–22.

our confession, the One who alone is worthy and who alone may offer appropriate intercessions for us and on our behalf. Worship, therefore, is not to be conceived in terms of the *dikaiomata sarkos* (Heb. 9:10). The essential argument here is directly parallel to Paul's constrast between living according to the flesh (in accordance with the *dikaiomata tou nomou*) and living through faith in the faithfulness that is offered vicariously by Christ on behalf of those who cannot of themselves fulfil the righteous requirements of the law.

In Romans 8 (vv. 26–27), Paul himself offers a doxological parallel to the above argument with respect to our failure to pray as we ought. The Spirit of Christ vicariously offers the prayer that we ought to provide but cannot provide for ourselves. In sum, when Paul writes earlier in the same passage (v. 3), 'For what the law was powerless to do in that it was weakened by the sinful nature or *flesh*, God did by sending his own Son in the likeness of sinful man to be a sin offering' he was speaking of a vicarious faithfulness which *includes worship within 'worthship'*. Consequently, faithfulness, righteousness, worthship and worship – the totality of the appropriate human response to God's unconditional, covenant commitment to his people held forth in the Torah – may be seen to be completed in the Second Adam, the one true human, who thus 'fulfils the law' on our behalf. It is this 'New Covenant' which constitutes that Gospel from which and for which that 'New Humanity' constituted as the 'Body of Christ' is brought to live by the Spirit as a New Creation.

The dynamics of grace denote, therefore, an 'enhypostatic' (human–Godward) movement realised in and through the Son and which constitutes, through a parallel movement of the Spirit, the ground of our communion in the divine life. This means that the trinitarian relations *ad intra* are to be conceived as open to us as creatures. It is this free and dynamic opening to humanity of the divine communion that constitutes worship as the transforming possibility for humanity – where worship is conceived as the gift of participating in the human priesthood of the Son through the presence of the Spirit.

What should be clear from this is that it is imperative for trinitarian theology to appreciate the inner connection between the ontology of grace and the vicarious humanity of Christ and that it not fail, therefore, to appreciate the interrelationship between the *Deus ad intra* and the *distinct* divine appropriations. Failure here can only lead to our reducing the trinitarian event of communion as it constitutes the very grammar of an integrated and integrative understanding of worship, worthship and epistemic communion to what will at best be simply an ethical or exemplary *principle* of communion or an epistemically crippled *structure* of revelation or divine Self-communication.

In sum, the strength of a doxological approach – a 'worship-oriented paradigm' as opposed to a 'revelation-oriented paradigm' – is its capacity to direct us to that event of triune communion which is conceived not as a 'mode of being' to be appropriated or taken on by the human subject, but as the gift of sharing in the life of the Second Adam as it is constitutive of the New Humanity – of sharing in and living out of *his* life lived in place of ours (his worthship), *his* continuing and vicarious priesthood (his worship) and in *his* union and communion with the Father in the Spirit.

Conceived in these terms, a doxological approach integrates a) the trinitarian grounds of that event of epistemic creativity that is revelation in Christ, and b) the trinitarian grammar of human participation in Christ (where the event of worship becomes inseparable from the divine dynamic of lived 'proclamation'). In this way, the worship model serves – more effectively than an epistemically-oriented revelation model or an ethically-oriented communion model – a conception of Christ in which the prophetic and priestly offices are inseparably integrated, where Christ's prophetic role in proclamation (the Logos who realises the hearing of the message) and his priestly role in the sacraments are irreducibly intermeshed.[37] In this way, we obviate the traditional

---

[37] When in the sacrament of communion we say that Christ 'took bread, gave thanks, broke it and gave', we refer to his taking human flesh, giving thanks in our

dichotomies between the soteriological and the doxological in such a way that a more integrated theological anthropology can emerge – one that is informed by, and oriented toward, the participation in the New Humanity of the One who constitutes in himself 'once and for all' the integration of the triune life and identity and ours.[38]

Semantic Participation

In his important essay 'Humanity in Correspondence to God', Eberhard Jüngel argues that 'theological anthropology has at least this in common with philosophical anthropology, that it regards language as constitutive for human being'. He then continues,

> Both agree that humanity is socialised through language and that it is this which makes us really human. But on the basis of its definition of humanity as justified through God's Word, theological anthropology identifies a problematic state of affairs in the linguistic being of humanity. Two basic characteristics define our linguistic being. We are both those who are addressed and those who state. We are both at one and the same time. However, theological anthropology makes an ontological distinction between these two basic characteristics in their very togetherness. It must be clarified

name, taking the brokenness of the cross to himself and giving his life for ours. Consequently, it points to God's taking what is ours that we might have what is his, a *mirifica commutatio* (Calvin) which denotes that exchange which is *katallage*. It is my view that neither Barth nor LaCugna sufficiently appreciated the vicarious event which stands at the centre of the sacraments. This is puzzling in the case of LaCugna, not least because the most useful exposition of Calvin's interpretation here is by LaCugna's fellow-Catholic colleague (Kilian McDonnell) with whom she has jointly written articles e.g. 'Returning from "The Far Country": Theses for a Contemporary Trinitarian Theology', *S. J. T.* 41 (1988), 191–215.

[38] In this context one appreciates Athanasius' concern to emphasise the priesthood of the Logos. The kind of participative and christological interpretation of doxological knowing I am advocating may be seen to lie behind the patristic emphasis, which T. F. Torrance highlights, on the *ecclesiastical* nature of all knowledge of God which can be described as *orthos* that is, rightly related to its object. For Athanasius, Torrance writes, 'theological statements have to be in accordance with the basic piety (*kata ten eusebeian*) of the Apostles and of the Church, and have to be in accordance with the mind of the Church (*to ekklesiastikon phronema*), if they are to be true and faithful to Christ.' (*Theology in Reconstruction*, London, 1965, 43.)

anthropologically not only that one of these two characteristics is the condition of the possibility of the other, but also that that characteristic makes it possible ... for us to be or to become again *human* persons.[39]

The 'problematic state of affairs' to which Jüngel refers is one of enormous significance. It has been seriously overlooked by much theology, and it is one for which a proper interpretation of human participation is profoundly significant. Theologians have generally been much too inclined to operate with a naïvely 'referential' and uncritically realist conception of the meaning of terms where it is assumed first that the meaning of a term is that to which it refers (be it a physical or spiritual 'object' or 'truth'[40]) and second that individual thought is historically and ontologically presupposed by language.[41] The world-view assumed by this suggests that there are 'things' (self-defining referents) to which we first *refer* by pure thought and second *express* where this 'expressing' is carried out by attaching terms to these mental acts of referring. Meaning is essentially describable, therefore, in terms of mental events and the *adaequatio intellectus et rei*,[42] in

[39] 'Humanity in correspondence to God. Remarks on the image of God as a basic concept in theological anthropology' in *Theological Essays*, ed. John Webster, Edinburgh, 1989, 145.

[40] A less naïve but equally inadequate form is the belief that the meaning of a term is 'the mode of designation of its reference' (Gottlob Frege).

[41] Susan Patterson makes an important and related point when reflecting on the approach of a certain school of liberal theology which makes much of the appeal to science but operates with a naïveté regarding science and the way it operates. She argues that science is thought by them 'to have a direct grip on reality of a kind denied to theology'. She states, 'For these theologians ... only descriptions of the physical world may be "reality depicting".' This means that 'these theologians are forced by their too-rigid understanding of the correspondence between words and world to withdraw from realism in theology. They thus deny their own models a referential function and justify their use only in terms of their "valuational significance". Their function is limited to evoking faith and hope and trust in the respondent, but, it may be asked, faith and hope and trust in what?' Susan Patterson, 'Janet Martin Soskice: Metaphor and a Theology of Grace', *S. J. T.* 46 (1993), 7–8.

[42] The inadequacy of this approach to meaning is revealed not simply by examples of non-referential words (a problem obviated by appealing to the referential capacity of sentential 'meanings') or, indeed, by appealing, for example, to the performative functions of 'meaningful' sentences (e.g., I name this ship the Titanic), but by the briefest consideration of metaphor. As Jüngel

such a way that a given correspondence between reality or '*things*', on the one hand, and *thought*, on the other, is simply presupposed. This world-view was reflected in the ancient (Platonic) world where 'logos in principle matched up to the whole of being; cosmos and logos were correlates'.[43]

Wittgenstein begins his *Philosophical Investigations* by discussing Augustine's 'primitive idea of the way language functions'.[44] What is outlined amounts to the same confused conception of meaning – as it continues to shape much Western theology. Opening with an extensive quotation from the *Confessions* (1:8) in which Augustine explains how we

points out, the 'judgement that metaphor is a non-literal mode of speech is connected at a very deep level with the understanding of truth as *adaequatio intellectus et rei*'. Meaning is interpreted in terms of correspondence. On this model 'metaphor has nothing to add in asking after the 'what' of things'. (Jüngel, 'Metaphorical Truth' in *Theological Essays*, ed. Webster, 22–3.) It serves a merely figurative function as a 'means of increasing the effect of a statement, of its attacking or striking home at its political or juridical opponents ...' (H. Blumenberg, 'Paradigmen zu einer Metaphorologie', *Archiv für Begriffgeschichte* 6 (1960), 8, cited by Jüngel in op. cit., 25). However, as Soskice shows, the assumption of a straightforward distinction between literal and metaphorical truth is woefully inadequate (cf. Janet Martin Soskice, *Metaphor and Religious Language*, Oxford, 1985, chapter 5).

Metaphor is reality depictive and succeeds in this in a manner that so-called 'literal' terms do not. Testimony to this is reflected not least in the use of metaphor in scientific theories which are laden with metaphors and where metaphors are used in scientific theories where 'a new hypothesis about the world, must use familiar terms to talk about unknown (or partially known) things or relationships'. (Susan Patterson, 'Janet Martin Soskice: Metaphor and a Theology of Grace', 7.)

[43] Jüngel in op. cit., 25. At the very least it is important to note that reference is often sustained precisely by virtue of the fact that words carry an irreducible "baggage" of associations' which may be necessary if they are to mean anything at all. This is particularly obvious when considering metaphors and models in science which are 'extenders of knowledge, the agents of discovery'. (Susan Patterson, 'Janet Martin Soskice: Metaphor and a Theology of Grace', 7.) As Patterson also points out, 'The meaning of a metaphor relies on its ability to make connections with the tacit reality of things and activities in the world.' (Ibid., 4.) Despite being a fundamentally important tool of our indwelling and discovering reality, the meaning of a metaphor cannot be determined either with respect to an object to which reference is being made or a particular, focally determinable thought in the mind of the person using the metaphor.

[44] *Philosophical Investigations I*, (Eng. trans. G. E. M. Anscombe), Oxford, 1974, sect. 2.

come to understand the signification of words by witnessing the manner in which our elders name objects, Wittgenstein comments,

> These words, it seems to me give us a particular picture of the essence of human language. It is this: the individual words in language name objects – sentences are combinations of such names. – In this picture of language we find the roots of the following idea: Every word has a meaning. This meaning is correlated with the word. It is the object for which the word stands.[45]

Augustine interprets language usage, therefore, as essentially a form of 'naming' where naming is carried out with respect to certain kinds of non-abstract objects (e.g. tables and chairs). He assumes, moreover, that the rest of language usage may be interpreted essentially along the same lines. As Wittgenstein comments later on,

> Augustine describes the learning of human language as if the child came into a strange country and did not understand the language of the country; that is, as if it already had a language, only not this one. Or again: as if the child could already *think*, only not yet speak. And 'think' would here mean something like 'talk to itself'.[46]

But this is patently not the way things are. A child is not born with a language, it cannot think in the sense of 'talk to itself' or analyse in any explicit way or divide up what amounts to a largely indescript (lit. 'un-de-scribed') blur. Language is a skill, a game with rules which one learns as one is brought to participate in this ongoing 'form of life' – rules which lead us to distinguish between certain kinds of things in certain kinds of ways. Although these distinctions are not arbitrary and are grounded in the structure of reality, the way these distinctions are made and the manner, therefore, in which the world is divided up are irreducibly bound up with the life of the community in which the child participates. Despite the extensive commonalities which characterise humanity as a whole and which are reflected in the fact that we can translate

---

[45] Ibid., sect. 1.
[46] Ibid., sect. 32.

one language into another – a factor with which the relativism of 'post-modern' theologies has failed to come to grips – there are differences to be found between different societies and the manner in which they distinguish objects and 'divide up' reality. These distinctions may be found to be immanent in the language and to shape the apperceptions of the members of that particular society. Even the grammar – the tense structure, for example – of a language may be influenced by the apperception of a particular socio-linguistic group, in such a way that its language both echoes and perpetuates that influence.[47]

The same mistake that we find in Augustine was perpetuated in Lockean essentialism as it has so shaped modernity. The supposition was that the meaning of generic terms was a fixed 'essence' which was present in every situation in which the relevant term was used and which constituted the 'meaning' of the word.[48] Again, Wittgenstein exposes this fallacy by simply encouraging us to 'look and see' the way in which generic terms actually function in particular cases. To this end he provides examples (e.g. games, as we shall discuss below) which show that the essentialist model fails abysmally as an attempt to describe the way in which language actually works.[49]

Several basic points require to be stressed over against the kinds of assumption underlying the Platonic-Augustinian-Lockean model. These are relevant to the whole debate concerning theological language and not only to the more obvious 'essentialist' elements underlying the Thomist conception of analogy.

[47] D. C. Williams offers a particularly interesting example of this in his discussion of the manner in which the Indo-European tense system of verbs conditions the way we understand time, leading us, in particular, to identify existence exclusively with 'existing in the present' and to the supposition that time 'moves'. Cf. 'The Myth of Passage', *Journal of Philosophy* 48, no. 15 (July 1951).

[48] This kind of approach we witnessed in Barth's attempt to assess the propriety of the notion 'person' by seeking a common denominator present in the *Seinsweisen* of the Father, Son and Holy Spirit as if this is how we establish the propriety of the function of a term or of the 'rules of use' of a term.

[49] *Philosophical Investigations 1*, sect. 66.

1) In the majority of cases the meaning of a word is its *use*.[50] As such it is not some abstract concept or 'essence'. Nor, indeed, is it a referent or class of referents. The meaning of a word relates, therefore, to the social rules which govern the appropriate use of that term. These determine whether someone is 'making sense' in what he or she says 'in public' to his or her hearer or hearers. Such rules determine, that is, whether or not that person is 'playing the game'.[51] If the speaker is not 'playing the game', communication breaks down, that is, communication ceases owing to the resulting 'meaninglessness' of the sounds uttered.

What is important to note is that these predetermined rules of use may sustain various usages which do not necessarily share some single common element. The use of a word is not determined by some fixed meaning which applies in each context of its use. And language is not used in a single uniform way, as, for example, 'to describe the world'. There is a whole multiplicity of ways of using language which much more closely resembles playing a game than attaching names to things. There is no more a single common essence to all that we call language than there is a common essence discernible in all games. This is demonstrated by Wittgenstein when he invites us to do the following:

> Consider for example the proceedings that we call 'games'. I mean board-games, card-games, ball-games, Olympic games, and so on. What is common to them all? – Don't say: 'There must be something common, or they would not be called "games"' – but look and see whether there is anything common to all. – For if you look at them you will not see something that is common to all, but similarities, relationships, and a whole series of them at that. To repeat: don't

---

[50] To quote Ludwig Wittgenstein, 'For a large class of cases – though not for all – in which we employ the word "meaning" it can be defined thus: the meaning of a word is its use in the language.' (Ibid., sect. 43.)

[51] Although it is Ludwig Wittgenstein's *Philosophical Investigations* to which this kind of emphasis is usually attributed, it was Ferdinand de Saussure who 'first realized that meaning resides in relationships between linguistic entities'. (Douglas Campbell, 'The Meaning of Pistis and Nomos in Paul: A Linguistic and Structural Perspective', *J. B. L.* 111.1 (1992), 91.) For a detailed discussion of Saussure's semantic theories cf. Jonathan Culler, *Saussure*, London, 1976.

think, but look! – Look, for example, at board-games with their multifarious relationships. Now pass to card-games; here you find many correspondences with the first group, but many common features drop out, and others appear. When we pass next to ball-games, much that is common is retained, but much is lost. ... – Are they all 'amusing'? Compare chess with noughts and crosses. Or is there always winning and losing ...? Think of Patience ...[52]

The analogy of 'family resemblances'[53] is used by Wittgenstein to denote the variety of different connections and associations between the various instantiations of the use of a term. That the uses of a term may be various certainly does not make its meaning in any way arbitrary. Quite the opposite! Public rules of use determine that it is appropriate to refer to chess and patience as games but not 'washing one's face', despite the fact that patience and washing one's face may have factors in common that patience and chess do not, for example, that they are 'solo' activities!

The significance of this for our argument is quite straightforward. To use a term such as 'person' of the Father, the Son and the Holy Spirit, or to use the term both of God and of human beings, does not necessarily imply that the meaningful use of the term is conditional upon its naming some fixed or determinate 'commonality' (some *tertium*) – an 'essence' or identity of substance that is present in all instances. There may simply be family 'resemblances' not between the referents but between the ways in which the term functions, that is, various and diverse series of connections and associations (with or without any essential 'continuity') involved. The underlying warrants for the usage of a term in diverse contexts may be substantially different across the various contexts of its use. There will, however, be rules of use which suggest when the use of the term is inappropriate. These rules which are intrinsic to the use of a term are open and not closed. As the briefest examination of the nature of metaphor suggests, they change, they are dynamic (i.e. they

[52] Op cit., sect. 66.
[53] Ibid., sect., 67.

are neither static nor fixed) and they are also 'fuzzy'. Most importantly, however, they are invariably 'public' – even their fuzziness is public – and they are defined in and through their adoption and appropriation by the community within which communication takes place.

One consequence of this is that it becomes inappropriate to think in terms of the traditional tidy distinctions between intrinsic attribution, extrinsic attribution and the various forms of analogy. There are fuzzy boundaries between terms and a semantic openness which must not be ignored if one is to avoid misinterpreting what one is doing when one engages in theological affirmation.

Certain forms of personalist ontology run the risk of being seduced by the fallacious assumption that there is a fixed commonality in the use of the term – and we have questioned whether the term 'person' or 'social' may not, in certain approaches, be supposed to have a single, univocal definition which spans the divine and human realms. Integral to theological approaches that are reverently *a posteriori* must be a willingness to acknowledge that, with respect to the theological uses of its terms, the various contexts of their use (for example, with respect to the Trinity on the one hand and humanity on the other) demand a degree of flexibility and open-endedness such that the relevant subject-matter can instigate the semantic shifting, conditioning or, indeed, 'commandeering' necessary to allow for objectivity in semantic reference.[54] Allowing for this stands to *serve* a proper theology of communion rather than the opposite. It reminds us when using the term 'person', for example, not to suppose that the whole 'family' of its rules of use in the human context applies

---

[54] Although some particular feature of the use of the term 'person' may be profoundly significant, we must actually 'look and see' whether the rules of use of that term may not also allow different sets of associations. For example, when we say that someone attended an event 'in person', there is no reference being made in this context to any relational *ekstasis* on the part of the 'individual' involved. One of the strengths of Barth's discussion is his determination to 'look and see' in considering the propriety of the language-game associated with this particular concept so that we do not 'buy into' series of associations which might confuse the debate.

appropriately when it is used of the intra-divine communion and that the degree of continuity between the two sets of rules of use must be determined reverently and *unius ad alterum.* This perception helps us to avoid the anthropomorphisms latent in approaches which operate in an essentialistic manner – which assume, that is, either univocality or an *analogia duorum ad tertium.*

At the same time, this also helps us to see why it may be important to use the same term in both contexts. The rules of use which apply to the term when used of the intra-divine life may 'feed into' and thus condition the rules of use when the term is used in the human context in such a way that there is a change in our perception and articulation of the human order. This creativity *vis-à-vis* our apperception that attends the commandeering of terms and of rules of use is integral to the dynamic of revelation. There can be no dichotomy between semantics and ontology in this respect. The very openness of the triune life means that the 're-ferring' of terms shaped by the divine communion to the ecclesial communion stands to extend and enrich our apperception, our whole sense of the purpose of the created order. There takes place, in other words, a kind of semantic *theopoiesis* which enables continuity in the use of terms in a manner that is precisely the opposite of mythological anthropomorphism.

It is in these terms that the element of intrinsic attribution required by Moltmann, Zizioulas and LaCugna needs to be interpreted. Its grounding must be in that 'intrinsicity' which attends ecclesial participation in triune *koinonia,* and in and through which the relevant rules of use require to be 'reconciled' or 'regenerated' by virtue of the dynamic presence of their reference. In sum, the whole conceptuality of personhood is *semper reformanda* and must not, without collapsing theology into anthropomorphism, be conceived in terms of the subliminal operation of categories which are anthropologically or ethically predetermined. However, as Zizioulas' discussion shows, the very strength of the term 'person' historically can be attributed to the manner in which it acquired its original theological currency. This was in and through an ecclesial context which allowed its rules of use so

to be defined by the eucharistic experience that the term
served to open new ways of conceiving of God and the world,
thereby helping to liberate theology from the confines of the
philosophies of the time. The West, by contrast, continues to
suffer from the warping or distortive conditioning of its
theological apperception mediated, not least, through the
rules of use attaching to its theological terminology. This is
because its categories were taken over, without sufficiently
reverent 'ecclesial' revision, from certain influential
metaphysical systems (Aristotelian, for example) as also from
contexts determined by judicial praxis and hence juridical
and contractual forms of thinking.

Within the theological context of the 'language-games'[55]
integral to the Body of Christ, 'actual' associations and
connections present themselves, not least between divine
and human communion, between theological ontology and
theological anthropology, and between elements of trans-
subjectivity between the Father and the Son and between the
Son and the Body of Christ. These associations and
connections alter our thinking in and through the shaping
of the rules of use which condition our language usage – and
which in turn shape the way we conceive of our world. It
should be plain from what has been said that it is our view
that the language-games associated with the term 'person',
when redefined by virtue of its use with respect to the triune
life, stand to sustain a 'gain' (Jüngel) to the use of the term
beyond that context. This is due not least to the potential to
associate and interrelate its rules of use with those of other
key theological language-games, such as those associated

[55] Wittgenstein provides the following list which represents the multiplicity of
kinds of language-games in the everyday world. This helps to illustrate what
Wittgenstein means by the concept – which we shall discuss later in the chapter.
His list runs as follows: 'Giving orders and obeying them – Describing the
appearance of an object, or giving its measurement – Constructing an object from
a description (a drawing) – Reporting an event – Speculating about an event –
Forming and testing a hypothesis – Presenting the result of an experiment in
tables and diagrams – Making up a story; and reading it – Play-acting – Singing
catches – Guessing riddles – Making a joke; telling it – Solving a problem in
practical arithmetic – Translating from one language into another – Asking,
cursing, greeting, praying.' (*Philosophical Investigations*, 23.)

with the terms 'communion', 'relation', 'participation', 'love' and so on – all of which also require similar 'commandeering' and the associated 'gains' to their rules of use. It is precisely here that our concerns about the term *Seinsweise*, whose rules of use are considerably more general and abstract than those attaching to the term 'person', are couched. In the public, 'intra-ecclesial' task of trinitarian description, associations with notions of participation, communion, love and relation are not served as effectively by this expression. Less constructive, impersonal associations and 'family resemblances' attaching to this concept risk being subliminally 'keyed in' to God-talk in place of the more *koinonial* notions associated with speaking of the 'person' of the Father, the 'person' of the Son and the 'person' of the Holy Spirit. An ill-conceived referential perfectionism here stands to deprive theology of some important series of connections inherent in its language usage.

As must also be plain, however, our judgement here is a contingent one – there is no 'absolute' need to use the term 'person' with respect to the members of the Trinity. But there is an absolute obligation, however, for our language-games to participate as effectively as possible in the triune dynamic which claims them. It is this that must be the all-controlling concern of theological description as a whole.

2) Since language is an irreducibly *social* medium, the very notion of a 'private' language is, as we have already emphasised, incoherent. To suggest that the meanings of terms may or can be 'private' is self-referentially incoherent. Clearly, if I suggest that meanings of the terms I use are on occasions 'private' or 'personal' to me, then I am undermining what I am saying in expressing this. Indeed, I am arguing that my utterance may be literally, socially 'in-significant', that is, meaningless babble – but where I fail even to argue this! In other words, this view can neither be expressed nor endorsed.

As we saw in chapter two, the incoherence of the notion of private language was illustrated by Wittgenstein's 'beetle in the box' analogy. Whatever is in the box 'has no place in the language-game at all; not even as something: for the box might even be empty'. One cannot 'divide through' by the thing in the box as 'it cancels out, whatever it is'.[56]

The significance of this lies not only, as Wittgenstein used it, in its exposure of the incoherence of Cartesian methodological solipsism, but in the critique it suggests of a Bultmannian interpretation of meaning where deeper levels of (spiritual) meaning are argued to be discerned with respect to 'my own' existential (or *existentiell*) experience. This is spelled out with devastating effect by Anthony Thiselton in his study, *The Two Horizons: New Testament Hermeneutics and Philosophical Description with special reference to Heidegger, Bultmann, Gadamer and Wittgenstein.*[57]

In sum, the use of a theological term presupposes a community which provides the context of its use, that is, the rules of use of the term. Terms are used in the context of social participation with respect to which certain rules of use apply. This adds support, therefore, to the insistence (implicit in the *analogia fidei*) that the commandeering of terms for theological usage takes place within the Church, that is, within the community of Christ. There is no unilateral, esoteric or inner transformation of meaning, there is simply the language-game which is constituted, which 'takes place' within the Body of Christ by the Spirit and which we are brought to indwell as the means of the communion which stems from the triune life. The very articulation of the Trinity takes place, therefore, within this context. What has traditionally been conceived, therefore, as theological *pre-dication* might be more properly (if somewhat clumsily!) interpreted as intra-ecclesial, objectively articulative, theologically 'ex-pressive' (in that the meaning of our terms submits to the 'pressure' of the God–humanward dynamic) *post-dication.*

Dogmatic theology is semantically grounded in the Church such that outwith that community of language-usage its meaningfulness is diminished to the extent that the conditions of meaning (and therefore of reference and truth) of its terminology rely on 'games' whose rules are simply not the

---

[56] *Ibid.*, Sect. 293.
[57] Exeter, 1980, 379–85.

same within the secular context as they are within the context of ecclesial participation. This means that part of being 'baptised into' the Church and sharing in the 'metanoia' which attends participation within the Body of Christ is that we are baptised into its language-games in such a way that one comes to share in the rules of use of its terminology. This may involve a semantic tension and the revision in one's thinking of rules of use associated with the secular context without which these rules stand to undermine that apperception (the 'mind of Christ') specific to life in the Body of Christ.

The *supposed* continuity of terminology, and therefore family resemblances between the usages of the terms that the two forms of life have in common (nominally), too often serves to subvert a proper appreciation of the discontinuity between the two domains and thus to confuse the theological or dogmatic task. This is the case not least when this 'continuity' is assumed (perhaps from an essentialist base) to involve a common referential capacity and thereby to denote a valid and necessary *Anknüpfungspunkt*! Concepts of law, covenant (conceived contractually), rights, reason, the individual, nature etc. constitute examples of terms which, when used within the ecclesial context without being sufficiently redefined (commandeered), have served seriously to distort the theological apperception of the community of the Body of Christ.

3) Language is the means of our making distinctions, of articulating and interpreting our experience, not least to ourselves. It is a condition of subjective interpretation. We interpret the world and compartmentalise the world by way of language. Language serves the processes of objective analysis, articulation and recognition. Human knowing and perception are semantically mediated, therefore, to a profound degree.

The element of truth in idealism is set forth in Bishop Berkeley's *New Theory of Vision*, where he shows the extent to which seeing is an interpretative act. As A. D. Ritchie discusses in his book on Bishop Berkeley, W. Chesselden's experiments on the removal of cataracts showed that a blind person given sight could not distinguish between a sphere and a cube until they could touch the objects presented before them and learn to integrate sight and touch.[58] Only then could they 'see' the shapes which they 'indwelled' by touch. Wittgenstein's arguments take the whole debate further still by showing the extent to which distinguishing between more abstract facets of objects involves semantic and linguistic skills. If touch is the *sine qua non* of our distinguishing between objects visually, language (of one kind or another) functions to interpret the whole analytic process underlying touch – that is, to guide the thought processes that underlie all perception. There is clearly a Kantian vein to Wittgenstein's arguments. Kant saw that perceptions without conceptual categories of understanding are mere "blind" events. The transcendental condition of understanding he interpreted in subjective terms. Consequently, his *Critique of Pure Reason* did not succeed in breaking adequately with the Cartesianism that had shaped European thought before him – and its interpretation of semantics. Wittgenstein, however, shows the extent to which our conceptual processes of interpretation belong to the public domain and take the form of obeying rules – a form of obedience that we do not choose but are born into. That is, we are irreducibly social creatures at the cognitive level and we find ourselves participating within rule-governed practices, customs or games which already function at the social level.[59]

There are four points of particular importance to note here. These are:

a) 'Obeying a rule is a practice. And to think one is obeying a rule is not to obey a rule. Hence it is not possible to obey a rule "privately": otherwise thinking one was obeying a rule

---

[58] A. D. Ritchie, *George Berkeley: A Reappraisal* (ed. G. E. Davie), Manchester and New York, 1967, 14–18.

[59] Wittgenstein undergirds this with the comment, 'The common behaviour of mankind is the system of reference by means of which we interpret an unknown language.' *Op. cit.*, sect. 206. Peter Berger and Thomas Luckmann have combined Kantian and Wittgensteinian elements in their notion of the 'social construction of reality'. (Cf. *The Social Construction of Reality: A Treatise in the Sociology of Knowledge*, New York, 1966.) Unfortunately, they open the door too much to relativistic conceptions of collective, social projection. To obviate this it is important to integrate Wittgensteinian insights with those which emerge from the post-critical realism of such as Michael Polanyi.

would be the same thing as obeying it.'[60] Following a rule, moreover, is 'analogous to obeying an order'.[61] It is something we are trained to do.

b) 'When I obey a rule, I do not choose. I obey the rule *blindly*.' In other words, *blind* participation is prior to the decision to participate! To a significant degree we are socially 'created' at the cognitive level prior to any decision to acquire these skills.

This stress on the priority of participation over interpretation and understanding is paralleled in the ecclesial context in various ways. The 'performative' logic of grace as held forth in infant baptism is irreducibly bound up with its purpose of training a child (in and through its being brought up to understand what its baptism means) in the 'skill' of interpreting the world from the perspective of the paradigm associated with the ontological and existential realities held forth in baptism. Being baptised into the Body of Christ is about being 'ecclesially created', or rather born into a context of speaking and thinking (about ourselves and the world) in ways that, by grace and through the presence of the Holy Spirit, constitute paradigmatic participation in the 'mind of Christ'.

Here also is appreciated the 'logic' of Zizioulas' interpretation of Christian communion and participation over against the extremes of individualistic and libertarian approaches to ecclesiology which are so much part of Western Christianity – and which so often operate with the dangerous myth of paradigmatic neutrality.

c) 'It is not possible that there should have been only one occasion on which someone obeyed a rule.'[62]

d) We cannot 'touch' or 'see' how our touching and seeing relates or connects with the world 'out there'. Any suggestion that we should or, indeed, can do so involves a category mistake. In a profound sense we *are* our touching and our seeing, our identity is given with them and what we would term 'world' includes these ways of being.

[60] Wittgenstein, ibid., sect. 202.
[61] Ibid., sect. 206.
[62] Ibid., sect 199.

To the extent that language serves to condition our interpreting the world and, indeed, the totality of our experience, it may be described as a 'universal medium'. Jaakko and Merrill Hintikka explain this notion (which they hold to be fundamental to the insights of the later Wittgenstein) in the following way:

> One cannot as it were look at one's language from outside and describe it, as one can do to other objects that can be specified, referred to, described, discussed, and theorised about in language. The reason for this alleged impossibility is that one can use language to talk about something only if one can rely on a given definite interpretation, a given network of meaning relations obtaining between language and the world. Hence one cannot meaningfully and significantly say in language what these meanings are, for in any attempt to do so one must already presuppose them.[63]

There is clearly an ambiguity in this argument in that it is not the case that one cannot describe what one is presupposing while one is presupposing it. However, what the Hintikkas are seeking to stress is clear. There is no Archimedean point outside of language from which we can speak or state or describe the relationship between language and the world. We cannot step out of language in order to articulate either to ourselves or others the way language 'connects' with 'the world'. Language is a universal medium and as such involves 'the inexpressibility of semantics' – the fact, that is, that 'one cannot transcend language in language or transcend one's thoughts in thinking'.[64] (We would add that this does not necessarily imply, as is too easily assumed, either relativism or idealism. The fact that linguistic mediation *underlies* the objective articulation of reality is no reason to conclude that it, therefore, *undermines* it or that it must be reduced to the 'ideal'.)

[63] Merrill B. and Jaakko Hintikka, *Investigating Wittgenstein*, Oxford, 1986. The element of truth in idealist insights mentioned above is reflected in the connections here with Kant which Wittgenstein himself notes, 'The limit of language shows itself in the impossibility of describing the fact that corresponds to a sentence ... without repeating that very sentence. ... What we are dealing with here is the Kantian solution to the problem of philosophy.' (Cited in Hintikka, ibid., 4.)

[64] Hintikka, op. cit., 185.

As Susan Patterson expresses the issue,

> When we think or talk about language we must perforce do it in language. If the nature of language, its structures and content, is primitive, that is, presupposed in all examinations or explanations of language, then such examinations or explanations are precluded. This seems to be irrefutable logic. The use of language to explain language entails that the conclusion will always be at least in part begged by the premise: *the way language is -> the way language is.*[65]

The consequences, therefore, of Wittgensteinian insights are summarised quite simply by Patterson in the following argument:

> 1. If all human experience requires language (verbal and non-verbal) for its comprehension and hence its accessibility, then language is universal medium.
>
> 2. If the linguistic and non-linguistic are both subsumed by physical reality and their relation therefore takes place in space-time, then language and world are integrated, not separate.
>
> 3. Therefore the language-game is basic or primitive.'[66]

It is not our concern here to offer an assessment of the ultimate plausibility of a Wittgensteinian approach. What we would suggest, however, is that it points to the extent to which human beings are constituted by language, that they are not social beings by choice but that their very thought, forms of analysis and reflection are socially constituted. It exposes, in other words, the extent of our semantic-linguistic sociality. Again this serves to emphasise the degree to which the event of revelation is integrally bound up with an event of communion which in turn conditions our 'sociality', by creating, sustaining and also commandeering our language-

---

[65] Patterson, 'The Theological Implications of the Relationship between a Wittgensteinian Understanding of the Relation of Language to World and the Role of Metaphor as an Agent of Revelation', unpublished doctoral thesis, University of Otago, Dunedin, New Zealand, 25 October 1991, 2. In this section I make use of material discussed in length in this thesis which was researched under my supervision.

[66] Ibid., 19.

games in such a way that we may participate cognitively (and *ergo* semantically) in the divine–human communion witnessed to and served by the kerygma.

A coherent exposition of revelation, therefore, requires very much more than the 'expressivist view of language' which Williams suggests is implicit in Barth's expression of his revelation model. It requires an 'in depth' exposition of human, semantic participation as it is created by the bestowal of communion and as it involves the creation of human participation in new forms and levels of (ecclesial) language-games as these are constituted by the Logos in and through the Body of Christ and by the *creative* presence of the Holy Spirit working a *meta-noia* with respect to our *noiein, logein* and *semainein* such that they may be brought into full participation with the one *Semeion* who is the incarnate *Logos*.

The extension of language is an essential ingredient in discovery. It has a fundamental role not simply in expressing but in generating new forms of perception. At the forefront of this is the semantically incremental function of metaphor, so important not only for scientific discovery but for theology where it is integral to that extension of language and thought associated with a theological heuristic – and where the Holy Spirit may be seen to be the 'bringer of intelligibility' (Patterson), and the Logos or Counter-Logos (Bonhoeffer) the control and atoning mediation of creative understanding and insight. In and through this process the triune God is perceived as one who 'enters the tacit patterns of our lives, confounds our logic and revises our concepts ...' as this reflects the fact that, to the extent that 'God is present to us in our world, God is also present to us in our language.'[67]

It is important to stress that there is no need for Wittgenstein's insights to be interpreted as committing us to a form of social determinism or behaviourism. First, in no sense do the insights we have listed above preclude our conceiving of an open, social structure in which God is dynamically present in triune ways. And, at the human level,

---

[67] Patterson, 'Janet Martin Soskice: Metaphor and a Theology of Grace', 23.

there is no sense in which our analytical capacities, acquired socially, cannot be applied in free critical engagement with the social structures which have 'formed' us. This is what does and must happen not least within the Church if it is to be reformed critically in the light of the Logos (the Counter-Logos) who never ceases to be the ground of its being and *is* its being precisely in and through this process.

4) We have seen that language is, therefore, an essential, social condition of our interpreting the world, i.e. our *indwelling* it 'in depth'. We indwell the world by means of words and by the use of language as much as we 'indwell' the world by means of visual, audial and tactile means. To this extent, language becomes essential to our being as persons. To put it in other words, to the extent that our 'indwelling' the world is a formal condition of our being persons, language, which is the ground of the 'immediacy' of this indwelling,[68] becomes a (socially mediated) 'given' constitutive of our personhood.[69]

It is only to the extent that we 'indwell' in this way, therefore, that we 'are'. We do not first 'exist' and then 'relate' in this sense[70] – there is no such Cartesian possibility. This is demonstrated by Wittgenstein's exposé of the incoherence of the notion of 'private language' and the extent, therefore, to which the entire Cartesian method of radical doubt is hoist on its own petard given that it is required to presuppose an irreducibly social, semantic enterprise.[71]

---

[68] The mediation of which we speak here gives rise in us to an overwhelming sense of 'immediacy'. Language is responsible for the 'mediated immediacy' in our experience of the world, to use John Baillie's expression. This makes it difficult for us to appreciate the extent of the semantic mediatedness (mediacy) that operates in discriminative perception of the world.

[69] Pertinent to the point I am making here is the thesis of Strawson's argument in *Individuals*, to which I referred earlier.

[70] Even the term 'exist' can be seen etymologically to be a relational term in origin: 'From *eksta*, stem of *existanai*, to put out of place ...' LaCugna, *God for Us*, 308, note 55. An existent exists by displacing other existents. An existent is constituted by its relations to other things. A personal existent is thus 'not an individual but an open and ecstatic reality, referred to others for his or her existence.' (Ibid., 260.)

[71] See Ludwig Wittgenstein's essay, *On Certainty* (1950–51), Oxford, 1969.

It is not the case, therefore, that we exist as persons, conceptualise, think and analyse and *then* attach words to our thoughts and express or communicate our conceptualising in language. As we have already argued, our very thinking and analysing presupposes our obedience to social rules, that is, *participation within a community.* The acquisition of the skills of communication (not only spoken language but at an even more primitive level – the rules of body language, physical communication and so on) is integral to our interpreting *world,* the totality of created being – world as it includes not merely physical entities but the whole network of connections, behaviours, rules and language.[72]

What is important to appreciate over and against the relativist or idealist rendering of these insights is the objective governing of these rules. The rules of activities such as verbal communication or, indeed, playing the piano, dancing, playing golf, or rock-climbing are all, in various and diverse ways, governed or conditioned by features which are 'given' in the sense of 'objective'. These 'conditionings' will be constituted by chemical, social, physical and biological factors, and will relate to our abilities, that is, our socio-linguistic, mental and physical capacities.

Two points of importance require to be recognised here. First, as we have already seen, we cannot 'step out' of our various forms of (physical, social, semantic …) indwelling in order to examine them. Second, the fact that we cannot do this does *not* mean that the distinctions we make are simply arbitrary projections and are not grounded in the nature of things. Epistemic objectivity, far from being compromised by this indwelling, is grounded in it. This applies even when the given conditions of some means of engaging with or discovering reality are obliged to change and to adapt. It is the case in the scientific enterprise where 'reality' may interrupt the processes (and paradigms) of scientific research, thereby forcing the revision of precisely the scientific hypotheses without whose

---

[72] Clearly, language and language-games are not extrinsic to, but integrally part of, what we are referring to when we use the term 'world'!

provisional adoption the process of indwelling could not take place. We use tools, therefore, and *must* do so even when they collapse in our hands. When they do, their very collapse becomes itself a tool in our attempt to interpret reality. Such failures generally lead to more successful forms of integrative engagement with parts of 'reality'.

The issues here are not unrelated to an apparent 'dilemma' concerning the nature of the self-relation. In his *Concept of Mind*,[73] Gilbert Ryle discusses 'The Systematic Elusiveness of "I"'.[74] He writes, 'To concern oneself about oneself in any way, theoretical or practical, is to perform a higher order act ...' This means that

> To try, for example, to describe what one has just done, or is now doing is to comment upon a step which is not itself, save *per accidens*, one of commenting ... the operation which is the commenting is not, and cannot be, the stem on which that commentary is being made ... A higher order action cannot be the action upon which it is performed. So my commentary on my performances must always be silent about one performance, namely itself, and this performance can be the target only of another commentary. Self-commentary, self-ridicule, and self-admonition are logically condemned to eternal penultimacy.[75]

In Ryle's discussion here we find expressed the essence of the problem involved in any attempt simultaneously to include the immediate act of articulating reality within the articulation of reality. This gap between first and second order examination is seen most clearly when one considers the self-relation in the act of self-description. Description cannot include within itself the description of its own self-description. The person who seeks to do so is 'always a day late for the fair'.[76] This pseudo-dilemma points to the confusion involved in our believing that we can 'indwell' our 'indwelling' by way of some secondary act. It is as confused as thinking that if our seeing

---

[73] *The Concept of Mind*, London, 1949 (see especially chapter 6, 'Self-Knowledge'). See also the section entitled 'Egoity' (chapter 4) in John Macquarrie, *In Search of Humanity: A Theological and Philosophical Approach*, London, 1982, 38–46.

[74] Ryle, op. cit., 186–9.

[75] Ibid., 186.

[76] Ibid., 187.

it is to be reliable it must be *seen* to be so, and that we must, therefore, be able literally to *look* and *see* whether our seeing is appropriate to its object. The (Cartesian) fear that the failure to be able to indwell our 'indwelling' in certain objectivist ways may lead to relativism and uncertainty is as foolish as believing that if we cannot visually see that our seeing is veridical while seeing something then our visual capacities may not be trusted. The very quest amounts essentially to a failure to appreciate the irreducible given-ness of our there-being or *Da-sein* (Heidegger). In other words, the self is not a detached thinking 'I' who attaches terms to thoughts about God and the world and infallibly checks out all one's stepping-stones to the 'outside world' before standing on them. The self is a 'person' who is constituted by his or her semantic indwelling and participation in a social context where thought and speech are irreducibly grounded in social rules and 'games'. Theological criticism begins with, and does not merely result in, *koinonial* 'there-being'. It begins with a stance, namely our standing within the Body of Christ under grace. Our stance is, therefore, 'relative' to the extent that it is relational and not self-sustaining. It is relative, moreover, in that, before God, it is provisional. None of these facets, however, mean that it is to be conceived in *relativist* terms – quite the opposite.

The structure of our *da-sein* conceived as indwelling (as this includes semantic indwelling and interpersonal knowing) is clarified by Michael Polanyi and his form of post-critical realism. This cuts through the traditional alternatives: idealism, relativism and naïve (or even 'critical') realism. What is distinctive about 'post-critical realism' is its ability to 'maintain the integral inter-wovenness of language and world (and subject and object)...'[77] What is distinctive about Polanyi's approach is his beginning with the world's giving itself to be known by us rather than the subject's seeking knowledge. '"What is out there" imposes its pattern on us, informing our language, revising and extending our concepts.'[78] Knowing,

---

[77] Patterson, 'Janet Martin Soskice: Metaphor and a Theology of Grace', 18.
[78] Ibid., 19.

speaking and understanding are grounded, therefore, in an event of the self-revelation of reality.[79]

5) Language is, not least in the form of metaphors and scientific models, an extender of knowledge, an agent of discovery and, as such, the condition and precursor of these rather than simply a secondary means or medium of the sharing of information. 'New knowledge is a product of the formation of new relationships between ourselves, our language and the rest of reality.'[80]

Perhaps the most serious weakness of Janet Martin Soskice's important discussion of metaphor and religious language relates to her argument that metaphor (which is at the forefront of semantic development and the creation of language) functions to 'depict' reality.[81] The interpretation of

[79] This is precisely Colin Gunton's argument in the second of his Warfield Lectures (1993), entitled, 'The authority of the other: towards a general theology of revelation'.

[80] Patterson, op. cit., 23.

[81] Elsewhere Soskice makes the case for 'perspectivalism' which acknowledges the extent to which various theological 'positions' may simultaneously and legitimately argue 'the truth looks different from here'. ('The Truth Looks Different from Here' in *Christ and Context*, ed. Hilary Regan and Alan J. Torrance, Edinburgh, 1993, 43–59) Despite the important element of truth here, this metaphor further supports the kind of 'visualistic' model of knowing which could be taken to suggest that the ideal model of theological knowledge is beatific vision, rather than, as I would wish to suggest, beatific *participation* – which conceives of personal knowing in rather different terms. It is interesting to note that already in the Middle Ages we find John Duns Scotus and Lady Julian of Norwich suggesting that the life to come is not just that of the beatific vision construed in Platonic terms of contemplating Truth, Beauty and Goodness (that is, the eternal Forms of these), but in terms of participating in the triune life of God. Lady Julian of Norwich writes, 'When Jesus appears, the blessed Trinity is understood ... The Trinity filled me with the greatest joy, and I understood that it will be so in heaven without end.' (*Revelations of Divine Love*, from *Showings*, translated Colledge and Walsh, New York, 1978, 181.)

For a devastating critique of the philosophical confusions associated with visualistic approaches to epistemology cf. Richard Rorty's important book, *Philosophy and the Mirror of Nature*, Princeton, 1979. For a critique of the excesses of Rorty cf. Ian Hacking's 'Is the end in sight for epistemology?' *Journal of Philosophy* 77, no. 10 (1980) 579–88, and for a defence of epistemology cf. Jaegwon Kim, 'Rorty on the Possibility of Philosophy', *Journal of Philosophy* 77, no. 10 (1980), 588–97. A highly critical response is to be found in Anthony Palmer's

metaphor as essentially 'reality *depictive*' falsifies the relationship between language and the world by undermining the essence of language as an indwelt tool. This Soskice does by making use of what is essentially a visual metaphor – reality *depiction* – whereas only a small minority of the pluriform functions of metaphor may be denoted with recourse to visual models. Patterson argues that by doing this Soskice 'in effect severs language from the world', suggesting that language be conceived as 'a self-contained system separate from physical reality if we are to have any pretensions to realism'.[82] A second weakness of this traditional form of approach is its tendency 'to operate from the perspective of the knowledge-seeking subject' in such a way that it implies a separation of subject and object, thereby placing 'the world (and God) in the position of passive substance to be sought out and known.'[83]

What we see here is that it is as confused to conceive of language as necessarily world-transcendent if things are to be understood, interpreted and communicated as it is to believe that human persons are to be conceived as 'transcendent' (in the dualist sense) if they are to know, interpret and assess the way things are! Theological reflection requires distinctions (and not dualisms) between beings and facets and, as Polanyi argues, interrelated 'levels' of reality. It also requires our 'indwelling' these 'levels'. Sometimes this will be by choice, but more often this indwelling will be 'given'. And, in the final analysis, the latter (the givenness of human indwelling) is presupposed by the former (the choice to indwell some particular domain).[84] A proper conception of theological

---

review in *Mind* 92, (1983), 446–8, and a much more appreciative discussion in Raimond Gaita's review in *Philosophy* 56 (1981), 427–9.

The issues raised by Rorty not least concerning 'oculistic' interpretations of an epistemological relation of self and world (which idealise the metaphor of the seeing eye) are of some significance for theological issues. Unfortunately, we do not have space to do more than mention this here.

[82] Patterson, op. cit., 18. As Patterson reminds us, 'Logically, language must be part of the reality of the world of which we are part, if it is to be the means by which reality becomes intelligible for us.'

[83] Ibid.

[84] This parallels Heidegger's notion of our 'thrownness' in time.

language, as a dimension of human being as this involves its specific forms of social and world relatedness, benefits substantially from being conceived in these terms.

It is here that the *post-critical* realism of Michael Polanyi has much to offer.[85] It seeks to press beyond the subject–object dichotomy which leads to the (supposedly) 'self-authenticating subjectivity of idealism' and the 'doubtful objectivity of critical realism'.[86] Post-critical realism conceives of the world as giving itself to be known – taking hold of our language, revising and extending our terminology and conceptualities, and compelling us to use semantically incremental metaphors in such a way that they receive a new and *a posteriori* propriety from the given structure of the world. The way in which things *are* is seen, therefore, as epistemically invasive, instituting heuristic leaps in our processes of understanding – an invasiveness that is, again, conceptually   mediated by our language and language-games (as these include the grammar of scientific models). There is a greater profundity, therefore, to W. H. Auden's words than may first meet the eye (or ear!): 'A sentence uttered makes a world appear.'[87]

What we are saying is that the nature of things actually imposes on the 'language-games' in and through which we interpret and engage with the way things are. In and through this 'imposition' these 'language-games' themselves undergo incremental changes which, in turn, enable more creative and profound forms of engagement *with* (and *in*) *world*. It should be clear that what is normally referred to as our engagement *with* (the) world is, properly conceived, a semantic engagement *in* and *within* reality, 'in world'.[88]

---

[85] Cf. also William H. Poteat's impressive and lengthy exposition of post-critical philosophy: *Polanyian Meditations: In Search of a Post-Critical Logic*, Durham, 1985.

[86] These are phrases used by Patterson.

[87] 'Words', in *Collected Shorter Poems*, New York, 1966, 320.

[88] What should now be clear is that this engagement with the world on our part is more 'auditory' than 'visual' or 'ocular' (Cf. footnote 81 above on Richard Rorty.) Moreover, this indwelling demands to be conceived in turn in quite strongly physical terms, as is suggested by W. H. Poteat's graphic discussion of the integrated and indeed, 'performative' interpretation of the relation between speaking and hearing and between word and deed in the Hebrew conception of

On Michael Polanyi's post-critical realist account the primary form of our indwelling the physical world is not 'focal' or 'conceptual', but rather sub-conceptual ('subceptual'). In tandem with the emphases of the philosopher John Macmurray, he stresses the primacy of doing over reflection, interpreting the latter as secondary.[89] The key to this distinction and his ability to explain the primacy of doing (without supposing that this primary doing is non-cognitive – and hence not 'doing' at all) is what he calls *tacit* knowing. This dimension of tacit knowing takes the form of 'subliminal' or 'subsidiary' forms of awareness. And it is this dimension that constitutes the essential facet of what he describes as his 'novel idea of human knowledge from which a harmonious view of thought and existence, rooted in the universe, seems to emerge'. The key to his whole system is, therefore, his insistence that '*we can know more than we can tell*'.[90] By incorporating tacit knowledge within the definition of knowledge, post-critical realism 'does not limit knowledge (nor language as both the vehicle and also a component of that knowledge) to that which is conceptual and explicit'.[91] This means that the person is conceived as drawing on a whole realm of tacit knowing (in the search for new and explicit forms of knowledge) – a realm which provides our sense of direction and informs and conditions our judgements and decisions in and through our negotiating and interpreting the way things are and in our knowing where to look for answers to problems which themselves may not be fully conceptualisable. The tacit dimension is, therefore, the *sine qua non* of our heuristic leaps

dabhar. Poteat refers to the inextricability of the 'dynamic audial event' associated with the term 'from the crude physicality of the muscular tensions of the face, lips, tongue, and torso that form it and of the speaker's breath that propels it forth.' (Op. cit., 116). With respect to Yahweh, 'this speaking word is not only the measure of reality; it is in its very utterance that reality takes up its abode between men and God and among men – literally hanging upon the "breath of God".' (Ibid.)

[89] John Macmurray, *The Self as Agent* (Gifford Lectures, 1953), London, 1957.
[90] *The Tacit Dimension*, London, 1967, 4.
[91] Patterson, op cit., 19.

of discovery – constituting Polanyi's means of solving the problem of the Meno. The tacit dimension, this subceptual form of indwelling by way of the epistemically 'subliminal', addresses the problem that the theory of Forms and the accompanying process of *anamnesis* were postulated to explain in Platonic thought.

Polanyi writes,

> the Meno shows conclusively that if all knowledge is explicit, i.e., capable of being clearly stated, then we cannot know a problem or look for its solution. And the Meno also shows, therefore, that if problems exist, and discoveries can be made by solving them, we can know things, and important things, that we cannot tell. The kind of tacit knowledge that solves the paradox of the Meno consists in the intimation of something hidden, which we may yet discover.[92]

Tacit knowing may thus be 'shown to account' for a) 'a valid knowledge of a problem', b) 'the scientist's capacity to pursue it, guided by his sense of approaching its solution', and c) a 'valid anticipation of the yet indeterminate implications of the discovery arrived at in the end'.[93]

As Patterson argues,

> Post-critical realism emphasises the reciprocal relationship between knower and known. From this perspective, knowing is inherently dynamic and participatory, not a static entity but constantly revised by our relationship to and involvement with the world. The post-critical realist understands knowledge of the world as coming to us from entities in the world via our (socially mediated) sensory contact which informs our tacit awareness. Our tacit knowing, in turn, provides the framework within which we interpret the world.[94]

Polanyi's theory of a 'tacit dimension' also constitutes the means by which the processes of 'discovery' and 'coming to know', which Polanyi interprets as skills, may be acquired. This is due to the way in which the tools one uses in the processes of discovery can only operate appropriately to the

---

[92] *The Tacit Dimension*, 22–3.
[93] Ibid., 24.
[94] Op. cit., 19.

extent that they become integral to one's indwelling of the world – and, therefore, to the sphere of one's subliminal awareness.

This may be made clear with recourse to the simple examples used by Michael Polanyi. In the process of learning or acquiring a skill such as riding a bicycle or playing the piano, one first has to concentrate (focally) on the technique involved and on the tool one is using. However, when the skill is mastered one is no longer 'focally' aware of balancing the bicycle or of pressing one's fingers on the keys of the piano and one is able to disattend *from* them in order to attend *to* where one is going or to the music one is playing. The bicycle or piano become 'proximal' in one's attending to the 'distal'.[95]

Indwelling the world involves, therefore, a process of 'interiorization'[96] whereby our awareness of the techniques involved in using the tools by which we indwell the world becomes subliminal so that they can be 'disattended from'. As such, this process of interiorisation becomes integral to the conditions of one's focal or distal awareness and involvement with the world (or, rather, various levels of 'world'). One's subliminal skills become, in effect, part of one, integral to one's being as a person, that is, as a rationally engaged active and relational being. When a blind man comes to rely on his stick, feels with his stick (i.e. 'touches' through his stick) and, thereby, comes to see and interpret reality through his stick, then that stick becomes, as it were, part of him. It becomes, like the rest of his body, integral to his indwelling the world. This *attending to* the meaning of the impact of the stick on the blind man's hand Polanyi terms 'the *semantic aspect* of tacit knowing'.[97] A feature of this dynamic, he points out, is that 'all meaning tends to be displaced *away from ourselves*', and it is this he takes as his warrant for using the terms *proximal* and *distal.*

The most essential or fundamental tool for our indwelling the world would appear, therefore, to be language.[98]

---

[95] *The Tacit Dimension*, 10.
[96] Ibid., 17.
[97] Ibid., 13.
[98] Patterson seems to understate her own arguments when she comments, quite simply, that 'for human beings ... words are part of the tacit learning process: language is an agent of knowing'. (Op. cit., 20.)

If Soskice's conception of metaphor as 'reality depicting' tends toward a falsification of the relationship between language and the world by undermining the essence of language as an indwelt tool, Eberhard Jüngel may be seen to convey in a more integrative way something of the essence of metaphor when he speaks of 'the transfer of being into language as *metaphora*' such that we may come to 'recognise *metaphora* itself as the event of truth'[99]. In this way metaphor may be seen as the paradigm of the way in which language and its dynamic interplay with that which it would communicate functions creatively to bring us to penetrate deeper, in both scientific and theological knowing, into what we might term 'epistemic communion' with the way things are. It becomes an essential means of indwelling the world (or, indeed, the world's indwelling us) in its newness and strangeness whereby, through the processes of 'interiorization', our understanding may come to penetrate the inner structures of the way things are in ever deeper ways.[100]

In the course of his discussion Jüngel reminds us of Luther's emphasis on the *creative power* of metaphorical language, arguing that it is this emphasis that lies behind his insistence that we take literally the term 'is' in metaphorical expressions.[101] It may be argued that the tension and interplay of contrasting metaphors such as 'wave' and 'field' served the scientific task by contributing to the creative, interpretative dynamic which helped to articulate something of the nature of light. Without the metaphorical function of such terms the heuristic process of interpretation becomes that much more difficult and

[99] 'Metaphorical Truth' in *Theological Essays*, ed. J. B. Webster, 53.

[100] Patterson argues, 'metaphor is the linguistic medium for the new knowledge which comes to us within the categories of the old, joining and rearranging them to express a more comprehensive reality. Metaphor is, therefore, our access to the reality which transcends our present conceptions; the greater intelligibility which comes to us within the patterns of our life and generates meaning out of the nonsense created by the juxtaposition of the old. It is the growing-edge of our understanding of reality.' (Op. cit., 22).

[101] 'Metaphorical Truth', op. cit., 51. Clearly, Luther has in mind here the debate concerning the Lord's Supper.

reality that much more obscure.[102] In a similar manner, the rich variety of scriptural terminology, as this includes the metaphorical dimension to the functioning of the trinitarian names, the 'parables' and so much more should not be seen as serving to obscure the specific Reality of God (and, therefore, as theologically peripheral), nor as unwarrantable forms of anthropomorphic projection (similes), but as essentially creative means through which the *dissimilar* God comes to us in an *assimilating* or 'theopoietic' event, articulating his own reality for our understanding (expanding and deepening our conceptual categories to this end) and reforming our apperceptions in such a way that we may be brought by the creative dynamic of the Spirit epistemically and semantically to *indwell* the triune life as created human beings and, thereby, to participate in created ways in the Son's eternal communion with the Father. As this happens the fully human semantic means of this indwelling are *interiorised* within us, becoming constitutive of our personhood at the most fundamental level.

Two important points require to be stressed at this point.

First, it is fundamentally important that nothing we have argued here be taken to suggest that the semantic dynamics of metaphor may themselves be conceived as offering some

---

[102] The significance of metaphor in scientific explanation is exhibited when, in a passage from *The Scientific Outlook*, Bertrand Russell describes what happens when we 'see' someone:

> Little *packets* of light, called 'light quanta' *shoot out* from the sun, and some of these reach a region where there are atoms of a certain kind, composing Jones's face, and hands, and clothes ... Some of the light quanta, when they reach Jones's atoms, *upset their internal economy*. This causes him to become sunburnt and to *manufacture* Vitamin D. Others are reflected, and of those that are reflected some enter your eye. They there cause a complicated disturbance of the rods and cones, which, in turn, *send* a *current* along the optic nerve. When this *current* reaches the brain, it produces an event. The event which it produces is that which you call 'seeing Jones'. (Cited in Soskice, *Metaphor and Religious Language*, 99.)

In this passage the more obvious metaphors are italicised. It is clear that other terms used here such as 'quanta', 'reach', 'enter' and 'produce' all acquired the capacity to be used in the these ways by way of a creative metaphorical extension of their original meanings. (See Soskice's interesting discussion of this passage, op. cit., 100.)

kind of heuristic for knowledge of God. And we are certainly not suggesting that this, or any other, semantic theory serve as the foundation for our interpreting revelation and the nature of God's engagement with us. The primary purpose of our discussion here is to help articulate more integrative (or rather less dichotomous) ways of conceiving of participation in the person of the Word made flesh than have traditionally operated in Western thought. It may be added that we detect an insufficiency here in Sue Patterson's characterisation of God in terms of our experience of 'the coming to us of greater intelligibility, of a more comprehensive involvement with reality through the "cracks" in our conventions of understanding' and the identification of this 'bringer of intelligibility' or, again, as the 'Relating Agent' who 'works within the gaps between our categories'. This comes too close to suggesting a *material* determination of God as a God of our 'semantic' gaps who perfects and fulfils rather than confounds and transforms our frameworks of 'intelligibility' – and does this concretely in and through that 'foolishness' that is the crucified Lord.[103]

Second, semantic participation in the triune life, as we have outlined it, remains inconceivable without the affirmation of the *homoousion* both of the Son and of the Spirit. It is here we find the essential grammar underlying that focal 'coincidence' of the divine *ekstasis* in the human *hypostasis* and of the human *ekstasis* in the divine *hypostasis* which takes place in Christ and which constitutes the semantic link without which there is no semantic participation in the divine life. It is in the one who is 'Immanuel' that we find the agent or mediator of the commandeering of our language, for it is in and through his vicarious humanity that we are brought, through the creative activity of the Holy Spirit, into the communion of his Body, and thus to participate in that renewed 'world' or New Creation which constitutes the very context of talk and thought about God.

---

[103] Patterson, op. cit., 23. In utilising Wittgenstein's insights it is imperative that we do not allow a concept of 'world' or a semantic ontology to introduce new forms of 'theology from below'.

Conclusion

There are several mutually interrelated conclusions which we would wish to draw. We shall begin by spelling out the conclusions of this chapter and move gradually toward conclusions which recapitulate the argument of this book as a whole.

1) There is an integral symbiotic link between doxological participation (*koinonia*) in Christ in worship and semantic participation in Christ. Semantic participation, as it includes – and, indeed, constitutes – our epistemic 'indwelling', is an essential *coefficient* of doxological participation in communion to the extent that worship is cognitive, conceptual and social (ecclesial), and thus grounded in the creative reconstitution in Christ, by the Spirit, of the language-games which constitute our 'capacity' for communion. If worship is 'the gift of participating by the Spirit in the Son's communion with the Father', then this includes semantic participation in such a way that the language–communion link (which parallels the language–world link) is constituted by the Logos. It is 'realised' both *objectively* in the union and communion of the High Priest of our humanity with the Father in the Spirit and also *subjectively* in Christ's union and communion with his Body in the Spirit.

2) The semantic dimension to this *may* be described in terms of an 'analogy of being', if this is carefully understood, in so far as we have in this 'hinge' of communion between the divine and the human a real and given event of *communion* between the divine and human orders. To the extent that created reality requires to be interpreted in the light of this communion – and not the other way round – we may speak of an 'analogy of being', of real participation[104] of created and

---

[104] It should be clear that by participation I mean *koinonia* and not some kind of Platonic *methexis*. The New Testament does employ the term *metechein* when referring to *koinonia* as, for example, in Heb. 3:1. It is important to note, however, that in its New Testament usage its meaning is profoundly different from that given to it by Plato when he is speaking of the participation of particulars in the eternal Forms.

contingent humanity in the triune life of God. This constitutes a '*koinonia*' and thus 'ontological' *ekstasis* involving an analogical extension of our conceptualities in the reconciling 'integration' of the human with the divine mediated by the *enhypostasis* of the Logos. In and through affirming that this is *sola gratia*, it is also appropriate to affirm here, with Zizioulas, that there is an identification of being and communion that is to be found in that triune event of epistemic communion (revelation) and semantic participation between humanity and God which takes place in Christ and in which humanity is given to share by the Spirit as the Body of Christ .

This 'analogical' function of human semantics demands a dynamic, participatory and theological interpretation of being (*ens*). *Analogein* is contingent on the free dynamic of divine creativity and remains, therefore, a 'possibility' affirmed *a posteriori*. We do not have here an *analogia entis* affirmed *a priori* with recourse to a metaphysic of being. It speaks of a commandeering integration of our semantic rules of use and the sets of family resemblances that constitute the meaning of our terminology *en Christo*. As such, the *analogia entis* requires to be conceived in *eschatological* terms in that it is only in the *eschaton* that human participation (as this includes semantic participation) is complete – where God will be all in all.

In the light of this it is clear that we cannot endorse any suggestion that the language-games and semantic rules associated with our *logoi* may 'naturally' circumscribe the cognitive reference or *Inhalt* of our 'attempts to speak of God'. Our language only becomes 'God-talk' (*Theos*-talk) *given* the creation and redefinition of our language-games instituted in and through the Word and which take place within the ecclesial community as the reconciled Body of the Word. There is clearly no sense here in which theology may be subsumed within the wider semantic domain of the word 'religion'. There are no grounds for conceiving the coincidence of their respective 'subject-matters'.

To affirm that theology cannot be subsumed within a wider semantic domain such as 'religion' is simply to echo Aquinas' insight that theology does not operate with an *analogia duorum ad tertium*. The implications of this for the way we conceive of the divinity of the Triunity is clear. In no sense may we speak of a *participatio tertiorum in quartuo quid*, where the Father, Son and Holy Spirit are conceived as participating in some fourth Reality, namely the divine substance or 'Being'. In this way, it is utterly inappropriate to operate with the traditional Western dichotomies between the questions *an sit* and *quid sit* or *qualis sit*, and, consequently, between apologetics or philosophy of religion on the one hand and Christian dogmatics on the other. It is precisely the communion of the Trinity that is the singularity and substance of the divine Being. To the extent that analogy is *unius ad alterum,* the *unius* refers to the triune communion. Human participation in the triune life at the semantic and every other level is participation in precisely this concrete singularity.

3) The theology of grace does indeed suggest an analogical parallelism between the intra-divine mutuality opened to us in Christ on the one hand and one level of human 'trans-subjectivity' on the other, namely the trans-subjectivity which is intrinsic to the communion of the Body of Christ. To what extent the further and wider form of trans-subjectivity which constitutes semantic sociality – and which, of course, provides a foundation for human relationships on a wider scale – may be deemed to constitute a further 'analogy' would seem to depend on the extent to which we can interpret obedience to social rules, which is the ground of semantic interaction, as a form of unconditional 'covenantal' commitment to others, that is, as a form of communion in itself.[105] It would appear to be difficult to argue for an easy identification between 'sociality' and 'communion' that does not commit us to a generic conception of *koinonia.* Moreover, without the supposition of *unconditional* love it is difficult to suggest that any analogy of *koinonia* as testified to in the theological context (which is how Barth seems to wish to interpret the *analogia relationis*) may easily be supposed in any context. The interesting feature of semantic sociality is that it *would* seem to repose on a degree

---

[105] As I mention in 7) below, there is certainly an element of 'intrinsicity' here as present in contexts of communion.

of unconditional commitment at the subliminal level – although one which may only manifest a 'marriage of convenience' rather than an intentional covenant commitment!

What is significant for both issues is Zizioulas' emphasis that 'communion', theologically conceived, requires our 'being born from above', which imples a degree of discontinuity with other forms of social interrelatedness. Only an over-realised eschatology (and a resulting isolationist ecclesiology) combined with a grossly inadequate doctrine of creation will suppose that the boundaries between semantic sociality within the secular context and semantic participation within the Church can or should be clearly drawn. Continuities between ecclesial communion and created sociality beyond the Body of Christ are the *sine qua non* of communicating with and hence loving – and hence hearing and speaking to – our neighbour. As such they are divinely intended. The outward dynamic of grace and the *ekstasis* of the ecclesial community mean the parallelisms in our argument here concerning semantic sociality and Barth's arguments *vis-à-vis* the *analogia relationis* are not coincidental. What is important to emphasise, however, is that we are talking of an 'analogy' and not of an equivalence and, given the *per prius et posterius* criterion, 'created sociality' requires to be understood in the light of ecclesiality (the sociality of the New Creation) and not the other way round – and certainly not as its 'natural' ground!

4) There is a correspondence between doxological and (ecclesial) semantic participation which may be spelled out in various ways.

a) Both the doxological and semantic-conceptual grounds of our faith are 'given' in Christ and realised in us by the Spirit. Humanity (or the New Humanity) lives 'out of' this givenness. Neither of these grounds are to be conceived in terms of some subjective accomplishment on the part of humanity.

The very grammar of the Gospel, conceived as an *eph 'hapax* atonement, suggests that just as no one knows the Father except the Son and those to whom the Son gives the Father to be known, there is only one who knows how to pray, to speak and to respond to God as he ought – there is only one true High Priest. Ecclesial and sacramental life and thought repose in our being brought to share in that which is objectively and vicariously *given* and fulfilled in Christ. Participation *en Christo* means therefore a) participation in *his* worship of the Father in the Spirit; b) participation in *his* knowledge of the Father in the Spirit; c) participation in *his* mission from the Father to the world in the Spirit.

Semantic participation means participation in a) *his* articulation of reality, that is, in *his* apperception and semantic 'form of life' – participating in the language-games, rules of use and sets of family resemblances introduced and sustained in his commandeering of language within the Body of Christ (in and through which we are brought to understand the world anew – given 'ears to hear' and thus 'eyes to see'); at the same time, it means participation in b) *his* vicarious life of prayer and intercession, *his* speech before the Father, *his* Amen addressed to the Father on our behalf, and c) *his* Word of grace to the world – participation in that One proclamation that is *his* Self-proclamation by the Spirit in and through his Body. 'Semantic participation' is thus an irreducibly trinitarian event.[106]

b) The givenness of the ecclesially (and hence socially) conditioned semantic relation is thus integral to our participation in the *leitourgia* of the *Leitourgos*. The 'speaking the Christian faith' of the Body stems from participation in the life of the One who fulfils the prophetic office in his being the *priestly* Word. To the extent that the Word of grace that is spoken (and not merely verbalised) is spoken by being 'realised' in his own person, Christ is seen to be the agent of the *metaphorein* of theological semantics – and to be so as the *Counter-Logos* (Bonhoeffer), the One who is a stumbling-block or foolishness to our alienated (*echthroi*) *dianoiai* and who stands to reconcile our language-games in order to realise in

---

[106] It is interesting to note that Christopher Kaiser argues, in a particularly interesting article, that the prayer life of Jesus 'as observed by the disciples and the early church, is a suitable empirical basis for the apostolic discernment of triunity ...' ('The Discernment of Triunity', *S. J. T.* 28 (1975), no. 5, 457.)

us his priestly, semantic communion, as the Word made flesh, with the Father.

It is in these terms that the communion to which the Gospel testifies in Christ, to which we are called and into which we are brought, demands to be articulated. Failure to interpret worship *and* God-talk together as participation in the triune life can only fall short of that quite specific and concrete 'communion' that is the *telos* of creation and which is radically different from 'religion' where God-talk and worship become the blind projections of human language-games on to the divine.

c) Clearly, both forms of participation involve interrelated forms of *ekstasis* – not only of the Father and the Son, but also of the Son and humanity and, finally, of humanity and world.

At the human level, both forms of indwelling by the Spirit involve not only the reconciliation of our focal awareness, but also the radical *metanoia* of our 'tacit dimensions'.

By way of summary, the integration of these in the theological context means that there can no more be a final distinction between the doxological and the semantic than between the priestly and prophetic offices of Christ. Any attempt to make such a distinction can only lead to a *metabasis eis allo genos* of the Gospel itself. The bestowal of meaning in and through the activity of the One who is the 'Bringer of Intelligibility' or the 'Relating Agent' is an event of participatory worship – of theopoietic participation in the communion of the triune life. In this alone is found the single co-ordinating ground not only of theology but of Christian *praxis*, ethics and also of 'apo-logetics' which, to be theological, must recognise that it is the Logos alone who *utters*, on his own behalf, the Word that creates or inaugurates that *metanoietic* event of semantic, epistemic and noetic communion which is the perception of the Truth and which is also Gospel.

5) To return now once more to the theme of analogy, it should be clear that any endorsement of a distinction between an *analogia entis* and an *analogia fidei* which assumes that both are simultaneously valid because they relate to different forms of reality becomes problematic. Despite his moving toward a much more constructive definition of the *analogia entis* (as we

discussed in chapter three), Gottlieb Söhngen, in his book *Die Einheit in der Theologie*, fails to move beyond the attempt to endorse a 'unity in distinction' between the *analogia entis* and the *analogia fidei*. The *analogia fidei* concerns, he suggests, the 'Erlösungsordnung' and the *analogia entis* the 'Schöpfungsordnung' such that, for example, we construe the relationship between Christ and his Church in terms of the former and the relationship between man and wife in terms of the latter.[107] He writes, 'Die *analogia entis* ist zuerst Analogie in der Wesensordnung des Seienden und folglich auch in der Tätigkeitsordnung, weil die Gnade keine neue Wesens-, sondern eine neue Tätigkeitsordnung setzt ...'[108]

Later in the same book Söhngen addresses the question of participation in Christ, arguing that 'Darum bedeutet unser "Sein in Christus" auch weniger ein Sein im Wesen Christi als ein Sein im *Tun* oder Handeln Christi ...'[109] The apparent benefit of this kind of approach would seem to be its perceived potential to safeguard the freedom of Christ over against Platonist conceptions of a mystical union. However, any such misconstrual of *koinonia* as *methexis* is much more effectively avoided if we are willing to conceive of Being in more dynamic, personal terms, as suggested by Zizioulas. If we interpret Being in the light of the triune communion and not the other way round, a whole range of new categories emerges which obviates the traditional Western dichotomies between a) Being and act; b) nature and grace (where the latter is believed to perfect the former, where grace perfects law[110]), and c) personhood and its *koinonial* constitution. These all too widespread dichotomies fail ultimately to construe God's creative purposes for humanity in terms of our sharing in the triune life, the objective and 'vicarious' nature of participation in Christ and the full import of both of these for the

---

[107] See his 'Schaubild', in *Die Einheit in der Theologie*, Munich, 1952, 247.

[108] Ibid., 238. See also his discussion that follows this on 'Die theologische Einheit von beiderlei Analogie', 238–47.

[109] Ibid., 363. Söhngen is willing to speak of our being 'im Wesen Christi', but he defines this in terms of the 'Tun Christi'.

[110] See the discussion in chapter 2.

reconstitution and radical realisation of our own (subjective) human being at every level.

Such traditional dichotomies fail, therefore, to appreciate that worship, properly construed, is about our 'being true' in the same way that 'worth-ship' also concerns our *being true* – so Paul, in Ephesians 4:15, speaks of *aletheuontes en agape*, that is, '*being-true* in love'.[111] And both forms of 'being true' involve 'faithful' semantic relations, i.e. our subliminal participation in the entire semantic process in so far as this is not merely an extrinsic event but constitutive of human *being*. The semantics of ecclesial existence includes and embraces, therefore, all that we 'are' to the extent that our very apperception is constituted by this event of communion.

6) In chapter 2 we pointed to what we described as a form of *intrinsicity* or 'intrinsic relation' to be found in the event of revelation. It should now be clear that a parallel intrinsicity characterises participation (*theosis*) as a whole, and all that pertains to it. Participation speaks of the fact that 'we live, no, Christ lives in us'; that we pray, no, the Spirit intercedes for us and in us; we understand, no, we are brought to participate in the understanding that is Christ's; we interpret, no, the Logos (Counter-Logos) brings us to participate in his extended and transformed semantic categories; we speak and proclaim, no, the Word speaks in and through us, defining and extending the rules of use of our terms; we worship, no, our High Priest worships on our behalf and unites us in his true and worthy worship ...

We have seen that there is an important analogy to be found here with that 'intrinsicity' which is the relation between language and world, where the language–world link may not be conceived as a merely *extrinsic* one.[112] We now see how

---

[111] Unfortunately, this is translated in at least two English versions as 'speaking the truth'.

[112] I discussed above the understanding of language which assumes an intrinsic connection between the semantic function of the terms used and *world*. Patterson uses the insights of the Hintikkas here to critique Soskice's conception of metaphor as reality-*depicting*.

much more this is the case at the theological level given the conception of Christ as Logos, where there is thus an intrinsic relation between Christ's being the Word, our being *in* Christ, and the Spirit's being *in* us on the one hand and the (ecclesial) semantics of theological 'expression' and affirmation on the other.

Revelation involves a semantic *ekstasis* of the Spirit in and through the very functionality of the language of revelation. Intrinsic to this *ekstasis* is our participation, by the Spirit, in an event that is *simultaneously* the bestowal of reality and an engendering of communion as this takes place in and through the presence of the Word. As such, revelation is an event of 'communication-within-communion',[113] where the impetus and semantically generative 'control' in this event is the human Jesus as he mediates (enhypostatically) our participation in the triune life of God.

What emerges here is a way into the interpretation of the full significance of the doctrine of the Trinity in terms not of the structure of revelation but of a no less epistemically relevant and considerably more integrative dynamic of communion and participation than that which Barth expressed in terms of his revelation model. This interprets the intrinsicity which we saw to lie at the heart of his interpretation of revelation in much fuller terms. Put quite simply, the communion which is intrinsic to God and to the Second Adam is seen to be intrinsic to the New Humanity, to the Body of Christ. Approaches to God-talk, apologetics or worship that fail to take full cognisance of this cannot do justice to the dynamic at the very heart of the Gospel as it constitutes the rationale of the Christian life.

It is not our intention in this critique of Barth's revelation model to detract in any way from his critique of the dangers of 'Religion' and 'Culture Protestantism'. His insights into the nature of proclamation seem to us to be of profound importance and continuing relevance. Moreover, the central methodological insights outlined in chapter 1 are as deeply

---

[113] Despite the clumsiness of this expression, I prefer it to 'speech-act' for reasons which should be clear.

relevant today as they were earlier this century – if not more so! Nor would we wish to deny that the orientation of much of his later discussion in the *Church Dogmatics* (particularly in Volume Four) may be seen to integrate with some of the central emphases in our discussion. To this extent, our critique of Barth amounts essentially to a modification which seeks to support rather than to repudiate his primary aims and central concerns. What we *would* suggest, however, is quite specific, namely that a) Barth's exposition of the Trinity as we have it in Volume One of his *Church Dogmatics*; b) the influence on it of what we have termed his 'revelation model' and, in particular, c) the outworking of this on the manner in which he explores the question of triune personhood require a degree of controlled reinterpretation. This, indeed, is vital if the full significance and implications of the triune communion for a participative interpretation of human communion, that is, of our doxological and semantic participation, are to be understood – and if the full depth and scope of its anthropological and ecclesiological significance are to be appreciated. Only in this way is it possible to come to a proper evaluation of the primordial place within a theology of worship, of sacramental participation and ecclesial existence as these relate to the irreducibly participative nature of human personhood – that participation in the New Creation which is the *telos* of creation as a whole. Our concern is that Barth's revelation model and exposition of the Trinity and the Word of God were too narrowly conceived and thus constrictive of his ecclesial vision as a whole.

At the very centre of a theology of personhood, therefore, stands the acknowledgement of the ecclesial dynamic of God's grace – a dynamic that is integrally bound up with the *praxis* of the sacraments. Through the event of baptism the unconditionality of grace and our participation by it in the redeemed life of the New Humanity, as perfected in the Second Adam and High Priest of our confession, is written into our existence. We are baptised into the Body of Christ prior to the satisfaction of any conceivable epistemic or semantic conditions on our part. As such, infant baptism constitutes – as Luther saw but Barth failed to appreciate – a crucially significant means of our personal liberation to live in the light of grace. As such, it serves uniquely, as a converting ordinance, the evangelical *ekstasis* of the *koinonia* of the Body of Christ. In continuity with this the communion of the Lord's Supper becomes a continually converting (metanoietic) ordinance. As a means of affirming the value of the person under grace it serves that inner transformation by holding forth Christ's communing presence with and for us as the priest of our confession. Uniquely in the eucharist the One who has vicariously fulfilled and realised on our behalf all that we are obliged (by God's unconditional covenant commitment to us) to be, presents himself and his life to us as ours. In this way, we are brought to live out of that healed communion that is Christ's, such that, by the Spirit, the exchange (*katallage*) completed in him may be realised in us. As he took what is ours that we may have what is his, so the fullness of his personhood as the Son comes to be realised in us by the Spirit.[114] It is thus

---

[114] It should be plain that the 'intrinsicity' to which we referred in chapter two with respect to the revelation event is also profoundly important *not only* for a proper understanding of the relationship between the incarnation and the atonement, *but also* for a proper interpretation of the sacrament of the Lord's Supper. The potential of 'Zwinglian' conceptions of the Lord's Supper conceived in terms of our feeding upon Christ by faith rather than, as Calvin emphasised, *Christ's feeding us* by making us participants in his vicarious life and priesthood, can too easily be reduced to a scenario in which the Lord's Supper is conceived merely as a memorial of the death of Christ rather than as an event of real and dynamic communion with God *in Christ*. When this happens the relationship between Christ and humanity in the sacraments is reduced to a merely extrinsic one. A doctrine of the 'real presence' of the whole Christ (as Luther emphasised) in the sacrament of communion flows from the perception that love and communion are intrinsic to God in his Self-giving in Christ and, further, that, by the Spirit and through the celebration of the Lord's Supper, this communion becomes *intrinsic* to our being. The Lord's Supper is thus a 'converting ordinance', the receiving of the bread and wine an event which radically reconstitutes and reorientates our horizons, our apperception and humanity as a whole.

It is surprising that Barth did not appreciate more fully the parallelism between what I have termed the 'intrinsicity' advocated in his interpretation of revelation and that involved in the 'event' of eucharistic communion. His adherence in this context to a distinction between 'vehicles of *God's* action' and vehicles of *our* action seems inconsistent. (Cf. A. I. C. Heron's *Table and Tradition*, Edinburgh, 1983, 157 and the footnote on this question in chapter two.)

Similarly, the (trinitarian) emphasis that love and communion in the Body of Christ are intrinsic and not extrinsic to the humanity of its participants means

in and through this dynamic that we are created, recreated and 'reformed' for that celebration and participation, through the Holy Spirit, in the glory of the triune life of God that is the New Creation – which will be fully realised in the *eschaton.* One of the greatest disappointments of Barth's *Church Dogmatics,* therefore (in particular, the arguments of Volume Four, part 4), is his failure to appreciate the anthropological significance of the sacraments. His reluctance to endorse infant baptism and his weak doctrine of the eucharist point to an inadequacy in his appreciation of the continuing priesthood of Christ and, at root, an insufficient grasp of the theology of communion. As we have suggested already, in chapter two, the weaknesses were inherent in (and further confirmed by) his treatment of the doctrine of revelation from the very beginning of the *Church Dogmatics* .

7) Finally, we now find ourselves in a position to gauge more adequately the extent to which the Trinity may be said to create and to sustain an *image* in us of its own communion *in such a way* that we can suppose a direct semantic continuity between using the term 'person' of the communion of the Trinity as also of human participants in the communion of the Body of Christ.

It should be clear from the discussion that the ecclesial creation of the New Humanity represents the profoundest expression of our creation in God's image. A little more, however, requires to be said on this issue. The 'image' metaphor has too often opened the door in the West to static (Platonic), exemplarist and individualistic interpretations of both God

---

that worship and communion may not simply be considered to be 'activities' in which we engage occasionally. They are the continuing and ceaseless expression of our real being – of our love for God. In the language of John Duns Scotus, we are made (created) to be *condiligentes* – sharers in the communion of the divine nature.

It should also be clear from the thrust of this chapter as a whole that the intrinsicities to which I refer here, together with the integral connection I have asserted between 'semantic' and 'doxological' participation, emphasise further the vital link between divine Self-communication and preaching and also the 'intrinsic' connection between preaching and the sacraments.

and humanity, and it has much too often served as the linchpin of rather over-confident approaches to theological description. In radical contrast to the suppositions of certain forms of Western theology, the *imago Dei* in humanity requires to be interpreted in terms of the participative life of the Body of Christ that we have been expounding, namely, that form of participation by grace within the Triune life of God and which 'in Christ' constitutes a *vestigium trinitatis* and thus an *imago Dei.*

As we learn from Barth, the *imago Dei* must be seen to refer to the whole person *as person*, that is, as participant in the New Humanity – and not to some subjective dimension or capacity. But, as we have also seen in dialogue with Zizioulas, this in turn speaks of the dynamic and free 'co-presence' of the open Triunity, that is, of the divine *Koinonia* that freely and creatively takes within its own Life by grace that human *koinonia* constitutive of the New Creation, of the New Humanity of the Second Adam. To affirm humanity's creation in the image of God is thus to speak first of the one true Adam. It is then that we can affirm that 'in and through him', as a restored humanity, we creatures are (become) persons in the image of the triune God. This we become as participants in the Body of the Second Adam, that is, in the New Creation – the creating anew of humanity in the image of God.

Being created in the image of God should not be conceived, therefore, as referring to a past or original historical event conceived in independence of the New Creation and the Second Adam, any more than *creatio ex nihilo* should be identified with *creatio originalis.*[115] Consequently, it certainly should not be interpreted as a natural 'state' possessed by individuals. It requires to be interpreted theologically in terms of the reconciling creativity of God, and this leads us to affirm that we remain 'on the way' to becoming fully and in

---

[115] To argue this would be to fail to appreciate that 'creation out of nothing' is not an event in time but an event which includes time. *Creatio ex nihilo* relates directly, therefore, to the totality of spatio-temporal identities – wherever and whenever their existence is to be found.

truth 'images' or 'reflections' of the Being of God and the communion of the triune life in ourselves; thus we remain 'on the way' to full subjective participation in the One in whom alone this ontological corresponding is realised.

The implications for our understanding of theological description suggested by interpreting the *imago Dei* (or, indeed, the *analogia entis* or *vestigium Dei*) in this manner are that the communion, love and mutuality internal to the Triunity as these are freely and dynamically present in the divine 'becoming' that is Christ confirm two primary obligations *vis-à-vis* the language we use. First, it demands the fullest semantic expression of the language of communion – a facet less than adequately served both by the notion of *Seinsweisen*, with its inherent lack of relational connotations[116], and by traditional Western interpretations of the *imago Dei*. Secondly, however, it also demands the fullest acknowledgement that any theological propriety on the part of our language and any perceived capacity on the part of our vocabulary to express or mediate anything whatsoever of the communion of the triune God reposes precisely on the very dynamic of God's grace that it would seek to articulate. Semantic at-one-ment is realised in Christ alone and is not a property of our language. 'Proper functionality', to utilise Alvin Plantinga's phrase, is not yet fully realised in the 'cognitive environment' of our semantic community any more than in the individual human subject – the two, of course, being irreducibly interrelated, as Plantinga has also shown.[117] Our language, just as the thinking mediated

---

[116] It is precisely this that Cornelius Plantinga is seeking to express when he writes: 'Barth wants in heaven a model of covenant fellowship, the archetype of mutuality that we image as males and females, and a ground for the ethics of agape ... But, to tell the truth, his theory cannot consistently yield these fruits. For modes do not love at all. Hence they cannot love each other.' ('The Threeness/Oneness Problem of the Trinity', *Calvin Theological Journal* 23, no. 1 (April 1988), 49.)

[117] In a profoundly important discussion of the relationship between warrant and the testimony of the community in which one lives and thinks, Alvin Plantinga writes, 'The human design plan is oriented toward a certain kind of cognitive environment: the sort of cognitive environment in which our faculties originally arose, whether by the hand of God or of evolution (or both). But from the point of view of the individual person, other people are part of the cognitive

in and through it, remains dysfunctional therefore, remains *echthros*. It is thus 'not yet' fully reconciled and perfected *in and of itself.*

There is, therefore, a parallelism here – one which denotes the intrinsic connection between who we are (and thus our thought processes) and the language we use. Just as we are *simul iusti et peccatores* – and the Church, the semantic community within which theology lives and functions, is *semper reformanda* – so our language, its underlying semantic frameworks, the network of rules of use constitutive of it and the understanding of God mediated in and through it, possesses an intrinsic provisionality, inadequacy and incompleteness under grace, despite being simultaneously affirmed and indeed 'commandeered' by the Logos through the presence of the Spirit. This means that our very forms of communication, expression and articulation, although sanctified in Christ, remain 'on the way' and therefore *semper reformanda.*

The grace of the triune embrace which claims us, together with all that constitutes our identities (our language, action and thought) *en Christo*, simultaneously judges and exposes the inadequacies in all that we are 'in the flesh', both as individuals and as communities. If, therefore, a doxological model of the theological enterprise, as we have outlined it, encourages us to speak of the Trinity as a Triunity of 'persons', this expression itself and the ways in which it functions –

environment; the design plan does not cover my cognitive faculties in isolation from yours or yours from mine: as it applies to my faculties it presupposes that you and *your* faculties will function and react in certain ways.' (*Warrant and Proper Function*, Oxford, 1993, 82.)

In sum, warrant only ultimately occurs within the context of the redemption (and hence proper functioning) of our minds and our thinking (*noiein*) and this cannot be separated from the proper functioning of the epistemic processes of our cognitive environment. Knowledge of God is to be found in the context of the redeemed cognitive environment of the reconciled community of the Church. Although this is 'in a manner present', it remains, however, 'in a manner absent' this side of the *eschaton*. The proper epistemic functioning of the Body of Christ awaits ultimately that day when we know even as we are known, when we shall know the Son as the Father knows the Son and we shall know the Father as the Son knows the Father.

together with the rest of our language as a whole and the semantic rules of use which underlie it – must be seen as having validity only provisionally and by grace alone.

Theological description, therefore, as it stems from our human participation in the triune life, remains *sola gratia*. Far from suggesting, however, that this means we dare not speak of God, it means that we dare not keep silent, that we ought not to keep silent and that we should not wish to keep silent.

Select Bibliography

Aquinas, Thomas: *Summa contra Gentiles* (Eng. trans. by fathers of the English Province), Burns and Oates, London, 1920.

Auden, W. H.: *Collected Shorter Poems 1927–1959*, Random House, New York, 1966.

Austin, J. L.: *How to Do Things with Words*, Clarendon Press, Oxford, 1962.

Baillie, John: (ed.) *Natural Theology*, Geoffrey Bles, The Centenary Press, London, 1946.

Our Knowledge of God, Oxford University Press, London, 1939.

The Sense of the Presence of God, Oxford University Press, London, 1962.

Balthasar, Hans Urs von: 'Analogie and Dialektik', *Divus Thomas* 22, no. 2 (1944), 171–216.

'On the Concept of Person', *Communio* (Spring 1986), 18–26.

Karl Barth, Cologne, 1952.

On Prayer (Eng. trans. by A. V. Littledale), SPCK, London, 1973.

Bantle, F. X.: 'Person und Personenbegriff un der Trinitätslehre Karl Rahners', *Münchner Theol. Zeitschrift*, 30, 1979.

Barth, Karl: *Briefe 1961–1968*, Theologischer Verlag, Zürich, 1979.

Church Dogmatics, Volumes 1–4 (Eng. trans. edited by G. W. Bromiley and T. F. Torrance), T. & T. Clark, Edinburgh, 1956–75.

The Epistle to the Romans (Eng. trans. by Edwyn C. Hoskyns), Oxford University Press, London, 1933.

Fides Quarens Intellectum, 2nd edition, Evangelischer Verlag A. G., Zürich, 1958.

The Göttingen Dogmatics, Instruction in the Christian Religion, Volume 1 (Eng. trans. by Geoffrey Bromiley), Eerdmans, Grand Rapids, 1990.

How I Changed My Mind (Introduction and Epilogue by John Godsey), Saint Andrew Press, Edinburgh, 1969.

Die Kirchliche Dogmatik, Erster Band, Die Lehre vom Wort Gottes, Chr. Kaiser Verlag, Munich, 1932.

Letters: 1961–1968 (Eng. trans. by Geoffrey W. Bromiley),
    T. & T. Clark, Edinburgh, 1981.

Die Protestantische Theologie im 19. Jahrhundert, Evangelischer Verlag
    A. G., Zollikon, Zürich, 1952.

The Theology of Schleiermacher (Eng. trans. by G. W. Bromiley),
    T. & T. Clark, Edinburgh, 1982.

Unterricht in der christlichen Religion, Theologischer Verlag, Zürich,
    1990.

Bax, Douglas: *A Different Gospel: A Critique of the Theology Behind
    Apartheid*, P. C. S. A., Johannesburg, n.d.

Berger, Peter L. and Luckmann, Thomas: *The Social Construction of
    Reality: A Treatise in the Sociology of Knowledge*, Doubleday, New
    York, 1966.

Berkhof, Hendrikus: *The Doctrine of the Holy Spirit*, Epworth Press,
    London, 1965.

Boff, Leonardo: *Trinity and Society* (Eng. trans. by Paul Burns), Orbis,
    Maryknoll, 1988.

Bonhoeffer, Dietrich: *Christology* (Eng. trans. by John Bowden),
    Collins, London and New York, 1966.

Creation and Fall, SCM Press, London, 1959.

Botha, J.: 'A Critical View of the Use of the Scriptures in the Kairos
    Document', *Orientation: International Circular of the Potchefstrom
    University for Christian Higher Education*, March, 1988.

Bouillard, Henri: *Karl Barth: Parole de Dieu et Existence Humaine*, Vol.
    3 (or Vol. 2, Part 2), Aubier [Paris], 1957.

The Knowledge of God, Burns and Oates, London, 1969.

Bowden, John: *Karl Barth: Theologian*, SCM Press, London, 1983.

Busch, Eberhard: *Karl Barth: His Life from Letters and Autobiographical
    Texts*, SCM Press, London, 1976.

Cajetan, Cardinal: *The Analogy of Names* and *The Concept of Being* (Eng.
    trans. and annotations by Bushinski and Koren), Duquesne,
    1953.

Calvin, John: *Institutes of the Christian Religion* (edited by John T. McNeill;
    trans. by Ford Lewis Battles), Westminster, Philadelphia, 1960.

Campbell, Douglas: The Crisis of Faith in Modern New Testament
    Scholarship' in Simon Rae and Peter Matheson (eds.), *Religious
    Studies in Dialogue: Essays in honour of Albert Moore*, Otago
    University Press, Dunedin, 1991.

'The Meaning of Pistis and Nomos in Paul: A Linguistic and
    Structural Perspective', *J. B. L.* 111.1 (1992).

The Rhetoric of Righteousness in Romans 3:21–26, J. S. N. T.
    Supplement, Sheffield, 1992.

Collingwood, R. G.: *An Essay on Metaphysics*, Oxford University Press, London, 1940.

Combrink, H. J. B.: 'Perspektiewe uit die Skrif' in J. Kinghorn (ed.), *Die NG Kerk en apartheid*, Macmillan Suid Afrika, Capetown, 1986, 219–23.

Culler, Jonathan: *Saussure*, Fontana (Modern Masters), London, 1976.

Dickie, John: *The Organism of Christian Truth: A Modern Positive Dogmatic*, James Clarke, London, 1930.

Dowey, Edward A.: *The Knowledge of God in Calvin's Theology*, Columbia University Press, New York, 1952.

Ferré, Frederick: 'Analogy in Theology' in Paul Edmonds (ed.), *The Encyclopaedia of Philosophy*, Vol. 1, Collier-Macmillan, New York, 1967.

Ford, David: 'Conclusion: Assessing Barth' in Stephen Sykes (ed.), *Karl Barth – Studies of his Theological Methods*, Clarendon Press, Oxford, 1979.

Frege, G.: 'On Sense and Reference' in P. Geach and M. Black (eds.), *Translations from the Philosophical Writings of Gottlob Frege*, Blackwell, Oxford, 1952.

Gaita, Raimond: 'Review of Richard Rorty, *Philosophy and the Mirror of Nature*', *Philosophy* 56 (1981), 427–9.

Gilson, Etienne: *The Christian Philosophy of St Thomas Aquinas* (Eng. trans. by L. K. Shook), Random House, New York, 1956.

Gruchy, John de: *The Church Struggle in South Africa*, SPCK, London, 1979.

Gunton, C. E.: 'Augustine, the Trinity and the Theological Crisis of the West', *S. J. T.* 43 (1990), 33–58.

'Barth, the Trinity, and Human Freedom', *Theology Today* 18, no. 1 (April 1986).

Being and Becoming: The Doctrine of God in the Theology of Charles Hartshorne and Karl Barth, Oxford University Press, London, 1978.

A Brief Theology of Revelation: the 1993 Warfield Lectures, T. & T. Clark, Edinburgh, 1995.

Enlightenment and Alienation: An Essay Towards a Trinitarian Theology, Marshall, Morgan and Scott, Basingstoke, 1985.

The One, The Three and the Many: God, Creation and the Culture of Modernity (The 1992 Bampton Lectures), Cambridge University Press, Cambridge, 1993.

The Promise of Trinitarian Theology, T. & T. Clark, Edinburgh, 1991.

Yesterday and Today: A Study in Continuities in Christology, Darton, Longman and Todd, London, 1983.

Hacking, Ian: 'Is the End in Sight for Epistemology?', *Journal of Philosophy* 77 (1980), no. 10, 579–88.

Haering, Theodore: *The Christian Faiths: A System of Dogmatics* (Eng. trans. Dickie and Ferries), Hodder and Stoughton, London, 1913.

Hardy, D. W. and Ford, D. F.: *Jubilate: Theology in Praise*, Darton, Longman and Todd, London, 1984.

Hardy, D. W. 'Christ and Creation' in T. F. Torrance (ed.), *The Incarnation*, Handsel, Edinburgh, 1981.

'The Spirit of God in Creation and Reconciliation' in Hilary Regan and Alan J. Torrance (eds.), *Christ and Context*, T. & T. Clark, Edinburgh, 1993.

'Theology, Cosmology and Change', unpublished paper presented to the Society for the Study of Theology, Cardiff, 1993.

Heron, A. I. C.: *A Century of Protestant Theology*, Lutterworth Press, Guildford, 1980.

The Holy Spirit, Marshall, Morgan and Scott, London, 1983.

'Homoousios with the Father' in T. F. Torrance (ed.), *The Incarnation*, Handsel Press, Edinburgh, 1981.

Table and Tradition: Towards an Ecumenical Understanding of the Eucharist, Handsel Press, Edinburgh, 1983.

Hick, John: *Philosophy of Religion*, Prentice-Hall, New Jersey, 1963.

Hill, William: *The Three-Personed God: The Trinity as a Mystery of Salvation*, Catholic University of America Press, Washington D. C., 1982.

Hintikka, Merrill B. and Jaakko: *Investigating Wittgenstein*, Basil Blackwell, Oxford, 1986.

Hume, David: *Dialogues Concerning Natural Religion* (edited by Norman Kemp Smith), 2nd edition, Nelson, Edinburgh and New York, 1947.

Imhoff, P. and Biallowons, H.: *Karl Rahner im Gespräch 1*, Munich, 1982.

Jenson, Robert W.: *The Triune Identity*, Fortress Press, Philadelphia, 1982.

Julian of Norwich: *Showings* (*Revelations of Divine Love*), trans. E. Colledge and J. Walsh, Paulist Press, New York, 1978.

Jüngel, Eberhard: *Christ, Justice and Peace* (Eng. trans. of *Mit Frieden Staat zu Machen* by Bruce Hamill and A. J. Torrance), T. & T. Clark, Edinburgh, 1992.

The Doctrine of the Trinity: God's Being is in Becoming (Eng. trans. of *Gottes Sein ist im Werden*, 2nd edition, by Horton Harris), Scottish Academic Press, Edinburgh, 1976.

God as the Mystery of the World (Eng. trans. by Darrell Guder), T. & T. Clark, Edinburgh, 1983.

Gott als Geheimnis der Welt, J. C. B. Mohr, Tübingen, 1982.

Gottes Sein ist im Werden. Verantwortliche Rede vom Sein Gottes bei Karl Barth: Ein Paraphrase, J. C. B. Mohr, Tübingen, 1976.

'Humanity in Correspondence to God. Remarks on the Image of God as a Basic Concept in Theological Anthropology' in John Webster (ed.), *Theological Essays*, T. & T. Clark, Edinburgh, 1989.

'Metaphorical Truth' in John Webster (ed.), *Theological Essays*, T. & T. Clark, Edinburgh, 1989.

'Die Möglichkeit Theologischer Anthropologie auf dem Grunde der Analogie: Eine Untersuchung zum Analogieverständnis Karl Barths', *Barth-Studien*, Gütersloh, 1982, 210–32.

Unterwegs zur Sache: Theologische Bemerkungen, Chr. Kaiser, Munich, 1988.

Kaiser, B. Christopher: 'The Discernment of Triunity', *S. J. T.* 28 (1975), no. 5, 457.

The Doctrine of God. An Historical Survey, Marshall, Morgan and Scott, London, 1982.

Kerr, Fergus: 'Rahner Retrospective III: Transcendence or Finitude', *New Blackfriars* 62 (September 1981), 370–9.

Theology after Wittgenstein, Blackwell, Oxford, 1986.

Kierkegaard, Søren: *Philosophical Fragments* (Eng. trans. by David Swenson and Howard Hong), Princeton University Press, Princeton, 1967.

Kim, Jaegwon: 'Rorty on the Possibility of Philosophy', *Journal of Philosophy* 77 (1980), no. 10, 588–97.

Klubertanz, George P.: *St Thomas Aquinas on Analogy*, Loyola University Press, Chicago, 1960.

LaCugna, Catherine Mowry and McDonnell, Kilian: 'Returning from "The Far Country": Theses for a Contemporary Trinitarian Theology', *S. J. T.* 41 (1988), 191–215.

LaCugna, Catherine Mowry: *God for Us: The Trinity and Christian Life*, Harper Collins, New York, 1991.

Lash, Nicholas: 'Up and Down in Christology', *New Studies in Theology 1* (edited by S. W. Sykes and D. Holmes), Duckworth, 1980, 31–46.

Lee, Jung Young: 'Karl Barth's Use of Analogy in his *Church Dogmatics*', *S. J. T.* 22 (1969), no. 2.

Lewis, Alan E.: 'The Burial of God: Rupture and Resumption as the Story of Salvation', *S. J. T.* 40 (1987), no. 3.

Louth, Andrew: 'The Doctrine of the Knowability of God in the Theology of Karl Barth', M.Th., Univ. of Edinburgh, 1968.

Lyttkens, Hampus: *The Analogy between God and the World: An Investigation of its Background and Interpretation of its Use by Thomas of Aquino*, Almquist and Wiksells, Uppsala, 1953.

McLean, Stuart: *Humanity in the Thought of Karl Barth*, T. & T. Clark, Edinburgh, 1981.

Macmurray, John: *The Clue to History*, Faber and Faber, London, 1938.

The Self as Agent (Gifford Lectures 1953), Faber and Faber, London, 1957.

Macquarrie, John: *In Search of Humanity: A Theological and Philosophical Approach*, SCM Press, London, 1982.

Marshall, Bruce D.: '*Review of Richard H. Roberts, A Theology on Its Way? Essays on Karl Barth*', *J. T. S.* 44 (1983), 453–8.

Mascall, Eric L.: *Existence and Analogy*, Darton, Longman and Todd (Libra edition), London, 1966.

The Triune God: An Ecumenical Study, Churchman, Worthing, 1986.

Words and Images: A study in Theological Discourse, Darton, Longman and Todd, London, 1957.

Meijering, E. P.: *Von den Kirchenvätern zu Karl Barth*, Amsterdam, 1993.

Moltmann, Jürgen: 'Die Einheit des dreieinigen Gottes: Bemerkungen zur heilsgeschichtlichen Begründung und zur Begrifflichkeit der Trinitätslehre', in *Trinität: Aktuelle Perspektiven der Theologie* (Sonderdruck), Herder, Freiburg, 1984.

In der Geschichte des dreieinigen Gottes: Beiträge zur trinitarischen Theologie, Chr. Kaiser Verlag, Munich, 1991.

God in Creation: An Ecological Doctrine of Creation (Eng. trans. by Margaret Kohl), SCM Press, London, 1985.

History and the Triune God (Eng. trans. by John Bowden), SCM Press, London, 1991.

'Inviting Unity', *Concilium* 177 (1985).

Theologie der Hoffnung, Chr. Kaiser Verlag, Munich, 1965.

The Trinity and the Kingdom of God: The Doctrine of God (Eng. trans. by Margaret Kohl of *Trinität und Reich Gottes*, Munich, 1980), SCM Press, London, 1981.

'The Unity of the Triune God', with responses by J. B. Cobb, S. B. Thistlethwaite and J. Meyendorff, *St. Vladimir's Theological Quarterly* 28 (1984).

Mondin, Battista: *The Principle of Analogy in Protestant and Catholic Theology*, Martinus Nijhoff, The Hague, 1963.

Montagnes, Bernard: *La Doctrine de l'Analogie de l'Etre d'apres Saint Thomas D'Aquin*, Publications Universitaires, Louvain, 1963.

Mühlen, Heribert: *Der Heilige Geist als Person: In der Trinität, bei der Inkarnation und im Gnadenbund*, Axchendorff, Münster, 1963.

Die Veränderlichkeit Gottes als Horizont einer zukünftigen altkirchlichen Christologie, Axchendorff, Münster, 1969.

Muller, Richard A.: *Christ and the Decree, Christology and Predestination in Reformed Theology from Calvin to Perkins*, Eerdmans, Grand Rapids, 1986.

'Perkins' *A Golden Chaine*: Predestinarian System or Schematised *Ordo Salutis*', *Sixteenth Century Journal* 9. 1 (1978), 69–81.

Nédoncelle, M.: 'Prosopon et persona dans l'antiquité classique', *Revue des sciences religieuses* 22 (1948), 277–99.

O'Grady, Colm: *The Church in Catholic Theology: Dialogue with Karl Barth*, Geoffrey Chapman, London, 1969.

The Church in the Theology of Karl Barth, Geoffrey Chapman, London, 1968.

Osthathios, Geevarghese Mar: *Theology of a Classless Society*, Geoffrey Chapman, London, 1979.

Padgett, Alan G.: 'God and Time: Toward a New Doctrine of Divine Timeless Eternity', *Religious Studies* 25, 209–15.

Palmer, Anthony: 'Review of Richard Rorty, *Philosophy and the Mirror of Nature*' *Mind* 92 (1983), 446–8.

Pannenberg, Wolfhart: 'Die Subjektivität Gottes und die Trinitätslehre', *Kerygma und Dogma* 23 (1977).

'Person', in *Die Religion und Gegenwart* (*V. Band*), Dritte Auflage, ed. Kurt Galling, J.C.B. Mohr, Tübingen, 1986 (1957), 230–5.

Parker, T. H. L.: *The Doctrine of the Knowledge of God: A Study in the Theology of John Calvin*, Oliver and Boyd, Edinburgh, 1952.

(ed.): *Essays in Christology for Karl Barth*, Lutterworth Press, London, 1956.

Patterson, Susan: 'Janet Martin Soskice: Metaphor and a Theology of Grace', *S. J. T.* 46 (1993) no. 1, 1–26.

'The Theological Implications of the Relationship between a Wittgensteinian Understanding of the Relation of Language to World and the Role of Metaphor as an Agent of Revelation', unpublished doctoral thesis, University of Otago, Dunedin, New Zealand, 1992.

Peters, Ted: *God as Trinity: Relationality and Temporality in Divine Life,* Westminster/John Knox Press, Louisville, 1993.

Phelan, Gerald B.: *Saint Thomas and Analogy,* The Aquinas Lecture, Marquette University Press, Milwaukee, 1941.

Plantinga, Alvin: *Warrant and Proper Function,* Oxford University Press, New York, 1993.

Plantinga, Cornelius: 'The Threeness/Oneness Problem of the Trinity', *Calvin Theological Journal* 23 (April 1988), no. 1.

Pöhlmann, H. G.: *Analogia entis oder Analogia fidei?, Die Frage der Analogie bei Karl Barth,* Vandenhoeck and Ruprecht, Göttingen, 1965.

Polanyi, Michael: *Personal Knowledge: Towards a Post-Critical Philosophy,* Routledge and Kegan Paul, London, 1958.

The Tacit Dimension, Routledge and Kegan Paul, London, 1967.

Poteat, William H.: *Polanyian Meditations: In Search of a Post-Critical Logic,* Duke Univ. Press, Durham, 1985.

Przywara, E.: *Polarity: A German Catholic's Interpretation of Religion,* (Eng. trans. by A. C. Bouquet), London, 1935.

Rae, Murray: 'By Faith Transformed: Kierkegaard's Vision of the Incarnation.', unpublished doctoral thesis, University of London, 1995.

Rahner, Karl: *Foundations of Christian Faith: An Introduction to the Idea of Christianity* (Eng. trans. by William Dych), Darton, Longman and Todd, London, 1978.

Spirit in the World, Sheed and Ward, London, 1968.

Theological Investigations V (Eng. trans. by Karl-H. Kruger), Darton, Longman and Todd, London, 1966.

The Trinity (Eng. trans. by Joseph Donceel), Burns and Oates, London, 1970.

Regan, H. and Torrance, A. J. (eds.): *Christ and Context,* T. & T. Clark, Edinburgh, 1993.

Ritchie, A. D.: *George Berkeley: A Reappraisal* (ed. G. E. Davie), Manchester University Press, Manchester, 1967.

Roberts, Richard: 'Barth's Doctrine of Time: Its Nature and Implications' in Stephen Sykes (ed.), *Karl Barth – Studies of his Theological Methods,* Clarendon Press, Oxford, 1979, chapter 4.

A Theology on Its Way? Essays on Karl Barth, T. & T. Clark, Edinburgh, 1991.

Rohls, Jan: 'Die Persönlichkeit Gottes und die Trinitätslehre, *Ev. Theol.,* 1985 (March/April), 124–39.

Rorty, Richard: *Philosophy and the Mirror of Nature,* Princeton University Press, Princeton, 1979.

Rumscheidt, H. Martin: *Revelation and Theology. An Analysis of the Barth–Harnack Correspondence of 1923*, Cambridge University Press, Cambridge, 1972.

Runia, Klaas: *Karl Barth and the Word of God*, Theological Students Fellowship, Leicester, 1980.

Ryle, Gilbert: *The Concept of Mind*, Hutchinson, London, 1949 (Penguin Books edn., 1963).

Schwöbel, Christoph and Gunton, C. E. (eds.): *Persons, Divine and Human*, T. & T. Clark, Edinburgh, 1991.

Schwöbel, Christoph: *God: Action and Revelation*, Kok Pharos, Kampen, 1992.

Slenczka, Reinhard: 'Zum Christologischen Personverständnis der Gegenwart', Antrittsvorlesung, Die Theologische Fakultät der Universität Heidelberg, 1966.

Smail, Tom: *The Giving Gift: The Holy Spirit in Person*, Hodder and Stoughton, London, 1988.

Söhngen, Gottlieb: *Die Einheit in der Theologie*, K. Zink, Munich, 1952.

Soskice, Janet Martin: *Metaphor and Religious Language*, Clarendon Press, Oxford, 1985.

'The Truth Looks Different from Here' in Hilary Regan and Alan J. Torrance (eds.): *Christ and Context*, T. & T. Clark, Edinburgh, 1993, 43–59.

Strawson, P. F.: *Individuals. An Essay in Descriptive Metaphysics*, Methuen, London, 1959.

Sutherland, S. R.: 'The Concept of Revelation' in S. R. Sutherland and T. A. Roberts (eds.), *Religion, Reason and the Self: Essays in Honour of H. D. Lewis*, University of Wales Press, Cardiff, 1989.

Sykes, Stephen W. (ed.): *Karl Barth – Studies of his Theological Methods*, Clarendon Press, Oxford, 1979.

Thatcher, Adrian: *Truly a Person, Truly God*, SPCK, London, 1990.

Thielicke, Helmut: *Der Evangelische Glaube*, J. C. B. Mohr, Tübingen, 1968.

Thiselton, A. C.: *The Two Horizons, New Testament Hermenentics and Philosophical Description with special reference to Heidegger, Bultmann, Gadamer and Wittgenstein:* The Paternoster Press, Exeter, 1980.

Thompson, John: *Christ in Perspective in the Theology of Karl Barth*, Saint Andrew Press, Edinburgh, 1978.

Tillich, Paul: 'Religious Symbol and our Knowledge of God', *The Christian Scholar* 38 (1955), 189–97.

'Theology and Symbolism' in F. E. Johnson (ed.), *Religious Symbolism*, Kennikat Press, New York, 1955, 107–16.

Torrance, A. J.: 'Christian Experience and Divine Revelation in the Theologies of Friedrich Schleiermacher and Karl Barth' in I. Howard Marshall (ed.), *Christian Experience in Theology and Life*, Rutherford House Press, Edinburgh, 1988, 83–113.

'Forgiveness; the Essential Socio-political Structure of Personal Being', *Journal of Theology for Southern Africa* 56 (1986).

'The Self-relation, Narcissism and the Gospel of Grace', *S. J. T.* 40 (1987), 481–510.

'On the Theological Derivation of "Ought" from "Is"' in *Religious Studies in Dialogue; Essays in Honour of Albert C. Moore*, Otago University Press, Dunedin, 1991, 195–204.

Torrance, J. B.: 'The Concept of Federal Theology – Was Calvin a Federal Theologian?' in Wilhelm H. Neuser (ed.), *Calvinus Sacrae Scripturae Professor,* William B. Eerdmans, Grand Rapids, 1994, 15–40.

'The Contribution of McLeod Campbell to Scottish Theology', *S. J. T.* 26 (1973), 295–311.

'Covenant and Contract, a Study of the Theological Background of Worship in seventeenth-century Scotland', *S. J. T.* 23 (1970), 51–76.

Torrance, T. F.: *Karl Barth: An Introduction to his Early Theology 1910–1931,* SCM Press, London, 1962.

Karl Barth: Biblical and Evangelical Theologian, T. & T. Clark, Edinburgh, 1990.

Theology in Reconciliation, Geoffrey Chapman, London, 1965.

Theology in Reconstruction, SCM Press, London, 1965.

'Toward an Ecumenical Consensus on the Trinity', *Theologische Zeitschrift* 31 (1975).

Trtik, Zdenek: 'Der Personbegriff im Dogmatischen Denken Karl Barths. Eine kritische Untersuchung', *Neue Zeitschrift für Systematische Theologie und Religionsphilosophie,* 5 (1963), 263–95.

Villa-Vicencio, Charles (ed.): *On Reading Karl Barth in South Africa,* Wm. B. Eerdmans, Grand Rapids, 1988.

Walker, Andrew (ed.): *Different Gospels,* first edition, Hodder and Stoughton, London, 1988.

Weber, Otto: *Karl Barth's Church Dogmatics, An Introductory Report on Volumes 1:1 to 3:4* (Eng. trans. Arthur C. Cochrane), Lutterworth Press, London, 1953.

Weir, David: *The Origins of the Federal Theology in 16th-Century Reformation Thought,* Clarendon Press, Oxford, 1990.

Welch, Claude: *The Trinity in Contemporary Theology,* SCM Press, London, 1953.

Williams, D. C.: 'The Myth of Passage', *Journal of Philosophy* 48, no. 15 (July 1951).

Williams, Rowan: 'Barth on the Triune God' in Stephen W. Sykes (ed.), *Karl Barth – Studies of his Theological Methods*, Clarendon Press, Oxford, 1979.

'"Person" and "Personality" in Christology', *Downside Review* 43, 253–60.

Willis, E. David: *Calvin's Catholic Christology*, E. J. Brill, Leiden, 1966.

Wittgenstein, Ludwig: *The Blue and Brown Books: Preliminary Studies for the 'Philosophical Investigations'*, Blackwell, Oxford, 1958 (dictated 1933–35).

On Certainty (1950–51), Blackwell, Oxford, 1969.

Philosophical Investigations (Eng. trans. by G. E. M. Anscombe), Blackwell, Oxford, 1967.

Zizioulas, John: *Being as Communion: Studies in Personhood and the Church*, St Vladimir's Press, New York, 1985.

'On Human Capacity and Incapacity, A Theological Exploration of Personhood', *S. J. T.* 28 (1975), 401–48.

Index